Web Journal of Current Legal Issues
Yearbook 1996

The Web Journal of Current Legal Issues is to be found at:
http://www.ncl.ac.uk/~nlawwww/

Web Journal of Current Legal Issues Yearbook 1996

edited by

Michael J. Allen
Professor of Law, Newcastle Law School

BLACKSTONE PRESS LIMITED

1996 Yearbook published in Great Britain 1997 by Blackstone Press Limited,
9-15 Aldine Street, London W12 8AW. Telephone 0181-740 2277

1995 Yearbook, 1996
1996 Yearbook, 1997

ISBN: 1 85431 690 7

British Library Cataloguing in Publication Data
A CIP catalogue record for this book is available from the British Library.

Typeset by Style Photosetting Ltd, Mayfield, East Sussex
Printed by Ashford Colour Press, Gosport, Hampshire

CONTENTS

PREFACE

The *Web Journal of Current Legal Issues* is the first UK general law journal to be published purely electronically using World Wide Web. The journal is refereed and aims to publish five issues each year. The focus of the journal is on current legal issues in judicial decisions, law reform, legislation, legal research, policy related socio-legal research, legal education, information technology and practice. The journal was first published in March 1995 in association with Blackstone Press Ltd and may be found at — http://webjcli.ncl.ac.uk/. This *Yearbook* contains all the articles originally published electronically in the 1996 issues. Casenotes, shorter comments and book reviews are not included. The number and quality of the articles included is an indicator of the success of the journal. Another indicator of its success is the fact that there have been over 31,000 visits to the 1996 issues of the journal and almost 70,000 visits to the journal site since its launch. The editorial team would like to thank all those who have contributed to the journal, acted as referees or simply read the journal. We would particularly like to thank Blackstone Press Ltd for their continuing support and their willingness to back this innovative venture.

Michael J Allen
Editor
April 1997

ANALYSIS OF THE POLICE AND CRIMINAL EVIDENCE ACT S. 69 — COMPUTER GENERATED EVIDENCE

Amanda Hoey LLM.

Lecturer in Law, University of Ulster at Jordanstown
<a.hoey@ulst.ac.uk>

First Published in Web Journal of Current Legal Issues in association with Blackstone Press Ltd.

SUMMARY

The law of evidence is concerned with the means of proving the facts which are in issue and this necessarily involves the adduction of evidence which is then presented to the court. At present there are special rules governing the admissibility of computer-generated evidence in criminal proceedings. In this article the issues of when computer output will be considered direct evidence or hearsay and the reliability of computer-generated evidence are discussed. In conclusion the article attempts to ascertain whether these special rules for computer output are necessary and, if so, whether the conditions established by the statutory provisions are appropriate.

CONTENTS

Introduction

We are living in what is usually described as an 'information society' and as the business community makes ever greater use of computers the courts are going to find that increasingly the disputes before them turn on evidence which has at some stage passed through or been processed by a computer. In order to keep in step with this practice it is vital that the courts are able to take account of such evidence. As the Criminal Law Revision Committee recognised, 'the increasing use of computers by the Post Office, local authorities, banks and business firms to store information will make it more difficult to prove certain matters such as cheque card frauds, unless it is possible for this to be done from computers' (CLRC 1972, para 259).

Admissibility

The law of evidence is concerned with the means of proving the facts which are in issue and this necessarily involves the adduction of evidence which is then presented to the court. The law admits evidence only if it complies with the rules governing admissibility. Computer output is only admissible in evidence where special conditions are satisfied. These conditions are set out in detail in section 69 of the Police and Criminal Evidence Act (PACE) 1984 (see further Nyssens 1993, Reed 1993 and Tapper 1993).

In general the principles of admissibility are that the evidence must be relevant to the proof of a fact in issue, to the credibility of a witness or to the reliability of other evidence, and the evidence must not be inadmissible by virtue of some particular rule of law (Keane 1994, pp 15–20; Tapper 1990, pp 51–61).

Real evidence usually takes the form of some material object (including computer output) produced for inspection in order that the court may draw an inference from its own observation as to the existence, condition or value of the object in question. Although real evidence may be extremely valuable as a means of proof, little if any weight attaches to it unless accompanied by testimony which identifies the object in question and explains its connection with, or significance in relation to, the facts in issue or relevant to the issue.

This is illustrated in the case of *R* v *Wood* (1982) 76 Cr App R 23 where the appellant was convicted of handling stolen metals. In order to prove that metal found in his possession and metal retained from the stolen consignment had the same chemical composition cross-checking was undertaken and the figures produced were subjected to a laborious mathematical process in order that the percentage of the various metals in the samples could be stated as figures. This was done by a computer operated by chemists. At the trial, detailed evidence was given as to how the computer had been programmed and used. The computer printout was not treated as hearsay but rather as real evidence, the actual proof and relevance of which depended upon the evidence of the chemists, computer programmer and other experts involved.

The difficulty in the application of this rule lies in its interaction with the hearsay rule. Evidence is hearsay where a statement in court repeats a statement made out of court in order to prove the truth of the content of the out of court statement (*Sparks* v *R* [1964] AC 964). Similarly evidence contained in a document is hearsay if the document is produced to prove that statements made in court are true (*Myers* v *DPP* [1965] AC 1001). The evidence is excluded because the crucial aspect of the evidence, the truth of the out of court statement (oral or documentary), cannot be tested by cross-examination.[1] The problem, however, occurs

1 *R* v *Blastand* [1985] 2 All ER 1095, per Lord Bridge at p 1099 where he stated that 'The danger against which this fundamental rule provides a safeguard is that untested hearsay evidence will be treated as having a probative force which it does not deserve'.

because some statements, although in form assertive and inadmissible if they were to originate in the minds of human beings, in fact originate in some purely mechanical function of a machine and can be used circumstantially to prove what they appear to assert.

The basis for this view was laid down in a case having little to do with computers. In the *Statute of Liberty* [1968] 2 All ER 195 a collision occurred between two vessels on the Thames estuary. The estuary was monitored by radar and a film of the radar traces was admitted into evidence. Simon P rejected the argument that the film was hearsay – he held that it constituted real evidence and not hearsay and he placed it on a par with direct oral testimony. Where machines have replaced human beings, it makes no sense to insist upon rules devised to cater for human beings but rather, as Simon P said 'the law is bound these days to take cognisance of the fact that mechanical means replace human effort' (at p 196).

This useful distinction was apparently overlooked in *R* v *Pettigrew* (1980) 71 Cr App R 39 where the prosecution wished to prove that some bank notes found in the possession of the accused were part of a particular consignment despatched by the Bank of England. A computer printout was used to prove this but the Court of Appeal held that such evidence was inadmissible under the statutory provision concerned (section 1 Criminal Evidence Act 1965 – now repealed). The Court took the view that the operator did not have the requisite personal knowledge of the numbers of the bank notes rejected from the machine since they were compiled completely automatically by the computer. This conclusion is quite accurate and a perfect application of the hearsay rule but it failed to consider the use of the print-out as real evidence. This confusion between hearsay and real evidence is unfortunate and it may explain why it was necessary to create special rules for computer evidence.

Criminal Proceedings

It is imperative that computer output should be readily used as evidence in criminal cases since otherwise many cases, particularly those involving dishonesty, would be immune from prosecution. At the same time one cannot be too complacent about the technology since computers are not infallible. It is widely acknowledged that 'hacking' and 'viruses' may affect information stored on a computer. These factors were obviously taken into consideration when enacting the provisions governing computer generated evidence in criminal proceedings.[2]

Section 69 of the Police and Criminal Evidence Act 1984 provides that:

> '(1) In any proceedings, a statement in a document produced by a computer shall not be admissible as evidence of any fact therein unless it is shown-
>
> (a) that there are no reasonable grounds for believing that the statement is inaccurate because of improper use of the computer and;
>
> (b) that at all material times the computer was operating properly or, if not, that any respect in which it was not operating properly or was out of operation was not such as to affect the production of the document or the accuracy of its contents.'

In addition any rules of court made under section 69(2) must also be satisfied (at the time of writing no such rules have been made).

2 See Steyn J in *R v Minors*; *R v Harper* [1989] 2 All ER 208 at p. 210; see also, to similar effect, Criminal Law Revision Committee, 11th Report, Cmnd 4991, 1972, para. 259.

Real evidence and hearsay

So far the discussion has focused on exceptions to the hearsay rule. However evidence derived from a computer constitutes real or direct evidence when it is used circumstantially rather than testimonially, that is to say when the fact that it takes one form rather than another makes it relevant, rather than the truth of some assertion which it contains.[3]

Direct evidence produced by a computer is not subject to the hearsay rule. As we have already noted, in *R* v *Wood* calculations were carried out by a computer specifically for the purpose of the trial to verify whether the composition of stolen metals matched original metals. Computer output was admissible as real evidence since it did not purport to reproduce any human assertion which had been entered into it. It was held that the machine was a tool and that in the absence of any evidence that it was defective, the printout, the product of a mechanical device, fell into the category of real evidence. The court did recognise, however, that the dividing line between admissibility of computer generated evidence as real evidence or hearsay would not always be easy to draw.

The same distinction and result were reached in *Castle* v *Cross* [1985] 1 All ER 87 and in *R* v *Spiby* (1990) 91 Cr App R 186, CA an automatic telephone logging computer which logged the call details without human intervention was admitted as real evidence. The Court also held that, in the absence of evidence to the contrary, courts would presume that such a computer was in working order at the material time. Thus as far as the common law is concerned the status of computer evidence as real or hearsay will depend, in each case, on the content of the computer record, the reason for using it in evidence and the way in which it was compiled. Cases like *R* v *Wood* and *R* v *Spiby*, however, must now be read in light of the decisions in *R* v *Shephard* [1993] 1 All ER 225, HL and *R* v *Cochrane* [1993] Crim LR 48, CA. In *R* v *Shephard* the House of Lords held that section 69 PACE 1984 imposes a duty on anyone who wishes to admit a statement in a document produced by a computer to produce evidence that will establish that it is safe to rely on the document; such a duty cannot be discharged without evidence by the application of the presumption that the computer is working correctly expressed in the maxim *omnia praesumuntur rite esse acta*; and it makes no difference whether the statement is or is not hearsay. In *R* v *Cochrane* it was held that before the judge can decide whether computer printouts are admissible, whether as real evidence or as hearsay, it is necessary to call appropriate authoritative evidence to describe the function and operation of the computer. In that case the prosecution wanted to prove that certain cash withdrawals were made from a particular 'cashpoint'. The machine would only dispense money if the correct Personal Identity Number was entered. The matching was carried out by a mainframe computer and evidence of its proper functioning was thus required by the court. The prosecution did not adduce this evidence and the conviction was set aside on appeal.

As we have seen, a printout from a computer which has been used as a calculating device, or which records information automatically without human intervention, is admissible as real evidence and involves no question of hearsay.[4]

---

3 See *R* v *Wood* (1982) 76 Cr App R 23; *Castle* v *Cross* [1985] 1 All ER 87; *R* v *Spiby* (1990) 91 Cr App 186.

4 See *R* v *Wood* (1983) 76 Cr App R 23 and *R* v *Spiby* (1990) 91 Cr App R 186 (but cf *R* v *Pettigrew* (1980) 71 Cr App R 23).

On the other hand, where the printout contains information supplied to the computer by a person, it is hearsay if tendered for the truth of what is asserted, but may be admissible under either sections 23 or 24 of the Criminal Justice Act 1988. A statement can only be admitted under sections 23 or s 24 if its maker (or the original supplier) had (or may reasonably be supposed to have had) personal knowledge of the matters dealt with. Furthermore, under section 24 the 'creator' of the document must have been acting in the course of a trade or business etc. A statement in a computer printout which has satisfied the foundation requirements of sections 23 or 24 can only be admitted on satisfaction of the *additional* requirements contained in section 69.[5]

Section 69 is couched in negative terms making it clear that evidence which does not satisfy its requirements is inadmissible. The object of section 69 is to impose a duty on anyone who wishes to introduce a document produced by a computer to show that it is safe to rely on that document and it makes no difference whether the computer document has been produced with or without the input of information provided by the human mind and thus may or may not be hearsay (per Lord Griffiths in *R* v *Shephard* at p 228). The operation of section 69, therefore, is not limited to printouts that fall within sections 23 or 24 of the 1988 Act.[6]

Reliability

If there is a dispute as to the admissibility of a computer printout in a criminal case involving a jury, the judge should hold a *voir dire.* A party seeking to admit a printout under section 24 (or section 23) must establish the foundation requirements of both that section and section 69. The judge, in deciding whether the *prosecution* has established these requirements, should apply the criminal standard of proof.[7]

Although, as we shall see, the additional requirements of section 69 can be proved by certificate, the foundation requirements of section 24 (or section 23) must be proved by evidence unless the other party makes admissions or allows the statement to be read. There is also a third common law requirement, before the judge can decide on admissibility, namely that appropriate authoritative evidence must be adduced to describe the function and operation of the computer (eg *R* v *Cochrane*).

In *R* v *Governor of Pentonville Prison ex p Osman* [1989] 3 All ER 701 it was argued that printouts were inadmissible because the prosecution had failed to prove the proper operation of the computers required by section 69. However Lloyd J held that 'where a lengthy computer output contains no internal evidence of malfunction . . . it may be legitimate to infer that the computer which made the record was functioning correctly' (at p 727).

In *R* v *Shephard* the House of Lords held that it will very rarely be necessary to call an expert to prove that the computer is reliable. The defendant was charged with theft from a store. A store detective gave evidence that she had examined all the till rolls for the relevant day from the tills, which were linked to a central computer, and that they contained no record of the unique product code for some

5 *R* v *Minors*; *R* v *Harper* [1989] 2 All ER 208 (CA) at pp 212–3.
6 *R* v *Shephard* [1993] 1 All ER 225, per Lord Griffiths at p 229, rejecting the construction adopted in *R* v *Minors*; *R* v *Harper* [1989] 2 All ER 208 and followed in *R* v *Spiby* (1990) 91 Cr App R 186.
7 *R* v *Minors*; *R* v *Harper* [1989] 2 All ER 208 (CA) at p 214. The standard of proof for the defence, presumably, is on the balance of probabilities.

goods found in the defendant's possession. She also said that there had been no trouble with the central computer. On appeal it was argued that the evidence did not satisfy section 69 since oral evidence that the computer was operating properly is not admissible unless given by a person qualified to sign the certificate under para 8(d) of Schedule 3 which provides that:

> 'In any proceedings where it is desired to give a statement in evidence in accordance with section 69 above, a certificate—. . .
>
> (d) purporting to be signed by a person occupying a responsible position in relation to the operation of the computer,
>
> shall be evidence of anything stated in it; and for the purposes of this paragraph it shall be sufficient for a matter to be stated to the best of the knowledge and the belief of the person stating it.'

Dismissing the appeal, it was held that section 69 can be satisfied by the oral evidence of a person familiar with the operation of the computer who can give evidence of its reliability and need not be a computer expert. Lord Griffiths said that:

> 'Computers vary immensely in their complexity and in the operations they perform. The nature of the evidence to discharge the burden of showing that there has been no improper use of the computer and that it was operating properly will inevitably vary from case to case. I suspect that it will very rarely be necessary to call an expert and . . . in the vast majority of cases it will be possible to discharge the burden by calling a witness who is familiar with the operation of the computer in the sense of knowing what the computer is required to do and who can say that it is doing it properly.'

This approach was adopted in *Darby* v *DPP The Times* 4 November 1994. The appellant had driven her car into an area of road subject to a 30 mph speed limit. At that point a police speed trap was being operated. A police officer was operating a device known as a GR Speedman and he concluded that the appellant had exceeded the speed limit by driving at 43 mph. It was submitted that the evidence of the reading of the GR Speedman was inadmissible if it was held to constitute a document. It was also contended that the evidence of the read-out required certification and that, whilst oral evidence of certification would be admissible, the police officer could not give such evidence as he was not an expert in the workings of the machine, only its operation.

Potts J adopted the approach of Lloyd LJ in the *Shephard* case and assumed that the machine was a computer and that the visual image was a document produced by a computer. He also referred to the principle enunciated in Lord Griffiths' speech above and accordingly found no problem in holding that, on the basis of the evidence of the police officer, who was a trained and experienced operator of the device, the machine was working correctly. The appeal was consequently dismissed.

Thus it seems that the provisions in section 69 are capable of being applied without undue difficulty. However, it is interesting to note that Rose LJ pointed out that if the GR Speedman had been central to this case and if it had produced a printout on which the prosecution had relied then it may well have been caught by section 10(1)(c)[8] of the Civil Evidence Act 1968 (section 118(1) of PACE 1984 provides that a 'document' within that Act has the same meaning as in Part I of the CEA 1968). This would have meant that as a document within the meaning of section 10(1)(c) it would have constituted a document requiring certification within the meaning of section 69 and the terms of para 8 of Sch 3. But it was the police officer's opinion evidence which was central to the case and that was capable of being corroborated by a technical device, the accuracy of which had been established. Thus it appears that the conditions for admissibility for computer output in a criminal case are less demanding if the evidence provided by the machine is merely corroborative.

The ambiguities and illogicality arising from the complex conditions for admissibility of computer evidence can clearly be seen in the recent case of *McKeown* v *DPP* [1995] Crim LR 69 where the Divisional Court held that if it cannot be proved that the computer was operating properly the computer evidence will be inadmissible. This flies in the face of Lloyd LJ's dictum in the *Osman* case since the conclusion was reached despite the fact that evidence showed that the malfunction did not affect the accuracy of the information. The case concerned an appeal by Miss McKeown against her conviction for driving after having consumed so much alcohol that she was over the legal limit contrary to s 5(i)(a) of the Road Traffic Act 1988 and Sch 2 of the Road Traffic Offenders Act 1988.

The appellant underwent a breath test using the Lion Intoximeter 3000 breath testing device. This machine has a visual display and a memory which stores a number of results. Four printouts were produced by the machine and these were certified by the officer in charge in accordance with s 69 PACE. On his statement the officer recorded the time shown on his watch as the machine was thirteen minutes out. The submission of the appellant was that the visual displays and printouts were inadmissible on the basis that since the timing device was thirteen minutes slow it could not be shown according to s 69(1)(b) 'that at all material times the computer was operating properly, or if not, that any respect in which it was not operating properly or was out of operation was not such as to affect the production of the document or the accuracy of its contents'. On behalf of the respondent it was argued that the words 'to a material degree' should be read into the statutory provision and that the incorrect timing did not in itself render the evidence from the machine de facto inadmissible.

Dr Williams, a director of the laboratories who supplied the breath testing machine, had been called as an expert witness on behalf of the prosecution. It was held that although he was not an electronics expert his qualifications and experience entitled him to give evidence in respect of the machine. The court accepted his evidence that the working and accuracy of the breathalyser was not affected in anyway by the clock. However, despite these findings the court took the view that there was substance in the appellant's submission that on the wording of s 69(1)(b) the inaccurate timing mechanism on the machine rendered the print outs produced by it inadmissible. The appeal was allowed and conviction quashed wholly on the basis that, despite the evidence, the prosecution could not prove that the machine was working properly. The outcome, although in line with the statutory requirements of section 69(1)(b), is quite absurd since there was no question as to the reliability of the evidence.

---

8 Section 10 (1) provides that:

'. . .document includes, in addition to a document in writing—. . .

(c) any disc, tape, sound track or other device in which sounds or other data (not being visual images) are embodied so as to be capable (with or without the aid of some other equipment) of being reproduced therefrom. . . .'

The *McKeown* case also gives rise for concern in that the defence raised the smoke-screen of concentrating on the fallibility of the computer evidence rather than the reliability of such evidence. This point was raised by Dr Castell when he delivered *The VERDICT Report* to the Treasury in 1987.[9] He was perturbed that the current law could be effectively exploited by defence counsel to undermine a prosecution. The Law Commission in its Consultation Paper (Law Com CP No 138) claim that there is support for this contention in that judges commented on the lengthy cross-examination of prosecutions' computer experts. It will be recalled that the standard of proof in a criminal case for evidence tendered by the prosecution is 'beyond all reasonable doubt'. The intricacy and complexity of many modern computer systems may make it relatively easy to establish a reasonable doubt in the juror's mind as to proper functioning of the computer. Using the example of the *McKeown* case it appears that in the absence of a presumption that the computer is working means that it may be quite easy to raise such a smoke screen. It would seem perfectly feasible that where there are doubts as to the reliability of computer generated evidence these doubts should not go to the issue of admissibility but rather to the weight of the evidence.

As we have seen in *Shephard* s 69 only applies where computer generated documents are tendered in evidence and there is an affirmative duty on those introducing computer evidence to show that at all times it is safe to rely on it. Thus when applying a literal interpretation of the statutory provision illogicality and confusion reigns as demonstrated by the *McKeown* case. Furthermore it has been held that s 69 does *not* apply where a witness uses computer generated evidence to refresh his or her memory nor where it is used by an expert to reach a conclusion. In *Sophocleous* v *Ringer* [1988] RTR 52, another driving with excess alcohol case, evidence was given against the accused by an analyst who had used a computer which produced a graph illustrating the levels of alcohol in the blood stream. The graph was not put in evidence but the analyst was allowed to look at it to refresh her memory. As the graph had not been put in evidence the court held that s 69 did not apply.

The same outcome is illustrated in a recent Court of Appeal case, *R* v *Golizadeh* [1995] Crim LR 232. In this case a brown substance was found in the possession of the appellant which turned out to be a Class A drug (opium). The substance was analysed through a machine which produces a print out in the form of a pattern; this pattern is then interpreted by an expert to determine the chemical constituents of the substance. In arriving at his conclusion that the substance was indeed opium the expert witness relied on his own interpretation of the print out and the opinion of another expert called to give evidence.

One ground of appeal was that under s 69 PACE the evidence should have been excluded on the basis that it was based on the computer print outs and was therefore inadmissible. The Court of Appeal rejected this argument and held that s 69 did not apply. Morland J reiterated Lord Griffiths' speech in the *Shephard* case whereby he stated that the object of s 69 'requires anyone who wishes to introduce computer evidence to produce evidence that will establish that it is safe to rely on the documents produced by the computer'. Thus it is clearly the case that s 69 will only apply where computer print outs are actually put in evidence. Since in the present case the print outs had merely been used by the experts in reaching their findings as to the chemical constituents of the substance s 69 had no

9 This report addressed the legal admissibility of digitally transmitted and processed data and information in the UK.

application on the facts of the case. In the words of the Law Commission in its recent Consultation Paper 'if it is safe to admit evidence which relies on and incorporates the output from the computer, it is hard to see why that output should not itself be admissible' (Law Com CP No 138, para 14.13).

The irony of the situation is that it appears perfectly acceptable for evidence to be adduced which is based on computer generated print outs but at the same time if the computer evidence itself was to be presented to the court then the hurdle of complying with s 69 would have to be surmounted.

Are the special provisions necessary?

As we have seen, the statutory provisions impose special conditions on the admissibility of computer output. Are these justified? What is it that is special about computer-generated documents and that distinguishes them from their paper equivalents? It is obvious from examination of the admissibility requirements that computer evidence is regarded as suspicious in several respects The main problem is concerned with the authentication and accuracy of computer records. It is almost as if the technology is believed to be inherently inaccurate.[10] Section 69 PACE requires some minimum proof of accuracy before the document is admissible. The court must be satisfied of the reliability of the statement as a true record of what the witness observed and also of its authenticity as an accurate record of what was intended to be recorded. As a result it is necessary to show that at all material times the computer had been functioning properly, or at least that any malfunction had not affected the accuracy of the information.

It was envisaged by the Criminal Law Revision Committee (CLRC 1972, para 259) that there would be many cases where the document might have become corrupted by software errors or hardware malfunctions. It is the contention of this article that this suspicion was probably unfounded on the basis that there has been no tangible evidence to date illustrating why computer records are likely to be less accurate than those contained on paper. Paper based records are also susceptible to alteration and deterioration yet, where it is alleged that such alteration has taken place, the paper document remains admissible and the challenge goes to the question of its weight as evidence, to be decided on the basis of the evidence called to prove falsification or authentication.

Regarding documentary evidence para 3 of Schedule 2 to the Criminal Justice Act 1988 provides that:

> 'In estimating the weight, if any, to be attached to . . . a statement [given in evidence under section 23 or section 24] regard shall be had to all the circumstances from which any inference can reasonably be drawn as to its accuracy or otherwise'.

Although no particular circumstances are specified, it seems safe to assume that regard may be had, for example, to the following matters: whether the person who made the statement in a document did so contemporaneously with the occurrence or existence of the facts dealt with in the statement; whether any person who supplied the information did so contemporaneously with the occurrence or

10 There has been no documented research that I am aware of to support this view but the question to be posed is why else do the statutory provisions concern themselves with the accuracy of the computer-generated documents?

existence of the facts dealt with in that information; and whether or not such persons or the 'creator' of the document containing the information had any incentive to conceal or misrepresent the facts.

In stark contrast to this, unless it can be shown that there is no chance of unauthorised use of a computer system, or of system failure, the same document stored on computer is inadmissible under the *additional* requirements of section 69 PACE (eg *McKeown* v *DPP*).

Doubts concerning the accuracy of information recorded on computers apply equally to paper-based systems, as do those concerning authentication. As with paper records, the necessary degree of authentication can be proved through oral and circumstantial evidence, if available, or via technological features of the system or record.[11]

Although a paper document can be authenticated by its author appending a signature, various technical ways of authenticating computer records have also been suggested.[12] These could include electronic signatures in the form of smart cards, PINS or passwords and, although arguably less secure than biometric systems such as finger and palm printing and retinal scanning, the fact that foolproof authentication of a computer record is rarely possible is no reason for imposing stringent conditions on the admissibility of computer evidence.

There appears to be no intrinsic reason why different rules should apply to different forms of record-keeping, particularly when there may be no obvious difference in the appearance between, for example, a document produced by a computerised word-processing system and one produced on an electric typewriter. It is interesting to note that this strict dichotomy between computerised information and manually compiled documents is witnessed, not only in the law of evidence, but also in the area of data protection.[13]

There seems to be a fundamental flaw in the statutory provisions in that they concentrate on the question of admissibility and not reliability. Analysis of section 69 PACE shows that by making the admissibility of computer output subject to conditions which are really concerned with the weight of the evidence, the UK legislation places a double hurdle in the path of the litigant. The legal system should be able to ensure that provably reliable computer generated evidence can be used in judicial proceedings yet it confronts us with formalistic rules which appear to ask the wrong questions and address the wrong issues.

Another flaw is clear in the interaction of the statutory provisions with the hearsay rule. Although it has been shown that computer documents are not necessarily hearsay, the approach of the English law has usually been to treat them as if they were by excluding them as evidence unless specified conditions are fulfilled. Where relevant computer-generated evidence and, indeed, all documentary evidence is provably reliable, it should be admissible in all circumstances regardless of the hearsay rule. This of course would necessitate solving the problem of what is acceptable as evidence of the reliability of the evidence.

Indeed in regard to the question as to whether special rules are necessary it is significant to note that in Scotland, New Zealand, America, Canada and some Australian states there is no separate regime for computer evidence. These

11 See *R* v *Shepherd* [1993] AC 380 and *Darby* v *DPP*, *The Times* 4 November 1994.

12 For a more detailed discussion see Heinriksen, 'Signature and Evidence' (UNECE doc TRADE WP.4/R98) in *Legal Acceptance of International Trade Data Transmitted by Electronic Means*, Special Paper No. 3 NORDIPRO, Universitets Forlaget., 1983, pp 40–101; and Reed, 'Authenticating Electronic Mail Messages – Some Editorial Problems' (1989) *Modern Law Review* 649.

13 The Data Protection Act 1984 applies *only* to computerised information.

jurisdictions appear to cope well without any special statutory rules (Tapper 1987, p 84) and as we have already seen, the problems associated with section 69 would suggest that there is obviously a strong case for abandoning the special regime for computer-generated evidence.

The Law Commission in its Consultation Paper (Law CP No 138) has suggested two options for reform; option one is to do nothing and option two is to repeal section 69 and leave it to the common law, relying on the presumption the machine works. It is the contention of this article that option two is preferable for the reasons discussed.

Conclusion

It is imperative that the law should give industry and commerce clear guidance on how to make their records acceptable to the courts (see further Miller 1990; Bradgate 1990). As technology develops evidential practice will need to be evolved to accommodate it. It is arguable that the judiciary themselves might be able to rescue litigants from some of the problems created by the special regime (as in the *Osman* case) but traditionally the law lags behind technological development. If there were no pre-conditions for the admissibility of computer generated evidence then litigants could rely on the presumption of regularity whereby it would be presumed that the machine was working properly unless there was evidence to the contrary. If this was the case the prosecution would not be under an 'affirmative duty' to lead evidence that the computer was working properly and would consequently avoid the problems faced by the prosecution in cases like *R* v *Cochrane* and *McKeown* v *DPP*. It is the contention of this paper that there appears no good reason for treating computer records differently from paper documents and the rules, based on false assumptions about the technology, only create anomaly and confusion.

Bibliography

Bradgate, R (1990) 'The Evidential Status of Computer Output' 6 *Computer Law and Practice* 142.

Criminal Law Revision Committee Eleventh Report (1972) *Evidence (General)* (London: HMSO) Cmnd 4991.

Keane, A (1994) *The Modern Law of Evidence* (London: Butterworths).

Law Commission Consultation Paper No 138 (1995) *Evidence in Criminal Proceedings: Hearsay and Related Topics* (London: HMSO).

Miller, C G (1990) 'Computer-generated evidence – implications for the corporate user, Part 1' 6 *Computer Law and Practice* 178.

Nyssens, P (1993) 'The law of evidence: on line with the computer age?' (1993) 15 *European Intellectual Property Review* 360.

Reed, C (1993) 'Computer records as evidence-back to the beginning?' *Journal of Business Law* 505

Tapper, C (1987) The VERDICT Report.

Tapper, C (1989) *Computer Law* (London: Longman).

Tapper, C (1990) *Cross on Evidence* (London: Butterworths).

Tapper, C (1993) 'Evanescent Evidence' 1 *International Journal of Law and Information Technology* 35.

THE POLICE SURGEON AND MENTALLY DISORDERED SUSPECTS: AN ADEQUATE SAFEGUARD?

*Judith M Laing**

Lecturer in Law, Faculty of Law, University of Liverpool <J.M.Laingwbt@liverpool.ac.uk>

First Published in Web Journal of Current Legal Issues in association with Blackstone Press Ltd.

**I would like to thank Professor Clive Walker at Leeds University and Professor Michael Jones at Liverpool University for their comments and advice on earlier drafts of this article.*

SUMMARY

This article examines the role of the police surgeon in identifying and assessing mentally disordered suspects in police custody. It suggests that police surgeons lack the relevant knowledge and expertise to deal with these people, and concludes that duty-psychiatrist schemes currently operating at magistrates' courts should be extended to police stations to ensure that mentally disordered suspects are assessed by medical professionals who possess the relevant psychiatric expertise.

CONTENTS

Introduction

The range of duties undertaken by the police surgeon is extremely varied and important. In recent years however, they have come under increasing attack, and a certain dissatisfaction has been expressed with regard to specific aspects of their work. What little research that has been undertaken has indicated that there is:

> '. . . sufficient information already available on which to raise concerns about the role currently undertaken by police surgeons within the British system of criminal justice' (Kelly *et al* 1993).

This research identified particular concerns with regard to the independence and impartiality of their work and also in respect of the police surgeon's ability to certify the detainee's fitness to be interviewed (Kelly *et al* 1993).

This article will focus on mental instability as a cause of unfitness and will in that context firstly explore the concerns which have been expressed about the ability of police surgeons accurately to identify and assess the mentally ill in police custody, and secondly suggest a possible solution.

The Problem of the Mentally Disordered in Police Custody

The role of the police surgeon has been transformed dramatically over the years.[1] Initially, they were simply physicians to the police and their families, but today, they are expected to perform a wide range of medical and forensic duties. The nature of their work no longer involves simply examining police injuries and illnesses at the request of the police. They may also be required to examine prisoners and the victims of their crimes, which may frequently result in them being required to give evidence in court. Indeed, research conducted by Graham Robertson found that over 80% of the police surgeon's work today involves conducting medical or forensic examinations of prisoners in police custody (Robertson 1993).

Recently, the work of the police surgeon has attracted criticism, most notably from the Royal Commission on Criminal Justice (Cm 2263). Concern has particularly been expressed over the ability of police surgeons to identify and deal appropriately with mentally disordered suspects. When a person in custody is believed to be suffering from a mental illness the police must seek a medical opinion to assess whether s/he is fit to be interviewed, which may indicate that the presence of an 'appropriate adult' is necessary to assist the detainee whilst being interviewed (as required under the Police and Criminal Evidence Act 1984),[2] or if a 'place of safety' is required under section 136 of the Mental Health Act 1983. Undoubtedly, the police rely upon the clinical expertise of the police surgeon to make this assessment.[3] The research conducted by Robertson found that whilst the majority of the police surgeon's work is confined to treating physical illness or injury, nearly 10% is concerned with identifying, diagnosing and assessing mental

1 See further Summers, R J (1988) *History of the Police Surgeon* (Association of Police Surgeons of Great Britain).

2 Code of Practice C (issued in pursuance of Police and Criminal Evidence Act 1984 s 66 which governs the treatment of detained persons) stipulates that the custody officer must immediately call the police surgeon if the detainee appears to be suffering from mental disorder/physical injury, does not show signs of sensibility or awareness or is failing to respond normally to questions or conversation (Para 9.2).

3 The Police and Criminal Evidence Act 1984 Code of Practice C Para. 9.2 states that where the custody officer suspects that the detainee is mentally disordered s/he must call a police surgeon for a medical opinion.

illness/handicap. Furthermore, an additional 19% involves dealing with drug/alcohol abuse problems, which may be related to an underlying mental illness (Robertson 1993). It is generally recognised that mentally disordered people are increasingly coming into contact with the criminal justice system, often as a result of the lack of care, support and treatment in the community (NACRO 1993a). Clearly therefore, the police surgeon will increasingly be called upon to provide on the spot medical opinion to the police.

Police surgeons are not required to receive any specific formal training, let alone require any specialist knowledge in the field of psychiatry. All that is officially required of them is that they are acceptable registered medical practitioners, and the vast majority of them are indeed busy general practitioners doing police work part-time. As the Royal Commission observed:

> '. . . GPs receive little or no training in police work nor does their training include psychiatry'. (Cm 2263, para 90)

Similar concerns have also been expressed by NACRO's (National Association for the Care and Resettlement of Offenders) Mental Health Advisory Committee. In a series of policy papers on the subject of mentally disordered offenders, it concluded that there is considerable room for improvement with regard to the quality of assessments and examinations provided to mentally disordered suspects by police surgeons. (NACRO 1993b, pp 15–16)

Accordingly, the Royal Commission recommended that a Working Party should be established to consider the urgent need for national standards and training for police surgeons, particularly in the role of psychiatry and the availability of psychiatric assistance. Furthermore, the report urged that it is imperative that the police should have access to psychiatric assistance whenever required. This is essential, because the mentally ill are highly vulnerable and suggestible whilst in police custody (Gudjonsson 1992, p 301; Gudjonsson *et al* 1993). The revised Code of Practice accompanying the Mental Health Act 1983 (which was published in August 1993 by the Department of Health and the Welsh Office pursuant to s 118 of the Act) stresses the need for all professionals involved to note the:

> '. . . vulnerability of people, especially those who are mentally disordered, when in police or prison custody. The risk of suicide or other self destructive behaviour should be of special concern'. (para 3.2 (a))

A recent joint Department of Health and Home Office Review of health and social services for mentally disordered offenders has echoed these sentiments (Reed Committee Report 1992, paras 2.17–2.19). It made sweeping recommendations to improve the treatment and provision of services. Amongst them was the proposal that the medical attention provided for mentally disordered offenders at police stations should be greatly improved.

A report by the charity MIND into the use of the Mental Health Act 1983 s 136 by the police reached similar conclusions (Bean *et al* 1991, pp 155–157). This section empowers a police officer to remove to a place of safety a person who is, or who appears to be suffering from mental disorder, for the purposes of carrying out a medical assessment and for making arrangements for that person's care and treatment. The study noted that the police routinely called out the police surgeon to make such assessments, but that the quality of advice provided was inadequate:

> 'Assessments by divisional surgeons were generally very brief and from officers' accounts provided little more information than they already knew' (Bean *et al* 1991, p 155).

Furthermore, should the s 136 detainee require hospital treatment, then the police surgeon cannot secure an admission – unlike a psychiatrist or a medical practitioner approved under the Mental Health Act 1983 s12(2) who have links with the local psychiatric services and are therefore in a better position to arrange admission. The study urged that custody officers should routinely call out a psychiatrist or an approved doctor in these cases 'then the need for divisional surgeons should reduce, if not diminish' (Bean *et al* 1991, pp 156).

Finally, an article in *The Guardian* has highlighted the disquiet in this area. A forensic psychiatrist in London was interviewed and speaking from years of experience, expressed his view that:

> 'Doctors in police stations often overlook mental illness. . . . In many cases their knowledge of psychiatry tends to be minimal. Their reports are often a scribbled, irrelevant, illegible note. They often have no more than five minutes. Unless someone is raving there is no time in which to assess them' (McFadyean 1993).

These concerns and the tragic consequences which can result are illustrated by the case of Travers Clarke, reported in *The Guardian* August 24, 1993. Clarke was a paranoid schizophrenic who vandalised his former wife's home and was consequently arrested by the police and taken into custody for questioning. Doubts were expressed regarding his mental condition and accordingly, the police requested the assistance of the police surgeon to make an assessment. Having examined Clarke, the police surgeon concluded that he was calm and 'perfectly logical' and that there were no indications that he would take his own life. The police released him and 12 hours later he set fire to himself and died in hospital suffering from 90 per cent burns.

Cases such as this, added to the findings of the Royal Commission, led the British Medical Association and the Association of Police Surgeons to conduct a full inquiry into the health care of detainees in police stations. The committee was critical of the increasing numbers of mentally ill being found in police cells (BMA 1994, pp 3, 24). One member of the report committee expressed the view that:

> 'There's an increasing problem with having to care for people who seem to have fallen through the safety net . . . It reflects badly on the current community care system'.[4]

Concerns were also expressed that the standards of care were well below those in the NHS and that inadequately trained police surgeons were putting detainees' lives at risk. Detainees should be entitled to the same standards of medical care as NHS patients,[5] and this is clearly not the case at present.

---

4 'Doctors warn on police cell care' *The Independent* June 21, 1994.

5 This may not be the case with regard to the standards of care required in the tort of negligence however. See *Knight* v *Home Office* [1990] 3 All ER 237 where a mentally disturbed prisoner, who was known to be a suicide risk hanged himself despite being observed every fifteen minutes by staff in the prison hospital wing. It was claimed that the prison authorities were negligent but the court said that they were not in breach of their duty of care towards the prisoner, as it was not correct to require a prison hospital to provide the same facilities and staffing levels as an ordinary psychiatric hospital.

The report findings were reinforced by an internal review conducted by Scotland Yard into the ability of police surgeons in London to recognise mental disorder and identify persons at risk during interview. The research found that the current situation was unsatisfactory as many police surgeons relied solely on a physical assessment which would not necessarily identify any mental health problems. Accordingly, Scotland Yard announced that it was recruiting an eminent forensic psychologist and a consultant psychiatrist to train the police surgeons to identify such prisoners correctly.[6]

Similar concerns have also been expressed about the inadequate level and quality of advice and protection currently afforded to suspects by their legal representatives at police stations (see McConville et al 1994, chs 4 & 5; Baldwin 1992; Cm2263 paras 55–63, Recommendations 65–69). In response, the Law Society and the Legal Aid Board have taken some action, and as from February 1995, legal executives and clerks attending suspects at the police station on behalf of solicitors will have to undergo a specific training regime. The training package has been developed by the Law Society and it is eventually hoped to extend this scheme to all trainee solicitors and duty solicitor representatives by February 1997 (Ames 1993).

It seems, therefore, that there is widespread dissatisfaction with the levels of advice and attention given by professionals to detainees in police stations. Police stations are extremely unfamiliar and distressing places and thus the provision of adequate safeguards is paramount. Doctors and solicitors are the only outsiders the detainee is likely to meet; their role is therefore vital in ensuring that no abuse or oppression on the part of the police takes place. Relevant action has been taken in respect of certain legal representatives. The same principles should apply to the relevant medical services.

A Possible Solution?

As outlined above, this article suggests that much more needs to be done with respect to police surgeons to improve health care conditions in police cells. The Royal Commission proposed that experiments should be set up to determine whether duty-psychiatrist schemes currently operating at magistrates' courts to provide speedy psychiatric assessments could be extended to busy police stations (Cm 2263, para 92). This is indeed an attractive solution, which is clearly in line with current government policy. In 1990 the government issued a policy statement by way of Home Office Circular 66/90, which provided that mentally disordered offenders in need of psychiatric care and treatment should receive it from the health and social services as soon as possible (HO Cir 66/90; see also HO Cir 12/95). Annexed to the Circular were examples of good practice which would enable this policy to be translated into practice. These included an account of a duty psychiatrist scheme operating at Bow Street and Marlborough Street Magistrates' Courts in London (Joseph 1990, 1992). Basically, the scheme enables defendants to be pro-actively screened by psychiatrists at court for mental health problems and also ensures that psychiatric assessments are readily available to the magistrates to help them make therapeutic disposals.

A natural and necessary extension of this type of scheme is the routine provision of psychiatric assessments in the police station as soon as possible after the point

6 *The Times* June 6, 1994 p 10.

of arrest, thereby saving both time and money and diverting mentally disordered offenders to receive health care at this earliest possible stage:

> 'It would greatly reduce prisoners' distress and save money if people were diverted at the point of arrest'. (*The Guardian* November 30, 1993)

Court psychiatric assessment schemes have been an extremely welcome development, but many mentally disordered offenders who are screened at court may have already spent damaging amounts of time in police custody. Extending the availability of psychiatric assessments to this earlier stage averts this, and enables mentally disordered defendants to receive appropriate psychiatric care at this early stage. This has indeed been found to be the case. A similar type of diversion scheme has been developed at the magistrates' court in Birmingham. This particular scheme involves Community Psychiatric Nurses attending the court every weekday morning to screen the defendants for mental health problems (Hillis 1993). However, it was felt necessary to extend the scheme to cover police stations to identify mentally ill suspects as soon as they came into police custody. Accordingly, in 1992, an assessment and diversion scheme was developed and is still operational at a busy inner city police station in Birmingham. This scheme involves a trained Community Psychiatric Nurse (CPN) who is present at Bournville Lane police station, to screen suspects for potential mental health problems. The scheme provides a 24 hour, 7 day week psychiatric service whereby the CPN is present at the police station for part of the day and on-call for the remainder. Should the mental disorder warrant it, then appropriate care arrangements can be made. During its first six months of operation, of all the detainees assessed by the CPN, only one proceeded as far as the court appearance. The scheme has been so welcome and made such an impact that it has now been extended to operate at several other police stations in the area. In other areas, for example in North Humberside, a court assessment scheme has been successfully extended to include the three main police stations in Hull. This scheme involves the project team (a Community Psychiatric Nurse, an Approved Social Worker and a Probation Officer) attending the police stations early every weekday morning to pro-actively assess police cell detainees for any potential mental health problems (Staite and Martin 1993). Thus, identification and assessment at this earliest possible stage by a person who is both trained and experienced in dealing with mental disorder is imperative. The scheme ensures that the police have instant access to psychiatric assistance and that detainees receive the appropriate level of care and treatment which they urgently need and to which they are entitled.

Conclusion

Police surgeons are being placed under mounting pressure today, particularly in light of the increasing numbers of mentally ill people coming into police custody. They are required to be a 'Jack of all trades', dealing with a wide range of medical complaints, and obliged to understand the laws of evidence, child neglect, driving offences, sexual offences and also the provisions of the Police and Criminal Evidence Act 1984. Furthermore, they are expected to be fully cognisant of court procedure, preparing witness statements and giving testimony, and to have a thorough knowledge of police organisation and structure (BMA 1994, p 41). Sadly, with so much required of them, they cannot also be expected to be 'Masters' of all their trades.

As an alternative, the Reed Committee Review recommended that:

> '. . . wherever possible, a mentally disordered person should be assessed by a qualified psychiatrist who is able, where necessary, to provide medical reports for the Crown Prosecution Service and the court . . . and to arrange admission to hospital if this is required in the interests of the person's mental health' (Reed Committee Report 1992).

In this way, serious consideration should be given to ensuring that, in the first place, qualified and experienced psychiatric staff are made available to safeguard and provide the help required by the mentally ill in police custody, and, secondly, that they are neither under-trained nor over-burdened like the generalist police surgeons they should supplant in this work. Indeed, this would be giving effect to official government policy. The Home Office Circular 66/90 expressly advises that:

> 'In the case of mentally disordered persons, chief officers of police may find it helpful to arrange with their local health authorities for psychiatrists to fill the role of police surgeon' (para 4(iv)).

Adopting such a measure however, clearly has far-reaching implications, most notably from a financial perspective. Consequently, a more practical solution might be to finance training in this specialism for existing police surgeons. However, this would also involve resource implications which may be even graver than for duty-psychiatrist schemes, for which the government and other organisations, such as the Mental Health Foundation, have allocated specific funding. Furthermore, in line with the government's diversion policy, health and local authorities are becoming increasingly aware of their responsibilities to this category of offender (Cm 2088, para 5.4). Funding for police surgeon training, by contrast, is not readily accessible. As has been outlined, they already receive only minimal basic training, and provision of the necessary finance is the responsibility of the police authority which employs them. It is doubtful whether police authorities would fund such intense training. Resources are limited, and, no doubt in the present climate, the funding of operational officers or crime prevention measures would prove more attractive.

Moreover, psychiatrists and psychiatric nurses receive years of specialist training to equip them with the relevant skills and expertise to help the mentally ill. Most police surgeons are physicians with a much broader knowledge and would require many more years of training to bring them up to the standard of the psychiatric personnel. Even then, however, training courses alone would not suffice, as most police surgeons are busy GPs and perhaps not sufficiently committed to this particular category of prisoners.

The value of developing duty psychiatrist schemes is further supported by the fact that such psychiatric personnel are likely to be based in local psychiatric hospitals or in the community and therefore have better and established links with local psychiatric facilities. Thus, having examined a detainee who is in need of psychiatric care, they are far better placed to secure that care and treatment, as the Reed Committee recommended. A further consequence is that the police are far more likely to negotiate over disposal where a prosecution does not clearly serve the public interest and care and treatment can instead be secured. This is clearly desirable and in line with government policy as expressed in the 1990 Home Office Circular:

'In some cases the public interest might be met by diverting mentally disordered persons from the criminal justice system and finding alternatives to prosecution, such as admission to hospital . . . or informal support in the community' (HO Cir 66/90 para 4(iii)).

Moreover, the police are continually expressing concern about the increasing numbers of mentally disordered offenders in their custody, particularly those homeless mentally ill offenders who continually pass through the 'revolving door' which leads to the cycle of homelessness, offending and imprisonment (Clarke 1994; Cherrett 1994). Many such offenders receive little or no support in the community and have lost touch with the psychiatric services. So, the presence of skilled and experienced psychiatric personnel at the police station would stop them from slipping through the net and undoubtedly go some way towards slowing down that 'revolving door'.

On balance therefore, it would seem that the case for psychiatric assessment at the police station is clear. However, it must be noted that this option also involves many practical problems in relation to achieving the diversion and psychiatric care of such mentally disordered offenders. As the Reed Committee noted (Cm 2088, paras 5.3, 5.4, 5.10–5.21, Annex E), diversion is a viable solution provided that adequate facilities exist into which the mentally ill can be diverted. Having established links with local psychiatric services, although a distinct advantage, is clearly not sufficient if the appropriate facilities do not exist in the first place. Mental health services have always been regarded as the 'Cinderella of Services'. Until the government provides greater resources to fund community, hospital and secure psychiatric provision for the mentally ill, they will still be remanded and sentenced to periods of imprisonment, no matter how well-meaning the intention of the medical and criminal justice professionals to the contrary (Allam 1995; Brindle 1994).

Bibliography

Allam, D (1995) 'Diversion Schemes for Mentally Disordered Offenders – A Service under Threat' 51 *The Magistrate* 90–91.

Ames, J (1993) 'Front-line defence – legal advisers test a crash course in standing up to the police' 90 *Law Society Gazette* 7.

Baldwin, J (1992) *The Role of Legal Representatives at the Police Station*, Royal Commission on Criminal Justice Research Study No 3 (London: HMSO).

Bean, P *et al* (1991) *Out of Harm's Way* (London: MIND Publications).

BMA (1994) *Health Care of Detainees in Police Stations* (London: BMA).

Brindle, D (1994) 'Cash urged for mental health care in crisis' *The Guardian* April 20, 1994.

Cherrett, K A (1994) 'Place of Safety' *Police Review* 14 October pp 16–17.

Clarke, M (1994) 'The Job that Nobody Wants' *Police Review* 26 November pp 26–28.

DoH/HO (1992) *Review of Health and Social Services for Mentally Disordered Offenders and others requiring similar services* Cm 2088 (London: HMSO)

DoH/HO Community Advisory Group Report (1992) *Review of Health and Social Services for Mentally Disordered Offenders and others requiring similar services* (London: HMSO).

Gudjonsson, G H (1992) *The Psychology of Interrogations, Confessions and Testimony* (Chichester: John Wiley & Sons).

Gudjonsson, G H *et al* (1993) 'Persons at Risk during Interviews in Police Custody: The Identification of Vulnerabilities', Royal Commission on Criminal Justice Research Study No. 12 (London: HMSO).
Hillis, G (1993) 'Diverting Tactics' 89 *Nursing Times* 24.
Home Office Circular 66/90 (1990) *Provision for Mentally Disordered Offenders* (London: Home Office).
Home Office Circular 12/95 (1995) *Mentally Disordered Offenders and Inter-Agency Working* (London: Home Office).
Joseph, P (1990) 'Mentally Disordered Homeless Offenders – Diversion from Custody' 22 *Health Trends* 51–53.
Joseph, P (1992) *Psychiatric Assessment at the Magistrates' Court* (London: HMSO).
Kelly, K *et al* (1993) 'The Role of the Police Surgeon' 9 *Policing* 148–159.
McConville, M *et al* (1994) *Standing Accused: The Organisation and Practices of Defence Lawyers in Britain* (Oxford: Clarendon Press).
McFadyean, M (1993) 'LAW: Locking away our problems: A fledgling scheme is struggling against the odds to keep the mentally ill out of jail' *The Guardian*, November 30, 1993.
NACRO (1993a) Mental Health Advisory Committee *Mentally Disturbed Offenders and Community Care Policy Paper No. 1* (London: NACRO Publications).
NACRO (1993b) Mental Health Advisory Committee *Diverting Mentally Disturbed Offenders from Prosecution Policy Paper No. 2* (London: NACRO Publications)
Reed Committee Report (1992) *Review of Health and Social Services for Mentally Disordered Offenders and Others Requiring Similar Services Volume 2: Service Needs – Community Advisory Group Report* (HMSO 1992)
Robertson, G (1993) *The Role of Police Surgeons*, Royal Commission on Criminal Justice Research Study No 6 (London: HMSO).
Runciman Commission (1993) *Royal Commission on Criminal Justice* (London: HMSO) Cm 2263.
Staite, C & Martin, N (1993) 'What else can we do? New Initiatives in Diversion from Custody' 157 *Justice of the Peace* 280–281.

CRIMINAL LIABILITY FOR THE TRANSMISSION OF HIV

*D. C. Ormerod**

Lecturer in Law, University of Nottingham
<david.ormerod@nott.ac.uk>

*M. J. Gunn**

Professor of Mental Health Law, De Montfort University
<mjgunn@dmu.ac.uk>

First Published in Web Journal of Current Legal Issues in association with Blackstone Press Ltd.

**Our thanks to Dr Keith Neal of the Department of Public Health and Epidemiology, and to Professor Herb Sewell and Dr William L Irving of the Department of Clinical Laboratory Sciences, University of Nottingham for their clarification on a number of issues relating to the medical aspects of the transmission of HIV. Thanks are also due to T K Baxter for her research assistance.*

SUMMARY

This article explores the issues arising when a person, knowing that he or she is anti-HIV positive, proceeds to engage in intimate sexual behaviour with another, and asks whether he or she is liable to criminal prosecution. It considers arguments for and against criminalisation. In the light of the Government's refusal to legislate in this area, the article considers the possible sanctions under existing criminal law, providing very detailed analysis of sections 23 and 24 of the Offences Against the Person Act 1861. It reviews and counters possible problems with the use of these sections and the defences available, especially consent, and concludes that they could be used successfully to prosecute this type of behaviour. Finally, consideration is given to proposed law reform and its effect on the criminality of the behaviour.

CONTENTS

1. Introduction

There are numerous recent instances of people who are aware that they have the human immunodeficiency virus (HIV) and yet engage in unprotected sexual activity with someone, involving the transmission of body fluids (in this case semen and/or vaginal fluids) without informing the partner of their condition.

One recent English case gave rise to considerable newspaper comment: the case of the now deceased Roy Cornes (Smith 1991; Bronnitt 1994; Alldridge 1993; Holland 1994; Harris 1993). Mr Cornes contracted HIV from an infected blood product which he received as part of the treatment of his haemophilia. He was aware of his HIV status from 1985, but claimed that he first learned of the risks involved two years later. It was alleged that Mr Cornes had infected a number of women in the Birmingham area. One of the women died at the age of twenty. A different woman went on to have his anti-HIV positive baby. There were calls for the man to be prosecuted, but the 'Crown Prosecution Service and the West Midlands police . . . suggested they were powerless to act against the man. . . .' (*The Guardian* June 23, 1992).

The question as to whether cases such as this give rise to criminal charges is one which 'academics have argued ad nauseam' (Brazier 1992). Nevertheless, it is our contention that insufficient consideration has been given to the possible criminal charges under sections 23 and 24 of the Offences Against the Person Act 1861.

We accept that there are real concerns when arguing about the criminalisation of sexual behaviour. Of necessity it interferes in what is usually a very private activity. In recognising these concerns, we seek to address only a limited issue, but one which might have wider implications. We will be considering a person's liability under the Offences Against the Person Act 1861 and an objection that might well be raised is that we are resorting to offences of violence to deal with a matter related to sexual activity. Indeed, one of the major objections which Lord Mustill had to the prosecution of people engaged in sado-masochistic behaviour was the inappropriate use of offences of violence to deal with what was essentially a private, sexual matter. This is echoed by the Law Commission in its 1995 Consultation Paper (Law Com CP No 139, p 145). We would argue that the type of case which we have in mind does not fall foul of such an objection, because of the consequences it produces and the frequency of those consequences, since the potential defendant typically wishes to infect as many people as possible. Of course, there might be liability for transmission of HIV or other diseases or viruses by other methods of transmission, most obviously by injection, falling within the same provisions which we consider and so, in fact, the topic is not necessarily limited to sexual activity.

However, we must accept that, for some, the fact that transmission occurs during sexual activity is sufficient to remove it from the attention of the criminal law. We are indeed concerned with what is apparently consensual sexual activity. Some would argue that the criminal law should have no role to play when individuals take risks about infection as a consequence of sexual activity. It is certainly difficult to believe that people are unaware of the risks of infection as a consequence of a sexual liaison, particularly casual sex and so it is possible to suggest that all involved should be regarded as taking the risk of the consequences that might develop. In so far as it goes, we do not necessarily have any difficulty with such an argument which presumes informed risk-taking. The scenario we have in mind is different. We envisage the case where one person is deliberately withholding information from the other with a desire to infect that other. We regard this as a very different case, deserving of criminal liability.

We accept that there is a real risk that our arguments for criminal liability might be used to pursue prosecutions in a discriminatory fashion. In particular, there is a risk that, proportionately, homosexual men (or women) would be prosecuted more frequently than some other categories of potential defendants. If that did happen, we take the view that such usage of the criminal law would be both unacceptable and contrary to the United Kingdom's international obligations (eg articles 8, 10 and 14 of the European Convention on Human Rights). It might be anticipated that the gay and lesbian community might fear prosecutions as a form of 'gay bashing'; but we would categorically resist the use of our arguments to support such discrimination.

The situation we have in mind is one where the defendant, as we will call him or her for these purposes, may be liable under sections 23 or 24 when engaging in intimate sexual activity, which we shall call sexual intercourse, and knowing that he or she has HIV which may be passed to the partner. We do wish to make clear that the people involved in sexual intercourse may be any combination of female and male, (Mastro et al 1994) since in all intimate sexual contact the transmission of body fluids, that is semen and/or vaginal fluids, is possible, although the virus is less easily transmitted via the mouth (Kingsley et al 1987, at p 348). We will be concerned with administration offences, but it is important to note that it is misleading to consider whether one person (male) is the actor and the other is passive (female) (cf. Law Com CP No 139, para 6.20). Both parties, whatever gender, may be active, and either party may be administering bodily fluids to the other. In passing we should note that the sexual offences do indeed perpetuate the myth of the man as having sexual intercourse and the woman permitting it. An 'active woman' would not thereby avoid conviction for a sexual offence, since her action would involve an indecent assault.

The defendant in this hypothetical situation is anti-HIV positive. Therefore, it is impossible to say that the virus will not be found in all blood, semen, or vaginal fluid samples. This does not mean that the partner will necessarily develop infection with HIV after sexual activity. Even if the partner does develop HIV infection, he or she may remain asymptomatic for many years, although the evidence suggests that most people who have the virus will eventually develop AIDS (Hessol et al 1988; Mayer 1990; Phillips et al 1994). AIDS is a fatal syndrome, in that the resultant lack of immunity will mean that some form of infection or disease will eventually lead to the death of a person with AIDS.

Little needs to be said to introduce HIV and AIDS: AIDS was first discovered in 1980 in five homosexual males in Los Angeles. (Mueller; McGuigan 1986; Burdt and Caldwell 1988). Human immunodeficiency virus (HIV) 'is present in all of the bodily fluids of an infected person. However it is only present in large enough quantities to be infectious in blood, semen and vaginal fluids' (Terrence Higgins Trust 1990, at p 7). Some early research had indicated that the HIV 'has been found in, but is not always present, in the blood, semen, vaginal secretions, saliva, breast milk, tears, urine, serum, cerebrospinal fluid and lung fluid of HIV infected persons' (Stauter 1989; Friedland & Klein 1987). It is still not known how many people who are HIV positive will go on to show symptoms of AIDS as currently defined (Terrence Higgins Trust 1990; Keenlyside and Adler 1993). 'Antibodies generally become detectable between two and four months after exposure. About 95% of infected individuals will register antibody positive within six months of exposure to HIV. Antibody tests taken during the 'window' period between exposure and seroconversion (the time when antibodies to HIV become detectable in the blood) may yield negative results, even though a person is actually infected' (Tierney 1992, at p 481). The degree to which this person can infect others during this period is unknown. Studies indicate that the median survival time for people with AIDS is 4 years after an AIDS diagnosis but that a few people have lived with AIDS for as long as 8 years.

Cases such as that involving Roy Cornes raise many difficult issues. As a result of this particular case two issues were publicly discussed: whether criminal charges could be brought and whether Parliament ought to create a specific offence to deal with wilful transmission. Before dealing with the central point of the article, it is necessary to consider the proposals for reform and the comments on the criminal charges currently available.

2. *New Legislation?*

At the height of the Cornes affair there were, predictably, many calls for Parliament to enact a new offence to deal with this problem of wilful transmission of HIV. Several States in the USA have enacted statutes to punish the wilful transmission of HIV; Indeed, the Presidential Commission on the Human Immunodeficiency Syndrome Epidemic recommended that States enact such specific legislation (Herman 1990). According to the Presidential Commission, an HIV-specific statute should provide 'clear notice of socially unacceptable standards of behaviour specific to the HIV epidemic, and tailor punishment to the specific crime of HIV transmission' (Tierney 1992, at p 499). The states which have enacted a specific statute include Arkansas, (Cook 1992) Idaho, Illinois, Louisiana, Missouri, Michigan, Montana, N. Dakota, Oklahoma, Texas and Washington. Some have criminalised HIV transmission in circumstances of prostitution: California, Colorado, Florida, Georgia, Kentucky, South Carolina and Tennessee (Holland 1994, at p 312). The criminalisation of this form of behaviour has already been utilised in the US Army (Deutschmann 1990, at p 33). One reason for the enactment of such legislation in so many States is the Ryan White Comprehensive AIDS Resources Emergency (CARE) Act 1990. This Act 'makes state emergency AIDS relief grants contingent upon a state's showing statutory capability to prosecute individuals infected with HIV who intentionally or knowingly infect or expose others through sexual contact, blood or tissue donation, or through the sharing of a hypodermic needle' (Kerney 1992, at p 247).

In Australia, four States have passed legislation which criminalises the transmission of HIV: Queensland, (Queensland Health Act Amendment Act (No. 3), 1988, s.48.); New South Wales, (NSW Public Health (Proclaimed Diseases) Amendment Act 1985, s 3; The Crimes (Injuries) Amendment Act 1990 No. 101); South Australia, (S Austl Pub & Envt'l Health Act, 1987, s 37(1)); Victoria (Vict Health (General Amendment) Act 1988, s 120(1)). The position in New Zealand is less clear (Rickett 1990). Discussion of the problem in Scotland has centred on the *dictum* of Lord Emslie, Lord Justice-General, in the case of *Khaliq* v *HM Advocate* (1983) SCCR 483 at p 492, a case concerned with the sale of glue-sniffing kits:

> '[t]here is ample authority for the view that the wilful and reckless administration of a dangerous substance to another causing injury or death is a crime at common law in Scotland' (Laurie 1991).

The specific calls for legislation in this country came from all quarters: Dr Patrick Dixon, medical director of ACET (AIDS Care, Education and Training) was reported in the *Daily Express* in June 1992 as saying 'I also think it is likely that the Government will want to consider the proposals by the Law Commission to extend the Offences Against the Person Act to include intentional or reckless infliction of illness or disease' and indeed, Dr Brian Mawhinney, Health Minister, suggested in *The Guardian* (June 24, 1992) that the Government would be looking at ways of bringing in legislation aimed at making the deliberate spreading of HIV a specific offence. There were also calls for legislation from many MPs, especially those with constituencies in the Birmingham area, for example, Andrew Hargreave, a Birmingham MP, calling for action from the Government. It was reported in the *Birmingham Evening Mail* (June 16, 1992) that Mr Cornes himself believed that the deliberate transmission of HIV should be a criminal offence. Mr Allen, father of the woman who died as a result of her infection in the Birmingham case, called for an urgent change in the law.

Arguments against criminalisation were voiced with equal force. The main arguments against appear to be: that the legislation would be intrusive into an area of intimate and private behaviour; that the legislation would not act as a deterrent; that the legislation would be counter-productive in that it would discourage people from being tested; that the legislation may be used in a discriminatory manner – ie anti gay. Some of those who expressed concern included Andrew Puddephat, general secretary of Liberty, who stated that

> 'Laws based on individual cases are generally bad laws. You cannot fight the spread of HIV and AIDS through the law, you can only fight it through public education.' (*The Guardian*, June 24, 1992)

Equally clear were the opinions of Professor Brazier who wrote of her concern as to the 'message' which criminalisation would 'send to the community' and Mr Partridge, Chief Executive of the Terrence Higgins Trust, stressed that 'we don't need a change in the law. We need a change in behaviour' (*Birmingham Post*, June 27, 1992). On the other hand, may it be by criminalising an activity that society aims to change behaviour? (Hart 1958). 'Realistically, criminal law is likely to be of minimal significance in influencing conduct: other factors such as fear of infection, are likely to be of greater effect in influencing sexual practices' (Holland 1994, at p 287).

It was obvious that the chances of legislation finding its way onto the statute book were not great. Despite the public demand to make wilful transmission of the virus a criminal offence, it was felt that such a law would be almost unenforceable. This practical difficulty stems from the necessity for an aggrieved party to prove the transmission took place as a result of a particular sexual act with a particular individual. The Home Secretary is reported in the *Daily Mail* (June 24, 1992) as stating that he was 'not instantly persuaded that the criminal law is the right way to help, and someone would have to come up with a very good case before [he] was persuaded that a new sex offence should be created.' Predictably, the Government decided in June 1992 not to introduce laws to prosecute such offenders. Virginia Bottomley stated the main ground for this decision:

> 'We need to encourage those who are at risk to come forward, not drive them underground by a coercive approach.' (*Birmingham Evening Mail*, June 26, 1992)

The Government's refusal to legislate in this area was criticised by several MPs: Clare Short thought that Virginia Bottomley was 'negligent in not extending [the law] to include those infected with HIV in very exceptional cases where people are irresponsibly passing on the infection' (*Birmingham Evening Mail*, June 26, 1992); the Liberal Democrat's Health Spokeswoman, Liz Lynn said 'Legislation might at least protect some people from being wilfully infected by a person carrying the HIV virus' (*Birmingham Evening Mail*, June 17, 1992).

It remains the case that no specific legislative provisions have been enacted in response to the problem under discussion.

3. Which Charges Have Been Considered

It has been generally asserted by both practitioners and academics that there is little chance of a successful prosecution. For example, the comments of Birmingham solicitor, Mr Malcolm Fowler, were reported widely at the time of the Cornes affair:

> 'It would be extremely difficult for the Crown Prosecution Service to bring a successful criminal action' and that 'the case presented the prosecution with a moral, legal and philosophical nightmare' (*Birmingham Post*, June 22, 1992).

Those commentators who suggested that criminal charges might be brought in the circumstances have focused their attention on the offences of grievous bodily harm (Dyer 1992; Hall 1992; Holland 1994) and/or of homicide (Hill 1992, Child 1992). It is worth considering these charges briefly, beginning with murder. Since the partner will not die within a year and a day, no prosecution for murder or manslaughter is possible. Although there have been recent proposals for reform of this aspect of the offence, it is at present an insurmountable hurdle to a prosecution (Law Com CP No 136). Even if the substantive criminal law problems are surmounted, there are also problems with the law of evidence. Given that the argument 'it was one of her other men' may be an argument in any case, the defending counsel may wish to question the victim as to his or her previous sexual experience. This could give rise to numerous difficulties for the rules of evidence. Even if he or she did die so suddenly, the prosecution would have to prove the causal connection between sexual intercourse, getting HIV, developing AIDS and then dying. This might not always be easy.

Attempted murder is a remote possibility, but necessitates not only that the person with HIV intends that the partner shall die, but also that the sexual act is an act more than merely preparatory to the death of the partner. Both might well be difficult to establish, perhaps the latter more than the former. Certainly a prosecution would face enormous obstacles (Bronitt 1994, at p 22). The mens rea which would have to be proved is that of intention (See Criminal Attempts Act 1981 s 1). This would be almost impossible to prove in all but the most clear-cut revenge-type cases where the defendant has transmission as his purpose or at least foresees that it is virtually certain that the disease will be transmitted. 'Having sex is a highly indirect *modus operandi* for the person whose purpose is to kill' (Field and Sullivan 1987, at p 47). Punishing for an attempt, even if it were possible on the facts, would serve no purpose in deterrence terms since the majority of transmissions would be reckless rather than intentional.

Similarly the Offences Against the Person Act offences appear unsatisfactory in that no injury or, in the language of the 1861 Act, no 'bodily harm' may occur at all or at least not for a considerable length of time. Prosecutions for offences involving the causing or inflicting of bodily harm become impossible or exceptionally difficult. Nevertheless, the New Zealand Court of Appeal in *Mwai* [1995] 3 NZLR 149 felt able to uphold a conviction for causing grievous bodily harm contrary to section 188(2) of the Crimes Act 1961 when Mwai had infected two women knowing that he was infected with the HIV virus. The court took the view both that HIV infection was 'grievous bodily harm' and that the women's HIV status could be caused by Mwai even though it may not have been the only cause as it was a substantial cause. In A's case the only cause could have been sexual intercourse with Mwai. 'It was the virus present in his semen that infected her' (*Mwai*, at p 155).

In the Canadian case of *R* v *Mercer* (1993) 84 CCC 3d 41, in the Newfoundland Court of Appeal, the accused pleaded guilty to two charges of criminal negligence for transmitting the human immunodeficiency virus and *thereby causing bodily harm* contrary to s 221 of the Criminal Code, and breach of an undertaking. Having been identified as a partner of a person who had tested HIV positive, the accused was contacted by the medical officer of health and advised that he should assume that he was a carrier of the virus and that he should not engage in unprotected sexual activity. The accused also supplied a blood sample which later confirmed that he was anti-HIV positive. The accused had established a relationship with a 16-year-old girl and he began to engage in unprotected sexual intercourse with her without advising her of his health condition and, in fact, he told the girl that there was no need for him to use a condom when she asked him whether he should. In a subsequent meeting with the medical officer of health, the accused was asked to identify any of his sexual partners but he failed to identify this girl. In the ensuing months, the accused continued to have unprotected sexual intercourse with the girl and she later was diagnosed as being [anti-]HIV positive. A different Canadian judge McDermid J, in deciding another Canadian HIV infection case, *Ssenyonga* (1993) 81 CCC 3d 257 took the more traditional view, remarking that 'The law of assault is too blunt an instrument to excise AIDS from the body politic.' *Ssenyonga* involved the transmission through sexual activity. One charge of common nuisance was rejected at the preliminary stage where the judge said 'Certainly the complainants are members of the public but I cannot accept that they, from a legal perspective, represent the community as a whole. The offence of common nuisance is, in my view, not appropriate based on the evidence presented on this preliminary inquiry.' In another Canadian case, *Thornton* (1993) 82 CCC 3d 530, the accused, who donated blood knowing that he was HIV infected, was convicted on a charge under s 180 [of the Canadian Criminal Code] 'common nuisance endangering the life and health of the public'. The New Zealand Court of Appeal in *Mwai* was also prepared to uphold a criminal nuisance conviction. No similar offence exists in English law.

In this country, the option of prosecution under sexual offence charges was also discussed. Professor Leigh was reported as stating 'If a woman didn't know her lover had AIDS, it could remove her consent to sex' (*The Sun*, June 24, 1992). One practitioner who was quite adamant that charges might be brought was Michael Arnheim, barrister (*The Guardian*, June 24, 1992). He also relied upon sexual offences suggesting that the three possible charges could be assault, indecent assault, and the offence under Sexual Offences Act 1956 s 3 of procuring sexual intercourse by false pretences. The assault and indecent assault charges raise the difficult question of consent, which will be dealt with more fully below. It is submitted that the charge under section 3 is probably inappropriate. If the defendant has infection with HIV and fails to inform his partner, then he may have deceived her as to an element of the act which is fundamental in nature, but it is, arguably, not by that deception that he procures the intercourse.

By far the most detailed treatment of the possible charges is provided by Professor KJM Smith (Smith 1991). Professor Smith highlights the difficulties with many of the charges under the 1861 Act, though his consideration of the offence under section 23 of the 1861 Act is brief. He comments that 'the willingness of some courts to construe the breadth of these administering offences in a liberal and flexible fashion suggests that their possible theoretical relevance to AIDS (and even venereal disease) cases may not be entirely fanciful, assuming the presence of the appropriate mens rea' (at p 316). He later goes on to state that '[e]ndangering life or injuring another by administering a noxious thing may well, as suggested, provide a prosecution vehicle, but the strained or awkward use entailed makes it an unrealistic proposition for any but the most desperate or vindictive of prosecutors' (at p 319).

4. Sections 23 and 24

Given the unsuitability of the charges which have been considered elsewhere, and the refusal of the government to enact legislation to deal specifically with the point, we believe that consideration of the more suitable offences is appropriate. These offences are those involving the administration of a noxious substance, which do not necessarily demand any consequent injury or bodily harm. It is not the function of this article to consider the possible criminal liability for transmission of the virus by sharing hypodermic syringes or being given a transfusion of infected blood.

Of the offences which exist, the most suitable are those to be found in the Offences Against the Person Act 1861, ss 23 and 24 (In addition to ss 23 and 24, there are relevant offences in ss 22 and 29 of that Act and in the Sexual Offences Act 1956 s 4 but these are not pursued in detail here). Section 23 provides that:

> 'Whosoever shall unlawfully and maliciously administer to or cause to be administered to or taken by any other person any poison or other destructive or noxious thing, so as thereby to endanger the life of such person, or so as thereby to inflict upon such person any grievous bodily harm, shall be guilty of an offence, and being convicted thereof shall be liable . . . [to a term of imprisonment not exceeding ten years]. . . .'

Section 24, is the less serious offence, and provides that a person who

> 'unlawfully and maliciously administers to or causes to be administered to or taken by any other person any poison or other destructive or noxious thing, with intent to injure, aggrieve or annoy, shall be guilty of an offence, and being convicted thereof shall be liable . . . [to a term of imprisonment not exceeding five years]. . . .'

(1) The actus reus of the offences

(a) 'administering'

Both offences require the prosecution in our hypothetical situation to prove that HIV was transmitted through sexual intercourse and that this transmission can be regarded as the 'administration of a noxious thing'.

The term 'administration' was defined by the Court of Appeal in *R* v *Gillard* 1988 87 Cr App R 189. The court, approving the approach of Mr Recorder Walsh QC in *R* v *Dones* [1987] Crim LR 682, rejected the idea that its definition could be left to the jury as a matter of the ordinary English language, a decision warmly to be applauded. The case was concerned with an appeal against a conviction under section 24, but is relevant, on the definition of 'administration', to both offences. The defendant sprayed the contents of a CS gas spray can at V. It was argued that the gas had not been administered because the defendant had not brought it into direct contact with V. McNeill J, giving the judgment of the court, referred to the *Oxford English Dictionary* in considering the meaning of 'administration' and found that the definitions proffered were 'too many and too diverse' to be of any assistance (*Ibid*). He was not persuaded that the two words appearing in section 24, 'administer' and 'take', were to be regarded as either synonymous or conjunctive. He thereby rejected the basis upon which Mr Recorder Walsh QC directed the jury in *R* v *Dones* which we consider below. McNeill J, stated (at p 194) that the proper construction was to include 'conduct which not being the application of direct force to the victim nevertheless brings the noxious thing into contact with the body.' The court also noted that, 'there is no necessity when the word 'administer' is used to postulate any form of entry into the victim's body, whether through any orifice or absorption. . . .' Bronitt comments that 'in cases where a person transmits a disease through coughing, sneezing or sexual intercourse, it would be difficult to describe these modes of transmission as 'administering' without distorting the ordinary and plain meaning of the words in the statute' (Bronnitt 1994, at p 25). With respect, unless the word were to be interpreted in the narrow manner discussed in the text above, it is difficult to see how the courts' interpretation of the word administering could fail to bring these activities within the section.

If this were the only decision on the meaning of administration, it would be relatively straightforward to state that the exchange of bodily fluids during sexual intercourse leading to the transmission of HIV would bring the virus into contact with the body of the partner and so there would be an administration of HIV. Further, even if the substance did have to enter the body in some way, this is true of the body fluids exchanged in the course of sexual intercourse.

Would *Gillard* be applied in this way in a trial of our defendant? Account must be taken of arguments which might be proffered to suggest that what we have described does not amount to an 'administration'. First, it might be suggested that 'administration' demands the use of some form of instrument. There is nothing in existing case law which would support such a view. In *R* v *Harley*, (1830) 4 C & P 369 the earlier case of *R* v *Cadman* (1825) 1 Mood CC 114 was explained on the basis that the judges had 'held that it was no administering unless the poison was taken into the stomach.' The poison was secreted in some cakes which were left to be taken by the victim. Despite this point seeming to draw a similarity between the concepts of 'administration' and 'taking', it is submitted that the general approach is a correct one, the administration of a noxious substance does not demand the use of an instrument. Criminal lawyers of all generations would be undoubtedly surprised at any other conclusion.

Secondly, and more realistically, it might be argued that administration has some sort of quasi-medical connotation which would exclude the activity under consideration being administration but would include, for example, the use of hypodermic syringes and the offering of food laced with poison. The argument would have to be based upon the direction, which is reported more fully in the course of the judgment of the Court of Appeal in *R* v *Gillard*, of Mr Recorder Walsh QC in *R* v *Dones* where he ruled that administration had a quasi-medical sense. In that case the defendant had squirted a solution of 7.7% ammonia from a plastic lemon at a man involved in a fight and was, on this interpretation of administration, found not guilty of an offence contrary to section 24. It followed from the Recorder's conclusion that administration in section 24 (and therefore also section 23) did not cover such activity as throwing something over another, because administering and taking were to be considered as similar concepts. The basis for the conclusion arrived at by Mr Recorder Walsh has been swept away by the Court of Appeal in *Gillard* where, as indicated above, the court rejected the idea of the two terms being synonymous. However, does that still leave any value in the idea of the administration having to be in some sense, quasi-medical?

The approach of the Recorder appears not to have been wholly unacceptable to Professor JC Smith who, in his commentary, stated, 'The opinion of the Recorder is very persuasive; but would not the football trainer who sprays a pain-killer on the injured player's leg properly be said to 'administer' it? The physical act is much the same as squirting the ammonia; but 'administer' is applied more naturally to an act done with a therapeutic purpose than to an assault.' We would respectfully agree that the trainer administers the pain-killer, but could not agree that the concept of 'administer' must have some 'therapeutic' sense. Section 23 criminalises the application of poisons, destructive and noxious things. They were not being therapeutically applied, or if they were the administrator would clearly have a defence because the administration would not be unlawful. Requiring 'administer' to have some 'therapeutic' sense cannot, therefore, be of any assistance. This does not entirely rid us of the problem of 'administer' having a 'quasi-medical' sense which is not synonymous with a 'therapeutic' sense. None of the older cases, *R* v *Cadman* (1825) 1 Mood CC 114; *R* v *Harley* (1830) 4 C & P 369; *R* v *Walford* (1899) 34 L Jo 116; *R v Wilson* (1856) 7 Cox CC 190; *R* v *Dale* (1852) 6 Cox CC 14, are of any assistance because they run the concepts of 'administration' and 'taking' together. More recently, in *Flack* v *Baldry* [1988] 1 WLR 393 the House of Lords held electricity to be a noxious thing in view of its stunning effect on its victims. If a requirement that 'administration' had to have a 'quasi-medical' sense were to be introduced, great care would have to be taken not to reduce the existing scope of the offences. For example, the administering of an electric shock to the victim could be an administration without being at all medical. The definition of 'quasi-medical' may present as many problems as it solves. For example, 'administer' in a quasi-medical sense cannot be limited to oral or intravenous administrations, since the transmission by an act such as shaking hands would then not be covered. Furthermore, a quasi-medical definition of 'administration' does not necessarily limit significantly the meaning of administration if the definition of that phrase in the Medicines Act 1968 s 130(9) is considered:

> 'administer' means administer to a human being or an animal, whether orally, by injection, or by introduction into the body in any other way, or by external application, whether by direct contact with the body or not; and any reference in this Act to administering a substance or article is a reference to administering it either in its existing state or after it has been dissolved or dispersed in, or diluted or mixed with, some other substance used as a vehicle.'

This definition is clearly wide enough to include the act of sexual intercourse.

Is there a conceptual basis upon which the quasi-medical sense has an appeal? The transfer of body fluids would undoubtedly be an administration in some instances, for example a blood transfusion, and there would still be an administration if that blood were contaminated, it being therefore a noxious thing. Infecting a person with smallpox by shaking their hand, thereby transferring the infection, would be the administration of a noxious substance. However, it might be suggested that if the transfer is brought about by sexual intercourse, there would be no administration. It is submitted that such a distinction would not only be contrary to what appears to be a generally applicable definition propounded recently by the Court of Appeal in *Gillard* 1988 87 Cr App R 189 but also would be an unfortunate development inappropriately narrowing the scope of an offence which ought to be able to deal with the infection of other people with diseases and poisons.

(b) 'A poison, destructive or other noxious thing'

Not only must the prosecution prove that there has been administration, but also it must prove that what was administered was a poison or other destructive or noxious thing. HIV is accepted by virologists to be a poison. In fact the definition of 'virus' taken from the *Oxford English Dictionary* is 'a morbid principle or poisonous substance produced in the body as a result of some disease, esp. one capable of being introduced into other persons or animals by inoculation or otherwise of developing the same disease in them.' If it were held that HIV is not a poison it would then be necessary to consider whether HIV is a 'noxious thing'. Although there is no direct authority, this is not a major obstacle, but necessitates careful consideration of the relevant applicable principles (Bronitt 1994 at p 25).

'Noxious' was defined by the Court of Appeal in *R* v *Marcus* [1981] 2 All ER 833. Tudor Evans J, giving the judgment of the court, stated that

> 'for the purposes of section 24 [and therefore also of section 23] the concept of noxious thing involves not only the quality or nature of the substance, but also the quantity administered or sought to be administered' (at p 837)

Tudor Evans J made quite clear that quantity was very important:

> 'we consider that the words 'a noxious thing' mean that the jury has to consider the very thing which on the facts is administered or sought to be administered both as to quality and as to quantity. The jury has to consider the evidence of what was administered or attempted to be administered both in quality and quantity and to decide as a question of fact and degree in all the circumstances whether that thing was noxious. A substance which may have been harmless in small quantities may yet be noxious in the quantity administered. . . .' (at p 837)

The first problem to be faced in our hypothetical situation is: what is the thing which is to be alleged to be noxious? It is either the virus itself or the body fluids within which the virus is contained. The discussion of 'administers' above can apply to either option. We presume that since the virus is inextricably linked with the body fluids that it is the latter, contaminated by the former, which should be alleged to have been administered. The medical evidence is highly technical, but supportive of our presumption:

> '[R]eports confirm the earlier findings that HIV is present in the semen of infected males. Assayed by virus infectivity, 30%, 16% and 9% of semen samples were positive for HIV. . . . Assayed by PCR 87% and 4% of samples were virus positive. . . . This wide range in semen virus detection undoubtedly reflects assay techniques as well as variations in patient population' (Kiessling 1992).

Other research has shown that 'HIV nucleic acid can be detected . . . in either the cell-free seminal fluid or non-spermatozoal mononuclear cells of 87% of semen samples, but not in the DNA of spermatozoa from HIV-infected men' (Mermin 1991).

The more important matter is to consider whether the body fluids so contaminated are a noxious thing. The decision in *Marcus* might be interpreted to mean that it is always necessary to consider the quantity of the thing administered to another. This would present at least two problems where the substance is body fluids contaminated with HIV which is administered to the partner. First, it will never be possible to prove how much of the virus was administered because viruses which have been transmitted cannot be measured in that way. Secondly, it might be presumed that the only way the quantity can be established is by assessing whether the other person also becomes anti-HIV positive. If he or she catches HIV, sufficient quantity was administered and so it can be stated the defendant's body fluids contained enough HIV to amount to a noxious thing. This raises a related problem of causation which is that in some cases it will be difficult for the prosecution to prove that the victim became HIV positive as a result of having sex with the defendant and not as a result of some other cause. However, the press have reported that recent medical developments have enabled scientists to identify 'to a high degree of probability, the particular person who transmitted the disease' (Bronitt 1994, at p 22).

It is submitted that there is an alternative and proper approach to the decision in *Marcus*. It applies properly to circumstances where the thing in question is only noxious in large quantities, and therefore the decision must be limited to that type of case. Where the thing is noxious whatever the quantity, quantity should be irrelevant and all that the prosecution should be required to prove is that the defendant did administer the virus to the other. The passage quoted may properly be interpreted to agree with this approach. The fact that a thing may not be noxious in small quantities does not, as a matter of law, mean that any substance in small quantities, however harmful that substance may be, is necessarily not noxious.

Further, the court in *Marcus* accepted that as noxious must be of less importance than a poison or a destructive thing, it has a relatively weak meaning, as indicated by the definitions to be found in the *Shorter Oxford English Dictionary*, which includes the word 'unwholesome'. Indeed the court thought that the presence of the snail in Mrs Donoghue's glass of ginger beer (*Donoghue* v *Stevenson* [1932] AC 562) would mean that the actus reus of the offence in section 24 would have been satisfied. It must, therefore, follow that body fluids contaminated by HIV, and the virus itself, are both a 'noxious thing.' Bronitt states that this is a difficulty because of the lack of clear authority on whether a virus is a 'destructive or noxious thing' (Bronitt 1994, at p 25).

In the Canadian case *Ssenyonga* (1992) 73 CCC 3d 216 (Preliminary Hearing); (1993) 81 CCC 3d 257 (Trial) the accused was charged 'that he did administer to a female person, namely each of the complainants, a noxious thing, to wit: bodily fluids containing the human immunodeficiency virus, with the intent to endanger life, contrary to s 245 of the Criminal Code.' For the purpose of the preliminary inquiry, counsel for the accused admitted that the semen of the accused who is infected with HIV would be a noxious thing. The court stated that

> '[t]he evidence I have heard is that each of the complainants had intercourse with the accused a number of times. On most occasions, he did not wear a condom. On many occasions he ejaculated inside their vaginas. The expert medical evidence was that unprotected heterosexual intercourse can result in the transmission of HIV, and that the accused was instructed to use a condom because he was [anti-]HIV positive.'

It is worth noting also that the court in *Ssenyonga* found it unnecessary to decide the issue as to what constituted an administration stating:

> 'Even if I were satisfied, based on the facts, that consensual intercourse is "administration of a noxious thing", I must also be satisfied that there is sufficient evidence to put before a jury that such "administration" was committed with intent to endanger life or cause bodily harm. . . . In the case before me, there is, in my view, no evidence that the accused could have foreseen the certainty or substantial certainty of infecting the complainants with HIV by having unprotected sex with them. From the evidence I have heard, I cannot infer subjective intent.'

Of course, if 'destructive' means not only something actually destructive, but also something potentially destructive, HIV is a destructive thing.

(c) Proving the administration even if the partner does not contract HIV

The chances of a woman who has unprotected sexual intercourse with an infected man contracting infection with HIV have been put at 20% (*The Guardian*, July 7, 1992). The difficulty with accuracy stems from the unsurprising fact that no-one is prepared to take part in any experiment which involves them, as a non-HIV infected person, having continued unprotected intercourse with (or insemination by) someone they know to be anti-HIV positive until they too are infected. It has been noted that

> 'experimental inseminations are elective procedures in healthy, HIV-negative women. Prospective volunteers and institutional review panels contemplating such experiments should be fully aware that they carry a risk of HIV transmission' (Edlin 1993).

A recent study concluded that 'the likelihood of a female seroconverting [a term meaning to develop antibodies against HIV] as a result of a single act of unprotected heterosexual intercourse with an infected male is about 1 in 500' (McGuire 1991, at p 97), while other research has suggested that a seroconversion rate of 7.2% is more accurate (Semprini 1993). It is difficult to give a precise figure and medical researchers have accepted that transmission rates of anywhere between 7% and 68% have been recorded (Krieger 1991).

But, if HIV is found to be a poison or noxious thing, it does not have to be proved that the other partner became anti-HIV positive in order for the offence to be made out. If a person is anti-HIV positive all samples of blood, semen and vaginal fluid contain the virus. Therefore, it only has to be shown that the defendant, who at the time was anti-HIV positive, had sex with him or her. It follows as a matter of science that the virus must have been administered to the other. There is no need to prove that the partner became anti-HIV positive and there is no need to be concerned with whether the other partner had contacts of some form from which he or she could have caught the virus.

(d) Life endangerment for the offence under section 23

If the charge is section 23, there is one more element of the actus reus which needs to be proved: that the life of the victim is endangered by the administration. It is unquestionably the case that life is endangered by having sex with someone who is anti-HIV positive. The partner runs the risk of getting the virus, and if so he or she will contract AIDS and, therefore, will die, at some stage in the future. If that is not life endangering, it is difficult to see what this requirement means other than 'causes death'!

It is submitted, therefore, that the actus reus of the offences in ss 23 and 24 are committed by a person who has infection with HIV having sex with another person.

(2) The mens rea

(a) The unaware defendant

Obviously the person who is anti-HIV positive, but is unaware that he or she has contracted infection with HIV, and has unprotected sexual intercourse with his or her partner will commit no offence as he or she clearly lacks mens rea. There is no foresight of any risk of administering the virus. Similarly any person who has protected sex, has no foresight of the risk of administering the virus, especially in view of all the advertising and educational campaigns which make it quite clear that protected sex is safe, subject to minimal risks such as breakage in a condom. *Mens rea* is a subjective concept so even if the defendant has made a mistake or taken inadequate precautions, he or she is not 'malicious' (See also *Ssenyonga*). It could be otherwise were the recklessness element of malice to have been interpreted in accordance with the House of Lords decision in *R* v *Caldwell* [1982] AC 341 and its progeny.

Several legislative responses to the AIDS transmission problem have required that the defendant 'know he or she has tested positive for HIV' (Arkansas Code 5–14–123(b) (Cook 1992, at p 524). In the Canadian case of *Ssenyonga*, the judge at the preliminary hearing, was certainly of the opinion that knowledge of the HIV status 'is a crucial difference which may alter the nature of the sexual act of unprotected sex.'

To be sure of a conviction the prosecutor would have to be certain of the defendant's HIV status. The defendant would have to submit to a HIV test. This involves further difficulties of an ethical nature (Somerville 1991; McGuire 1991). This has already been required in at least one US case (Herman 1990, at pp 364 and 370). In America, the Presidential Commission on the Human Immunodeficiency Virus, which was established by President Reagan in 1987 and reported in 1988, recommended that rapists be tested for HIV and that their victims be informed of the results. Furthermore, the results of such a test would have to be made available for use at the defendant's trial. In the US this has given rise to potential Constitutional difficulties with respect to the fourth and fifth amendments guarantees (Cook 1992, at p 524). Requiring the defendant to undergo a HIV test may also have repercussions for the presumption of innocence. If the defendant is known to be anti-HIV positive, he may face prejudice from the jury on that ground alone (McGuire 1991, at p 111).

There is an argument that the person who is aware that he or she is in a high-risk group may have sufficient mens rea for the offences even if he or she does not know that they have the disease (Taitz 1989, at p 219; Laurie 1991, at p 316; Field and Sullivan 1987, at p 52). Although technically possible, this would require proof that they foresaw the risk of administering the virus. This would improperly punish those who did not know that they were transmitting anything other than their normal bodily fluids.

(b) The aware defendant

In cases where the defendant knows that he or she has the virus, the required mens rea for the offence contrary to section 23 is simply that of 'malice', whereas there is the additional element for the less serious offence contrary to section 24 that the defendant must intend to injure, aggrieve or annoy the other person.

The concept of 'malice' was authoritatively considered by the Court of Criminal Appeal in *R* v *Cunningham* [1957] 2 QB 396. In considering the offence contrary to section 23, Byrne J, giving the judgment of the court, said at p 399:

> '. . . in any statutory definition of a crime 'malice' must be taken not in the old value sense of 'wickedness' in general, but as requiring either (i) an actual intention to do the particular kind of harm which in fact was done, or (ii) recklessness as to whether such harm should occur or not (i.e. the accused has

> foreseen that the particular kind of harm might be done, and yet has gone on to take the risk of it). It is neither limited to, nor does it indeed require, any ill-will towards the person injured.'

It is, therefore, the case that the defendant in our hypothetical situation must actually foresee something. In accordance with the traditional approach to English law, mens rea in the sense given would be required in relation to every element of the actus reus. Thus the defendant must foresee: (a) an administration; (b) that the substance is noxious; and (c) that HIV will be transmitted.

There is no difficulty in a jury finding that the defendant has the requisite malice in relation to all of these factors. The defendant will know that, in the ordinary course of things, unprotected sexual intercourse will involve the transmission of bodily fluids, that is the administration of something. He or she does not have to realise that it would legally be described as an administration. He or she will know of the noxiousness of the substance if aware of his or her own condition. Finally, it will not be difficult to show that the defendant foresaw the risk of the transmission of the virus, since, as has been indicated, it is necessarily the case that in all instances the virus is transmitted, although the other does not necessarily contract it. Even if a defendant claimed that, because not all partners would contract infection with HIV, he or she thought that the virus would not always be transmitted, it would be difficult for him or her to avoid the jury arriving at the conclusion that he or she foresaw the risk of transmission nevertheless.

In *Ssenyonga* the judge at the preliminary hearing was not prepared to find that the administration 'was committed with *intent* to endanger life or cause bodily harm' as required by the relevant Canadian legislation. Whilst recognising that the

> 'actor's foresight of the certainty or moral certainty of the consequence resulting from his conduct compels a conclusion that he, none the less, acted so as to produce it, then he decided to bring it about (albeit regretfully), in order to achieve his ultimate purpose.'

The judge concluded that:

> 'In the case before me, there is, in my view, no evidence that the accused could have foreseen the certainty or substantial certainty of infecting the complainants with HIV by having unprotected sex with them. From the evidence I have heard, I cannot infer subjective intent.'

As the mens rea requirements are peculiar to the specific offences, the decision has no effect upon the position under sections 23 or 24.

(c) Mens rea as to life endangerment for section 23?

The one difficulty in the section 23 offence in relation to mens rea is that it is unclear whether there is a further element of malice required. Must there, in addition, be malice as to the endangering of life? Parliament has left this point unanswered. There is little help from other offences since each offence depends upon its own construction. There is also little help from the decided cases on the section 23 offence. In *R* v *Dilworth* (1843) 2 Mood & R 531 it was held that 'if a noxious drug is administered which is likely to occasion death, and the party administering it is indifferent whether it occasions death or not, that party must be looked upon as contemplating the probable results of his own action.' (at p 535)

Whilst the Court of Appeal in *Cunningham* suggests that foresight of some injury is needed in addition to the foresight of the administration, more recently the Court of Appeal in *Cato* [1976] 1 All ER 260 has suggested, distinguishing *Cunningham,* that there need only be foresight as to the administration. In so far as *Cunningham* suggests that there must be foresight of injury, it is submitted that that decision is wrong. There need be no foresight of injury, if anything there would have to be foresight of life being endangered. Life may be endangered without an injury. For example, no-one would doubt that life is endangered by ingestion of a poison, but there is no obvious injury caused by that ingestion.

Even if a court decides that the defendant in our instance must foresee the endangerment of life in addition to the other elements of the mens rea, there is no reason why a jury could not find that the defendant also foresaw that life would be endangered. It is unlikely to be the case that a person infected with HIV could honestly and reliably claim that he or she did not realise that if a person has infection with HIV, that he or she will not at some stage get AIDS (it is just possible that advisers might hedge this point slightly, nevertheless he or she will realise at least that there is a significant risk of contracting AIDS), and therefore realise that he or she will die (it is unlikely to be the case that anybody with HIV will not realise that, if they contract AIDS, it will eventually cause their death). In any case, the general level of knowledge of all people is that HIV and AIDS are life threatening. Should HIV actually cause grievous bodily harm, it will be possible to convict him or her of the section 18 offence, but, as already indicated, it may well be extremely difficult to prove that this instance of contact with an HIV source was the cause of the victim having contracted that virus (See *Tulley* v *Corrie* (1867) 10 Cox CC 640 per Mellor J, at p 641).

(d) Intention to injure, aggrieve or annoy for section 24

Were the lesser offence contrary to section 24 to be charged, there is a clear extra mens rea element in addition to the need for the prosecution to prove the malicious administration of the noxious thing. The administration must be done with an intent to injure, aggrieve or annoy. Intention presumably bears the same meaning as it does in the law of murder (*R* v *Moloney* [1985] AC 905; *R* v *Hancock and Shankland* [1986] AC 455; *R* v *Nedrick* [1986] 3 All ER 1). The specific intention in section 24 was considered by the House of Lords in *R* v *Hill* (1986) 83 Cr App R 386. According to Lord Griffiths, the correct test is whether the defendant intended to cause harm to the victim's health. As discussed above in relation to the endangerment of life, there is little, if anything, to prevent the jury finding that the defendant intended to cause harm to the victim having had sexual intercourse knowing he or she was anti-HIV positive.

It is submitted that the mens rea of the offences may, therefore, be satisfied.

AIDS is fatal and incurable. Any offence which punishes its transmission ought to be able to reflect the gravity of harm caused in the severity of the sentence imposed (Field and Sullivan 1987 at p 50). The offence under section 23 is capable of satisfying this requirement with its maximum sentence of ten years, and the maximum five years under section 24 is a not inconsiderable period.

(3) A defence: consent

Having shown that the defendant could have fulfilled both the actus reus and the mens rea of the section 23 or section 24 offence, without having to prove actual harm to the partner, it is appropriate to consider the defences which may be available. The most obvious defence upon which the defendant may choose to rely is that of consent. The partner to whom he or she has transmitted HIV did, in our hypothetical situation, consent in fact to the sexual intercourse. Is this consent valid so as to prevent the commission of an offence contrary to either section 23 or section 24 of the Offences Against the Person Act 1861? For the sake of exposition we concentrate upon the defence of consent as relevant to the section 23 offence.

If the defence of consent applies to this offence, it will deprive the administration of the necessary unlawfulness. For the defence of consent to achieve such a result it must be established that the victim actually did consent, and that the defendant had an honest belief in the consent of the victim. But, first, what is it to which the partner is supposed to be consenting? The offence is concerned with the administration of a noxious thing, therefore, the consent must be to that administration (Bronitt 1994, at p 25; Alldridge 1993, at p 258). Broadly, there are two different aspects to this problem which must be considered. The first is the instance where the partner is not aware of the defendant's condition, but does consent to sexual intercourse. The second is where the partner is aware of the defendant's condition, but nevertheless still consents to have sexual intercourse.

(a) The partner is not aware that the defendant is HIV positive

The partner has consented to sexual intercourse, but is unaware of the defendant's condition. Has he or she thereby consented to the administration of a noxious substance? A similar, though not identical, question was considered by the Court of Crown Cases Reserved in *R* v *Clarence* (1888) 22 QBD 23 In that case the defendant husband had consensual sexual intercourse with his wife knowing that he was infected with gonorrhoea. The wife was unaware of his condition, and she contracted the disease. The defendant was charged with offences contrary to section 47 and section 20 of the Offences Against the Person Act 1861. (It is not known whether a charge contrary to section 24 was ever considered. There are comments in the various judgments of the Court which hint at some success had such a charge been framed, although it would have been necessary to have proved an intent to injure, aggrieve or annoy). His conviction was quashed by a 9–4 majority. The reasoning of the various judgments is somewhat obscured by the facts that first, there is clearly no need for there to be an assault when the charge is one of inflicting grievous bodily harm (*R* v *Wilson* [1984] AC 242. Judges in *Clarence* relying on this point included Stephen J, AL Smith J, Mathew J, Grantham J, Huddleston B., Pollock B. and Hawkins J, who nevertheless managed to give a judgment in favour of upholding the conviction. Secondly, a husband can be found guilty of raping his wife (*R* v *R* [1991] 4 All ER 481). The judges in *Clarence* who relied upon this point included AL Smith J and Wills J. Perhaps the most significant element of the case, for present purposes, is the point made, for example, by Stephen J, that fraud does not vitiate consent, but that if a person is mistaken as to the nature and quality of the act, there is no consent. (See also *R* v *Flattery* (1877) 2 QB 410; *R* v *Case* (1850) 4 Cox CC 220; *R* v *Williams* [1923] 1 KB 340; *R* v *Linekar* [1995] 2 WLR 237; *R* v *Elbekkay* [1995] Crim LR 163). It was then asserted that the wife was not mistaken as to the nature and quality of the act, she still had sexual intercourse with her husband.

When the nature and quality test is examined in detail, the argument is shown to be unconvincing. The types of instances when the judges in *Clarence* thought that there would be no mistake were not only those like the instant case, but also where the woman thought, wrongly, that she was married to the man, or where the woman was seduced in the expectation of marriage, or where the woman was a prostitute and thought she had been paid (Stephen J, at p 43). When these examples are considered, it will be noted that there is a significant difference between the facts of the case and the examples provided. The examples are all concerned with the morality of the sexual relationship, indeed that is explicitly stated by Stephen J (*Ibid*, at p 44). In all the examples sexual intercourse took place, but the woman was mistaken as to some aspect which would, if true, have made the sexual intercourse more acceptable to her. But the facts of the instant case are not about morals or acceptability, they are about health. We assert, as did Field J in the minority in *Clarence* (at p 59) that sexual intercourse with a diseased man is an act different in nature and quality from sex with an undiseased man. Sex with a man, for example, to whom a woman believes she is married is no different an act in nature or quality from sex with a man to whom she actually is married (*Papadimitropoulous* (1957) 98 CLR 249). The judges in *Clarence* would not be able to offer a counter argument, because their point is taken also on the basis of assertion (See assertions by Wills J at p 27 and Stephen J at p 44). If our point of view is accepted, the partner who believes that he or she is having sexual intercourse with a healthy person does not provide consent which prevents the defendant who in fact is anti-HIV positive being guilty of an offence contrary to section 23. *R* v *Bennett* (1866) 4 F & F 1105 and *R* v *Sinclair* (1867) 13 Cox CC 28 would both support this approach, but they were decided before *Clarence*.

A difficulty with this argument is its failure in the Canadian case of *Ssenyonga* (1993) 81 CCC 3d 257. The following evidence in relation to the accused was not disputed: (a) He already knew he was infected with HIV; (b) He knew of the risk of transmitting the virus to the complainants through unprotected sexual intercourse, ie, sexual intercourse without the use of a condom; (c) None of the complainants knew he was anti-HIV positive; (d) None of the complainants would have consented to have sexual intercourse with him had they known he was anti-HIV positive. There was evidence that after having sexual intercourse with the accused, each of the complainants tested positive for HIV.

The prosecution argued that 'the English case of *Clarence* should not be followed. . . . [on the basis that] the failure of a person who knows he is infected with HIV to disclose that fact before engaging in sexual intercourse constitutes fraud as to the quality of the act of sexual intercourse that will vitiate the consent of the complainant.'

McDermid J, ruled that 'fraud sufficient to vitiate consent must relate to the nature and quality of the act. In this case, the complainants were under absolutely no misapprehension as to the nature of the consenting to participate in acts of sexual intercourse with the accused. Nothing he said or did induced them to believe otherwise. Accordingly, on this branch of the Crown's argument, there is no evidence of fraud' (*Ibid*).

A further means of distinguishing *Clarence* is to ask to what it is the partner is supposed to be consenting? He or she may be consenting to sexual intercourse (subject to what has just been said), but is not consenting to the administration of a noxious substance. Of course by consenting to sexual intercourse, he or she is consenting to the transmission of body fluids, but not body fluids contaminated with HIV, nor to the administration of the virus itself.

In any case, we should be very careful in according the decision in *Clarence* too much significance in this debate. It is important to look carefully at the other arguments used to substantiate the quashing of the husband's conviction. The charges in that case, as already indicated, were of offences contrary to section 47 and section 20 of the 1861 Act. It is quite clear that some of the judges thought that these charges were inappropriate to deal with the conduct in question (Wills J, at pp 30 and 35 and Manisty J, at p 55.). This point has no relevance to the possibility of an offence contrary to either section 23 or 24 of the same Act being committed, indeed we would agree that the wrong charges were brought against Clarence. Some of the judges took the view that the common law, for example adaptation of the offence of public nuisance, (Stephen J at p 39.) should not be left to deal with the activity in question, but that Parliamentary action was necessary, if at all, to criminalise the sort of behaviour in question (Wills J, at p 33, Stephen J, at p 46, Hawkins J, at p 53 and Pollock B., at p 64). A simple answer to this problem is that had the judges given sufficient thought to sections 23 and 24, they would have realised that Parliament had provided the answer. Some judges were also concerned that conviction of the defendant would lead to hundreds of convictions (Wills J, at p 32, Stephen J, at p 38 and Hawkins J, at p 54). This is an irrelevant argument if there is an offence covering the activity in question. If the activity is criminal, as we argue, there is nothing necessarily wrong in there being hundreds of convictions. If the activity is that frequent, it is right that there should be convictions of people taking such advantage of their sexual partners. The truth of the matter is that the judges do not appear to have realised that Parliament had chosen to make criminal the administration of poisons, destructive and other noxious things, so that the person passing on smallpox to a friend or a child would be guilty of a crime which did not require improper extension of the concept of assault. Had that been realised then those judges who were of the view that Clarence should have been guilty of an offence would have been able to point out that he was prosecuted for the wrong offence.

Finally, it might credibly be argued that *Clarence* is a decision now over one hundred years old which reflects somewhat outmoded attitudes to sexuality, most clearly in the acceptance of the majority of the judges of the marital rape exemption, and, therefore, the case deserves to be re-examined. We accept that longevity of a case is sometimes a reason in itself for refusing to overrule it and, indeed, it is not necessary for the success of our argument that *Clarence* be overruled, provided the basis upon which it may be distinguished is accepted.

The Law Commission has resiled from a proposal that all fraud should vitiate consent (Law Com CP No 139, paras 6.15–6.18 and see Ormerod 1994). The Law Commission now proposes that fraud as to the nature and quality of the act or identity of the actor will nullify consent (Law Com CP No 139, para 6.18). It is, however, concerned about one particular case, that of ‘the case where a person agrees to allow another to have sexual intercourse with him or her after that other person has untruthfully said that he has been tested with HIV or other sexually transmitted diseases and that the findings were negative’ (Law Com CP No 139, para 6.19). A question then arises whether the failure to disclose HIV status goes to the nature and quality of the act, because, as the Law Commission asserts, it has a ‘morally different’ character when compared with the prostitute who is led to believe, mistakenly, that she or he will be paid or the woman who submits ‘to a vaginal inspection by an impostor doctor’ (Law Com CP No 139, paras 6.19 & 6.17). The distinguishing factor, as we see it, is the health risk involved as a consequence of the fraud, which, we have argued, should be sufficient to vitiate the consent. This is the sufficient moral distinguishing factor, which, we believe, should be identified by the Law Commission (Law Com CP No 139, para 6.19). We would argue that this principle applies to both an articulated and an unconscious assumption (Law Com CP No 139, para 6.29).

(b) The partner is aware that the defendant is HIV positive
At first glance it might well be assumed that this would undoubtedly mean that the defendant would not be guilty of an offence contrary to either section 23 or section 24 of the 1861 Act. However, the matter is by no means so straightforward. It is undoubtedly the case that a person may not consent to the administration of something which is fatal, because consent is no defence to a charge of murder. In *R* v *Cato* the defendant administered to another, consenting person a fatal dose of heroin which had been mixed by the deceased. The Court of Appeal held, inter alia, that the consent of the deceased was not relevant in considering the defendant's guilt except in so far as it went to the question of recklessness or gross negligence in relation to the manslaughter charge. In our hypothetical case, if the partner has consented to the administration of a fatal substance, this consent will not provide a defence to the defendant. However, it cannot be proved that HIV is necessarily a fatal substance.

Where the victim has consented in fact, and the substance is not fatal, it remains to be considered whether that consent is legally valid. The courts do not permit people to consent to activity which is contrary to the public interest. The transmission of HIV is life endangering, though not necessarily fatal, because not everyone having sexual intercourse with someone who is anti-HIV positive catches the virus themselves. It would seem possible that the courts would, therefore, decide that a person cannot consent to the transmission of the virus. In *Attorney General's Reference (No 6 of 1980)* [1981] QB 715, the Court of Appeal decided that 'it is not in the public interest that people should try to cause or should cause each other actual bodily harm for no good reason.' The court made clear that this approach was not meant to impugn the legality of 'properly conducted sports and games, lawful chastisement or correction, reasonable surgical interference, dangerous exhibitions, etc.' There is some good reason for such activity, despite the bodily harm which it causes or may cause.

This approach was expressly approved by the Court of Appeal and the House of Lords in *R* v *Brown* [1994] 1 AC 212. In this case the House of Lords, by a bare majority, upheld the convictions of offences contrary to sections 47 and 20 of the Offences Against the Person Act 1861 of 15 homosexual sado-masochists who performed various acts upon each other, including whippings, beatings and acts of genital torture. All the acts were done with the full informed consent of each of the adult males involved and none resulted in permanent injury or even required medical treatment. The majority explained that

> 'the authorities . . . do not establish that consent is a defence to a charge under the Act of 1861. They do establish that the courts have accepted that consent is a defence to the infliction of bodily harm in the course of some lawful activities. The question is whether the defence should be extended to the infliction of bodily harm in the course of sado-masochistic encounters' (per Lord Templeman at p 234).

One reason given by Lord Templeman for denying the defence in such cases was the 'obvious dangers of serious personal injury and *blood infection*' (at p 236 emphasis added). His Lordship went on to point out that two members of the group had died of AIDS and a third had contracted HIV, although it was not necessarily as a result of the practices of this group.

It is submitted that the transmission of HIV is more dangerous than such sado-masochistic behaviour, furthermore there is no apparent good reason at all why people should be permitted to transmit the virus, indeed it is arguable that all reasonable efforts should be made to prevent transmission, and that, therefore, consent to transmission of the virus is not legally valid. It is submitted, therefore, that the defendant who administers to his consenting and fully informed victim HIV would commit the offence under section 23. We consider this point further after looking at the need of the defendant to believe in the other's consent.

Where a defendant does not have the actual consent of the victim, but has an honest but mistaken belief in his or her consent, the defendant will, generally, escape conviction. This is not so in cases where the consent, if it had been present, would have been contrary to the public interest and therefore not legally valid. Thus, belief in the partner's consent to having sex with a person who is anti-HIV positive and making a mistake about the legal position will not avail, because it would be a mistake of criminal law, which is not relevant.

If the argument above is correct, the courts could convict in cases when both parties are consenting and both fully informed of the medical condition of one or both. This may well seem to be an outrageous proposition, but it does appear to follow. However, the object of the argument propounded in this paper has been to deal with the person deliberately trying to infect partners with the virus, for whatever motive. We still hold to the view that such people should be prosecuted. Unless a distinction can be drawn between loving couples and other relationships in a 'public interest' debate, the conclusion seems to be that it would also put loving couples at the potential risk of prosecution (see discussion of defence above). We would point out that no prosecution is possible without the problem being reported to the police and, if reported, it is not appropriate for the Crown Prosecution Service to go ahead with a prosecution where such a prosecution would be against the public interest. Whilst the public interest is firmly in favour of keeping the spread of HIV in check, there is, in an individual case, the countervailing public interest of not improperly interfering in the intimate relationships of people, one or both of whom have sadly contracted infection with HIV.

The prosecution in *Ssenyonga* argued that 'There is no good reason on moral grounds for permitting a person to have sexual intercourse without disclosing his HIV positive status. If an infected person chooses to engage in sexual activity, which he is under no duty to do, the privacy interest of the infected person should yield to the physical safety and autonomy of the partner.' This was rejected by the trial judge McDermid J who found that the limitations on consensual harm were to control the direct or indirect application of force and that '[t]he law of assault is too blunt an instrument to excise AIDS from the body politic.'

Where specific legislation has been enacted, it usually provides that there shall be a defence where the infected person has informed the 'victim' of his or her condition and that 'victim' has consented to the act of intimacy which may result in the transmission of infection' (See eg the Illinois Public Act 86-0897 D; Deutschmann 1990). Interestingly, the Florida statute Control of Sexually Transmissible Diseases Act 1986, provides a defence where the victim 'has been informed of the transmission of the sexually transmissible disease and has consented to the sexual intercourse' (Waters 1990, at p 35).

It has been suggested by Deutschmann (1990, at p 34), that it should be a defence to show that a condom or presumably a 'femidom' (a female condom) or 'dental dam' (a latex barrier originally developed for use in dental surgery which is placed over the vulva thus making oral sex safer) was used during the sexual act by which the virus was transmitted. There is, in this case, no need to speak of defences in the true sense of the word. It seems obvious that the defendant who has used a condom or other form of protection will lack the necessary mens rea for the offence under either section 23 or section 24. Medical research has confirmed that '[w]orldwide, the predominant mode of human immunodeficiency virus (HIV) transmission is heterosexual intercourse [and that c]onsistent use of condoms for heterosexual intercourse is highly effective in preventing the transmission of HIV' (De Vincenzi 1994). Anne Johnson has commented that the results of work done on condoms and protection from HIV are

> 'important in three ways. First, they demonstrate that even among repeatedly counselled European couples known to be exposed to HIV, nearly half continued to have unprotected intercourse. Second, the results show that among couples who used condoms inconsistently, there remained a considerable risk of infection. . . . Third, the data provides evidence of the protective effect of condoms in people known to be exposed to HIV. There was no seroconversion among the 124 couples who used condoms consistently.' (Johnson 1994)

Despite this, it is arguable that taking precautions *per se* ought not to be sufficient *defence* unless the defendant has also informed his sexual partner of his condition (Field and Sullivan 1987, at p 53). Condoms and femidoms can split. It is arguable that the defendant who knows of his HIV status and does not disclose it to his partner but takes the precaution of using a condom is still a conscious risk taker and will still have the mens rea as required by *Cunningham*. This is not a very strong argument. The converse of this is that it has been suggested that there is a strong case to be made for . . . not allowing informed consent to be a defence in the absence of precautions (Field and Sullivan 1987).

It has been suggested that there should be a special defence available for married couples (Deutschmann 1990, at p 34). A special defence in such cases would be wholly inconsistent with the policy underlying the recent decision of the House of Lords *R* v *R*, in which the husband's immunity from prosecution for rape of his wife was abolished. One proposal contains a defence for married persons who have disclosed the risk of infection (Robinson 1985, at p 101). The Queensland statute provides a defence for the spouse or 'connubial' who knew of the accused's infection and voluntarily took the risk of being infected (Queens. Health Act Amendment Act (No 2), No 103, 1984 Queensl Stat 1195, 3(h), (i) (1984)).

5. The Effect of Reform

Briefly we wish to draw attention to changes which would occur were the Law Commission's proposals on offences against the person to be legislated (Law Com No 128). The Commission adopts an earlier proposal made by the Criminal Law Revision Committee in its Fourteenth Report (CLRC 14th Report, 1980) that sections 23 and 24 be abolished. The Commission accepted that the proposals for offences to deal with the causing of serious injury would adequately cover all that is dealt with by sections 23 and 24.

The Law Commission's Proposals in relation to injury

In 1993 the Law Commission recognised the 'recent public concern over the possibility of the deliberate or reckless infection of others with life-threatening conditions, including the HIV virus' (Law Com No 128, at para 15.17). The Commission restated its view that 'the deliberate or reckless causing of disease should not be beyond the reach of the criminal law as restated by clauses 2 to 4 of the Criminal Law Bill' (*Ibid*). This would suggest that the offences of injury and serious injury contained in clauses 2 to 4 are intended to cover the situation. In addition, the proposed Criminal Law Bill, contained in the 1993 Report, provides in clause 5 that in respect of administering substances without consent:

> (1) A person is guilty of an offence if, knowing that the other does not consent to what is done, he intentionally or recklessly administers to or causes to be taken by another a substance which he knows to be capable of interfering substantially with the other's bodily functions.
> (2) For the purposes of this section a substance capable of inducing unconsciousness or sleep is capable of interfering substantially with bodily functions.

The Law Commission explained in the 1993 Report that there had been almost 'no opposition to the retention of such an offence . . . [but that it] nevertheless reconsidered the question whether it is necessary given that, in many serious cases, an offence under clauses 2 to 4 of the Criminal Law Bill will also be committed.'

The Law Commission went on to state that:

> 'On careful consideration, our view remains that the balance of the arguments is in favour of retaining the clause. The administration without consent of substances capable of interfering substantially with bodily functions is irresponsible and potentially highly dangerous conduct, serious enough in itself to warrant criminal sanctions, notwithstanding that in many cases a more serious offence will also often be committed.' (*Ibid*)

The Law Commission's Proposals in relation to consent

In its 1994 consultation paper on consent the Law Commission proposed that fraud should vitiate consent (Law Com CP No 134, para 26.1), but, as we have already noted, this proposal has been dropped in its latest consultation paper on consent (Law Com CP No 139). The Law Commission proposes that consent would normally be valid unless it was to 'serious disabling injury', but subject to some exceptions, e.g., in relation to medical treatment, medical research and recognised sports. 'Serious disabling injury' is defined as:

> 'Injury or injuries which -
> (1) cause serious distress, and
> (2) involve the loss of a bodily member or organ or permanent bodily injury or permanent functional impairment, or serious or permanent disfigurement, or severe and prolonged pain, or serious impairment of mental health, or prolonged unconsciousness;
> and in determining whether an effect is permanent, no account should be taken of the fact that it may be remediable by surgery. (Law Com CP No 139, para 4.51)

Serious disabling injury must include HIV, which means that it is something, the risk of which, a person cannot consent. This is a consequence which would have serious and unfortunate consequences for those engaged in relationships where each knows of the other's status, but the law should have no involvement. However, the Law Commission's proposals go further, because intentionally or recklessly causing a serious disabling injury would be an offence (Law Commission, 1995, para 4.48).

The full implications of these proposals are beyond the scope of this paper. However, issues related to our discussion include the effect of fraud, which we deal with above. Further, the Law Commission proposes that the 'victim' who has consented to a serious disabling injury, or the risk of it, would be dealt with according to the ordinary rules of accessorial liability. The Law Commission appears to mean that, although secondary parties cannot normally be guilty where they are victims, where a 'victim' positively seeks the commission of the principal offence, they should face criminal liability (Law Com CP No 139, para 1.22). This has very wide consequences and potentially criminalises any partner who engages in sexual activity knowing of his or partner's HIV status. This is potentially alarming.

The Law Commission proposes that there be an offence of procuring consent by deception (Law Com CP No 139, para 6.81). This would be a welcome addition to the criminal calendar, since its objectives would be consistent with the argument which we have propounded. Further, the Law Commission contemplates the possibility of imposing an 'express duty to communicate information' (Law Com CP No 139, para 6.84). Were such an offence to be created it would enable conviction for failure to provide information about HIV status which has, for example, lead to conviction for criminal nuisance in New Zealand (see *Mwai* [1995] 3 NZLR 149). The extent of a duty to disclose would apply only to the creation of injury.

Bibliography

Alldridge, P (1993) 'Sex, Lies and the Criminal Law' 44 *Northern Ireland Legal Quarterly* 250.

Andrias, RT (1993) 'Urban Criminal Justice: Has the response to the HIV epidemic been fair?' 20(3) *Fordham Urban Law Journal* 497.

Babinski, M, Closen, M, & Herman, D (1994) 'Criminalisation of an epidemic: HIV-AIDS and Criminal Exposure Laws' 46(4) *Arkansas Law Review* 921.

Bronitt, S (1994) 'Spreading Disease and the Criminal Law' *Criminal Law Review* 21.

Burdt, LK & Caldwell, RS (1988) 'The Real Fatal Attraction: Civil and Criminal Liability for Transmission of AIDS' (1988) 37 *Drake Law Review* 657.

Burris, Dalton, Miller and the Yale Aids Law Project (1993) *Aids Law Today – A new Guide for the Public* (New Haven: Yale University Press).

Cook, MS (1992) 'Criminal Liability for attempting to inflict the Aids virus: Possibilities in Arkansas' future' 25 *Arkansas Law Review* 505.

Criminal Law Revision Committee Fourteenth Report (1980) *Offences Against the Person* (London: HMSO) Cmnd 7844.

De Vincenzi, I (1994) 'A longitudinal study of human immunodeficiency virus transmission by heterosexual partners' 331 *New England Journal of Medicine* 341.

Deutschmann, J (1990) 'Criminal Sanctions for Transmission of AIDS – An analysis of new Illinois legislation' *Chicago Bar Association Record* 32.

D'Orio, LB (1993) 'What to do when the charge is criminal sexual conduct and the complainant is HIV positive' *Michigan Bar Journal* 922.

Edlin BR and Holmberg, SD (1993) 'Insemination in HIV-negative women with processed semen of HIV-positive partners' 341 *The Lancet* 571.
Field, MA and Sullivan KM (1987) 'Aids and the Criminal Law' 15 *Law Medicine and Health Care* 46, 47.
Friedland, G and Klein, R (1987) 'Transmission of the Human Immunodeficiency Virus' 317 *New England Journal of Medicine* 1125, 1132.
Glenn, HP, Gilmore, N, Somerville, MA and Morissette, YM (1990) *HIV Infection, AIDS and Privacy* Working Paper McGill University Montreal.
Gostin, LO (1990) *Aids and the Health Care System* (New Haven: Yale University Press).
Haigh, R and Harris, D (eds) (1995) *AIDS: a guide to the law* (2nd ed) (London: Routledge).
Harris, KA (1993) 'Death at First Bite: A Mens Rea Approach in Determining Criminal Liability For Intentional HIV Transmission' 35 *Arizona Law Review* 237.
Hart, H (1958) 'The Aims of the Criminal Law' 23 *Law and Contemporary Problems* 401.
Herman, DJH (1990) 'Criminalising Conduct Related to HIV Transmission' 9 *Saint Louis University Public Law Review* 351.
Hessol, NA, Rutherford, GW, Lifson, AR, et al (1988) *The Natural History of HIV Infection in a Cohort of Homosexual and Bisexual Men: A Decade of Follow-up* Fourth International Conference on AIDS, Stockholm.
Holland, WH (1994) 'HIV/AIDS and the Criminal Law' 36 *Criminal Law Quarterly* 279.
Johnson, MA (1994) 'Editorial' 331 *New England Journal of Medicine* 341.
Keenlyside, RA and Adler, MW (1993) 'Definitions and epidemiologies of AIDS' *Medicine International* 29.
Kerney, SV (1992) 'Criminalizing HIV Transmission: Lessons from history and a model for the future' 8 *Journal of Contemporary Health Law and Policy* 245.
Kiessling, A (1992) 'Semen transmission of human immunodeficiency syndrome' 58 *Fertility and Sterility* 667.
Kingsley LA et al (1987) 'Risk factors for seroconversion to Human Immunodeficiency Virus among male homosexuals' 336 *The Lancet* 345.
Krieger, et al (1991) 'Fertility in men infected with HIV' 164 *Journal of Infectious Diseases* 464.
Laurie, GT (1991) 'AIDS and Criminal Liability Under Scots Law' *Journal of the Law Society of Scotland* 312.
Law Commission No 218 (1993), *Legislating the Code: Offences Against the Person and General Principles* (London: HMSO) Cm 2370.
Law Commission Consultation Paper No 134 (1994) *Consent and Offences Against the Person* (London: HMSO).
Law Commission Consultation Paper No 139 (1995), *Consent in the Criminal Law* (London: HMSO).
Leng, R (1994) 'Consent and Offences Against the Person' *Criminal Law Review* 480.
Mastro, TD, Satten, GA, Nopkesorn, T, Sangkharomya, S, Longini, IM (1994) 'Probability of female-to-male transmission of HIV–1 in Thailand' 343 *The Lancet* 204.
Mayer, KH (1990) 'The Natural History of HIV Infection and Current Therapeutic Strategies' in Gostin, LO (ed) *Aids and the Health Care System* (New Haven: Yale University Press).

McGuigan, S (1986)'The Aids Dilemma, Public Health vs. Criminal Law' 4 *Law and Inequality* 545.
McGuire, KA (1991) 'AIDS and the Sexual Offender: The Epidemic Now Poses Threats to the Victim and the Criminal Justice System' 96 *Dickinson Law Review* 95.
Mermin, JH, et al (1991) 'Detection of HIV DNA and RNA in semen by polyerase chain reaction' 164 *Journal of Infectious Diseases* 769.
Mueller, P (1986) 'The Epidemiology of the Human Immunodeficiency Virus Infection' 14 *Law Medicine & Health Care* 150.
Ormerod, DC (1994) 'Consent and offences against the person: Law Commission Consultation Paper No 134' 57 *Modern Law Review* 928.
Phillips, AN, Sabin, CA, Elford, J, Bofill, M, Janossy, G, Lee, CA (1994) 'Use of CD4 lymphocyte count to predict long term survival free of AIDS after HIV infection.' 309 *British Medical Journal* 309.
Rickett, CEF (1990) 'AIDS, Sexually Transmitted Diseases and the Criminal Law' 20 *Victoria University of Wellington Law Review* 182.
Robinson D (1985) 'AIDS and the Criminal Law : Traditional Approaches and a New Statutory Proposal' 14 *Hofstra Law Review* 91.
Semprini, AE (1993) 'Insemination of HIV-negative women with processed semen of HIV-positive partners' 341 *The Lancet* 1344.
Sloan, IJ (1988) *Aids Law: Implications for the Individual and Society* (London: Oceana Publications).
Smith, JC and Hogan, B (1992) *Criminal Law* (7th ed) (London: Butterworths).
Smith, KJM (1991) 'Sexual Etiquette, Public Interest and the Criminal Law' *Northern Ireland Legal Quarterly* 309.
Somerville, MA and Hamblin, D (1991) 'Surveillance and Reporting of HIV infection and AIDS in Canada: Ethics and Law' 41 *University of Toronto Law Journal* 224.
Somerville, MA and Gilmore, N (1988) *Human Immunodeficiency Virus Antibody Testing in Canada* (Report submitted to and approved by the National Advisory Committee on AIDS) (Ottawa: Health and Welfare Canada).
Stauter, RL (1989) '*United States* v *Moore*: AIDS and the Criminal Law. The Witch Hunt Begins' 22 *Akron Law Review* 503.
Taitz, J (1989) 'Legal Liability for Transmitting AIDS' 57(4) *Medico-Legal Journal* 216.
The Terrence Higgins Trust (1990) *HIV and AIDS: Information for Women* (London).
Tierney, TW (1992) 'Criminalizing the Sexual Transmission of HIV: An international analysis' 15 *Hastings International and Comparative Law Review* 475.
Waters, RC (1990) 'Liability Under Florida Law for Exposing Others to Infectious Disease' 64 *Florida Bar Journal* 35.
Woodhouse, DE, Math, JB, Potterat, JJ and Riffe, LD (1993) 'Restricting Personal Behaviour – case study on legal measures to prevent the spread of HIV' 4(2) *International Journal of STD and AIDS* 114.

CHARITY LAW – A POLITICAL SCANDAL?

Alison Dunn

Newcastle Law School

First Published in Web Journal of Current Legal Issues in association with Blackstone Press Ltd.

SUMMARY

The extent to which charities may pursue political activities, and political campaigning is a contentious issue. Whilst Parliament has steadfastly refused to embrace political aims as charitable purposes, charities are nevertheless permitted to undertake a degree of political activity. In order to assist charity trustees to remain within the law, the Charity Commission has updated its guidelines on the types of political activity and political campaigning that charities may pursue, and the penalties involved for breach. Whilst advice in this uncertain area is to be welcomed, the Charity Commission guidelines have limitations. These limitations reflect problems in charity law, an area that is ripe for reform. This article examines the guidelines, their limitations, and argues for greater clarification in the area.

CONTENTS

Introduction

In 1995 the Charity Commission updated its guidelines concerning the involvement of charities in the political sphere.[1] The guidelines, published as 'Political

1 The Charity Commission's Home Page may be viewed at **http://www.open.gov.uk/charity/cchome.htm**

Activities and Campaigning by Charities' (leaflet CC9), replace a set previously issued by the Commission in 1994. They cover a range of situations straddling the sphere of political activity and political campaigning, providing charities with advice, *inter alia,* upon influencing public opinion; supporting, opposing or promoting legislation; commenting on public issues; providing information; seeking support for government grants, and concluding with an examination of penalties. The stated aims of the guidelines are threefold: in the context of political involvement they aim to assist trustees of charities to remain within the law; secondly, to outline what actions the Charity Commission will take if trustees stray beyond the law; and, finally, to provide reassurance – effectively a safeguard – for those trustees who adhere to the guidelines (Preface, p 2).

The rationale for restricting charities from engaging in political activities lies in the notion that a political purpose fails to satisfy the requirement of public benefit, an essential qualifier for a purpose to be charitable. This is due in part to the wide diversity in political tenets, the need for the judiciary to remain politically neutral, and, as Lord Parker stated in *Bowman* v *Secular Society Ltd* [1917] AC 406 at 442, 'because the Court has no means of judging whether a proposed change in the law will or will not be for the public benefit'. So, for example, charities whose purposes have been to support a political party, or reform a particular law, have been held to be political and not charitable.[2] However, charities may engage in political activity where that activity is *subsidiary* to the principal purpose of the charity, for example see *Re Koeppler's Will Trusts.*[3] The practical dividing line between a political purpose and a political activity ancillary to a charitable purpose, however, remains largely unclear. As Parliament has steadfastly refused to either incorporate political purposes into charitable trusts, or indeed provide any form of clarification upon the issue, the position of charity trustees precariously attempting to walk the tightrope between what is and is not permitted remains.[4] In the context of providing support for trustees, the updated guidelines issued by the Charity Commission are invaluable in their attempt to clarify an unacceptably uncertain area.

The 1995 Charity Commission Guidelines

Under the 1995 Charity Commission guidelines, charities are given a fairly wide ambit to enter into the political sphere. Whilst they cannot be political organisations and cannot support a particular political party, the guidelines stress that they may nevertheless be involved in political processes and political activation, with the caveat that such activities must be subsidiary to, and in furtherance of, their principal charitable purposes (para 7).

According to the Commission, a political activity is acceptable if :

> 'there is a reasonable expectation that the activity concerned will further the stated purposes of the charity, and so benefit its beneficiaries, to an extent justified by the resources devoted to the activity; the activity is within the powers which the trustees have to achieve those purposes; the activity is consistent with

2 See, for example, *Bowman* v *Secular Society Ltd* [1917] AC 406, *National Anti-Vivisection Society* v *IRC* [1948] AC 31, *McGovern* v *Attorney General* [1982] Ch 321.

3 [1986] Ch 423. In this case a gift was made to a non-party political association ('Wilton Park') whose purpose was to promote greater co-operation in Europe. This was accepted as a valid charitable purpose.

4 Legislating upon the political activities of charities was discussed and dismissed in the 1989 White Paper, *Charities: A Framework for the Future* (Cm 694) Chapter 2.

[the] guidelines; [and] the views expressed [by the charity] are based on a well-founded and reasoned case and are expressed in a responsible way' (para 12).

This embracing statement is elaborated in greater detail in paragraphs 15–62 of the guidelines. To take a few examples, a charity may influence government and public opinion, though it should only do so through accurate, well founded and reasoned argument based upon research or experience, and then only upon a matter directly related to the charity's purpose or the charitable sector as a whole (para 23). Additionally, a charity may comment upon changes in the law or government policy (para 33), and advocate or oppose such change (para 34). Whilst a charity cannot support a political party, it may nevertheless have a political view and advocate particular political solutions, providing it makes it clear that its views are independent of any political party (paras 39, 40). Charities may organise and present petitions to the Houses of Parliament or local government (para 26), and in a well-received change from the previous guidelines, a charity may both inform its supporters or the public how Members of Parliament have voted on particular issues, and provide them with material (such as the previously banned pre-printed postcards) to send to Members of Parliament to express the charity's and the supporters' viewpoint on a given political issue (paras 24, 25).

In carrying out the above a charity may not, *inter alia*, participate in party political demonstrations (para 28); attempt to influence government or public opinion through inaccurate or distorted data (para 27); invite either its members or the public to support its position without providing them with sufficient information (para 31); overstep the boundary between education and propaganda (para 32); persuade the public to vote for or against a particular candidate or political party (para 49); or undertake research with another body where it is clear that the latter's intention is to use the research for party political or propagandist purposes (para 53).

The penalties for breaching the restrictions against political activities are elaborated in the final section of the guidelines (paras 56–60). They emphasise that a breach will amount to a misapplication of charity funds, and could, for example, lead to withdrawal of taxation relief.[5] Where a breach is suspected, the Commission will first seek an explanation from the charity. If that explanation is unsatisfactory, the Commission will use their discretion in imposing a suitable penalty. Depending upon the circumstances, the Commission may purely provide the charity trustees with advice, or, at the other end of the scale, it may initiate formal proceedings to recover the misapplied funds and restrict the charity from further political activities (para 58). It is unlikely that a breach of the restrictions on political activities would cause the Charity Commission to remove the charity from the Charities' Register. However, any charity seeking to exploit this detail should beware of the ultimate consequences, for as paragraph 60 of the guidelines states:

5 The statutory provisions providing taxation relief are various and include: Income and Corporation Taxes Act 1988 (consolidating the 1986 Finance Act) s 505 (exemption from income or corporation tax on a charity's income); Taxation and Chargeable Gains Act 1992, s 256 (exemption from tax on capital gains); Local Government Finance Act 1988, s 43(5) (local taxation relief at 80% of non-domestic rate); Finance Act 1982, s 129 (exemption from stamp duty); Finance Act 1977, s 57 (exemption from National Insurance Surcharge). Relief for donors which can also aid charities include: Income and Corporation Taxes Act 1988, ss 660–662 (enabling charities to recoup tax on covenanted sums over 4 years); Inheritance Tax Act 1984, s 23 (no inheritance tax on charitable legacies); Taxation and Chargeable Gains Act 1992, s 241 (disposition to charity does not cause donor to be saddled with tax on a capital gain otherwise taxable).

> 'If . . . the trustees could argue successfully that the express purposes of the institution were wide enough to cover impermissible political activities, then the question of whether the organisation was established for exclusively charitable purposes would arise, and could lead to its removal from the Register of Charities.'

Interestingly, as well as the more specific penalties, the guidelines further stress the *wider* risks for a charity, and indeed for the sector as a whole, of embarking upon unacceptable political activities and misapplying funds. That wider danger is the loss of public support – be it financial or moral (para 56). Whilst this may be a risk that some charities are willing to take in furtherance of their aims or principles, it remains clear that in the present climate of declining donations and donor scepticism on the efficiency and efficacy of the sector, this could prove in fact to be the most compelling of 'penalties'.

Two useful developments

One introduction in the 1995 guidelines on political activity is the inclusion of objective assessment criteria. This is a change from the subjective standards that had been in place in the 1994 Charity Commission guidelines. Under paragraphs 36, 37 and 39, a charity is advised that it may support, oppose or promote legislation, or advocate political solutions 'which can reasonably be expected' to achieve, hinder or further its charitable purpose. The change to this objective standard increases certainty, and is in line with the trend towards more stringent regulation of charitable behaviour, in the sense that it requires an internal check to trustee activities through consideration of a notional common standard rather than by individual rationalisation. This reinforces the need for charities to have in place a procedure for accountability in order to evaluate their political activities, the importance of which is a point forcibly made in the guidelines (para 14). Regular evaluation by charities of trustee activity is, of course, advantageous, and objective standards by which to assess such activities should provide certainty where trustees are in doubt.

On a topical note, the 1995 guidelines include advice on the political use by charities of emotive advertising material. Enormous pressures have been put upon charities' fund-raising in recent years. Despite moves to introduce more and easier methods of planned donations, charities have seen their income diminish in real terms.[6] This fall has been exacerbated by the introduction of the National Lottery. For example, the National Council for Voluntary Organisations (NCVO) has estimated that during the first year of operation of the Lottery, £276 million of charitable donations would be lost (NCVO 1995). (It does not appear that this fall in donations will be offset by grants made to charities by the National Lottery Charities Board. An overall loss is therefore expected.) Whilst the long term effects of the latter cannot as yet be predicted, charities have been forced to reassess traditional modes of fund-raising. Some charities have become more aggressive in their advertising techniques in order to counter the decrease in donations. As a

6 Donations may be made to charities by a variety of tax efficient methods: for example, by deed of covenant, gift aid, and Give As You Earn (G.A.Y.E). Charity accounts and affinity cards have also been introduced. Some charities also receive income from the Government. Central Government funding to voluntary organisations in the period 1993/4 amounted to £3,567 m., and in the period 1994/5, £19,663m was given to organisations in England under the Health Services and Public Health Act 1968, s 64 General Scheme.

result, the use of emotive material to highlight issues and engage the compassion of the public is becoming increasingly common. In terms of campaigning and of seeking to influence government and public opinion, the Charity Commission guidelines emphasise the need for 'well-founded, reasoned argument based on research or direct experience' (para 23). Whilst the use of emotivity is not ruled out, the circumstances in which it may be used are circumscribed: paragraph 20 of the guidelines states:

> 'Provided all other requirements are met, material produced in support of a campaign may have emotional content. Indeed, the Commission accepts that the areas in which many charities work it is difficult to avoid engaging the emotions of the public. *But it would be unacceptable (except where the nature of the medium makes it impracticable to set out the basis of the charity's position) for a charity to seek to persuade government or the public on the basis of material which was merely emotive.*' (emphasis added – see also para 30)

Further, if the medium used to advertise prohibits factual support for a charity's position, they must nevertheless be able to provide evidence of that factual support if questioned. The explicit inclusion by the Charity Commission of guidelines upon emotive material is a welcome move forward, and may combat the rise in 'shock' advertising techniques increasing prevalent in print and other forms of advertising medium. In some circumstances regulation already occurs through the operation of the Advertising Standards Authority (ASA), who touched on the use of emotive material in advertising by charities in a recent report. In upholding complaints against a cinema advertisement of a particular charity, the ASA acknowledged the financial pressures placed upon charities, but cautioned against the wide effects of claims that did not 'stand up to scrutiny'. The wider effects highlighted by the ASA mirror those emphasised by the Charity Commission, that is, the penalty of loss of public support. The ASA commented (ASA 1995, p 1):

> 'Overstepping the line between presenting a possibly distressing, but accurate, picture of their cause and misinforming people about an issue by exaggerating or stretching the truth, *exploits the trust* that the public have in charities and certain pressure groups.' (emphasis added)[7]

However, whilst tighter regulation of the use of emotive material is foreseen, the Charity Commission provide little indication in their guidelines as to the precise dividing line between what is an acceptable or non-acceptable use of such material. The dividing line is important if, for example, the powerful and intrusive nature of audio and audio-visual advertisements is not to be abused.[8]

---

7 The ASA upheld complaints against the National Society for the Prevention of Cruelty to Children (NSPCC) for a cinema advertisement which featured a foetus disturbed by arguing parents. The ASA decided (at p 20) firstly, that the NSPCC had not 'demonstrated to be true' its implication that a foetus could be emotionally disturbed and, secondly, that the advertisement could cause unjustified distress. The ASA Report also concerned complaints against advertisements made by Friends of the Earth, International Fund for Animal Welfare and Greenpeace. However, whilst those bodies do have charitable branches, the advertisements were made by the non-charitable sections of those organisations.

8 One argument in *R* v *Radio Authority, ex parte Bull* [1995] 4 All ER 481, at 492 was that freedom of speech had to be weighed against 'the right of listeners to the radio not to be bombarded with information which they may not wish to receive. When an advertisement is on a hoarding or in a newspaper the reader can decide at a glance how much, if any, of it he wishes to read. If it is inserted into a radio programme which he wants to hear he has no similar way of curtailing it. The medium is intrusive. That is why it is powerful.'

Causes for concern?

It is in this lack of precision upon acceptable behaviour that the Charity Commission's guidelines disappoint. In certain instances, unequivocal statements and explanations are provided by the Charity Commission in the guidelines: for example, in explaining that a charity may advance education, but must not overstep the boundary separating education from propaganda, the distinction between the two is explained (para 32); so too is the notion of an ancillary purpose (para 9). Yet, despite the cogency these guidelines have in an abstract context, when assessed in a practical environment their immediate boundaries become less obvious. The Commission acknowledge that 'the dividing line between proper debate in the public arena and improper political activity is a difficult one to judge' (para 8). Even so, the use by the guidelines of concepts such as 'acceptability' and vague advice that charities should express their views 'with a proper sense of proportion' (para 10) can cause confusion. The failure to clarify these terms does not aid the guidelines to attain the first of their stated aims, to assist trustees to remain within the law. The lack of explanation of the law, however, is not so much symptomatic of the guidelines as it is of a lack of clarity in the charity arena as a whole. A 1989 White Paper which partly examined political activities by charities, freely admitted (in para 2.38) that 'the precise extent to which a charity may properly seek to influence the Government and public attitudes is a difficult question'. It is just unfortunate that the question remains as difficult with the aid of the Charity Commission's guidelines on political activity and campaigning, as without.

On a point associated with the demarcation of boundaries, it should be noted that whilst the Charity Commission give an indirect interpretation of political activity through identifying various forms of permissible and non-permissible actions by charities, the guidelines do not directly ascertain the breadth of the term 'political'. Reference is made within the guidelines (see paras 5, 6 and the Annex) to established case law, which indicate that the term 'political' is to be construed widely, though it has limits. This was recognised by Slade LJ in *McGovern* v *Attorney General* [1982] Ch 321, at 340, when he stated:

> 'Trusts for political purposes . . . include (*inter alia*) trusts of which a direct and principal purpose is either – (i) to further the interests of a particular political party, or (ii) to procure changes in the laws of this country, or (iii) to procure changes in the laws of a foreign country, or (iv) to procure a reversal of government policy or of particular decisions of governmental authorities in this country, or (v) to procure a reversal of government policy or of particular decisions of governmental authorities in a foreign country.'

The construction of the term was recently considered by Kennedy LJ and McCullough J in the case of *R* v *Radio Authority, ex parte Bull* [1995] 4 All ER 481. Bull concerned an application by the British Section of Amnesty International for judicial review of a decision made by the Radio Authority (the body which regulates commercial radio) in which the Radio Authority refused to broadcast an advertisement on behalf of Amnesty. Under the Broadcasting Act 1990, s 92(2)(a) the Radio Authority is required not to broadcast an advertisement:

> '(i) . . . by or on behalf of any body whose objects are wholly or mainly of a political nature, (ii) an advertisement which is directed towards any political end.'

According to Rule 8(a) of the Radio Authority Code of Advertising Standards:

> 'The term 'political' here is used in a wider sense of 'Party Political'. The prohibition precludes, for example, issue campaigning for the purposes of influencing legislation or executive action by local or national government.'

One of the questions before the Court was whether the Radio Authority had correctly interpreted the term 'political' in the Broadcasting Act. In construing the term and interpreting s 92(2)(a) of the Act, the Court found that 'political' as a concept was a wide one – going beyond the notion of party politics, and encompassing any activity which transcended into government policy. In reaching this conclusion the Court sought assistance from Slade LJ in *McGovern*, and also drew support from the House of Lords in *Tzu-Tsai Cheng* v *Governor of Pentonville Prison* [1973] AC 931, where Lord Diplock stated (at 945):

> '. . . politics are about government. 'Political' as descriptive of an object to be achieved must, in my view, be confined to the object of overthrowing or changing the government of a state or inducing it to change its policy.'

However, whereas *McGovern* and *Tzu-Tsai Cheng* seemed content to leave political activities at procuring change in policy, McCullough J in *Bull* seemed to cast the net wider – an activity would be political if it *pertained* to government policy. Whilst McCullough J stated (at p 500) that the fact something could be achieved by legislation would not make it political, the point was added that:

> 'Once the matter has become the subject of government policy, or once the need for legislation about it is advocated, particularly if the matter has become contentious, then, as it seems to me, it is open . . . to treat it as ''political''.'

This construction could have potentially wide reaching consequences, not least because a majority of charities, whilst not procuring change in government policy, nevertheless are concerned with politically sensitive areas which pertain to government policy, such as housing, health, education and welfare. If one takes McCullough J's view of 'political' to its natural limits, it could embrace all those activities falling short of procuring a change in policy, the everyday work of charities. Admittedly, *Bull* was not a case concerning construction of the term 'political' in the charity context, it concerned judicial review and interpretation of the Broadcasting Act. Nevertheless its view of the extent of the term is significant. Future editions of the Charity Commission's guidelines would benefit from clarification upon the grey area of activities which pertain to government policy.

The explicit demarcation of acceptable and non-acceptable political or campaigning activity by charities in guidelines such as the ones published by the Charity Commission would, however, be resisted by many – the basis of that resistance following the same rationale that has prevented Parliament legislating in this area. In considering the issue of whether to embrace political purposes as legitimate charitable purposes, the 1989 White Paper ultimately opposed the making of such a recommendation, since legislation would 'have the disadvantage of laying down inflexible rules instead of allowing the law to develop in the light of particular cases which may present features which cannot now be foreseen' (para 2.44). But it is a paradox that the preservation of flexibility highlighted in the White Paper, and which has so dominated the thrust of charity law, can actually exist as both the area's strength and its weakness. On the positive side, charities, in the main, act in response to social need, and thus must retain enough flexibility to mirror the changes in society, social expectations and social attitudes. In this context, the inflexibility of specific legislation (or guidelines) would hinder the effectiveness of charities. Here, the quick and unfettered ability to respond to change is a strength. Conversely, the attempt to preserve the pliancy and diversity of charities from the impediment of rigid legislation (or guidelines) can be stifling, especially in the context of political activity. For example, to stave off strict regulation an emphasis is placed in the guidelines upon charities to self-regulate their political activities (para 14). Yet, without unambiguous guidelines concerning the boundaries of acceptable political behaviour, self-regulation becomes difficult. In a climate of uncertainty, moreover, the threat of penalties for unlawful activity will tend to preclude participation in the political arena, which ultimately prevents the area from developing and changing. Here then, the preservation of diversity becomes the stick of restraint.

A second concern arising from the Charity Commission guidelines relates to the ability of smaller charities to influence government or public opinion. Paragraph 23 of the guidelines states that whilst charities may influence government or public opinion, they may only do so 'through well-founded, reasoned argument *based upon research or direct experience*' (emphasis added). The requirement of accurate and justifiable argument is essential for informed debate. In a democratic society, so too is the ability for *all* voices to be heard. It has been stated that 'The voice of charity can be the voice of conscience in a society where such voices are often drowned out'[9], and smaller charities often represent the only outlet for those in society who are not accommodated by the large main stream charities, but who are vulnerable and require representation nevertheless. The main pressure that smaller charities are under is a strain upon resources. They have been hit hard by falling donations, and whilst some may benefit from the grants made by the National Lottery Charities Board, those grants may not be received in time to offset the fall in donations.[10] In this climate, the requirement for charities to undertake research to support argument, though laudable, is likely to be beyond their resources. Further, the use of charity funds to undertake research must in any event be within a charity's ambit, and must be for the public benefit. (The Charity Commission is currently taking consultation on the issue of research.) Additionally, those with insufficient direct experience to support their argument will have a diminishing opportunity to present their views, and participate in political activities.[11] This could prove to be regrettable. One of the chief characteristics of current charity law is its great diversity. The legal structure and the looseness of the categories of charitable status evident from *Commissioners for Special Purposes of Income Tax* v *Pemsel* [1891] AC 531, the Preamble of the 1601 Statute of Charitable Uses, and up to four hundred years of case law, has enabled a myriad of charities with a myriad of purposes to come into existence. Despite criticisms in some quarters[12] as to the effectiveness of a huge body of organisations enjoying charitable status,

9 per Alun Michael MP, Labour Party Press Release, 26th January, 1995.

10 Cancer charities have been particularly vulnerable in this respect. Many have been hit by the Lottery 'Instants' and are not to be included within the National Lottery Charities Board programme of grants until the 'Health, Disability and Care Theme' in Spring 1996.

11 This may occur, for example, where a charity wishes to argue against the enactment of particular legislation, but has insufficient experience of the practical consequences of the proposed legislation to support an argument against it.

12 Notably the Duke of Edinburgh in delivering the 11th Annual Arnold Goodman Lecture, June 1994.

overall their diversity enriches society and enables the spirit of philanthropy to be accommodated alongside the wide relief of vulnerability. A threat to this diversity – be it via the extinction of individual charities through financial pressure, or effective exile from the political framework because of a lack of resources to fund research – is a threat both to the spirit of the area as a whole, and to adequate representation for vulnerable individuals in particular.

One absence from the 1995 guidelines is the form of any practical advice to trustees of those charities who have entered into contracts with the government to provide state services, such as healthcare. The growth in a 'contract culture' over recent years raises many concerns (see Knight 1993, ch 3), including how far humanitarian ideals are being subjugated in order to relieve government burdens. In the political context, however, it raises the issue of how far charities have created a conflict of interest with their – albeit limited – political freedom by effectively compromising their independence. Whilst the Government have stated that they 'seek a free, vigorous and creative partnership with the voluntary sector' (H M Government 1992), the price charities may be forced to pay for this 'partnership' could possibly be the forfeiture of their ability to undertake a degree of political activity in order to safeguard their contract. Admittedly, this type of political issue is more oblique than those considered by the Charity Commission in its guidelines, but nevertheless it is an example of an additional *practical* issue facing charities when they consider whether or not to campaign.

Reform

The 1989 White Paper stated, at paragraph 2.41, that:

> 'The safeguards which the law provides are indispensable to prevent what are essentially political factions or pressure groups from assuming the guise of charity. It is vital in the longer term interests of the public and charities alike, that political and charitable purposes should remain distinct.'

In an attempt to prevent fringe groups or extreme political activists gaining a degree of legitimacy through charitable status (and hence from receiving public subsidisation through generous taxation exemptions), the current law has overlooked the *full* potential charities have to act for the common good. If the Government is seeking a successful union with the charitable and voluntary sector it will need to take on board the political aspects of charities, and consider the role charities could usefully play in a social and political order. They have the experience. Charities and their legal structure were founded in an overtly political climate, and both have the competency to take on a political role. The Preamble to the 1601 Statute of Charitable Uses was reputedly enacted to quell possible social disturbance and formed part of a systematic and tight programme of Elizabethan social reform (see Holdsworth 1922, pp 396 ff).[13] Further,

13 Three statutes were enacted in 1601 along the theme of relief: one concerning the poor law (43 Eliz. c.2), another concerning the relief of poor mariners and soldiers (43 Eliz. c.3), and the Act of Charitable Uses (43 Eliz. c.4). Further, earlier statutes also indicated the state's preoccupation with the maintenance of order and the nature of society. See: 22 Hen. VIII c.12 a statute designed to keep the poor within their own parish, and to apprentice poor boys, 27 Hen. VIII c.25 setting up penalties for giving money to unlicensed beggars, 14 Eliz. c.5 defining the professional and the real poor, 39 Eliz. c.3 permitting taxation of the parish to set the poor to work, and finally 39 Eliz. c.4 concerning 'houses of correction' for the vagabond poor.

the framework for charitable purposes enabled private philanthropy to be channelled into easing parochial burdens; be they the relief of the aged, the impotent and poor people, the education of orphans, or the maintenance of houses of correction. Charity has not shaken free from those origins and continues to exist in a political environment dealing with political issues, such as poverty or education. Given their lineage, and the unique position they occupy in society, charities have the singular ability to directly assess the efficiency and effectiveness of current Government policy or legislation, and upon the basis of that experience they have a valid contribution to make in the political arena. Charities may, of course, establish non-charitable bodies to take on a political role. But that non-charitable arm remains financially distinct from the main charity, and as a result it is not a feasible option for smaller organisations. In any event, separation is not a long term solution to the cut in freedom of speech.

In the context of trends in the sector as a whole, this is, moreover, a particularly judicious time for reform. The area is experiencing a challenging period, uncertain of its own identity and direction as it moves towards the third millennium. Cracks are surfacing in a legal structure principally designed for flexible operation, but which has increasingly to combat criticism and calls for tighter regulation. The particular timing of a number of recent reports on the sector calling for a reorganisation, a 'renaissance', have resulted in an intense focus on the charitable arena (see Mulgan & Landry 1995, p 8; Knight 1993). For example, whilst the financial advantages afforded charities via taxation exemptions have continually been questioned, those questions only appear now to be gathering any impetus. Additionally, donors and beneficiaries, disillusioned by a climate of corporate fraud, are demanding that charities too display a greater degree of accountability and business acumen.[14] In the last twelve months moreover, the National Lottery has added the final touch, principally by placing pressure upon charitable donations as a consequence of a widespread public misconception concerning the precise proportion of each lottery stake siphoned off to the National Lottery Charities Board (currently only 5.6 pence in the pound).

These diverse pressures have political consequences, and despite the wide range of activities identified by the Charity Commission in their guidelines as acceptable for a charity to pursue, many charities are nevertheless held back by current law from campaigning against Government policy. For some the political restrictions will not present too onerous a problem, though that position is not applicable to all, in particular, to those charities that deal with health or poverty and for whom current law and government policy directly impacts upon their work, and, ultimately, their effectiveness. Admittedly, effectively securing and implementing change on a political level will not be free from difficulty. There are many barriers to overcome. For example, one objection to political legitimisation has been the

14 This has been reflected in the trends of recent charity legislation. For example, stringent duties to account may be found in the Charities Act 1993, ss 41–49 (re-enacting the Charities Act 1992, ss 19–27 and coming into force on March 1st 1996). In October 1995 *Accounting by Charities – Statement of Recommended Practice* was published by the Charity Commission, examining, *inter alia,* charitable funds, donations and classifying expenditure. Control of fund-raising may be found in Part II of the Charities Act 1992, and the Charitable Institutions (Fund-Raising) Regulations 1994. There has also been a focus upon the investment duties of charity trustees, a topic recently considered in this journal by D. Morris in *Charity Investment in the UK: Some Contemporary Issues for the 1990s* [1995] 3 Web JCLI. The corporate ethos is, moreover, permeating into the attitude of many charity managers, as well as into legislation, and business concepts are beginning to dominate managerial agendas in a greater degree than before. Whilst the move towards improving efficiency and accountability is a trend to be welcomed, that welcome remains a cautious one. Charities should beware of marginalising the needs of their beneficiaries and the loss of sight of their ultimate purposes in an attempt to increase cost-effectiveness.

exploitation of donors (see the 1989 White Paper, para 2.41) who may find that their donations are being used to fund actions that are adverse to their own political principles. This is a valid objection. For charities that wish to pursue an active political function, full and accessible information as to their political stance and objectives should be freely available to donors, so that the latter have the opportunity to make up their own mind whether to donate. Another valid objection arises from *R* v *Radio Authority, ex parte Bull.* In a postscript to his judgment, Kennedy LJ stated, (at 496), that 'it is worth recognising that something which may appear to be an unnecessary restriction upon a good cause could also usefully restrain something manifestly less worthy.' It is implicit from this that safeguards will need to be built into the legal structure to prevent extreme fundamentalism prejudicing the common good. This will not be easy. But despite the barriers and the difficulties, the opportunities that currently present themselves for sensible revision need to be grasped. At the moment, charities exist in a form of political limbo. It is anomalous that many perform political functions, but do not have a clear and unequivocal political voice.

The Charity Commission guidelines highlighted above do not provide charities with that clear voice, and they do not resolve the anomalies in the law – nor should they, since such an embrace properly rests with Parliament. Nevertheless, the 1995 guidelines have significance. On a practical level, they are clearer and better organised than the ones they replace and provide essential support to charity trustees as they walk through the political minefield. On a more fundamental level the guidelines serve, albeit unconsciously, to highlight the need for reform, or at least for Parliament to provide clarification in the area. On a final note, whilst it may be said that 'where there is no vision, the people perish' (Proverbs 29:18), in the context of charities, it should be added that in addition to vision, there also has to a be a clear opportunity for expression.

Bibliography

Advertising Standards Authority (1995) Report Number 53 (London: ASA).

Charity Commission (1995) *Political Activities and Campaigning by Charities* (London: CC).

Charity Commission (1994) *Political Activities and Campaigning by Charities* (London: CC).

Duke of Edinburgh (1994) *11th Annual Arnold Goodman Lecture* (London: CAF).

Gaines, A (1995) *'Stand by your claims'* 69 NCVO News (November) 8.

H M Government (1992) *The Individual and the Community: The Role of the Voluntary Sector* (London: HMSO).

Holdsworth, W (1922), History of English Law, Vol. 1, (London: Methuen & Co).

Knight, B, (1993) *Voluntary Action* (London: Centris).

Mulgan, G & Landry, C (1995) *The Other Invisible Hand: Remaking Charity for the 21st Century* (London: DEMOS).

NCVO (1995) *The Impact of the National Lottery on charitable donations from the general public* (London: NCVO).

White Paper (1989) *Charities: A Framework for the Future* (London: HMSO) Cm 694.

*DRUG OFFENDERS AND SENTENCING POLICY**

Ralph Henham

Reader in Law, Nottingham Trent University

First Published in Web Journal of Current Legal Issues in association with Blackstone Press Ltd.

**Revised version of a paper delivered at the British Criminology Conference, Loughborough University, July 1995.*

SUMMARY

This paper is concerned to illustrate how recent sentencing policy has precipitated a reversal of the apparent welfarism in the treatment of drug offenders evident in the Criminal Justice Act 1991. An increasingly retributivist penal climate has produced a situation where drug offenders are likely to receive more frequent and lengthier custodial sentences. Since neither the executive nor the judiciary appear able to contribute towards the development of a coherent sentencing strategy for dealing with drug related crime it is argued that the introduction of strategic incentives to treatment in the criminal process may provide a solution.

CONTENTS

Introduction

In February 1994 the Home Secretary, Mr Michael Howard, announced a proposal to increase the maximum fines for cannabis possession fivefold to £2500 by an amendment to the Criminal Justice and Public Order Bill 1993. Fines were also to be increased from £500 to £2500 for illegal possession, production and supply of amphetamines and barbiturates. The announcement was justified by reference to the Government's 'get tough' approach to law and order, sources close to the Home Secretary being quoted as stating that:

> 'His view is that if these are fines, they ought to be stiff ones, in order to drive home the message that illegal conduct is not acceptable. People who transgress should realise that they face a fine, not a minor financial penalty they can view as an occupational overhead' (*Sunday Times*, 13 February 1994).

Predictably, the announcement met with almost universal condemnation.[1] The most telling criticism concerned the Government's apparent determination to eschew the trend towards liberalisation despite Home Office statistics which showed that 51% of those arrested for cannabis possession received a caution in 1991. The main implication of the proposals was a predicted significant increase in custodial sentences for drug offenders resulting from their inability to pay increased fines. Notwithstanding, Schedule 8, Part II, Criminal Justice and Public Order Act 1994 contained (*inter alia*) increases in maximum fines for offences relating to possession of Class B drugs (s 5(2) and Schedule 4, column 5, Misuse of Drugs Act 1971) from £500 to £2500 and offences relating to the possession of Class C drugs (s 5(2) and Schedule 4, column 6, Misuse of Drugs Act 1971) from £200 to £1000 which apply to offences committed after 3rd February 1995.[2] These provisions may be seen as enacted in pursuit of a political agenda which seemingly chooses to ignore the fact that the consequences of failure to meet these increased financial penalties will be a continuing contribution to the rising prison population. Home Office statistics continue to reveal that possession of cannabis is by far the most common drug offence accounting for almost 90 per cent of 48,900 convictions in 1992 (Home Office 1993a, paras. 12 and 15). Some 7 per cent of this total (about

---

1 Mike Bennett, chairman of the Metropolitan Police Federation; 'This is absurd. Just to announce a fivefold increase in the fine instead of looking at the problem won't make it go away. You'll end up with an awful lot of unpaid fines. That will deplete court resources. These proposals are not well thought out. Many people who use cannabis simply won't be able to afford the new fines and may end up in prison.'

Anthony Scrivener Q.C., former chairman of the Bar Council; 'This is a ridiculous waste of resources. All this will do is lead to an increase in people going to prison.'

– both quoted in the *Sunday Times*, 13 February 1994.

Richard Coyles, chairman of the Police Federation; 'It is what magistrates decide that matters. They deal with the reality of the people before the courts. We know there is a link between crime and drugs. Fines at this level will mean more people committing crime to pay them.'

Mike Goodman of Release commenting on the tougher penalties of the last 25 years; 'Drug seizures have increased, drug offences have increased, and drug use has increased. The policy has not worked and in our view won't work.'

– both quoted in *The Times*, 14 February 1994.

2 Criminal Justice and Public Order Act 1994 (Commencement No. 5) Order 1994. Fines were also increased in the case of the following offences by Schedule 8, Part II of the 1994 Act – Production or being concerned in the production of Class C drugs; s 4(2) Misuse of Drugs Act 1971 – from £500 to £2500.

Supplying or offering to supply Class C drugs or being concerned in the doing of either activity by another; s 4(3) Misuse of Drugs Act 1971 – from £500 to £2500.

Having possession of Class C drugs with intent to supply; s 5(3) Misuse of Drugs Act 1971 – from £500 to £2500.

Being the occupier or being concerned in the management of premises and permitting or suffering certain activities concerning Class C drugs to take place there; s 8 Misuse of Drugs Act 1971 – from £500 to £2500.

3400 offenders) were given immediate jail sentences. This represents approximately 9.6 per cent of prisoners in Prison Service establishments or 7.4 per cent of the average population in custody in 1992 (Home Office 1993b, Tables 4 and 5) and is clearly a significant component of the prison population. With substantially increased Class B and C drug seizures being reported[3] the proportion receiving custodial sentences for possession will inevitably reflect this trend. The upward trend will itself be inflated by those additionally receiving custodial sentences for breaches of financial orders or crime to finance payment.

The Retreat from Welfarism

This latest twist in Government sentencing policy for drug offenders is symptomatic of the anomalies and confusion persisting in this area of policy-making during recent years. For example, there has been a bifurcation of approach, fostered by recent criminal justice legislation, which is exemplified by the failure to distinguish between drug takers and suppliers with regard to the scaling of penalties. As Collison (1993) has pointed out drug users rapidly assume the status of suppliers and traffickers once they have been drawn into the criminal justice system. This results in punitive and deterrent measures designed only for the so-called 'villains' being applied to both groups. Since, the largest prisoner group relates to Class B drug offenders rather than Class A suppliers and traffickers (Home Office 1992, Table S2.12) it is arguable that the relevant legislative provisions are failing to make a significant impact upon this important group. The implications of blurring the distinction between custody and treatment are profound since it results in the criminalisation of less serious offenders with consequential increases in drug related activity with its attendant social consequences. Such a policy eventually contributes to an increase in the numbers of recidivist drug offenders who become locked in a cycle of increased prisonisation. Hence, the serious nature of the prison drug problem is continually exacerbated by the failure of sentencing policy for drug offenders to address this issue. The bifurcation of approach is further perpetuated within penal institutions where the relationship between custody and treatment is tenuous. As a result there is a tendency for treatment initiatives to become diluted within the mainstream prison system. Not only is any form of compulsory treatment invariably defined as punishment by prison inmates but treatment may also become a guise for control within a penal institution. Since custodial and treatment objectives may be seen as mutually contradictory there is no doubt that any system of specialised treatment has to recognise that inmates must contribute to the maintenance of the prison. Hence, the prospect of treatment-oriented penal institutions is limited by two factors:-

1. The attitudes and demands of inmates exist in an environment characterised by inmate hostility. Attempts to apply individualised treatment criteria may be interpreted as the administration of special favours or privileges.

3 Ecstasy seizures increased by almost 40 per cent to 2400 compared with 1700 in 1991 and 400 in 1990. Seizures of amphetamines rose 55 per cent to 10600, more than three times as many as in 1989. LSD seizures increased by 50 per cent to 2500, the number of doses recovered totalling 540000 compared with 170000 in 1991. Heroin seizures were up 12 per cent to around 3000 and cocaine seizures rose by 20 per cent. Fifty one tonnes of cannabis were found, 60 per cent more than in 1991 although seizures actually dropped by 3 per cent to 57700 (Home Office 1993a, paras. 8 and 9).

2. Any system of specialised treatment must accept that the maintenance of the prison needs the co-operation of the inmates. It is certainly arguable, therefore, that the recent introduction of random drug tests in prison will serve to undermine prison treatment initiatives.[4] In any event, there is no doubt that the endemic nature of the drug culture in British prisons[5] and the power hierarchy it sustains exacerbates attempts to foster individual or group treatment programmes.

The impact of recent Criminal Justice Legislation

Nowhere is the retreat from welfarism more apparent than in the recent history of criminal justice legislation. The Criminal Justice Act 1991 appeared to herald an era of progressive change through the introduction of a requirement to be added to a standard probation order that an offender should receive treatment with a view to the reduction or elimination of the offender's dependency on drugs and alcohol (Schedule 1, Part II, para. 6 (2)). Paragraph 6(1), not only made it a condition of the order that the drug or alcohol dependency must be treatable (Schedule 1, Part II, para 6 (1) (c), it also made it a condition of such an order that the offender is dependant on drugs or alcohol but also that his dependency caused or contributed to the offence in respect of which the probation order is made (Schedule 1, Part II, para 6 (1) (a) and (b).[6] The 1991 Act provisions marked a significant change to welfarism in comparison with the pre-Act probation alternatives.[7] The most significant aspect of the changed criteria relates to the wide definition of drug dependency as including a propensity towards the misuse of drugs or alcohol, thus moving away from the restrictive psychiatric requirement (Schedule 1, Part II, para 6 (9). Lee (1993) has observed that drug agencies were advised to regard the 1991 Act's approach as a major policy initiative requiring significant forward planning.

4 It was reported in *The Guardian* 7 July 1994 that random drug tests would be carried out on 12000 prisoners each year following a prison service drugs survey which had revealed a 58 per cent increase in Class A drug finds in the previous year. The tests would apply to 5 per cent of inmates with a further 5 per cent being tested on suspicion. Inmates who refused would be disciplined and lose privileges.

Section 151 Criminal Justice and Public Order Act 1994 introduced powers for prison officers to require prisoners to provide a sample of urine for drug testing purposes (operative from 9 January 1994; Criminal Justice and Public Order Act (Commencement No 2) Order 1994). The Prison (Amendment) Rules 1994 (No 3195) made under the Prison Act 1952, s 47 (also operative from 9 January 1995) amended SI 1964 No. 388 to allow for collection of samples from prisoners for drug testing and introduced a new disciplinary offence (*inter alia*) of unlawful administration of a controlled drug.

5 See, for example, Maden et al (1991). Maden et al estimated that 11 per cent of the imprisoned male population and approximately 25 per cent of the female population were dependent on drugs whilst it is acknowledged that a significant number of imprisoned drug offenders do not admit their problem to the prison medical service.

6 It was suggested by Wasik and Taylor (1994, p 67) that the provisions could be used where the offender had committed an offence to obtain money for drugs, or assault to obtain drugs or robbery or burglary of a chemist's shop. In other words the offence does not have to be directly drug or alcohol related or committed under the influence of either. Many such offences would not qualify for a probation order in any event, since they would be regarded as 'so serious' that only a custodial sentence could be justified.

7 The first of these was a probation order containing a requirement as to psychiatric treatment available where the offender was not found to be suffering from one of the forms of mental disorder which would have justified the making of a hospital order. Such an order was regarded as appropriate where it was felt that it would have such beneficial effects on the offender as would outweigh the risk to the public; *R* v *Mcdonald* (1983) 5 Cr App R (S) 419. The other two pre-1991 Act probation orders were orders made with a residential requirement in a drug rehabilitation unit or as directed by a probation officer. The use of such orders is discussed by Collison (1994, p 29).

However, Lee reported several weaknesses in the 1991 legislative framework indicating a failure to provide a community based sentencing alternative for recidivist drug offenders. Lee also suggested that sentencers might prefer the pre-Act conditional residence requirement rather than conditional treatment since the former can be used as a punitive restriction on liberty (see further Lee and Mainwaring, 1995).

The welfarism of the 1991 Act probation provisions was, of course, against the overriding policy contribution of the Act with its emphasis on just deserts (Home Office 1990, para. 1.6, 2.3 and 2.9. The subsequent amendments to the 1991 Act made by the Criminal Justice Act 1993, s 66.[8] provided further evidence of a concerted re-alignment of policy towards punishment and deterrence. These provisions appeared to signal the end of any deliberate sentencing policy aimed at diverting the petty persistent or recidivist offender away from custodial to community based sentencing alternatives. This would ensure a return to punishment at the expense of treatment for many drug offenders. These difficulties were compounded by the impact of s 29(1) (as substituted by s 66(6) Criminal Justice Act 1993)[9] since Ashworth and Gibson suggested that the wording of the substituted s 29(1) would have the effect of allowing previous convictions and sentences to lift a particular offence over the custody threshold.[10] Wasik and von Hirsch (1994, p 415) however, retorted that in their opinion reference to 'failure to respond' in the new s 29(1) had to be construed narrowly and was relevant only 'in considering the seriousness of the offence'.[11] Even if this limitation were accepted there was considerable doubt concerning what could be regarded as a 'response' to previous sentences. Ashworth and Gibson opined (1994, p 105) that any conduct following the imposition of a sentence could be construed as a 'response' including breach or failure to respond to a community order, and also reconviction (and perhaps even other behaviour falling short of criminality or conviction) after the termination of such an order. As Collison has pointed out (1993, pp 390, 393) drug addicted offenders who lack the motivation to give up and who have demonstrated this through their past behaviour may become suitable cases for prison more quickly. Furthermore, the drug-related nature of many

8 Section 66(1) of the 1993 Act amended s 1 of the 1991 Act to permit the court to look at the offence and all associated offences (or any combination thereof) when considering whether to impose a custodial sentence on the basis of its seriousness. This removed the controversial restriction that the courts were only allowed to take account of the offence and one other associated offence in considering whether to impose a custodial sentence or a community penalty on the basis of its seriousness. Section 66(2) made corresponding amendments to allow a court to consider all associated offences when determining the length of a custodial sentence. Finally, s 66(3) amended s 3(3) (a) of the 1991 Act by requiring that in forming an opinion as to whether a custodial sentence is justified and as to the length of any such sentence, the court must take into account all such information as is available to it about the offence and any associated offences combined with it under ss 1(2) (a) or 2(2) (a) (as amended).

9 The subsection states that 'in considering the seriousness of any offence the court may take into account any previous convictions of the offender or any failure of his to respond to previous sentences'.

10 'Thus, the notion of proportionality to the seriousness of the current offence, so pivotal to the scheme of the 1991 Act has been weakened. Prisons and young offender institutions may once again fill with people who have been sentenced on their record rather than for a serious offence (Ashworth and Gibson, 1994 p 106).

11 The logic of their argument is that an offender's failure to respond is relevant only when it impinges on the offender's culpability which is in turn circumscribed by the concept of seriousness embodied in the 1991 Act. It is, therefore, consistent with the notion of just deserts that the current offence should be regarded as a ceiling of 'seriousness' beyond which the sentencer cannot go. A weakness in this approach lies in the implicit assumption that it is possible to know how aggravating factors such as previous convictions, operate on sentencers' decision-making processes and raise the sentence for the present offence above one threshold to another.

offences involving recidivist offenders often remains undisclosed. Such offenders may perceive the custodial option as less unattractive than what they perceive to be strict breach and treatment conditions. There is no doubt that drug addicted offenders are more likely to be disadvantaged by the 1993 Act amendments to the 1991 Criminal Justice Act considered herein.

There remain several other policy implications of the 1991 and 1993 Criminal Justice Acts requiring comment in so far as they impinge on the sentencing of drug offenders. Firstly, it is arguable that the early release procedures introduced by the Criminal Justice Act 1991 may result in longer terms of imprisonment being served by drug offenders in common with offenders in general (Thomas 1992, Home Office 1994a, para 14) and, in addition, that the strict breach criteria introduced by the 1991 Act for community service and probation orders will result in an increase in custodial sentences for drug offenders where drug dependency renders them more likely to commit breaches of such orders (Collison 1993, p 393). The second point concerns the protective sentencing provisions introduced by ss 1(2)(b) and 2(2)(b) 1991 Act[12] allowing a protective element to be added to the sentence in the case of violent and sexual offences (defined by s 31(1)) where necessary to protect the public from serious harm from the offender (defined by s 31(3)). Section 31(3) currently states that any reference to protecting the public from serious harm is to be construed as a reference to protecting members of the public from death or serious personal injury, whether physical or psychological which would be occasioned by future violent or sexual offences committed by the offender. Since *R* v *Bowler* [1993] Crim. L.R. 799 the Court of Appeal has been prepared to recognise that in assessing the incidence of serious harm a court may have regard to the degree of vulnerability of potential victims and it is certainly arguable that the definition of serious harm in s 31(3) is capable of including such harm as is caused by the supply and sale of dangerous drugs.[13] Although doubt exists as to the protective efficiency of the life sentence as a maximum sentence in serious Class A supply cases protective sentences under s 1(2)(b) of the 1991 Act are currently restricted by the upper limit of the maximum term available for the offence (Thomas 1993, p. 978). Finally, it should be remembered that s 4 of the 1991 Criminal Justice Act introduced an apparently progressive requirement concerning mentally abnormal offenders which provides that in addition to requiring a medical report in all cases where an offender is or appears to be mentally disordered (unless the court deems it unnecessary) the court must also consider the likely effect of a custodial sentence on any mental condition and

---

12 Section 1(2)(b) provides that a court shall not pass a custodial sentence on an offender unless it is of the opinion, where the offence is a violent or sexual offence, that only such a sentence would be adequate to protect the public from serious harm from him.

Section 2(2)(b) provides that the length of the custodial sentence, where the offence is a violent or sexual offence, shall be for such longer term (not exceeding the permitted maximum) as in the opinion of the court is necessary to protect the public from serious harm from the offender.

For the sentencing policy implications of these provisions see Henham (1995b).

13 Since there is no definition of 'dangerousness' and no legal test or guidance in its prediction contained in the 1991 Act or elsewhere it is open to suggest that the danger presented by drug suppliers and pushers approximates that of an imminent danger (see Walker 1985, p 363). There would be no difficulty in accommodating the danger in terms of the sorts of harm against which precautions are justifiable in the terms postulated in Floud and Young (1981) *viz* 'any offence which caused or was intended to cause; death; serious bodily injury; serious sexual assault; severe or prolonged pain or mental distress; loss or damage to property which results in severe personal hardship; damage to the environment which has serious adverse affects on public health or safety; serious damage to the security of the state'. The change required would be in terms of the behaviour which produces the harms in question.

treatment that may be available (see Henham 1995a). It is arguable that these provisions should apply equally in the case of drug addicted offenders generally as regards the necessity to consider the likely effect of a custodial sentence on the offender's drug problem and treatment availability. At present, unless the drug offender is specifically selected by the court for a treatment-oriented option, he or she will be subject to the general provisions contained in the 1991 Act.[14] However, it should be noted that the requirement to obtain a medical report under s 4 does not apply where a pre-sentence report has been dispensed with under s 3(2) on the basis that the court is of the opinion that it is unnecessary to obtain one in the circumstances of the case. There has been a general relaxation in the legal requirements regarding pre-sentence reports following amendments to Criminal Justice Act 1991, ss 3 & 7 by Schedule 9, paragraph 10 Criminal Justice and Public Order Act 1994 which apply to any sentence passed after 3rd February 1995 (Criminal Justice and Public Order Act 1994 (Commencement No 5) Order 1994). These amendments (*inter alia*) enable a court in any case of an offender aged 18 or over to dispense with a pre-sentence report as unnecessary when forming an opinion as to the need for, or the appropriate length of a custodial sentence.[15] There seems little doubt that these new provisions will adversely affect prospects for the individualisation of sentences and, therefore, treatment initiatives for drug addicted offenders. Even before the pre–1994 Act provisions the court was only under an obligation to take into account the content of the pre-sentence report together with any other relevant information about the offender and the offence, including aggravating and mitigating factors. The provisions did not oblige the court to consider the impact of imprisonment on the offender's condition or treatment potential.

The drift towards punishment and retribution has recently received further impetus following the announcement by the Home Secretary of the Government's proposals to abolish existing non-custodial sentences and to create a single community sentence (Home Office 1995). The Green Paper suggests that magistrates would decide the type of community punishment and would be empowered to impose extra conditions such as attendance on a drug treatment course. Probation officers would lose their discretion over such matters and magistrates would become involved in decisions regarding the supervision of community sentences by probation and social services departments. It is proposed that magistrates could specify penalty combinations and conditions designed to correspond to the seriousness of the offence and an offender's behavioural or other problems. Magistrates would therefore not only specify the type of punishment in any particular case but also impose conditions such as treatment for alcohol or drug abuse. The proposals have predictably met with considerable opposition[16] and there

14 If the offence is so serious it may merit a custodial sentence; ss 1(2)(a) and 2(2)(a).

15 Under the original provisions contained in Part I of the 1991 Criminal Justice Act a sentencing court was required to obtain and consider a pre-sentence report when making a decision whether a custodial sentence is justified and as to the appropriate length of a custodial sentence. Section 3(3)(a) requires the court to take into account 'all such information about the circumstances of the offence (including any aggravating or mitigating factors) as is available to it. Further, s 28(1) provides that 'nothing shall prevent a court mitigating an offender's sentence by taking into account any such matters as, in the opinion of the court, are relevant in mitigation of sentence.' Finally, s 29 (1) permits the court to have regard to the offender's previous convictions and responses to previous sentences. In all these matters the pre-sentence report is a vital source of information. The only exception to the original mandatory requirement for a pre-sentence report in custody cases was under s 3(2) which provided that no pre-sentence report needed to be obtained where the offence was triable only on indictment and the Crown Court judge took the view that obtaining one was 'unnecessary'.

16 See comment in *The Times* on 16 March and 4 April 1995 and, particularly, the letter from Paul Cavadino, Chair, Penal Affairs Consortium, *The Times* 28 March 1995.

is no doubt that a reduction in the social welfare input relating to treatment decisions and supervision of drug-addicted offenders is a retrograde step.

The Role of the Criminal Courts

Further evidence of the recent increased emphasis on punishment and retribution in the sentencing policy for drug offenders can be derived from a comparison of Court of Appeal sentencing principles and the Magistrates' Association sentencing guidelines introduced in 1993.[17] Detailed guidelines for drug offences were laid down by Lane C.J. in *R* v *Aramah* (1982) 4 Cr. App R (S) 407) and *R* v *Bilinski* (1987) 9 Cr App R (S) 360. In cases involving simple possession of Class A drugs Lord Lane in *Aramah* suggested that the possible variety of individual circumstances was so wide that it was not possible to lay down any meaningful guidelines but that custody would be 'both proper and expedient' in many cases. Where possession is for personal use typical sentences have been in the range of six to twelve months in recent years; eg *R* v *Gallagher* (1990) 12 Cr App R (S) 224. However, although the National Mode of Trial Guidelines[18] advocate that possession of Class A drugs cases should be committed (now transferred) for trial unless the amount is small and consistent only with personal use, the 1993 Magistrates' Association sentencing guidelines (p 23) recommend the entry point as community service. The former Magistrates' Association guidelines (p 22) starting point for possession of a small quantity was a guideline fine of 30 units (under the now abolished unit fine system). It has been argued that sentencing levels in such cases will be raised since the existence of the entry point under the new guidelines will dissuade magistrates from considering lesser alternatives such as the fine and they will be more inclined to move up the penal severity scale. Justification of the reverse will be more difficult. Magistrates may also simply fail to take proper account of those factors which might make an offence less serious or neglect those factors relevant to personal mitigation which are crucial in many drug offence cases. Where the offence is simple possession of Class B drugs Court of Appeal sentencing principles indicate that a fine is usually considered appropriate; *R* v *Jones* (1981) 3 Cr App R (S) 51. Although the National Mode of Trial Guidelines point out that possession cases should be committed (now transferred) for trial where the quantity is substantial, both the former and new Magistrates' Association sentencing guidelines (pp 24 and 25 respectively) reflect agreement on the appropriateness of a fine in normal simple possession cases. However, general principles have established that continued flouting of the law may justify a short

---

17 The introduction of revised sentencing guidelines for magistrates in September 1993 was treated with some suspicion that the courts would be reluctant to depart from the prescribed 'entry points' to take account of the factors relevant to the seriousness of the offence and mitigating factors. See, for example, comments by Roger Ede, Secretary, Law Society's Criminal Law Committee and Frances Crook, Director, Howard League in *The Gazette* 21 September 1993, p 4. Scepticism was also voiced by Lord Taylor CJ in his speech to NACRO in September 1993. It was felt that the new guidelines would contribute to an increase in the prison population because of the fundamental change in their recommended approach to sentencing. The former guidelines (issued in June 1992) had provided a number of 'starting points' for each offence and magistrates were invited to consider tougher sentences on the basis of weighing up aggravating and mitigating circumstances and rejecting lesser alternatives. The new guidelines provided that the term 'entry point' was simply used as a guide for an offence of average seriousness. The main criticism was that the entry points had been fixed at a higher level in the case of certain offences and magistrates would be deterred from considering lesser alternatives as they would have been forced to do by the approach adopted in the former guidelines.

18 See *Practice Note (Mode of Trial: Guidelines)* [1990] 1 WLR 1439.

prison sentence (*R* v *Robertson, Coupar and Baxendale* (1982) 4 Cr App R. (S) 150) and even possession of a small amount may result in a short custodial sentence where the offender has a persistent record of cannabis related offences (*R* v *Osborne* (1982) 4 Cr App R (S) 362). Notwithstanding the continued existence of these sentencing principles and guidelines there is no doubt that the dominant trend in simple possession cases is towards release with a caution. This reflects a trend towards general relaxation of penalties for soft drug use in European countries. For example, in Germany a number of lower courts recently appealed to the Constitutional Court alleging that they were unable to pass judgment on soft drug users on the basis that the present law was incompatible with the constitutional right to equal treatment with alcohol and nicotine users. The Constitutional Court judgment of 28th April 1994 rejected this argument but advised lower courts to show tolerance to individuals possessing small quantities exclusively for personal use.[19] It is interesting to note that while some 16 per cent of Germans aged between 12 and 39 admit to having consumed illegal drugs at least once (cannabis predominating) findings from the 1992 British Crime Survey reveal that some 28 per cent of UK citizens aged between 16 and 29 admit to some drug use (again, cannabis predominating) (Home Office 1993c). Nevertheless although 24 per cent admitted cannabis use this fell to one per cent for those aged 12 to 13 admitting cannabis use in 1991.[20] It is consequently apparent that *de facto* decriminalisation of soft drug use and possession has occurred in certain European countries without necessitating deliberate sentencing policy changes.

Drug Trafficking and Sentencing Principles

The continued emphasis on punishment and deterrence is clearly discernible in recent sentencing legislation and principles aimed at curbing drug trafficking. Although such developments are understandable and necessary it is arguable that their introduction has been at the expense of a diminution of offenders' due process rights. Whilst there are several major erosions of due process discernible in the Drug Trafficking Act 1994 (see Henham 1994, p 225) the most significant is that contained in s 2 (8) of the 1994 Act which reverses the rule in *R* v *Dickens* (1990) 12 Cr App R (S) 191 by requiring the civil standard of proof to determine whether a person has benefited from drug trafficking or the amount to be recovered. Sallon and Bedingfield (1993) have questioned the efficacy of a policy which drastically erodes some of the fundamental rights of an accused in a criminal trial without establishing the potential for any perceptible reduction in drug use. In March 1994 the Court of Appeal in *R* v *Richardson, Teixeira, Dean, Tredwin* (*The Times*, 18 March 1994) felt obliged to provide detailed sentencing guidelines for abnormal

---

19 See *The Times* 29 April 1994 where some of the other legal problems raised by the court judgment are referred to eg the reporting by police of increasing numbers of car accidents caused by soft drug users, the problem being that drink-drive tests do not show up the use of marijuana although the effects are similar.

20 These figures are supported by research carried out by Leitner, Shapland and Wiles (1993). Their research also confirmed (*inter alia*) that:–

(i) only a small minority of the population admitted ever taking illicit drugs;
(ii) there were regional variations in admitted drug use in addition to variations by drug type;
(iii) 'recent' usage was much less extensive than 'ever' usage;
(iv) drug usage was spread generally across different social classes;
(v) generally whites were more likely than non-whites to have used illicit drugs;
(vi) men were more likely than women to have taken illicit drugs.

crimes of Class A drug trafficking. Lord Taylor CJ, giving the judgement of the court pointed out that the existing guidelines laid down in *Aramah* (and revised in *R* v *Bilinski*) were inadequate. In *Aramah* it had been suggested that where the street value of the consignment was of the order of £1 million or more 12 to 14 years' imprisonment was the appropriate sentence whereas in *Bilinski* Lord Lane CJ had felt compelled to increase that figure to '14 years and upward'. Since the present case involved the importation of hard drugs worth £50 million in street value, the question of what was meant by 'and upwards' had to be explored and some guidance provided for what was becoming an increasing trend. The Court of Appeal agreed with the approach adopted by Lord Lane C.J. in *R* v *Scamaronie* (1992) 13 Cr App R (S) 702 that in such cases sentences in the order of 25 years were not inappropriate reduced to 20 years to reflect mitigating circumstances such as plea and assistance given.[21] Finally, in *R* v *Aroyewuni* [1994] Crim. LR 695 the Court of Appeal again amended existing sentencing guidelines relating to the importation of Class A drugs. The court held that street value would no longer be used as a basis for determining the sentence in such cases and that a better way to measure the relative significance of any seizure of Class A drugs is by weight. Following the increase in the maximum sentence for importing Class A drugs (from 17 September 1985) the Court of Appeal in *Bilinski* had increased the suggested sentences to 10 years and upwards where drugs had a street value of around £100,000 and (as stated earlier) to 14 years and upwards where the street value was in the order of £1 million or more. Lord Taylor CJ in *Aroyewuni* stated that the Court of Appeal has decided to substitute the *Bilinski* guidelines with the following:- where the weight of the drugs at 100 per cent purity[22] is in the order of 500 grammes or more sentences of 10 years and upwards are appropriate. Where weight at 100% purity is in the order of 5 kilogrammes or more sentences of 14 years and upwards are appropriate. The Court did not think it appropriate to extend the guidelines to other Class A drugs such as LSD and Ecstasy (MDA)[23] or to the Class B drug amphetamine sulphate. With regard to the latter, there already existed numerous reported decisions of the Court of Appeal confirming its treatment along broadly similar lines to cannabis offences, within the *Aramah* guidelines, although the Court emphasised the importance of taking into account the purity level as well as weight or quantity in such cases. One of the main reasons given by the Court for preferring weight to street value in assessing the relative significance of Class A drug seizures concerned the ready availability of heroin and cocaine causing a fall in the consumer price. Thus increasing drug imports were lowering the street value per gramme. By taking the street value as the criteria, the sentencing level for like quantities of the drug became lower as the drug became more plentiful. It

---

21 Lord Taylor CJ again repeated that a plea of guilty in such cases should result in a substantial discount. As regards assistance to the authorities the discount would depend on a number of factors such as: the actual value of the assistance, the extent to which it demonstrated contrition, the risk to the offender and his family of possible reprisals and any evidence of the results of the assistance given.

22 The court decided that in order to achieve an accurate and fair standard applicable to all cases it was necessary to calculate the weight of the drug of 100 per cent purity contained in each seizure. By calculating the weight at 100 per cent strength, a consistent approach could be made to the significance of each consignment.

23 In *R* v *Warren, Beeley, The Times*, 3 July 1995 the Court of Appeal produced sentencing guidelines for Ecstasy (MDA). Lord Taylor CJ stated that the criteria should be based on the drug's active constituents which in most tablets was approximately 100 mg. On this basis 5,000 tablets would be assumed to contain 500 g of Ecstacy. Following *R* v *Aranguren* (1994) 99 Cr App R 347 (heroin and cocaine) the Court stated that where 5,000 tablets were involved the appropriate sentence would be in the order of 10 years and upwards whilst 14 years or more was appropriate where 50,000 or more tablets were involved.

could not serve Parliament's purpose if the more drugs imported and the lower the street price, the lower the sentencing level. In a recent study Green, Mills and Read (1994, p 183) confirm that both previous sentencing guidelines and previous findings appeared to indicate that the crucial determinant in the sentencing of drug importers was estimated street value of the drug imported yet their analysis found only a moderate positive correlation between the estimated street value of the drug imported and the length of sentence. Green et al state that in their view a substantial proportion of the variation in sentence length was attributable to factors other than the estimated street value of the drug and that judges appeared prepared to depart from the guideline sentences in more serious cases by exercising their discretion thus 'obscuring the apparent proportionality implicit in the *Aramah* and *Bilinski* guidelines'. The result is perhaps not surprising in that the Court of Appeal had frequently recognised the shortcomings in the provision of street value estimates (see Kay 1987) and had itself stated in *R* v *Patel* (1987) 9 Cr App R (S) 319 that so long as they were used as a rough yardstick there was no reason why judges should not measure the length of a sentence to some degree by them. With cocaine and crack seizures increased by 20 per cent and heroin 10 per cent during 1991–92 (Home Office 1993a, paras 8 and 9) it may be surmised that the Appeal Court has responded with uncharacteristic speed to a perceived need to maintain the elements of retribution and deterrence in sentencing levels for large scale drug importation. There is also evidence to suggest that this view is not simply confined to drug importation. For example, in *R* v *Kempley* (*The Times*, 4 April 1994) the Court of Appeal held that there had to be a deterrent element in any sentence imposed on someone found in possession of the Class A drug Ecstasy with intent to supply it to others. In this case the Court upheld the defendant's five year prison sentence for this offence although it was his first offence.

Concluding remarks

The implications of the drift towards retribution and deterrence in the sentencing policy for drug offenders is all too apparent. The increased numbers imprisoned will contribute to an already grossly overcrowded and deteriorating prison situation (Home Office 1994, para 20) and drug-related crime will increase. There is a danger that the UK could follow the United States where Bureau of Justice Statistics recently revealed that the prison population had almost tripled during the period 1980–93, from 329,821 to 948,881. The Bureau attributed almost half the increase in prisoners to the US Government's war on drugs with stiffer sentences and limits on parole.[24] It has been argued in this paper that the welfarist provisions contained in the Criminal Justice Act 1991 seem destined to be subsumed by the general climate of punishment and deterrence evident in recent government sentencing policy. In the medium to long term recent changes will neither reduce drug use nor the imprisonment of drug offenders. I would argue that certain strategic sentencing provisions would repay closer scrutiny and provide constructive alternatives. For example, in Germany, drug sentencing law not only reflects a clear distinction between repressive and therapeutic measures it also integrates therapy into the sentencing process and uses it as an incentive enabling the offender to mitigate or suspend the punitive aspects of the sentence (see Council of Europe 1991). Under s 56 of the Criminal Code the public prosecutor may with the court's

24 See comment in *The Times* 23 April and 3 June 1994.

consent temporarily refrain from charging the defendant if he proves that he has been undergoing treatment for drug addiction with a view to rehabilitation for at least three months provided the expected sentence is not more than two years' imprisonment. The proceedings are themselves terminated after four years provided treatment has been completed, the defendant has not re-offended, and there is no fresh evidence indicating a more severe sentence for the initial offence. In the case of imprisonment for up to one year (exceptionally two) the court will suspend the sentence on probation for two to five years if it expects the defendant to be deterred from future offending merely by the fact of conviction, even without the impact of a prison sentence. The court may impose conditions and directions such as the direction (with the defendant's consent) to undergo curative treatment or a residential requirement. If the defendant fails to comply the suspension of the sentence is revoked; if he does comply the sentence is remitted at the expiration of the probation period. Section 57 of the Criminal Code provides for the suspension of the remaining part of a sentence after two-thirds (exceptionally one-half) has been served if the court is satisfied that the defendant will not re-offend following release. These measures are mainly applied where a defendant has a good prognosis and displays a willingness to undergo treatment. Where a sentence is not suspended due to unfavourable treatment prognosis ss 35 and 36 of the Narcotics Act allow the public prosecutor, with the court's consent, to postpone execution of a prison sentence (or the remainder of one of not more than two years) for up to two years where the defendant's offence was connected with his drug addiction and he is undergoing treatment for the purpose of rehabilitation or definitely about to commence it. The duration of the treatment counts towards the sentence and successful therapy may result in suspension and finally remission of the sentence. Failure to complete the therapy may result in revocation of sentence postponement and continued execution of the sentence, although renewed postponement is a possibility. Finally, s 64 of the Criminal Code allows a court to order in a sentence for admission of an addicted offender to an institution for drug addicts if the prognosis is that he may commit serious offences in the future because of his disposition.

Collison (1994, pp 28 and 37) has indicated that changes in cautioning policy with respect to Class A drug offenders are inconsistent. Further, not only do referral practices differ between police forces, cautioning policy may be attributable to organisational demands for efficiency and production. Since the majority of Class A drug offenders will find their way to court it becomes imperative for sentencing policy to adopt strategic proposals for harm reduction to halt the post–1991 Act slide towards the increased criminalisation of addicted offenders. With criminal justice and Government agencies each pursuing separate agendas compromise solutions must be urgently pursued. I would argue that for sentencing policy such a compromise should represent a reduction in penalty levels and the implementation of suspended sentences of imprisonment by strategic postponement in sentence execution provided therapeutic measures are completed.[25]

---

25 The relative merits of voluntary and compulsory treatment strategies for addicted offenders are not discussed here (see Council of Europe 1991, Ch 2).

Regrettably, very little of substance as regards sentencing policy appears in the recent White Paper (Home Office 1995b). The Government re-affirmed its opposition to decriminalisation of any controlled drug set out in the Green Paper. (Home Office 1994b, Annex C, C 19, p. 55). In Chapter 2, 2: 5, p 8 and Annex B, B.25, p 44 it is simply stated that the Green Paper (Home Office 1995a) provides an opportunity to consider the role of treatment for drugs misuse in the rehabilitation of offenders serving a community sentence.

Bibliography

Ashworth, A and Gibson, B (1994) 'The Criminal Justice Act 1993: Altering the Sentencing Framework' *Criminal Law Review* 101.

Collison, M (1993) 'Punishing Drugs: Criminal Justice and Drug Use' 33 *British Journal of Criminology* 382.

Collison, M (1994) 'Drug Crime, Drug Problems and Criminal Justice: Sentencing Trends and Enforcement Strategies' 33 *Howard Journal of Criminal Justice* 25.

Council of Europe (1991) *Study and Synopsis of Basic Criminal Law Concepts of Pompidou Group Member Countries on the Prevention of Drug Trafficking and Abuse*, Strasbourg: Council of Europe.

Floud, J and Young, W (1981) *Dangerousness and Criminal Justice* (London: Heinemann).

Green, P, Mills, C and Read, T (1994) 'The Characteristics and Sentencing of Illegal Drug Importers' 34 *British Journal of Criminology* 479.

Henham, R (1994) 'Criminal Justice and Sentencing Policy for Drug Offenders' 22 *International Journal of the Sociology of Law* 223.

Henham, R (1995a) 'Dangerous Trends in the Sentencing of Mentally Abnormal Offenders' 34 *Howard Journal of Criminal Justice* 10.

Henham, R (1995b) 'Sentencing Policy, Appellate Guidance and Protective Sentencing' *Journal of Criminal Law.*

Home Office (1990) *Crime, Justice and Protecting the Public* (London: HMSO) Cm. 965.

Home Office (1992) *Statistics of Drug Seizures and Offenders dealt with, UK, 1991, Supplementary Tables* (London: HMSO).

Home Office (1993a) *Statistics of Drug Seizures and Offenders dealt with, UK, 1992* (Statistical Bulletin 30/93) (London: Home Office).

Home Office (1993b) *The Prison Population in 1992* (Statistical Bulletin 7/93) (London: Home Office).

Home Office (1993c) *Self Reported Drug Misuse in England and Wales: Main Findings from the 1992 British Crime Survey* (London: Home Office).

Home Office (1994a) *The Prison Population in 1993 and Long Term Projections to 2001* (Statistical Bulletin 16/94) (London: Home Office).

Home Office (1994b) (Green Paper) *Tackling Drugs Together : A Consultation Document on a Strategy for England 1995–1998* (London: HMSO) Cm 2678.

Home Office (1995a) (Green Paper) *Strengthening Punishment in the Community* (London: HMSO) Cm2780.

Home Office (1995b) (White Paper) *Tackling Drugs Together: A Strategy for England 1995–1998* (London: HMSO) Cm2846.

Kay, L (1987) '*Aramah* and the Street Value of Drugs' *Criminal Law Review* 814.

Lee, M (1993) 'The Unspoken Sentence? Treatment Conditions for Drug Using Offenders under the 1991 Criminal Justice Act' 12 *Criminal Justice Matters* 15.

Lee, M and Mainwaring, S (1995) 'No Big Deal: Court Ordered Treatment in Practice' *Druglink*, January/February 14–15.

Leitner, A, Shapland, J and Wiles P (1993) *Drug Usage and Drugs Prevention: The Views and Habits of the General Public* (London: HMSO).

Maden, A et al (1991) 'Drug Dependance in Prisoners' 302 *British Medical Journal* 880.

Sallon, C and Bedingfield, D (1993) 'Drugs, Money and the Law' *Criminal Law Review* 165.

Thomas, D A (1992) 'Towards a New Tariff' 4 *Sentencing News* 12.
Thomas, D A (1993), 'Commentary on *R* v *Coull*' *Criminal Law Review* 978.
Walker, N (1985) *Sentencing Theory: Law and Practice* (London: Butterworths).
Wasik, M and Taylor, R D (1994) *Blackstones Guide to the Criminal Justice Act 1991* (London: Blackstone Press).
Wasik, M and von Hirsch, A (1994) 'Section 29 Revised – Previous Convictions in Sentencing' *Criminal Law Review* 409.

GOOD CHARACTER DIRECTIONS AND BLEMISHED DEFENDANTS

Jennifer James LLB, BCL

Senior Lecturer in Law, University of Reading
<j.james@reading.ac.uk>

First Published in Web Journal of Current Legal Issues in association with Blackstone Press Ltd.

SUMMARY

Since the Court of Appeal decision which clarified the direction to be given to a jury in respect of an accused with a good character, the issue of who possesses such a character has become highly relevant. This article provides a brief introduction to the admission and effect of good character evidence before concentrating on the blemished defendant, that is a defendant whose record is not above reproach. Three categories of blemished defendants are considered and the cases analyzed with some suggestions for rationalization of the principles applicable in such cases.

CONTENTS

Introduction

It is now almost three years since the landmark decision on the appropriate direction to give to a jury in respect of an accused of good character handed down by the Court of Appeal in *R* v *Vye*; *R* v *Wise* and *R* v *Stephenson* [1993] 1 WLR 471, CA, (hereafter *Vye*). The decision which was designed to give 'clear guidance on the relevant principles', while followed in innumerable cases did not dam the flood of litigation on the issues of good character directions which had begun with *R* v *Berrada* (1989) 91 Cr App Rep 131, CA.[1] Despite Lord Taylor CJ's attempt to provide clear guidance on good character directions there have been at least eighteen Court of Appeal decisions in this area since *Vye*.

One significant stream of cases[2] has concerned the appropriate direction to give in respect of an accused, who while not of absolutely good character, is at least of goodish character – the so-called blemished defendant. The House of Lords has also had one bite at this particular cherry in *R* v *Aziz* [1995] 3 WLR 52. Has this extensive appellate activity left us with clear principles applicable to character directions in respect to blemished defendants? Let us consider first the context in which this issue arises.

What is evidence of character?

Generally, when evidence of character – good or bad – is admissible at all it must be illustrative of the disposition of the accused. Moreover, the law does not, other than in exceptional cases (see for example *Lowery* v *R* [1974] AC 85, PC), admit such evidence unless the accused has manifested this disposition by objectively demonstrable actions. Hence, for bad character, previous criminal acts (whether the accused has been convicted or not) or other highly relevant, proven discreditable conduct is required. Traditionally, for evidence to be probative of good character (see for example the Criminal Evidence Act 1898, s 1(f)(ii)), good works or positive, demonstrable character trait, were required. However, for the purposes of the *Vye* direction the absence of discreditable acts or convictions may suffice.

A line of cases deriving from *R* v *Rowton* (1865) LJMC 57, CCR, has taken a different view of what constitutes evidence of character. It held that evidence of character (good or bad) must be limited to testimony as to the general reputation of the accused without reference to any specific acts. According to *Rowton*, a witness can refer neither to his own knowledge of the accused nor to specific incidents involving the accused since neither reveal general reputation. The decision has been much criticised; clear judicial criticism is to be found in *Selvey* v *DPP* [1970] AC 304, HL and there are many cases in which *Rowton* is just ignored. Academic criticism of *Rowton* began early (see Stephen 1882, p 450); more recent criticism can be found in Cross and Tapper (Cross and Tapper 1995, p 349) and Murphy (Murphy 1995 pp 114, 115). *Rowton* cannot be applied if it is the accused who is giving evidence for he can hardly be limited to relating the reputation he has in the eyes of other people. In the recent case of *R* v *Durbin* [1995] 2 Cr App Rep 84, CA, the court took the view that character was not synonymous with reputation although evidence of reputation could be relevant to the issue of character.

---

1 The decision in *Vye* was a trifle slow in percolating through to some courts and appeals are still being heard on cases where the judge failed adequately to implement that decision. It seems that there is only one case where a court has expressed reservations about the correctness of *Vye*: *R* v *Wood*, *The Times*, July 11, 1995, CA.

2 The other major source of litigation has been the appropriate direction when an accused of good (or goodish) character is tried with a person of bad character.

The admission of good character evidence

No clear explanation of why good character evidence can be given by an accused is to be found in the law reports; it is usually described as a concession to the accused (see, for example, *R* v *Miller* [1952] All ER 667, CA). Stephen said that: '[e]vidence as to the character of the accused person is admitted in criminal cases as a sort of indulgence though character is usually treated as irrelevant.' (Stephen 1882)[3] Nor is it certain when good character evidence became admissible although the practice is hallowed by long usage (see for example *R* v *Turner* (1664) 6 St Tr 565 and *R* v *Harris* (1680) 7 St Tr 926) although a clear rule emerges in the eighteenth century – see particularly, *R* v *Hardy* (1794) 13 St Tr 267 and *R* v *Horne Tooke* (1794) 14 St Tr 123. Evidence of good character may be given in evidence in chief by a defendant or his witnesses or be elicited from a witness in cross-examination on his behalf.

The evidential effect of good character evidence

In 1989, in *R* v *Berrada*, the Court of Appeal took the view that where a defendant of good character has given evidence, the judge must direct the jury about the relevance of good character to the credibility of the defendant – this is now known as the 'first limb' of a good character direction: *Berrada* did not deal with a non-testifying defendant nor did it consider the issue of co-accused with different characters. In *Vye*, Lord Taylor CJ confirmed the necessity for a 'first limb' (credibility) direction where the accused testifies. He then ruled that a non-testifying defendant is also entitled to a 'first limb' direction: 'when the defendant has not given evidence at trial but relies on exculpatory statements made to the police of others, the judge should direct the jury to have regard to the defendant's good character when considering the credibility of those statements.' He added that the judge would be entitled to point out that such statements were not on oath.[4] The justification for the mandatory direction being 'when the jury is considering the truthfulness of any such statement it would be logical for them to take good character into account, just as they would in regard to a defendant's character.'

Lord Taylor CJ further ruled that where a defendant is of good character, whether he had testified or not, the judge should give a 'second limb' direction, namely the effect of good character on the issue of propensity. The court accepted that the form of the direction is for the judge to determine and it should be tailored to the particular circumstances but that the appeal court 'will be slow to criticise any qualifying remarks he may make based on the facts of the individual case.'

Cases since *Vye* have stressed that failure to give both limbs of the good character direction where appropriate (the credibility direction will depend upon the accused testifying or relying on out of court exculpatory statements; the second limb direction applies to any defendant, since propensity is relevant even in respect of a non-testifying defendant who has made no exculpatory statement) will

3 The concession is two-edged since a defendant by adducing evidence of general good character opens up the possibility of specific incidents of bad character being given in rebuttal by the prosecution or a co-accused.

4 Section 35 of the Criminal Justice and Public Order Act 1994 would now require the judge to direct the jury that they can draw such inferences as appear proper from the failure to testify.

generally lead to a conviction being quashed.[5] This may be the case even where the jury have heard all the character evidence but the direction is omitted or incomplete.[6] Given the importance now laid upon the appropriate directions for an accused with a good character it is critical to discover who falls within this category.

The Court of Appeal in *Vye* did not provide guidance on what constituted evidence of good character, while accepting that the defendants in the three cases there considered fell within that category.[7] Particular difficulty has arisen in respect of 'blemished defendants', that is defendants whose record is not wholly free of discredit.

Blemished defendants

The court in *Vye* seemed willing to treat an accused with convictions or other blemishes as being of good character and thus entitled to one or both (depending on the case) limbs of the good character direction. Indeed, the co-accused in the third of the *Vye* cases was so treated despite having a youthful conviction. This raises two possibilities: either, an accused with a blemished character may be of 'good' character and entitled to a *Vye* direction, albeit tailored to the facts of the case: or, such an accused may be regarded as not of good character at all and thus not entitled to any part of the *Vye* direction.

The House of Lords has recently had its first opportunity to consider the appropriate direction to be given to a jury when faced with a defendant of 'good' character, that is with no convictions, whose character is in fact blemished. In the case in question, *R* v *Aziz* [1995] WLR 53, A, Y and T had been convicted of conspiracy to cheat the public revenue by the evasion of VAT and offences contrary to the Value Added Tax Act 1983, s 39(3). Their convictions were quashed by the Court of Appeal; the prosecution appealed to the House of Lords and the Court of Appeal certified the following question:

> 'Whether directions in accordance with *R* v *Vye* [1993] 3 All ER 241 must be given in all cases in which a defendant has adduced evidence of previous good character, and if not, in what circumstances must such evidence be given?'

---

5 See, for example, *R* v *Liacopoulos, Ifill and Marulanda* (1994) unreported – no first limb direction, retrial ordered; in *R* v *Heath, The Times*, February 10, 1994; *R* v *Micallef, The Times*, November 25, 1993, no second limb direction was given and the convictions were quashed; in *R* v *Durbin* [1995] 2 Cr App Rep 84, CA and *R* v *Wood, The Times*, July 11, 1995, CA – no second limb direction – a retrial was ordered. However, in *R* v *Hitchens, The Times*, February 13, 1995, CA, the judge's failure to refer to the accused good(ish) character when defence counsel had made much of that evidence and the other evidence against the accused was 'overwhelming' was not treated as sufficient to quash the conviction.

6 Where, however, the judge omits the credibility direction but the case manifestly raises the issue of credibility, ie the issue is anyway before the jury, such an omission should not, it is argued, lead to a conviction being quashed. It also seems arguable that to omit the second limb direction, particularly in respect of an accused whose good character evidence is limited to an absence of convictions, should not be an automatic ground for quashing a conviction.

7 The relevant good character possessed by the defendants or co-defendants in *Vye*, *Wise* and *Stephenson* were as follows: *Vye*, 50 and with no previous convictions; *Wise*, 35 and 'had worked in the secondhand car trade for some eight years and had not fallen foul of the law'; and while *Stephenson* was not of good character his co-accused, H, was 'save for one ''peccadillo'' at the age of 16'. H was treated as of good character despite the blemish on his record.

In fact the appeal was concerned with a narrower question.[8] Namely, whether a defendant with a good character, but who admits he has committed crimes (there are other types of character blemish: see below for an analysis of differing types) was entitled to a direction on character in accordance with *Vye*. Who may be said to fall into the category of a blemished defendant?

Who is a blemished defendant?

A defendant may have a blemish on his character in any number of ways. There are three main categories:

(a) The accused who has minor or long past convictions (the convictions group).
(b) An accused who has no convictions but who admits the commission of other crimes or in respect of whom there is evidence that he has committed other offences (the criminal group – the category in *Aziz* itself).
(c) The accused with no past convictions who is charged with two offences based on the same incident, to the lesser of which he pleads guilty (the concurrent group).

a. Minor or long-past convictions

First, it should be noted that the Rehabilitation of Offenders Act 1974 does not apply to evidence in court although a spent conviction can be referred to only with the leave of the judge. However, it seems arguable that, at least in relation to the scope of the judicial direction in respect of good character, a defendant can have past convictions and still be of good character. It is clear that whether such a defendant is to be treated as of good character is for the judge to determine. Equally clearly, if a convicted person is ruled to be of good character the two limbs of the *Vye* direction (appropriately modified if necessary) must be given.

In a number of cases a convicted person has been treated as being of good character for the purposes of the direction on character. Lord Taylor CJ in *R* v *Horrex* (1993) unreported, CA, put it thus: '[i]t must be a matter for the judge's discretion where the previous character is not absolutely good, in the sense of there being no blemish upon it at all' and in *R* v *Micallef*, *The Times*, 25 November 1993, the Court of Appeal took the view that: '[u]nless the trial judge reaches a clear conclusion that a defendant is not a man of good character the direction should be given.' Not all cases are as inclined towards giving the accused the benefit of the doubt. In *R* v *O'Shea* [1993] Crim LR 951, CA, the accused who was charged with possession of cannabis with intent to supply, had two convictions for minor offences many years previously (1962 and 1973) and his counsel argued that he should be treated as a man of good character. The judge had ruled that the issue of whether a person was of good character was a matter of judicial discretion but was resolute in refusing to disregard convictions (even long past convictions) in his direction on character if he would, in any way, be misleading the jury. In this case the judge had told the jury that the accused's convictions were minor, that he was sure the jury would not hold such convictions against him and that he had never been in trouble over drugs. The Court of Appeal upheld the conviction.

8 In addition the House of Lords considered arguments adduced by counsel for the Crown that *R* v *Sharp* [1988] 1 All ER 65, HL, was wrongly decided.

O'Shea, a case decided some months after *Vye* and which case was not cited, can not mean that a person with convictions can never be of good character (and thus never entitled to either limb of the *Vye* direction) since that would be contrary to *Vye* itself. However, the case seems to suggest that a defendant with minor, long past and non-relevant convictions must always have those convictions referred to in any character direction since to say that such a person had no convictions would mislead the jury. While Lord Taylor CJ in *Vye* spoke of tailoring the direction to the accused the tenor of that case seems to support the notion that such a defendant could be treated as of absolute good character and that the judge need not refer to the past convictions at all; this interpretation seems more consistent with other post-*Vye* decisions. *O'Shea* was referred to by the Court of Appeal in *R* v *Hitchens* (1995) unreported, CA, but its import was not discussed since the judge in this case fell into the larger error of failing to say anything about the character of the appellant because of the markedly different character of a co-accused. However, the court seemed to suggest, obiter, that the appropriate direction in respect of *Hitchens* would be to describe him as of good character, and thus entitled to both limbs of the *Vye* direction, albeit he had one minor conviction many years previously. This seems to offer some support to the *O'Shea* view.

Some past offences may be such as to lead to the accused losing the mantle of good character entirely. Similarity between the offences emerging and the current trial tend to diminish the chances of the accused being of good character as will repeated offences and more recent criminal activity. Lying about the existence of past convictions is also likely to lead a judge to rule a defendant is not of good character.[9] Blemishes which have not precluded the accused being treated as of good character include: a recent conviction for possession of cannabis (*R* v *Wren* [1993] Crim LR 952, CA, charge of indecency against qualified barrister, aged 39, practising in industry); convictions for dissimilar offences 12 years previously (*R* v *Arif*, *The Times*, 17 June 1993, CA, reputable restaurant owner charged with fraudulent importation of cannabis): a conviction five years previously for a drink-driving offence (*R* v *Timson and Hales* [1993] Crim LR 58, CA, unqualified solicitor's assistant charged with the solicitor with obtaining property by deception by making fraudulent claims on the 'Green Form' Legal Advice scheme); a conviction 13 years before for possession of an offensive weapon (*R* v *H* [1994] Crim LR 205, step-father charged with indecent assault on his step-daughter); and, two convictions for theft 20 years previously (*R* v *Heath*, *The Times*, 10 February 1994,CA, long distance lorry driver charged with fraudulent importation of 211 kilogrammes of cannabis).

Apart from the inherent uncertainty of knowing in advance whether a court will disregard past convictions, the approach manifested in these cases seems eminently sensible.

b. Unconvicted criminals

Turning to cases involving an accused with no convictions but who has committed other offences, which fact emerges during the trial. In *Aziz*, for example, a number of people were prosecuted in respect of a widespread scheme to evade income tax and VAT; three of the defendants were A, Y and T, none of whom had prior

9 *R* v *H* [1994] Crim LR, CA, was a case where the accused may have lied about the circumstances of the conviction. The Court of Appeal refused to find him disentitled to the good character direction because there was no certain evidence that he had lied. It might be preferable to find that lies about the circumstances of a conviction should be disregarded, and the conviction alone considered, in determining if a person is of good character.

convictions. A did not testify but put forward the defence that he had been misled by his co-defendants. A had made exculpatory statements to investigating officers but had also made damaging admissions. The judge gave the second limb direction (propensity). Y and T did testify, both of them admitted they had committed offences for which they had not been prosecuted (knowingly making a false mortgage application, under-declaring income to the Inland Revenue and allowing employees to under-declare income to the Revenue). The judge gave the first limb direction (credibility) in respect of both of them. The House accepted that the judge had erred in failing to give both the credibility and the propensity direction if the accused were of good character and that the conviction was rightly quashed by the Court of Appeal.

Of wider interest is the discussion of whether the accused who admitted other offences (Y and T) were of good character at all and thus entitled to a *Vye* direction. Lord Steyn (with whom the rest of the House concurred) considered two propositions. First, that an absence of convictions meant an accused was of good character and the *Vye* directions, qualified if necessary, must be given. Second, that an accused's criminal behaviour may, despite the absence of convictions, permit a judge to terminate the accused's status as a person of good character and decline to give a *Vye* direction. He plumped unhesitatingly for the latter saying that 'a sensible criminal justice system should not compel a judge to go through the charade of giving directions in accordance with *R* v *Vye* in a case where the defendant's claim to a good character is spurious.' Hence, he ruled, a judge has a discretion to decline to give a character direction if to do so is an insult to common sense. He added that the discretion to dispense with a *Vye* direction is of a limited variety and prima facie the direction should be given.

Thus, in many cases it may be appropriate to give the directions and then add words of qualification concerning other proved or possible criminal conduct of the accused which has emerged during the trial in order to ensure the jury receive a fair and balanced picture. However, in those limited cases where it would make no sense to give directions they may be dispensed with altogether. Lord Steyn left the determination of whether the accused receives a qualified direction or no direction to the good sense of the trial judge.

Two earlier cases, approved in *Aziz*, provide some guidance on the type of situation where it would be farcical to give *Vye* directions. From these one could conclude that the critical issues appear to be the relative degree and type of criminality which the accused has admitted. In *R* v *Zoppola-Barraza*, *The Times*, 6 May 1994, CA, the court was strongly influenced by the similarity between the offences admitted (illegal importation of gold in order to evade VAT) and that with which he was charged (illegal importation of cocaine). In *R* v *Buzalek and Schiffer* [1991] Crim LR 116, CA, B and S were charged with fraudulent trading. The dishonesty they admitted at trial was in respect of false financial references and similar incidents; the accused were held not of good character since they had admitted dishonesty in respect of incidents other than that with which they were charged. Further, in *R* v *Akram* [1995] Crim LR 50, CA, a case in which the jury knew that the accused, who was charged with possession and possession with intent to supply heroin, had used heroin, he was not treated as of good character. Little enthusiasm can be felt for this decision in which the Court of Appeal seemed to suggest that, since A could have been cross examined about his use of heroin because he had cast imputations on a prosecution witness (i.e. under the Criminal Evidence Act 1898, s 1(f)(ii) – the second part) this justified failure to give the full character direction. However, cross examination under section 1(f)(ii) is aimed only at the credibility of the accused and is anyway subject to a discretion to disallow it where it might, as here, lead a jury to argue that previous use of heroin was relevant to the issue of guilt. Surely, that A might, or might not, have been cross examined with a view to shaking his credibility should not affect whether there should be a direction on propensity for a person with no convictions.

Cases involving an unconvicted, but criminal, accused give rise to greater difficulty than those relating to defendants with petty past convictions. It has been argued by Professor Birch (Birch 1994, p 834) that the simplest approach would be to treat all unconvicted defendants as of good character and leave it to the judge to tailor the character direction appropriately when the defendant has, until now, evaded detection rather than failed to commit crimes and this approach finds support in *R* v *Micallef* which was not discussed in *Aziz*. In support of Lord Steyn, it would seem very odd for a judge, who has admitted evidence of past criminality under the similar fact rule as demonstrating a propensity to commit the crime charged, still to give, even in suitably tailored form, a character direction saying that the accused's lack of convictions can be taken into account in determining whether he has the propensity to commit the type of crime with which he is charged.[10] Consequently, the House of Lords decision in *Aziz*, provided the directions are not lightly discarded, is to be welcomed.

Perhaps surprisingly, the House in *Aziz* did not refer to the Court of Appeal decision in *R* v *Durbin* [1995] 2 Cr App Rep 84, CA, decided some two months before the hearing in *Aziz* (and some four months before judgment). In *Durbin*, the accused, a lorry-driver, was charged with knowing importation of a controlled drug. D admitted that he was engaged in smuggling goods (which he believed to be computers) across borders in mainland Europe to evade VAT or other Customs duties and also had two minor, old convictions; the judge did not give any direction in his summing up on the issue of D's character (having fallen into the same trap as in *Hitchens*, above, of saying nothing about the character of one co-accused when the other co-accused was of manifestly bad character). The facts of this case bear a similarity to those of *Zoppola-Barraza* where Alliott J had described it as 'an affront to common sense to hold that such a person is entitled to the same direction that is intended to benefit those who can truly be regarded as of good character.' The Court of Appeal agreed that, on its facts, *Zoppola-Barraza* was correctly decided but felt able to distinguish it in this case. In the former case, the accused had a smuggling business of which the importation which formed the subject matter of the charge was but a part, whereas here the smuggling was put forward by the accused as an explanation of the particular transaction in which the importation of drugs was discovered but he was not admitting an organised smuggling business. Clearly, held Evans LJ, D could not be regarded as a model citizen but the circumstances did not disentitle him to any direction on character. The appropriate course where a defendant was 'entitled to a good character direction, based on his previous good character' was to give a good character direction 'even though its terms may have to be modified in the light of admissions made by the defendant as to the circumstances of the offence charged against him'. Where a qualified direction is given it should be 'in realistic terms, taking account of all the facts as they are known to the jury. The jury should not be directed to approach the case on a basis which, to their knowledge, is artificial or untrue.' On the facts, D was to be regarded as of good character and a direction should have been given – a retrial was ordered.

10 See the comment of Lord Taylor CJ in *Vye* discussed below concerning the accused whose conduct in participating in the incident at all could be said to affect good character.

c. No convictions prior to the current incident

Finally, what of a defendant who pleads guilty to an offence arising out an incident but not guilty to a more serious charge based on the same event – a special type of the previous category of defendant. Four Court of Appeal cases are in point: *R* v *Teasdale* [1993] 4 All ER 290; *R* v *Challenger* [1994] Crim LR 202; *R* v *Micallef*, *The Times*, 25 November 1993; and *R* v *Shepherd* [1995] Crim LR 153.

In *Teasdale*, there had been a fight between the former and current boy friends of J at J's home; the fight turned into a fracas and J and T became involved. J suffered minor and serious injuries. The accounts given by J and T differed markedly as to the cause of the serious injury (an attack by T or an incidental blow emanating from the principal fight between the boyfriends) but T admitted the minor assault. The case turned on the jury's assessment of the evidence of J and T; the Court of Appeal considered a character direction was required – particularly since the relative credibility of the protagonists was crucial to the issue. Morland J pointed out that in *Vye* the Court of Appeal agreed that a character direction on credibility was mandatory even in respect of an accused who had lied to the police so that similar credit must be given to an accused 'who has frankly admitted an offence in the indictment.'

This case was not followed in *Challenger* in which C, who had no prior convictions, pleaded guilty to possession of cannabis but denied the further charges arising from his arrest – possession of cannabis with intent to supply and possession of an offensive weapon (a knife). The judge declined to give any direction on character. The Court of Appeal upheld the convictions in respect of all counts and distinguished Teasdale on the basis that it was applicable only where the charge to which the accused pleaded guilty was, in effect, a lesser alternative to the charge in issue. As Roch LJ put it:

> '[i]n our judgment, once a person has pleaded guilty to an offence he ceases to be a person of good character and the full character direction becomes inappropriate in such a case, unless the offence to which he has pleaded guilty is an alternative to that on which he is being tried and the facts are such, that if his conviction on the greater offence is brought home then his guilty plea on the lesser offence has to be vacated, so there is no conviction.' (Lexis Transcript)

The court then accepted that, depending on the circumstances of the case, a judge had a discretion as to whether to give a direction on the defendant's character in so far as it related to credibility.

The basis of the distinction between these cases seems unconvincing and introduces a yet further twist in respect of the direction to be given in respect of defendants with no previous convictions. The *Teasdale* approach requires the judge to give a direction and then leave it to the jury to determine the weight the unsullied character has in the scales – such an approach seems both more consistent with *Vye* and more likely to promote consistency of practice.

Neither of these cases was discussed in *Micallef*[11] or *Shepherd*. In *Micallef* there was history of acrimony in respect of custody and access to C, the son of the accused and X. The accused approached X (in itself a breach of undertakings) and tried to talk to her, he admitted he had a knife with him and waved it about near her face in order to emphasise his words. During this discussion X's face was cut.

11 The existence of these cases was drawn to the attention of the court after the judgment was drafted and the court said they did not affect its judgment.

M admitted reckless wounding (Offences Against the Person Act 1861 s 20) but denied wounding with intent (contrary to s 18). The full character direction was not given. The Court of Appeal, in quashing the section 18 conviction, concerned itself principally with the previous breach of undertakings by M (see above) and, rather surprisingly, ignored the contemporaneous offence. The court was clearly of the view that the full good character direction should be given to a person with no convictions other than in the most exceptional of cases, albeit suitably tailored in the light of any adverse character evidence. Clearly, this case could come within *Teasdale* as explained in *Challenger* but the tenor of the judgment is markedly in favour of treating an accused without prior convictions as of good character in most cases.

Finally, in *Shepherd* the accused was charged with multiple counts of obtaining state benefits by deception and obtaining property (mortgage advances) by deception. He pleaded guilty to the social security frauds. The court upheld the convictions for the mortgage frauds and did not dispute the judge's decision not to give a direction that S was of good character: ie the contemporaneous fraud rendered S other than of good character. This decision is in line with *Challenger* rather than *Teasdale* but neither case seems to have been discussed and the appeal was principally concerned with implicit comment on S's character provided by the good character direction about a co-accused. It should be noted that counsel for S had down-played the social security frauds so that the failure to give a *Vye* direction, which would have been heavily qualified to reflect the admitted fraud, was probably beneficial to S.

Conclusion

The valiant attempt by the Court of Appeal in *Vye* to clarify the position relating to good character evidence has solved one question but rendered another – is the accused of good character – of crucial importance. Perhaps no consistent pattern can be expected given the differing types of blemish which an accused of predominately good character may manifest. However, it seems desirable for some attempt to be made to classify some common blemishes as fatal or otherwise to the possession of a good character.

Perhaps convictions which are for other purposes spent should be disregarded in determining if the accused is of good character. More recent convictions might also be disregarded if non-relevant to the current charge though this seems less satisfactory and more productive of uncertainty. It could be argued that more recent (or more serious) convictions should be drawn to the attention of the jury who should be directed as to the relevance or otherwise of such convictions.

An accused who admits criminal acts but who has no convictions is perhaps best left to the discretion of the judge who can assess the relative degree of good and bad within the accused's character and this may also be appropriate for an accused who admits a contemporaneous offence. However, even in these cases it is surely appropriate to remember that the starting assumption is that an accused is entitled to be treated as of good character unless the contrary is established.

Judges are surely capable of distinguishing those accused with long-past, minor convictions (who could be regarded as of good character) from those who have committed serious crimes which have remained undetected until raised at the trial for some other offence (not of good character). Certainly what should be avoided is the pre-*Vye* free for all which seemed to appeal to the Court of Appeal in *R* v

Wood. Perhaps even more fervently to be resisted is statutory intervention: a cry of trust the judges or even trust the juries is not always heard in the field of evidence but the cry of trust the politicians is a very rare bird.

Bibliography

Birch, D (1994) comment on *R* v *Zoppola-Barraza* [1994] *Criminal Law Review* 833, 834.

Cross, R and Tapper, C (1995) *On Evidence*, 8th ed. (London: Butterworths).

Murphy, P (1995) *A Practical Approach to Evidence,* 5th ed. (London: Blackstone Press).

Stephen, J (1882) *History of the Common Law* (London: MacMillan & Co).

FAMILY REDEFINITION UNDER PART III OF THE FAMILY LAW BILL 1996

Craig Lind

Lecturer in Law, University of Wales, Aberystwyth
and

Anne Barlow

Lecturer in Law, University of Wales, Aberystwyth

First Published in Web Journal of Current Legal Issues in association with Blackstone Press Ltd.

SUMMARY

We aim to assess the potentially wide-ranging effects of Part III of the Family Law Bill 1996 on the legal position of unmarried couples in domestic violence law, and on the jurisprudential scope of family law itself. We begin by considering the social reality of family structuring, noting the erosion of the dominance of the traditional married family. Then we consider the equivocal and, consequently, incohesive legal response to this social diversification (particularly in the context of heterosexual cohabitation). In the analysis of Part III of the 1996 Bill which follows we examine the implications of the proposed reforms for all unmarried cohabitants, and examine the adequacy of the new remedies available to expanded categories of victims of family violence. We conclude by arguing that the Bill significantly improves current law, but that by creating three tiers of legal regulation to distinguish the remedies available to spouses, unmarried heterosexual cohabitants, and other home sharers (notably homosexual cohabitants), it unnecessarily and inappropriately complicates the resolution of comparable disputes. The ideological importance of the superiority of the married state has prevented pragmatic and coherent reform.

CONTENTS

Introduction

The Family Homes and Domestic Violence Bill 1995 was withdrawn by the government in October 1995 because of pressure from Conservative back bench Members of Parliament (prompted by the *Daily Mail*, 23 October 1995) concerned that privileges reserved to married couples were being extended to unmarried couples. When the Lord Chancellor yielded to the pressure he vowed that he would not abandon the legislation. He was adamant that current law on domestic violence and occupation of a family home was long overdue for reform and rationalisation. He promised revised legislation before long.

True to his word Lord Mackay's first Bill presented to the House of Lords in the 1995/6 parliamentary session was the Family Law Bill. Whilst originally intended only to radically overhaul the law of divorce, in Part III the Bill has been used as the vehicle to reintroduce (with minor alterations) the amendments he intended for the law on family homes and domestic violence. Thus not only does the proposed legislation remove fault almost entirely from formal divorce, in the field of domestic violence law, it also extends the categories of 'family' for jurisdictional purposes. While both reforms are primarily aimed at giving effect to recommendations made by the Law Commission (Law Com No 192 and 207) their ambit is guaranteed to provoke controversy especially amongst conservative thinkers whose fears have long been that the traditional family is under legal attack.

In this article we intend to examine Part III of the Bill focusing on its effect on the rights of both homosexual and unmarried heterosexual cohabitants. While the proposed reform of law in respect of the latter has been responsible for much of the controversy that has surrounded this piece of legislation, the creation of family law remedies for the former may, in the end, be the more ideologically significant reform. In broadening the application of remedies for domestic violence and the resolution of family homes disputes to unmarried heterosexual couples family law is clearly expanding. But in extending some of those remedies to lesbian and gay couples, and others sharing a household, the jurisprudential scope of family law is beginning to be radically revised. And yet the Bill is not uncompromising in its progressive trend. It still harbours a tendency to cling to a tradition of family law that is exclusively marriage centred and heterosexual, and insists upon cohabitation as the central focus of family relationships. This ideological allegiance, it is submitted, prevents it from offering a rational and cohesive set of solutions to the domestic violence and property disputes of all 'romantic' and cohabiting relationships (whether or not sexual).

Reconstructing the Family

The family idealised in film, fiction and even in law is not the family that prevails in our society (O'Donovan 1993, ch 3; Bainham 1995; Weeks 1991, 134; Esseks 1990, p 192; Coote *et al* 1994). Indeed empirical research on the family supports the proposition that even within the dominant realm of heterosexual partnerships our society is undergoing a period of radical family restructuring; the traditional married family is visibly in decline. The number of marriages in the UK is falling dramatically: between 1971 and 1991 it fell by 24% (*Social Trends* 1995, p 36). And even then, more than one out of every three marriages ends in divorce. In contrast, heterosexual cohabitation is on the increase. Almost one third of non-married men and women in their mid-twenties to mid-thirties now choose to cohabit (compared with less than 10% in 1979) (*1993 General Household Survey* 1995, p 6). A significant and rising proportion of children are no longer born or raised in married families; in 1993 32% of all children born were born to unmarried parents (*1993 General Household Survey* 1995, p 29) and almost one in five mothers with dependent children were lone mothers (*1993 General Household Survey* 1995, p 34). While there is anecdotal evidence that lesbian and gay cohabitation is increasing, and that their lives are conducted on lines similar to heterosexual cohabitation and even marriage, no empirical data are routinely kept on these relationships.

Thus, while some married couples do have children and do sometimes live together until one of them dies, it is not uncommon for the marriage to end in divorce. Nor is it unusual for couples never to marry, or never to have children. There are also those who have children without involving themselves in a long term, monogamous, relationship. And those whose relationships are with members of their own sex. Some relationships are asexual. And some households consist of more than two adults, who may or may not share sexual intimacy. The variety is almost infinite. The most that can be said with any certainty, in an attempt to define the family, is that it usually involves significant emotional and material relationships between people (whether adults or children) born of a genetic, social, legal or sexual connection. While there may be some definitions which are more widely used than others, and while particular conceptions are applicable in particular contexts, it is clear that 'family' means many things to many people, and that the social expectations of families cannot be regarded as anything like as uniform as some would have us believe.

Law and the Social Family

This diversity in family reality has gradually entered the culture of legal regulation. The focus of family law has been shifting and its reform in the last two or three decades has seen its overwhelming concentration on the problems of married couples diminish in favour of greater recognition of the need to regulate the problems of other domestic relationships (principally unmarried, heterosexual cohabitation). The altering social attitude towards these relationships, and towards single parent families, and even homosexual families, required (and continues to require) a response that seriously addresses the real and parallel problems that all these relationships produce. While that may mean that family law has become, in the words of some authors, 'domestic relations law' (Wadlington 1990) there seems to be no need for an alteration in the rubric describing this area of law if it is accepted that the family itself is merely undergoing a process of redefinition.

That this broader ethic should be (and has, to some extent, been) adopted does not necessarily mean that society should stop privileging the marriage state.[1] But it does dictate that the law should acknowledge the existence and at least some of the needs of other families in various important spheres of their lives. This has occurred in a number of piecemeal legal developments in the last few decades.

In property disputes between cohabitants the courts acknowledged the real parallels between unmarried heterosexual cohabitation and marriage. Indeed, Lord Denning in *Bernard* v *Josephs* [1982] 3 All ER 162 at 163 said:

> 'In my opinion in ascertaining the respective shares, the court should normally apply the same considerations to couples living together (as if married) as they do to couples who are truly married.'

However, after the Denning era the courts retreated from this liberal position despite the increasing numbers of unmarried cohabitants (*Burns* v *Burns* [1984] Ch 317, *Thomas* v *Fuller-Brown* [1988] FLR 237 CA, *Rossett* v *Lloyds Bank PLC* [1990] 2 WLR 867, cf. *Midland Bank* v *Cook* [1995] 4 All ER 562). Whereas they had been prepared to imply resulting and constructive trusts to achieve fairer settlements of disputes, they began to adhere to a stricter application of property law. They would only use their equitable jurisdiction to allow cohabitants to assert rights in the property of their partners where a common intention could be inferred that each party should have an interest in the property. This inconsistency led to the Law Commission's current review of the property rights of cohabitants (Harpum 1995).

There have also been a number of legislative developments which have seen unmarried cohabitants emerge as a recognised, although inferior, form of family in law. In the case of social security law, it did not escape the notice of the legislature that to ignore the existence of unmarried cohabiting couples would be to disadvantage married couples dependent on means-tested state benefits. The latter's entitlement (as a couple) is less than that of two unconnected individuals. Thus very early (Supplementary Benefits Act 1966) the introduction of the much hated 'cohabitation rule' ensured that no such advantage was gained by unmarried cohabitants (Social Security and Contributions to Benefits Act 1990 (SSCBA 1990) ss 136(1) and 137(1)). Conversely, where non-means tested contributory benefits are concerned, unmarried cohabitants are usually denied an adult dependent's allowance for their partners where married claimants would receive one, however good their national insurance contribution record (see, for example, SSCBA 1990 ss 82–4). Furthermore, the married couples' allowance providing greater personal relief against income tax does not extend to those living together as husband and wife however stable and long-standing their relationship (ICTA 1988 s 257A, see *Rignell (Inspector of Taxes)* v *Andrews* [1990] STC 410). Yet there was no hesitation in making heterosexual cohabitants liable for their partners' council tax (Local Government Finance Act 1992, s 9). It is noteworthy that lesbian and gay cohabiting couples are not covered by the 'cohabitation rule' or the rule making cohabitants liable for their partners' council tax. Thus, they enjoy a rare advantage in law because it ignores their shared existence and treats them as unconnected individuals merely sharing accommodation.

Another notable recognition of the family status of unmarried cohabitants came in the guise of the extension to them of the right to succeed to public and private

1 Of course, there are many (particularly feminist) writers who question the privileges that are associated with marriage: see Herman 1990; Rubin 1993; and Ettelbrick 1993.

sector tenancies on the death of their partners (Housing Act 1985, s 87 with s 113(1) & (2); Housing Act 1988 (HA 1988), s 17(4); Rent Act 1977, sch 1 as amended by HA 1988 sch 4, part I). This time the courts excluded lesbian and gay cohabitants from the ambit of this rule (*Harrogate Borough Council* v *Simpson* [1986] 2 FLR 91).

Two further statutes have focused on the length of relationship to confer marriage-like benefits on unmarried heterosexual cohabitants. Section 1(3) of the Fatal Accidents Act 1976 extended to them the right to bring a dependant's action where they had cohabited for at least two years and the applicant had been financially dependent upon the deceased. Most recently cohabitants of two years' standing have been given improved succession rights under section 2 of the Law Reform (Succession) Act 1995. These people are now recognised as a separate category of eligible applicants under sections 1A and 2A of the Inheritance (Provision for Family and Dependants) Act 1975 entitled to make a claim for financial provision against a deceased's estate.[2]

Finally, the need for legal protection from domestic violence for unmarried cohabitants was acknowledged by legislation passed in 1976. Rushed through Parliament in the wake of revelations in Erin Pizzey's *Scream Quietly or the Neighbours will Hear* about the shocking effects of violence in the home, the Domestic Violence and Matrimonial Proceedings Act 1976 (DVMPA 1976) gave cohabitants protection from their violent partners (s 1(2)). Perhaps the hurry to pass this Act was responsible both for the incomplete protection it offered victims of domestic violence, and for the inconsistency of the remedies available in different courts. Its shortcomings were the subject of judicial comment (see, for example, *Davis* v *Johnson* [1979] AC 264, per Lord Kilbrandon at p 338) and, as long ago as 1992, the Law Commission described the existing remedies as 'complex, confusing and lack[ing] integration' (Law Com No 207, para 1.2) and called for their reform.

That reform was finally introduced in the Family Homes and Domestic Violence Bill 1995 which sought to codify domestic violence law in a more consistent and cohesive statutory framework. Thus protection against molestation was made almost universal and the courts' discretion to settle occupation of the family home was extended and rationalised. Moreover, the courts were given jurisdiction to make transfer of tenancy orders between unmarried heterosexual cohabitants on relationship breakdown where previously there had been no remedy. In addition it sought to extend to these couples the procedures available to spouses and engaged couples under section 17 of the Married Women's Property Act 1882 (MWPA 1882) for resolving property disputes. Whilst most of these reforms have survived largely intact, in the redraft the latter purely procedural remedy has, inexplicably, disappeared. As John Eekelaar has written (Eekelaar 1996, at p 48.):

> 'It is hard to see how maintaining procedures which benefit only lawyers, even those of the Chancery Bar, help the institution of marriage, but political compromise seldom produces rational results.'

Ironically, despite the fact that the bill extended protection against domestic violence to lesbian and gay cohabitants, and gave the courts a measure of discretion to order occupation of their family homes, this did not feature in the moral controversy which led to its demise. Consequently these reforms have remained intact in the new Bill.

2 Previously cohabitants could only claim if they could show dependancy and this is still the case for those who cannot show two years' cohabitation: see Inheritance (Provision for Family and Dependants) Act 1975 s 1(1)(e).

Unmarried Cohabitants under the Family Law Bill 1996

Part III of the 1996 Bill for the first time provides a uniform code of domestic violence remedies available, in the main, in all courts with jurisdiction in family proceedings (clause 52). It is much more victim and child-centred, concentrating on the harm being suffered within the household, and the remedies available to victims. In this respect it removes a large measure of the discrimination suffered by heterosexual cohabitants, and for the first time, introduces a lesser measure of protection for lesbian and gay cohabitants.

The Bill will repeal and replace the whole of the DVMPA 1976 together with the relevant sections (ss 16–18, s 28(2) and para 53 of Sch 2) of the Domestic Proceedings and Magistrates' Courts Act 1978. It will introduce two types of order: (i) non-molestation orders (clause 37), and (ii) occupation orders (clause 34), available to newly defined classes of applicants (clauses 28, and 30–33).

i. Non-molestation orders

In line with the Law Commission's recommendations, the term 'non-molestation order' has been retained in clause 37 of the Bill which governs the making of these orders. 'Molestation' is not expressly defined. The omission is deliberate, designed to ensure that the current level of protection is not reduced.[3]

The criteria for granting non-molestation orders also follow the Law Commission's recommendation that they be broad rather than specific. Consequently, clause 37(5) provides that in deciding whether to exercise its powers under the clause and, if so, in what manner, the court shall have regard to all the circumstances including 'the need to secure the health, safety and well-being' of the applicant and any relevant child. The term 'well-being', it is submitted, is sufficiently wide to ensure that courts do not feel restricted to making orders only in cases where violence or a threat of violence can be proven.

The range of potential applicants under the Bill is far wider than those encompassed within the 1976 Act. This is perhaps the most radical of the Bill's reforms. Those entitled to apply for non-molestation orders must be 'associated' with the respondent. 'Associated' persons are defined by clause 56(3) to include a wide variety of different people. Most obviously it covers spouses and former spouses, and heterosexual cohabitants and former cohabitants (clause 56(1)(a)). Perhaps most radically, it includes those living or having lived in the same household otherwise than merely by reason of one of them being the other's employee, tenant, lodger or boarder. Significantly, this includes lesbian and gay cohabitants.[4] It should be noted, however, that the Bill prescribes no minimum period of cohabitation or of 'living together in the same household' before a cohabitant or associated person becomes an eligible applicant under clause 37.

Whilst this definition includes a far wider range of applicant than under the current law, one important vulnerable group have been denied protection. The Law

---

3 Thus authorities such as *Vaughan* v *Vaughan* [1973] 1 WLR 1159, *Horner* v *Horner* [1982] Fam 90 and *Jones* v *Walton* [1990]1 FLR 350 (all examples of non-violent behaviour amounting to molestation) will remain good law. Clause 37(6) also makes it clear that molestation of both a general and a specific nature may be prohibited by an order.

4 The other associated persons are:

those falling within a defined group of close relatives;

those who have at any time agreed to marry each other, parents with a child of the relationship or a child in respect of whom they both have or have had parental responsibility;

those who are both parties to the same family proceedings other than proceedings brought under Part III of the 1996 Bill: clause 56(3).

Commission recommended (Law Com No 207 para 3.24) that persons in a 'romantic' relationship (such as boyfriend/girlfriend) who had had a sexual relationship (whether or not involving sexual intercourse), should have a remedy against molestation. However, these people do not fall within the definition of 'associated' persons in the Bill and will not, therefore, be able to avail themselves of the protection it provides. This leaves those who have had a relationship but who have never cohabited, agreed to marry, or had a child together (including a couple who are expecting a child) without a domestic violence remedy in family law.

From the perspective of lesbian and gay couples the proposed legislation represents a significant step forward. Although the Law Commission did not feel able to include them within the definition of 'cohabitants' and, indeed, specifically excluded them, they do fall within the more general category of those who have lived together in the same household other than on a commercial basis (clause 56(3)(c)). The Law Commission foresaw (Law Com No 207 para 3.21) that the test for determining whether people are 'living together in the same household' would be that developed in the matrimonial law context to establish the degree of community of life between them (see, for example, *Fuller* v *Fuller* [1972] 2 All ER 650 and *Mouncer* v *Mouncer* [1972] 1 WLR 321). Although there may be difficulties in interpretation of the definition of the 'same household' with regard to persons who have not had a sexual relationship (such as friends who are also flatsharers), it is submitted that these problems would not present themselves in the case of lesbian and gay cohabitants. Whilst all the authorities relate to married or heterosexual cohabiting couples, the existence of an intimate relationship together with shared meals and domestic arrangements should bring them within the definition. Indeed, the Law Commission report specifically refers to homosexual couples as falling within this broad family relationship (para. 3.19).

In addition several significant improvements are in evidence in clause 37. Former cohabitants and former spouses are included in the Bill where they were previously largely unprotected. Moreover, former 'associated persons' will also be eligible to apply for non-molestation orders. It will not be necessary for those who seek non-molestation remedies to remain in the violent home.

ii. Occupation Orders

Part III of the 1996 Bill replaces both ouster orders under the DVMPA 1976 and the Matrimonial Homes Act 1983 and exclusion orders under the DPMCA 1978 with new forms of orders to be known as 'occupation orders.' These are detailed in clauses 28 and 30 to 33 of the Bill. The aim of this part of the proposed statute is to harmonise and improve what had become a confusion of remedies available under the 1976, 1978 and 1983 Acts for the resolution of disputes about rights of occupation of the family home in domestic violence situations. It also contains the more marked distinction between the rights of spouses and cohabitants in this regard. The most significant distinction, however, is drawn between 'entitled' and 'non-entitled' applicants. Although both will, for the most part, be able to obtain occupation orders, their scope and the ability to seek them will be more restricted in the case of non-entitled applicants.

The fact that cohabitants with no right as a matter of property law to occupy the family home would be able to obtain occupation orders excluding their partners in whom the legal right to occupy vested, provoked the controversy which resulted in the ultimate withdrawal of the 1995 Bill. That this was already a possibility in the same exceptional (domestic violence) context under section 1(1)(c) DVMPA

1976 as confirmed some fifteen years earlier in the leading case of *Davis* v *Johnson* [1979] AC 264 did nothing to prevent those opposing the Bill from claiming that this amounted to a new and unacceptable assault on marriage and property rights.

Notwithstanding this, Part III of the 1996 Bill has retained the majority of these reforms completely intact, whilst attempting to satisfy its conservative critics by focusing the court's attention when deciding whether to make an occupation order on the fact that the parties have not made the same commitment as married couples (Clause 36). While the bill treats heterosexual cohabitants on an almost equal footing with spouses, it distinguishes them from homosexual cohabitants who are only able to apply for an occupation order if they can show their own legal entitlement to occupy the property (Clause 28).

a. Unmarried Entitled Applicants

To be able to apply for a clause 28 occupation order, an applicant must be able to show two things: firstly, that they have an entitlement to occupy the accommodation and secondly, that the accommodation either was or was intended to be their home jointly with a person with whom they are associated. Clause 28(1) defines entitlement to occupy, either through having a legal or beneficial estate or interest, or by virtue of contractual or statutory rights (including 'matrimonial homes rights' defined by clause 25 for spouses). Therefore both heterosexual and lesbian and gay cohabitants who are sole or joint owners, or tenants (whether contractual or statutory) in the rented sector may apply for an order against their partner or former partner. This is because an order can be sought against any person with whom the applicant is associated within the meaning of clause 56(3).

The clause 28 order is an improvement upon the protection currently available to cohabitants and will entitle an applicant to secure her/his occupation of their home (and even its precincts) against intrusion by the respondent for a specified period, or even indefinitely (clause 28(10)). It will give all family courts greater flexibility in terms of the type of orders that can be made and will extend to all entitled applicants remedies that are currently only available to spouses under the MHA 1983. In particular the bill will enable courts to attach conditions relating to matters such as maintenance of the property, taking care of furniture and the payment of rent, mortgage or other outgoings to any clause 28 order (clause 35). Thus unmarried entitled cohabitants, whether or not heterosexual, will make significant advances in terms of the protection available.

A major distinction between occupation orders and ouster injunctions under the DVMPA 1976 is that a violent situation will not be a necessary prerequisite to the making of the order. In deciding whether or not to make an order, and if so what order to make, the courts will have to consider all the circumstances, including the parties' financial resources, their housing needs and resources, and the effects of any order on their (or any relevant child's) health, safety, or well-being (clause 28(6)). Furthermore the court will be compelled to make an order if one party or any child is likely to suffer significant harm if no order is made. This can only be avoided in a situation where it can be shown that *as great or greater* harm is likely to be suffered by the respondent or child if the order in favour of the applicant is made (the 'balance of harm' test) (clause 28(7)). However, in deciding whether or not to exercise its powers under clause 28 in respect of heterosexual cohabitants the court will have to have regard to the fact that the parties have not 'given each other the commitment involved in marriage' (clause 36). However, even then, where at least one of the parties (or their children) is likely to suffer significant harm the balance of harm test will prevail.

Because the Bill defines cohabitants heterosexually, and because clause 36 applies to cohabitants only, the courts will not be required to make the same assumption about commitment when they are dealing with lesbian and gay cohabitants. Ironically, this seems to make the criteria applicable to these couples, who are legally unable to marry (Matrimonial Causes Act 1973, s 11), more closely analogous to spouses than to unmarried heterosexual cohabitants.

b. Unmarried, Non-entitled Applicants

To be able to apply for a clause 31 order giving them a protected right to occupy a family home, an applicant must be a heterosexual cohabitant (or former cohabitant) and be able to show three things: firstly, that their partner has a right to occupy the home;[5] secondly, that they have no such entitlement, and thirdly, that their accommodation either was or was intended to be their mutual home.

The nature of this occupation order is the same as the order granted under clause 28 except that its maximum duration is one year (clause 31(10)). But the criteria governing the discretion of the courts in deciding whether or not to make the order have been weakened in the 1996 version of the reforms. While all the circumstances remain relevant, and while the courts must consider the parties' financial resources, their housing needs and resources, and the effects of any order on their (or any relevant child's) health, safety, or well-being they will also be obliged to consider the nature of the parties' relationship, the length of cohabitation, and whether or not there are children (clause 28(6)). Furthermore while the court must consider the balance of harm, in contrast to the position under clause 28, it will not be obliged to make an order in favour of an applicant suffering greater harm (clause 31(7) & (8)). The courts must also have regard to the fact that the parties have not 'given each other the commitment involved in marriage' (clause 36).

As in orders under clause 28 the court may, in making an order under clause 31, attach conditions relating to matters such as maintenance of the property, taking care of furniture and the payment of rent, mortgage or other outgoings (clause 35). Whereas the House of Lords had decided in *Davis* v *Johnson* [1979] AC 264 that cohabitants who had no estate or interest in the family home were able to obtain ouster orders against their partners under the DVMPA 1976, their legal position as against third parties remained precarious. Difficulties arose as a result of the court's inability under that statute to make orders, for example, with respect to payment of outgoings in respect of the property or removal of furniture. Thus the 1996 Bill considerably enhances their position. Indeed, given that a violent situation will not be a prerequisite for the making of an occupation order under clause 31(6), it may be a useful tool for deserted non-entitled former cohabitants to secure a legal status with third parties such as a mortgagee or landlord.

iii. Transfer of Tenancies

In current law unmarried cohabitants who have no children of their relationship[6] and whose home is rented have no means of resolving transfer of tenancy disputes when their relationship ends. Thus a joint tenancy cannot be transferred to one

5 In the rare circumstance where neither cohabitant has a right to occupy the home, clause 33 provides for an occupation order (on the same criteria as those enumerated in clause 31) regulating only the right to occupy the home inter se. The order cannot affect third party rights.

6 Those who have 'natural' children of their relationship can apply for a transfer of property order (which includes transfers of tenancies: *K* v *K* [1992] 2 All ER 727) under Sch. 1 of the Children Act 1989 for the benefit of the children. Where the child is a child of only one of them the schedule cannot be used: *J* v *J* [1993] 2 FLR 56. Thus lesbian or gay couples are definitively excluded.

party, and any tenancy in the name of one cohabitant only cannot be transferred to the other. Where a relationship is disrupted by violence, or is breaking down for any other reason, the courts are powerless to provide a final remedy to the parties in dispute concerning their tenancy rights. The unresolved deadlock that this lacuna in the law permits was the subject of critical commentary by the Law Commission (Law Com No 207 Pt VI). It felt that the problem had to be resolved by the enactment of legislation which would give the courts a discretionary remedy to transfer tenancies between former cohabitants whose family home comprised rented accommodation. To provide no remedy at all was unacceptable.

Schedule 7 of the 1996 Bill (to be enacted by clause 48) provides the recommended remedy. It will empower the courts to exercise a discretion to reallocate tenancies. In re-enacting schedule 1 of the MHA 1983 it provides for the transfer of tenancies between spouses and then goes on to create a mechanism for the transfer of the tenancies of unmarried heterosexual family homes when the couple cease living together as husband and wife. The criteria for the exercise of the discretion in respect of joint tenants are the same as those applicable to 'entitled' applicants seeking an occupation order under clause 28 (clause 28(6)(a)(c)). And in the case of a sole tenancy vesting in the respondent the criteria are the same as those applicable to non-entitled occupation order applicants under clause 31 (clause 31(5)(d)(g)). When making an order under the schedule the court may direct the party to whom the tenancy is transferred to make a compensatory payment to the other party, having had regard to the financial loss of the transferor and the financial needs, resources and obligations of both of the parties (Part III of Sch 7).

What is disconcerting about the schedule is that it is inapplicable to homosexual cohabitants. This leaves them without the remedy the Law Commission regarded as essential for unmarried cohabitants in their position. Lesbian and gay couples whose relationships end will continue to have no recourse to the courts to resolve their joint tenancy disputes. And non-tenant lesbian or gay partners will go on having no legal protection at all. Where the relationship is being brought to an end by the violence of a legal tenant that violence is likely to decide the future occupation of the family home, leaving the most vulnerable party least protected. Where the violent partner is a sole-tenant the law bolsters her/his physical power by enforcing it with a property right. It is anathema that anyone should be capable of being evicted from her/his habitual home, without recourse to the courts, by the brutality of anyone else, least of all an unmarried partner. This permits those in close personal relationships to do something which the criminal law prevents landlords from doing.

Conclusion

For reasons of public policy and political expediency the government has, in this Bill, created three layers of family definition. It has reinforced the distinction between married and unmarried heterosexual couples in a number of ways. It creates a formal commitment test as a factor to be considered by courts being asked to make occupation orders for unmarried cohabitants (clause 36). Moreover, the revised Bill amended its 1995 predecessor by dividing the two clauses dealing with unentitled applicants for occupation orders into four: two relevant to spouses and two separate clauses relevant to cohabitants (clauses 9 and 10 of the 1995 Bill became clauses 30 – 33 of the 1996 Bill). Some minor distinctions between the proposed law relating to married and unmarried couples were introduced into these revised versions. Thus occupation orders for unentitled cohabitants can never be indefinite, while they can be for former spouses, and unentitled spouses. Finally, the government in the 1996 version refused to extend the procedural advantages to be derived from the application of the MWPA 1882 to unmarried cohabitants. Thus a number of immaterial considerations have been introduced, and an effective mechanism for the pragmatic and effective resolution of disputes has been sacrificed for the sake of the symbolic superiority of the married state.

The Bill goes on to establish its third tier of family regulation by distinguishing between unmarried cohabitation and a variety of other domestic relationships classified under the heading of 'associated persons'. These include almost all those who live together in domestic (rather than commercial) relationships.

Most significantly the Bill will, if enacted, represent the first legal acknowledgment of the family status of lesbian and gay couples. But instead of grouping together like relationships, the Bill severs homosexual cohabiting relationships from heterosexual cohabiting relationships. This separation must be artificial when one considers the similarity of the practical and legal problems to which they are likely to give rise. Where two women or two men who have a 'romantic' relationship share a household they do so in exactly the same circumstances as cohabiting, or even marrying, heterosexual couples. They will generally be mutually dependent and will often make joint contributions to their mutual home. In their social context their interdependence is observable. They socialise together, and will generally be treated as a couple by their friends and families. They rely on one another when they are ill. They may even raise their own children. Clearly their emotional ties and their domestic lives are no different from the emotional ties and domestic lives of heterosexual cohabitants. In the context of domestic violence, neither its incidence nor the problems it creates for its victims are different (Taylor and Chandler 1995). For that reason its legal control ought to be no different. And yet it is. Once again the government has sacrificed legal coherence in the resolution of parallel disputes for the sake of maintaining the symbolic and moral superiority of heterosexual relationships over homosexual relationships.

While the more comprehensive extension of remedies for domestic violence to unmarried cohabitants, and to homosexual families and other associated persons in this Bill will be a remarkable step for family definition in itself, the tiered protection available under the Bill is difficult to rationalise when its protective context is considered. Although the applications of the property provisions are not explicitly linked to domestic violence their proposed enactment in that part of a Bill which sets out to resolve the anomalies of domestic violence legislation indicates that they are perceived to be relevant in that context. Thus, occupation orders, while not reserved to the victims of molestation, are likely to be sought to bolster non-molestation orders. That harm (and the balance of harm test) are important criteria when courts decide whether or not to make occupation orders must, it is submitted, indicate the deep concern of the Bill to protect from violence those who share domestic premises. In these circumstances it seems perverse that a tiered approach has been adopted to provide different levels of personal security to victims while protecting the property interests of some (lower tier) violent partners in domestic relationships. In order to maintain the distinctions between married and unmarried cohabitation, and between heterosexual and homosexual (and merely friendly) cohabitation the personal security of those involved the 'lesser' relationships has been sacrificed in this Bill. Moreover, this tiered approach is not all encompassing. There are significant omissions. Thus those involved in uncohabiting 'romantic' relationships, for example, remain unprotected. None of the remedies provided for in the Bill (contrary to the Law Commission's recommendations (para 3.26)) are available to them. This denies the reality of the parallel problems to which all 'romantic' relationships are susceptible.

In contemporary Britain (as in many other, particularly western, jurisdictions) the parameters of the legal family are being reconsidered. Where a national society demonstrates the kind of social and cultural diversity that is evidenced in the United Kingdom the imposition of a limited but universally applicable family definition on a diffuse population cannot continue to satisfy the expectations and aspirations of all the citizens of this nation. Already British law has begun to distance itself from particular moral and social traditions in both its definitions of family relationships and in its expectations of them. What seems most necessary in the realms of legal discourse on the family is the recognition that the need for effective legal remedies is more important than the moral status of particular relationships. In no context is this more obvious or more urgent than in the context of family violence.

Bibliography

Bainham, A (1995) 'Family Law in a Pluralistic Society' 22 *Journal of Law and Society* 234.

Church, J (ed) (1995) *Social Trends 25* (London: HMSO).

Coote, P, Harman, H, Hewitt, H (1994) 'Changing Family Structures and Family Behaviour' in Eekelaar, J and Maclean, M (eds) *A Reader on Family Law* (Oxford: OUP).

Eekelaar, J (1996) 'The Family Law Bill – The Politics of Family Law' [1996] *Family Law* 45.

Esseks, J D (1990) 'Redefining the Family' 25 *Harvard Civil Rights-Civil Liberties Law Review* 183.

Ettelbrick, P (1993) 'Since When is Marriage a Path to Liberation?' in Rubenstein, W B *Lesbians, Gay Men, and the Law* (New York: The New Press).

Foster, K, Jackson, B, Thomas, M, Hunter, P and Bennett, N (1995) *1993 General Household Survey* (London: HMSO).

Harpum, C (1995) 'Cohabitation Consultation' *Family Law* 657.

Herman, D (1990) 'Are We Family?: Lesbian Rights and Women's Liberation' 28 *Osgoode Hall Law Journal* 789.

Law Commission No 192 (1990) *The Ground for Divorce* (London: HMSO).

Law Commission No 207 (1992) *Domestic Violence and Occupation of the Family Home* (London: HMSO).

O'Donovan, K (1993) *Family Law Matters* (London: Pluto Press).

Pizzey, E (1974) *Scream Quietly or the Neighbours will Hear* (London: Penguin Books).

Rubin, G S (1993) 'Thinking Sex: Notes for a Radical Theory of the Politics of Sexuality' in Abelove, H, Barale, M A, Halperin, D M, *The Lesbian and Gay Studies Reader* (New York: Routledge).

Taylor, J and Chandler, T (1995) *Lesbians Talk Violent Relationships* (London: Scarlet Press).

Wadlington, W (1994) *Cases and Materials on Domestic Relations* (3rd ed) (Westbury, NY: Foundation Press).

Weeks, J (1991) *Against Nature: Essays on History, Sexuality and Identity* (London: Rivers Oram Press).

PROBLEM-SOLVING THROUGH REFLECTIVE PRACTICE: THE OXYGEN OF EXPERTISE OR JUST SWAMP GAS?

*Caroline Maughan**

Senior Lecturer, Faculty of Law, University of the West of England, Bristol <c-maughan@uwe.ac.uk>

First Published in Web Journal of Current Legal Issues in association with Blackstone Press Ltd.

**With thanks to Mike Maughan and Julian Webb for their help and advice in the preparation of this article.*

SUMMARY

The notion of reflective practice as a means of developing professional expertise has been gaining ground. Very little evidence exists about the effectiveness of such an approach to legal problem-solving. Donald Schön provides us with a theory of professional knowledge and its development through 'reflection'. He claims it is the ability to practise reflectively which distinguishes the expert from the merely competent professional. The central question for this paper is the value of developing reflective practice skills and processes at the 'novice' level. Drawing on the evidence of running an undergraduate Legal Process course over five years, the author argues that novice lawyers can be enabled to develop reflective skills and habits. However, the paper also indicates that there are still unanswered questions about the transferability of the skills and processes learned as students progress into the vocational stage of legal education and the early years of practice.

CONTENTS

Introduction

In recent years there has been an increased interest in the nature of legal problem-solving and the development of strategies through which it can be taught (Nathanson, 1989; Cruickshank, 1996). One link between legal problem-solving and learning theory that remains under-developed is the role of 'reflective practice'. In this paper the significance of reflective practice as a means of developing expert problem solvers will be explored.

Although the concept of reflective practice is becoming a major theme in debates about both academic and professional legal education, it is important that we do not lose sight of the fact that the 'reflective practitioner' is a Weberian ideal type. There remains much uncertainty about how a 'real' reflective practitioner thinks and acts, and consequently about how this being might be created. The focus will be an aspect of educational development for reflective practice which the author has found especially challenging: by what processes does the novice practitioner move towards expertise, and how can we develop these processes? In so doing the author will draw on her experience of facilitating a 'lawyering skills and legal process' course for undergraduates at the University of the West of England[1] (see Maughan and Webb 1995). Although the practical focus of the paper is therefore on 'academic'[2] legal education, it is suggested that the experience is relevant to the whole question of professional development.

The principles underlying the clinical dimensions of the programme can be stated as follows:

(a) that professional expertise is developed through processes of reflective practice.

(b) the development of reflective practice capability at the undergraduate level will enable those students who subsequently practise law to become proficient and effective practitioners more rapidly and more confidently.

What is a Reflective Practitioner?

It is easy to reduce the reflective practitioner to an image of someone who is simply thoughtful about their own practices. In fact the notion of reflective practice describes a completely different way of thinking about professional knowledge and professional education from the traditional one. It is about creating a different kind of knowledge from the rule-based knowledge which is created and transmitted in law schools. It therefore involves a challenge to both the skills/knowledge and academic/vocational divides.

---

1 This programme is facilitated jointly with Julian Webb.

2 The approach in this course, and to legal education generally, is a 'holistic' one which plays down the significance of the academic/vocational divide (see Webb 1995).

The reflective practitioner constructs professional knowledge through integrating her rule-based knowledge with 'know-how', which derives from a range of personalised skills, strategies and values developed through experience. It is not, therefore, something that can be acquired through a 'technical-rational' (Schön 1983, 1987) education. This is an education which is grounded in rule-based knowledge and which lacks the element of experience necessary to enable the individual both to live through their propositional knowledge and to develop the heuristics needed to deal with the unpredictability of real world problems.

Creating the Reflective Practitioner

To date the most influential writer on education for reflective practice is Donald Schön (1983, 1987). Schön's approach, it has been said, requires:

> 'diagnosis, testing and belief in personal causation. Diagnosis is the ability to frame or 'make sense of' a problem through use of professional knowledge, past experience, the uniqueness of the setting and people involved, and expectations held by others. Once framed, the reflective practitioner engages in on-the-spot experimentation and reflection to test alternative solutions. Finally, the courage to act in situations of uncertainty . . . requires that the practitioner accept responsibility for action.' (Kirby and Paradise 1992: 70)

Schön draws a fundamental distinction between two reflective processes: reflection on action and reflection in action. Reflection on action describes the process of reflection which takes place after the event where the practitioner makes explicit and evaluates the theories of action used to solve a problem. Reflection in action describes interaction with a 'live' problem as it unfolds. The capacity to reflect in action assumes that the problem-solver has the capacity to surface their 'knowing in action', that is, the hidden or tacit knowledge which we use to deal with particular tasks. Where a problem does not create a sense of uncertainty or surprise we will tend to deal with it spontaneously on the basis of that tacit knowledge. However, where a problem contains an element of uncertainty or value conflict, Schön suggests we must consciously confront our tacit theories of action and their underlying values in order to reframe the problem and make it capable of resolution. Schön calls this process 'the reflective conversation'.

The essence of Schön's model of professional education is the creation of an environment in which students can confront simulated or live problems and engage reflexively with them. This he calls the 'reflective practicum.' It is a safe environment in which students put their rule-based knowledge into action and develop a repertoire of responses and judgements which become progressively more complex and sophisticated as they develop to cover a wider and wider range of experiences.

The concept of reflection in action is one of the cornerstones of Schön's theory. It is this process which integrates theory, intuition and action in situations of uncertainty. It is understandable, therefore, that it is reflection in action which has been the principal focus of analysis and critique.[3]

3 Philip Jones has usefully drawn together much of the critical literature in a forthcoming paper: (see Jones, 1996).

Jones (1996) sees it as one of the major criticisms of Schön's work that it derives a model of professional education from his own analysis of expert narratives, i.e. that it seeks to build a system of developing novices from an expert perspective on problem-framing and problem-solving. It is open to debate whether the exemplar of the expert is appropriate for developing the capability of the novice.

Problem-Solving: Novice and Expert Approaches

Studies of the cognitive processes involved in problem-solving provide a valuable starting point to an analysis of the role of reflection. Problem-solving, it has been said, is determined both by the situations (or 'task-conditions') in which the professional must think (Hammond 1978, 1981; Hamm 1988) and by the professional's level of expertise (Dreyfus & Dreyfus 1986; Schmidt et al 1990). Studies of variations in task-conditions suggest that the form of thinking adopted will differ according to whether a problem presents itself in a form that is well-defined or ill-defined, both in terms of what is presented and how it is presented. Well-defined problems are generally resolvable by analytical, or 'technical rational' problem-solving, whereas ill-defined, or 'swamp' problems in Schön's terms, require a form of reasoning that is far more intuitive. The Dreyfuses' work, on the other hand, suggests that it is more the professional's level of expertise which will determine the nature of problem-solving. In essence, they argue, experts are necessarily intuitive: it is a defining characteristic of their expertise. Novices, by contrast, use far more analytical forms of reasoning. More recent research similarly stresses the importance of heuristics in the development of expertise. A study of medical problem solving by Schmidt *et al* (1990) identifies a temporal shift from technical rational – in this context pathophysiological – 'scripting' of problems amongst newer trainees to an increasingly intuitive 'idiosyncratic experience-based knowledge' (ibid, p 618) scripting of problems by experienced practitioners.

Despite their obvious differences, both the 'cognitive continuum' model of Hammond and others, and the experiential model of the Dreyfuses, place significant doubts on (1) the idea first advanced by Newell & Simon (1972) that *all* problem-solving is grounded in analytical reasoning, and (2) that performance is closely related to the availability of content-based knowledge, so that expert problem-solvers are 'expert' because they have a substantial body of propositional knowledge to apply to problems (Elstein *et al* 1978).

Hammond's work suggests that Schön's distinction between high ground and swamp is a valid one, and that swampy situations require intuitive processing. But this research says little about novices' capacity to deal with the swamp.

Jones (1996) and Eraut (1994) make the point that the Dreyfuses' work suggests that novices may encounter major difficulties when they first experience professional work. From this a concern arises about whether reflection in action is an over-ambitious process for developing the novice.

What is a Novice?

Jones cites the work of Dreyfus and Dreyfus in analysing the defining characteristics of the novice. The novice is someone who

> '. . . applies rules and plans rigidly, who has little situational understanding, and who has no judgement of a situation. . . .'

This contrasts with their description of the expert, who

> '. . . no longer relies on rules, who has an intuitive grasp of situations based on deep tacit understanding, and who has a vision of the whole. . . .' (Jones 1996)

But how valuable is this contrast in the real context of learning?

The Legal Process Course at UWE provides a particular focus on what is meant when reference is made to the 'novice'. Novices are undergraduates in their second and third year of a law degree. They have all opted to take the course. Most have no experience of any kind of legal practice, though a small minority work casually as paralegals. The course attracts a number of mature students who bring experience of other professional and occupational activities with them.

Thus the notion of the 'novice' is not clear cut. There are those students who have little knowledge of substantive law and have little or no experience or knowledge of the professions. There are those who have valuable practical experience of the law in operation, and there are those who bring with them a wealth of knowledge and experience from other backgrounds, and who are able to transfer the value of that experience into a legal context. There are, indeed, those who would be regarded as experts in another field.

The above would suggest that any group of 'novices' is not homogeneous. There are many things which distinguish them one from another.

What unites the Legal Process group at UWE is that they are all studying academic law, and that none of them have yet begun their vocational training. Do these factors preclude them from developing the skills and processes of reflective practice?

The Novice in the Swamp

The main issue arising from the above discussion is the degree to which novices operate effectively in conditions of uncertainty and unpredictability. (I will continue to refer to 'novices' in spite of the misgivings about the term outlined above.) The work of the Dreyfus brothers would have us believe that they do not, or are unable to.

While it is accepted that the novice is subject to a greater degree of uncertainty than the expert, the latter is likely to be sure of the substantive legal aspects of her work. Her experience will give her much more confidence to take action in the contexts in which she finds herself. She has very likely had time to reflect on and clarify her personal values and integrate these with the ethical requirements of her profession. The novice has none of these advantages. What is completely routine and run of the mill to an expert can give rise to uncertainty and anxiety for the novice.

Research suggests that novices actually store substantive knowledge differently from experts. Jill Larkin (1979), for example, in her work on how students solve textbook physics problems shows that while novices solve problems by retrieving isolated blocks of information serially from long-term memory, experts retrieve information much more conceptually; in clusters of equations, for example. This would seem to indicate that access to substantive knowledge is much more problem-driven in experts.

What arises from the UWE course is the possibility that the technical rational approach, both to the teaching of substantive law and to the teaching of skills, may indeed be a barrier to developing expertise if it is not accompanied by an encouragement to reflect in and on the learning that takes place. The law may have been learned only at a surface level. Students frequently lack a deep, contextual understanding of the legal rules because they are taught in an environment remote from experience. They cannot easily make sense of that knowledge in the context of their own individual life worlds. This lack of confidence and understanding is revealed through a 'check list' approach some students take to activities such as client interviewing and negotiation. Checklisting signifies a desire to over plan and a rigid, structured preparation. Students are essentially attempting to ensure control over an otherwise open-ended situation. The following illustration is taken from an assessed interview (from Maughan 1996):

> Lawyer and client are discussing the client's house sale.
> Client: (Near start of interview) I'm really worried that Mr Crabbe (the buyer) might convert the house into a bail hostel. I don't think my neighbours would want that. Can I stop him?
> Lawyer: We'll come back to that. Did you say you had put the property with an estate agent?
> Client: I really need to know this before I decide if I want accept his offer.
> Lawyer: Just let me get some other details first. Who's your estate agent?

Anxieties about giving legal advice, and a mechanistic approach to interviewing, have combined to prevent this student from listening to the concerns of her client. In this case the interviewer's tacit interpersonal knowledge about how to converse with someone else and to respond with appropriate questions has been interfered with by her lack of confidence in using her rule-based knowledge, which is not yet adequately personalised.

The student in such a case would be invited to give feedback on her performance and encouraged to reflect *on* the theories of action in play during this interaction. Ideally she will consider the underlying theory she used which said that her checklist overrode the need to listen and respond to her client. She will hopefully recognise why this approach is likely to lead to an unsatisfactory outcome. This will enable her in a subsequent interaction to be aware of what she is doing, and perhaps to modify her behaviour as the interaction unfolds.

The danger is that the emphasis on, and the perceived prestige of, a technical rational approach to professional practice will seriously impede other, non-legal, theories of action which are nevertheless needed in order to bring about a satisfactory solution to the problem.

Mary Tuck (ACLEC 1995, p 17) makes the same point:

> 'Even when learning skills at the vocational stage, it was difficult for students to get beyond handling facts and procedures to the point of dealing with other parties, whether a client or otherwise, whose responses would be unpredictable.'

The key feature of reflection in action is that it enables the practitioner to surface implicit theories of action as a situation unfolds. The novice, as well as the expert, is working from theories of action. There may be fewer of them, or they may be less developed and complex, and they will certainly be based on a smaller repertoire of experiences, but they nevertheless are determinants of how that person will behave. Work in the cognitive domain suggests that novices rely on far more naive representations of problems. They focus on the superficial characteristics of the problem and draw on everyday concepts and experience, rather than on the specialized knowledge utilised by experts (Chi *et al* 1981; Larkin 1983). Understanding that they are using a theory of the situation which determines how they will act to resolve the situation is in itself a useful developmental experience for the novice, hopefully enabling her to move beyond these naive representations. The subsequent awareness that alternative theories may be brought into play which may provide a more appropriate outcome for a given situation would seem to be self evidently valuable. The development of this awareness is a strength of programmes which develop reflection in action.

None of this is to say that technical rationality has no part to play in the development of professional expertise. It does however serve as a reminder that technical rationality is only part of a complex web of processes and theories of action which enable students to become aware of the swamp and increase their confidence to operate in it.

Where technical rationality has an important part to play for the novice is in helping her to categorise and explain the world of the practising lawyer. The rules and procedures learned in the law school, as well as the discourse of legal problem solving, is an indispensable starting point. But it is only a starting point. It enables a novice to 'see' issues with a lawyer's eye. It is not, however, a complete toolkit, the application of which to any given problem will bring about a satisfactory outcome.

Postponing the encouragement and development of reflection in action is doubly problematic. Firstly, we have seen that the novice has as great a need as the expert for those processes which help the building of a repertoire of exemplars of effective behaviour. Reflection *on* action without subsequent reflection *in* action (in a new situation) seems not to make any sense. The capacity to articulate and consider what happened, why it happened, what implicit theories were at work which required one course of action rather than another is of crucial importance. But if that reflection is not followed by the ability to surface and select from the repertoire *during* a subsequent interaction, it is effort wasted. Reflection *in* and reflection *on* action constitute an axis of effective development. You cannot have one without the other.

Secondly, there is the notion of the 'masterclass' approach. Those who would deny novices the benefit of reflective development would restrict it to experienced, competent practitioners. The analogy is with a masterclass in music. The expert/mentor deals only with the artistic refinements to a technically adept performance. Implicit in this idea is that it is possible to become technically adept without any of those reflective skills which enable development from the competent to the highly proficient. The author would take issue with this. The need to make sophisticated judgements about the requirements of a given situation are just as present in the work of the novice as they are in that of the expert.

The Nature of the Swamp

Mention has been made of the unpredictable nature of professional work, even at the level of the novice. To understand the nature of this unpredictability is to begin to see the inadequacy of a purely technical-rational approach to professional education.

Clients present themselves with problems which are unique to them. They may or may not be clearly defined as problems. In any event, the professional has to go through a complex process of negotiation, consultation, decision-making and discussion before the outcome that is best for that client in that context is arrived at. Probably only a part of this process is to do with the law itself. A number of other issues may well arise to affect the way any particular case is dealt with.

First, any professional work is premised on the ethical behaviour of the professional practitioner. Equally, the practitioner is not simply the unquestioning follower of the professional codes of conduct. She will have her own set of values which may from time to time come into conflict with the requirements of professional life. How she deals with these conflicts is part of her professional make-up.

Second, different clients need the lawyer to take on different roles. While one client may be articulate and assertive, and require the lawyer to be a professional advisor, another may want a counsellor, while another may expect her to take complete charge of the case. Exercising judgment about what role is appropriate is part of her expertise.

Third, the lawyer is expected to work with peers, colleagues from other professions and a variety of lay people in addition to her clients. Again this demands a sensitivity to the varying expectations of these others.

Fourth, all lawyers have to work within economic constraints. Those in private practice have also to be aware of the commercial imperatives of their work. This has implications for what work is done, the quantity of work taken on, the time available to deal effectively with cases, etc.

Fifth, the lawyer has consequently to be personally well organised to handle these pressures.

Lastly, she has to operate in a particular organisational culture. Therefore she has to understand the micro-political issues which exercise the organisation as well as the influencing processes that enable her to have a voice in the organisation's decision making mechanisms.

Most of the above points are not addressed by the more technical rational approach to learning the work of the lawyer. Yet they are all factors which may come into play when trying to perform professionally and effectively. For every interaction with a client, there are a number of stakeholders who need to be considered. The ability to be sensitive to this is part of professional expertise.

Moreover, these swampy issues are not confined to the legal professional world; rather, they involve skills and processes which we need to develop in order to fulfil our various roles in society, be it within the family, the school, work or university. In other words, we need them for our personal as well as our professional development. It therefore follows that every member of the group of UWE 'novices' will bring to the programme some measure of experience or expertise in dealing with these problems.

The purpose of a reflective practicum in legal practice, therefore should surely be (at least in part) to encourage learners to transfer the reflective skills and processes they have acquired in these other contexts to the legal context. It should help them to personalise the content knowledge of law so that they begin the process of making that knowledge part of their tacit knowledge.

The evidence from the Legal Process course that has been running now for almost five years, is that, with guidance, students can manage this transfer. This provides some justification for the belief that the development of reflective skills and processes will subsequently be transferred into professional practice.

Although a Legal Process programme like that at UWE may not be able to replicate all the swampy issues discussed, it can certainly address some of them.

It can also present the learners with surprise and uncertainty so that they are not sure whether they are looking at a problem which comes under a particular head of law, or even any head of law.

Developing the Habit of Reflection in Action

From what has been said it should be clear that the kind of reflection to be encouraged is broader and deeper than that often found in the competence-based performance/feedback approach of skills courses. The experience at UWE over five years indicates that reflective learning is more likely to be encouraged if the learning theory and objectives are discussed with the group at the beginning of the course (Maughan and Webb 1995: chs 1, 2; and see Maughan and Webb 1996).

It is worth pointing out that it has taken us some time to surface and clarify our own action theories. They are still being revised! Currently, the course begins by asking the group to reflect critically on their experiences as law students and from there to broaden their analysis to consider the separation of theory and practice in traditional legal education; the nature of legal professional knowledge; and their perceptions of the role of the lawyer in society. This provides a framework within which to introduce and discuss the concept of the reflective practitioner.

Up to this point, the approach is technical-rational. The students are asked to think about how they, and others, might react in various swampy situations. This approach is used because it has been observed that students tend to feel more comfortable with a learning environment and method they are used to. The familiar lecture/seminar method tends to develop and reinforce those learning styles and preferences which are associated with technical rationality, namely 'converger/ assimilator' styles (Kolb 1984), also known as 'theorist/reflector' styles (Honey and Mumford 1992). Learners with these styles like to carry out methodical and detached analysis of concepts, rules, systems. They may feel uncomfortable with open-ended, experiential learning activities, distrust intuition and question the value of 'letting it all hang out.'[4]

When these learners first enter an unfamiliar learning environment, some feel anxious and threatened. It is made clear that everyone will be expected to participate. All general discussion takes place 'in the round'. There are no desks or tables between them and staff, and thus nowhere to hide. There will be a number of people in the group they do not know. All these factors, together with some intellectually challenging subject-matter, are sufficient shock for the first week.

The approach changes, however, in week two. The group is introduced to Schön's concepts of reflection in action and reflection on action by placing each individual in a swampy situation and asking them to work through their reflective conversations to try to identify the reasoning processes they used when confronted with something unexpected. The exercise also provides a useful introduction to experiential learning theory. This is the basis on which it is hoped to create the conditions for reflective learning.

It is only fairly recently that the decision to make the learning theory explicit was taken. This was done because, on the whole, there was dissatisfaction with the quality of reflection demonstrated by the students. It was thought this might be linked to a failure to articulate and clarify the course objectives adequately. The

4 The point has been made before that lawyers tend to prefer learning styles and approaches that are 'left-brained', i.e. logical, analytical, controlled, conservative. (see Armytage, 1995). Are these orientations likely to be reflected in their approach to problems?

group could not be expected to engage in deep reflection if they were not clear about why they were doing it and how it helped them to learn. Through experiential exercises they are encouraged to make the link between the experiential learning cycle (Kolb 1984) and Schön's model of reflection and to use these processes to identify their strengths and weaknesses as learners and then use their new experiences to modify and refine their action theories. They are asked then to record these processes in a learning journal.

This two-week excursion into learning theory has been effective in the sense that the 'novices' quickly come to a deeper awareness of how they learn and to feel much more in control of their learning. They appear to have become more confident and flexible learners by the end of the course. What is less clear is the extent to which they have developed the capacity for reflective practice. Other strategies are used throughout the course which are aimed at developing this capacity.

Reflection in action involves uncovering processes of discrepant reasoning. This occurs when our action theories are in conflict so that we act inconsistently with our professed beliefs and values (Schön 1987, Argyris 1989). It can easily happen in situations of unpredictability and value conflict. Those theories underlying our behaviour in the situation are usually tacit, and failure to confront and challenge them may lead to a rationalisation of intuitive action after the event in which an unsatisfactory outcome is attributed to some external cause. Argyris and Schön call this process *distancing*. For example, when asked to say why she had spent twenty five minutes going round in circles in an attempt to reach an agreement, a negotiator might put it down to lack of time, rather than reflecting on the use she and her opponent made of the time available.

One way in which novices are encouraged to begin to develop awareness of these discrepant reasoning processes is to construct exercises which specifically highlight them. An attempt is made to construct a situation in which the discrepancy will be so self-evident by the end of the exercise that no one will fail to spot it. This should enable each individual to understand how the processes of discrepant reasoning work, and to this extent it is usually successful. However, it does not necessarily mean that in future situations they will be able to recognise and articulate their own discrepancies. It is therefore essential, as with all experiential activities, to design techniques of feedback which seek as far as possible to elicit the student's reflection in action (See Maughan 1996).

Furthermore, the feedback process should be made as painless as possible. Confronting and challenging deeply held values and beliefs can be disturbing, even threatening, and all the more so if it is done in public.

This is why the learning journal can be an effective device for novices to surface and review their personal theories. A student can record here things she would prefer not to reveal in oral feedback within the group. Moreover, the process of deep reflection can take a long time. For example, a student may need to review a performance on video a number of times before she gets a clue as to what led her to frame a problem in a particular way. If she is in the habit of keeping a journal, it can provide a blueprint of this lengthy reflective process on which to base future action.

Over the five year period that this programme has been running the author has become convinced that the reflective approach to developing students at this stage is extremely valuable. They become much more aware of their own learning processes. They begin to develop their individual approaches to framing and solving complex problems. They feel more confident when placed in open-ended, unpredictable situations.

However, this is a programme that forms an optional part of the law degree. The approach and content of the programme are determined by the tutors. It therefore remains ultimately a dependency model of learning. Consequently, the extent to which students are able to use the problem-solving skills they have acquired in Legal Process *outside* the context of the course is unclear. A further concern is the time lapse between developing these reflective skills and the students' entry into professional practice.

Like all skills, those of reflection need constantly to be practised. There is a danger that if these skills are not practised and developed during the Bar Vocational Course or the Legal Practice Course and the training contract, they will fall into disuse. The development of expertise in practice thus becomes haphazard and unpredictable.

Conclusions: Challenges for the Future.

If, as Schmidt *et al* suggest, expertise seems to consist of matching a problem with similar ones seen before (1990: 619), then developing the novice's capacity to do this through their reflection in action would seem to be an appropriate method to set them on the road towards expertise. However, it is clear that much more work needs to be done to discover how the transfer from 'novicehood' to expertise works in specific domains, like law. To date, the experience of operating a Legal Process course based on the principles of reflective practice has convinced the author of the value of this approach at this stage of a student's development. That is not to say it is a cure-all. The experience with Legal Process also shows just how difficult it is to inculcate effective habits of reflection in a one year course that is one-twelth of an LLB. In common with more traditional approaches to learning, there remain a number of questions about the development and transferability of what has been learned.

The following issues therefore need to be addressed:

1. Most fundamentally, as a prerequisite to curriculum development, a clearer, research-based understanding of the legal problem-solving process needs to be developed. In particular:

(a) Should an attempt be made to further unpack the Dreyfuses' model of development from novice to expert? Is the notion of a 'novice' as unproblematic as this appears to assume?

(b) To what extent are the skills and processes of reflective practice, if taught at the undergraduate level, transferable to the vocational stage and early professional life?

(c) More generally, how can we enable students to move from dependency to independence through reflective practice? Just how generalisable are the skills that we teach?

2. Then, if it is accepted that a primary aim of legal education (viewed as a continuum from the academic to continuing phases) is to develop professional expertise in problem-solving, consideration must be given to the implications this has for the curriculum. At present, there are a variety of competing models – problem-based learning; Nathanson's problem-solving approach, and a range of discovery and clinical methods which address problem-solving processes perhaps less directly and less coherently. Is there a 'right' way?

Bibliography

ACLEC (1995) Lord Chancellor's Advisory Committee on Legal Education and Conduct, *Review of Legal Education: Third Consultative Conference* (London: ACLEC).

Argyris, C (1989) *Reasoning, Learning and Action*, (San Francisco: Jossey Bass).

Chi, M T, Feltovich, P J & Glaser, R (1981) 'Categorization and representation of physics problems by experts and novices' 5 *Cognitive Science* 121.

Cruickshank, D (1996) 'Problem Based Learning in Legal Education' in Webb, J & Maughan, C (eds) *Teaching Lawyers' Skills* (London: Butterworths), in press.

Dreyfus, H L & Dreyfus, S E (1986) *Mind Over Machine: The Power of Human Intuition and Expertise in the Era of the Computer* (Oxford: Blackwell).

Elstein, A S, Schulman, L S & Sprafka, S A (1978) *Medical Problem-Solving: An Analysis of Critical Reasoning* (Cambridge, Massachusetts: Harvard University Press).

Eraut, M (1994) *Developing Professional Knowledge and Competence* (Lewes: Falmer Press).

Hamm, R M (1989) 'Clinical expertise and the cognitive continuum' in Dowie, J & Elstein, A *Professional Judgment: A reader in clinical decision making* (Cambridge: Cambridge University Press).

Hammond, K R (1978) 'Toward increasing competence of thought in public policy formation' in Hammond (ed) *Judgment and Decision in Public Policy Formation* (Boulder. Co: Westview Press).

Hammond, K R (1981) 'Principles of organization in intuitive and analytical cognition' *Report No. 231, Center for Research on Judgment and Policy* (Boulder: University of Colorado).

Honey, P & Mumford, A (1992) *The Manual of Learning Styles* (Maidenhead: Honey).

Jones, P A (1996) 'We're All Reflective Practitioners Now: Reflections on Professional Education' in Webb, J & Maughan, C (eds) *Teaching Lawyers' Skills* (London: Butterworths).

Kirby, P C & Paradise, L V (1992) 'Reflective Practice and Effectiveness of Teachers' 70 *Psychological Reports* 1057.

Kolb, D A (1984) *Experiential Learning: Experience as the Source of Learning and Development* (Englewood Cliffs, NJ: Prentice-Hall).

Larkin, J H (1979) 'Information Processing Models and Science Instruction' in Lochhead, J & Clements, J (eds) *Cognitive Process Instruction* (Philadelphia: Franklin Institute).

Larkin, J H (1983) 'The role of problem representation in physics' in Gentner, D & Stevens, A (eds) *Mental Models*, (Hillsdale, NJ: Lawrence Erlbaum Associates).

Maughan, C & Webb, J (1995) *Lawyering Skills and the Legal Process*, (London: Butterworths).

Maughan, C & Webb, J (1996) 'Taking Reflection Seriously: How Was It For Us?' in Webb, J & Maughan, C. (eds), *Teaching Lawyers' Skills* (London: Butterworths).

Maughan, C (1996) 'Learning How to Learn: The Skills Developer's Guide to Experiential Learning' in Webb, J & Maughan, C (eds), *Teaching Lawyers' Skills* (London: Butterworths).

Nathanson, S (1989) 'The Role of Problem Solving in Legal Education' 39 *Journal of Legal Education* 167.

Newell, A & Simon, H A (1972) *Human Problem Solving*, (Englewood Cliffs, NJ: Prentice-Hall).

Schmidt, H G, Norman, G R & Boshuizen, H P A (1990) 'A Cognitive Perspective on Medical Expertise: Theory and Implications' 65 (10) *Academic Medicine* 611.
Schön, D A (1983) *The Reflective Practitioner* (Aldershot: Avebury).
Schön, D A (1987) *Educating the Reflective Practitioner* (San Francisco: Jossey Bass).
Webb, J (1995) 'Where the Action Is: Developing Artistry in Legal Education' 2 *International Journal of the Legal Profession* 187.

STATUTORY REFORM OF CHOICE OF LAW IN TORT AND DELICT: A BITTER PILL OR A CURE FOR THE ILL?

*Dr Abla Mayss**

Lecturer in Law, Faculty of Law, University of Liverpool
<mayss@liverpool.ac.uk>

First Published in Web Journal of Current Legal Issues in association with Blackstone Press Ltd.

**My sincere thanks to Brian Thompson, Sue Nott and Alan Reed for their invaluable comments on an earlier draft of this article.*

SUMMARY

The common law rules on choice of law in tort in the field of Private International Law had long been criticised. The double-actionability rule in *Phillips* v *Eyre* (1868) tended to operate in favour of defendants. The exception, established in *Boys* v *Chaplin* (1971) and expanded in the *Red Sea Case* (1994), had created much uncertainty. To alleviate such anomalies, Part III of the Private International Law (Miscellaneous Provisions) Act 1995 has been recently adopted. This article examines the new provisions vis-à-vis the common law and its drawbacks, and addresses the question of whether Part III is likely to be a cure for the ills suffered as a result of the shortcomings of the common law.

CONTENTS

Introduction

Apart from being out of step with almost every other area of English Private International Law,[1] save for certain aspects of Family Law, and apart from the uncertainty created by the operation of the double-actionability rule and the boundaries of its exception, the major deficiency of the common law rules on choice of law in tort was stated by the Lord Chancellor, Lord Mackay of Clashfern, in the course of the proceedings of the Special Public Bill Committee (hereafter SPBC 1994–95) in the following terms:

> 'The law is to the advantage of the defendant because, as a general rule, the plaintiff cannot succeed in any claim unless both the law of the forum and the law of the place where the wrong occurred make provision for it, whereas the defendant can escape liability by taking advantage of any defence available under either law. This appears unfair to plaintiffs because it ensures that they cannot generally succeed to a greater extent than is provided by the less generous of the two systems of law concerned.' (HL Paper 36, March 1995, p 3)

Indeed, Lord Mackay's views on the unsatisfactory effect of the double-actionability rule had been shared by many, including academics and members of the judiciary and had provoked calls for reform. This dissatisfaction was primarily levelled at two particular issues. First, the general rule had attributed unique importance to the law of the forum in such cases. Secondly, the exception to the rule, as established in *Boys* v *Chaplin* [1971] AC 356 and extended in *Red Sea Insurance Co Ltd* v *Bouygues SA* [1995] 1 AC 190, had created much uncertainty. Accordingly, in 1984, the English and Scottish Law Commissions (Law Com WP No 87) suggested two models for reform and without a preference to either. Following extensive consultations, the Law Commissions adopted Model One (Law Com No 193) as the basis for reforms, and drafted a Bill to this effect. An amended version of this Bill has now been incorporated in Part III of the Private International Law (Miscellaneous Provisions) Act 1995. This Act received Royal Assent on 8 November 1995.

In general terms, Part III (not yet in force)[2] of this Act repeals the common law rules on choice of law in tort, save for the tort of defamation. It introduces a new general rule in favour of the *lex loci delicti* as the *prima facie* applicable law. Hence, the main purpose of this article is to review the common law rules, examine their strength and weaknesses, and then assess the impact of the new law. Bearing in mind the field of law Part III of the Act caters for, where the question of choice of law had been repeatedly described as raising 'one of the most vexed questions

---

1 In all such areas, clear and general rules allow UK courts to apply the provisions of a foreign law exclusively in an appropriate case rather than its concurrent application with the law of the forum.

2 Part III will come into force on such day as the Lord Chancellor and the Lord Advocate may by order made by statutory instrument appoint.

in the conflict of laws', it is intended to explore the extent to which the new law is likely to remedy the anomalies of the common law rules and address the question of whether Part III of the 1995 Act has improved the situation.

The Common Law and its Drawbacks

Where the tort was found to have been committed abroad, the general rule of double-actionability applied. This rule was established in *Phillips* v *Eyre* (1870) LR 6 QB 1, and was subsequently modified in *Boys* v *Chaplin* [1971] AC 356.

1. The general rule

As a general rule, to found a suit in England for a wrong alleged to have been committed abroad, two conditions had to be satisfied:

(i) the alleged wrong must have been actionable as a tort if committed in England; and
(ii) it had to be actionable in the *lex loci delicti.*

The much criticised first limb of this rule had derived from the Privy Council decision in *The Halley* (1868) LR 2 PC 193. Here an action was brought against a shipowner for damage caused by a collision due to the negligent navigation of a pilot he was compelled to employ by Belgian law. The action was dismissed on the ground that English law did not at the time recognise such vicarious liability though it was recognised under Belgian law. In other words, English courts would not allow a claim for a tort which was unknown to English law. As for the second limb, when initially formulated by Willes J in *Phillips* v *Eyre*, it had imposed a requirement of non-justifiability rather than actionability in the *locus delicti.* This phrase led English courts, at one stage, to take the view that the rule was satisfied where the defendant's conduct attracted criminal, but not civil, liability under that law.[3] Such an interpretation, however, was rejected in *Boys* v *Chaplin* [1971] AC 356, where the House of Lords adopted the view that civil actionability rather than non-justifiability had to be satisfied.

The general rule was also greatly criticised because it operated in favour of the defendant and to the disadvantage of the plaintiff. Whilst the plaintiff could only succeed in his claim where both the law of the forum and that of the place of tort made provision for such a tort, the defendant could easily escape liability where either system of law allowed for a defence. This disadvantage became more apparent where such a defence formed a part of the law of the forum, in the sense that a defendant who had committed a tort in a foreign jurisdiction, knowing his act to be wrong, could avail himself of a defence available to him only under English law. Clearly in such cases, a plaintiff would be more inclined to bring suit elsewhere. This inadequacy alone might be said to account for the relatively few cases in English courts in respect of foreign torts.

Such anomalies could be illustrated by the often cited Scottish case of *M'Elroy* v *M'Allister* 1949 SC 110, where a widow claimed damages for the death of her husband as a result of a lorry accident in England. Both, the deceased who was a passenger and the driver, a fellow employee, were at the time conducting work for their Scottish employer. The widow's claim entailed the following:

3 See *Machado v Fontes* [1897] 2 QB 231.

(1) solatium under Scots law, the *lex fori*;
(2 & 3) by English law, the *lex loci delicti*, on behalf of his estate and under the Fatal Accidents Act 1846; and
(4) by both laws, the funeral expenses.

The Court of Session applied the double-actionability rule and held that the widow was merely entitled to recover the funeral expenses, that is the only common head of damages under both laws, and regardless of the slight connection with England which was the place where the accident had occurred.

The major problem, in the view of the Law Commissions, with the double-actionability rule was with the first limb of the rule. This limb, which had originated in *The Halley,* had received unquestioned judicial acceptance, constituted the unwarranted anomaly and was central to any proposed reforms. The main criticisms against this first limb of the rule were rehearsed by the Law Commissions in Report No 193. The Report stated that the exceptional role given by this rule to the substantive law of the forum could be described as 'parochial' in appearance, for it presupposed that it would be inherently just for English domestic law of tort to apply irrespective of the circumstances of the case and the connection or non-connection of the parties with the forum. Indeed, apart from matters of procedure and subject to overriding public policy considerations, the Law Commissions saw no reason for retaining the application of the law of the forum to all cases involving foreign torts or delicts. After all, *The Halley* (1868) LR 2 PC 193, which was the nexus of the first limb, could be justified on the historical ground that the law of tort was formerly seen as 'having a punitive rather than compensatory function'. In other words, it used to be more closely allied to criminal law, an area of law which courts in the UK are always expected to apply UK law. As this is no longer the case, the Law Commissions concluded that the purpose of the first limb of the rule has been defeated.

2. *Boys* v *Chaplin*: An exception to the general rule?

Boys v *Chaplin* was of great importance in the sense that it had paved the way towards the recognition of an exception to the general rule. Prior to this case and for almost a hundred years, the general rule had been applied rigidly and to the advantage of the defendant who could not be held liable unless both English law and that of the *locus delicti* recognised liability. In this case, the plaintiff and defendant were both resident in England, but temporarily stationed in Malta serving in the British armed forces. Whilst off-duty, the plaintiff was seriously injured in a road accident as a result of the defendant's negligent driving. The question before the House of Lords was whether the plaintiff's claim for damages should be restricted to special damages for incurred expenses and proved loss of earning as allowed under both systems of law, or whether it should also extend to general damages for pain and suffering as provided under English law. Ultimately, it was unanimously held that the plaintiff should recover damages assessed according to English law. It should be borne in mind, however, that this was a most unsatisfactory decision for, on the face of it, it appeared to have introduced a degree of flexibility into the double-actionability rule by applying the law of the forum by way of exception. Ambiguities, however, surrounded the nature and extent of that flexibility. This was due to the fact that their Lordships reached the same conclusion but for divergent reasons. Whereas Lord Hodson and Lord Wilberforce, with whom Lord Pearson concurred by way of second preference, applied the law of the forum on the basis that the general rule should apply with flexibility, Lord Guest and Lord Donovan were of the view that English law should apply to the right to claim damages for pain and suffering as the law of the forum which governed procedural questions.

Despite the variety of reasons expressed by their Lordships, academics and judges in subsequent cases tended to view Lord Wilberforce's judgment as authoritative and to accept the proposition that the rule should apply with flexibility, as amounting to an exception to the double-actionability rule (see eg Fawcett 1992, p 535; Stone 1995, p 278; *Johnson v Coventry Churchill International Ltd* [1992] 3 All ER 14). In fact *Dicey & Morris on The Conflict of Laws* (Collins 1993, pp 1487–1488) stated the rule (rule 203) in the following terms:

> '(1) As a general rule, an act done in a foreign country is a tort and actionable as such in England, only if it is both (a) actionable as a tort according to English law, or in other words is an act which, if done in England, would be a tort; and (b) actionable according to the law of the foreign country where it was done.
> (2) But a particular issue between the parties may be governed by the law of the country which, with respect to that issue, has the most significant relationship with the occurrence and the parties.'

In spite of the recognition of such an exception, there has been a reluctance to invoke it. In the very few instances where it was successfully applied it resulted in ousting the application of the *lex loci delicti* in favour of English law as the law of the forum. Moreover, the implication of paragraph (2) of rule 203, if taken to have represented the law correctly, had meant that only a particular issue could be governed by another law by way of exception. This appeared to have ruled out the possibility of applying the exception to the whole of the cause of action. It was not until July 1994, when the Privy Council decided the case of *Red Sea Insurance Co Ltd* v *Bouygues SA* [1994] 3 WLR 926, that the uncertainty surrounding the extent of the exception was somewhat elaborated.

3. The impact of *Red Sea*

This revolutionary judgment of the Privy Council has indeed extended the application of the exception to govern the whole of the cause of action and in favour of the *locus delicti*, but as Lord Slynn stated, the answer to many questions remained elusive. However, prior to considering the pros and cons of this judgment in detail, a brief and simplified account of the facts must be made.

The 23 plaintiffs, who were involved in various ways in connection with construction work at the university of Riyadh in Saudi Arabia, brought an action in Hong Kong against Red Sea, an insurance company incorporated in Hong Kong with its head office in Saudi Arabia, for indemnity under an insurance policy claiming loss and expense incurred in relation to correction and repairs of certain structural damage. The first to third plaintiffs were employed as main contractors, the fourth to thirteenth plaintiffs (a consortium 'PCG') were suppliers of precast concrete building units, and the fourteenth to twenty-third plaintiffs acted as architectural and design consultants. Red Sea argued that the loss claimed by the plaintiffs was not covered by the policy, and counterclaimed that PCG was in breach of its duty of care to the other plaintiffs for having supplied faulty precast units, but if Red Sea was liable under the policy it was entitled to recover the loss from PCG by way of subrogation to the rights of the other plaintiffs. On PCG's application to strike out the counterclaim, Red Sea applied for leave to amend the counterclaim to the effect that the law governing the relationship between the plaintiffs and Red Sea was that of Saudi Arabia, under which Red Sea was entitled to sue PCG directly for the damage caused to the other plaintiffs.

The High Court of Hong Kong, applying the double-actionability rule, refused leave to amend and ordered the counterclaim to be struck on the grounds that (a) the right of subrogation under Hong Kong law could not arise until payment had been made by the insurer; (b) in any case proceedings had to be brought in the name of the insured; and (c) that the law of Saudi Arabia could not be relied upon exclusively to determine the liability in tort in the courts of Hong Kong. The Court of Appeal appeared to have applied a wider interpretation to the rule by setting aside the order striking the counterclaim and holding that Red Sea should be permitted to establish that it could pursue the claim by way of subrogation under Saudi Arabian law, but also decided that the company could not sue PCG directly for negligence relying solely on the *lex loci delicti*. On appeal to the Judicial Committee of the Privy Council, Lord Slynn delivered their Lordships' judgment which allowed the defendant to recover its loss by exclusively relying on the *lex loci delicti* and irrespective of the fact that it had no remedy under the *lex fori*.

Following a brief exposition of the background and development of the double-actionability rule, Lord Slynn went on to say that if the law of England was as stated in rule 203 of *Dicey & Morris*, the defendant would win since that law equally applied in Hong Kong. If it was not, it would be necessary to consider what was the then current position. Having endorsed both limbs of the general rule as incorporated in Clause (1) of rule 203, he proceeded to consider the exception and the doubts surrounding its extent by addressing the question of whether rule 203(2), which recognised an element of flexibility, was correctly stated. As a starting point, he examined the House of Lords decision in *Boys* v *Chaplin* [1971] AC 356 and concluded that, although this part of the rule reflected Lord Wilberforce's views in that case, their Lordships' reasons for reaching the same conclusion varied to such an extent that it made it impossible to extract a binding *ratio decidendi*. Consequently, he explored relevant English and Australian decisions[4] in order to ascertain whether or not the exception existed. If so, whether there was any indication that it could extend to the case in hand which raised different considerations. He also found it helpful to review relevant extracts from both the Law Commission Report (No 193) and the American Restatement of the Law, Second, Conflict of Laws. Indeed the Law Commission (Report No 193, 1990, paragraph 2.7, at p 7) had expressed the view that there was no reason why the existence of a foreign element should not make it just to apply a foreign law to determine a dispute in tort, even though the substantive provisions of that law might be different from English law. Similarly, section 145 of the Restatement of the Law implied that the US courts had long recognised that they were not compelled to decide all issues under the local law of a single state. The end result of this lengthy overview was that the Privy Council recognised the reality of the conflict which had arisen since *Boys* v *Chaplin*. On the one hand, there was detected the desire to apply a rule which was certain and clear and, on the other hand, there was a need for flexibility whereby injustice could be avoided. Nevertheless, the fact remained that the way in which the exception had been applied left many questions unanswered, and it was unfortunate that only two of those questions were considered in this case.

The first question addressed the issue of whether the exception could be relied upon to invoke the application of the *lex loci delicti* even if the claim was not

4 Such as, *Church of Scientology of California* v *Commissioner of Police of the Metropolis* (1976) 120 SJ 690; *Coupland* v *Arabian Gulf Oil* [1983] 1 WLR 1136; *Johnson* v *Coventry Churchill International Ltd* [1992] 3 All ER 14; *Warren* v *Warren* [1972] QdR 386; and *Corcoran* v *Corcoran* [1974] VR 164.

actionable under the *lex fori*. Lord Slynn, while recognising that to do so would be a departure from the strict rule in *The Halley* (1868) LR 2PC 193, took the view that it would be unrealistic to limit the exception to the application of the law of the forum. This would clearly contradict the degree of flexibility envisaged by Lord Wilberforce in *Boys* v *Chaplin* [1971] AC 356 where he stated that (at pp 391–392):

> 'the necessary flexibility can be obtained . . . through segregation of the relevant issue. . . . For this purpose it is necessary to identify the policy of the rule, to inquire to what situations, with what contacts, it was intended to apply; whether not to apply it . . . would serve any interest which the rule was devised to meet. . . . No purely mechanical rule can properly do justice to the great variety of cases where persons come together in a foreign jurisdiction for different purposes with different pre-existing relationships, from the background of different legal systems.'

Lord Slynn concluded by adding that the fact that the forum was being required to apply a foreign law in a situation where its own law would not give a remedy, would also be a factor to be taken into account when the court was to decide whether the exception should apply.

The second question, which required an answer, was whether the exception could extend to govern a whole case rather than specific isolated issues as was the case in *Boys* v *Chaplin* and indeed the opening words of rule 203(2) of *Dicey & Morris*. Again, Lord Slynn's reasoning had the impact of further extending the application of the exception by stating that, although such instances might be rare, the exception was not limited in application to isolated issues but might also apply to the whole claim. This should take place in circumstances where all, or almost all, the significant connecting factors point in the direction of the *lex loci delicti*. In this instance, the policy of insurance was subject to the law of Saudi Arabia, the work was carried out in Saudi Arabia, all the contracts were to be performed in Saudi Arabia and were all made subject to the law of that country. The breaches, alleged damage and the cost of repairing such damage occurred in Saudi Arabia. The only connection with Hong Kong was that the defendant company was incorporated there, but then its head office was in Saudi Arabia. All of the above factors tipped the scales in favour of applying the exception to the double-actionability rule and allowing the defendant to rely exclusively on the *lex loci delicti*.

The above judgment was greatly commended and frequently described as an essential step in the right direction, for it resolved many ambiguous questions which had surrounded the exception. The fact remained, however, that many other questions still required elaboration and amplification (see Fawcett 1984, pp 665–669). Moreover, the general rule of double-actionability, which had frequently been criticised for having caused injustice in some instances, was confirmed.

4. Torts committed in England

A further drawback under the common law rules had been that of the distinction made between English torts on the one hand, and foreign torts on the other. In the former case, English courts consistently applied English law, irrespective of, and despite the existence of foreign elements. In the latter, however, they applied the double-actionability rule. Apart from being described as discriminatory and nationalistic in character, this distinction had the disadvantage of having to determine the place of tort, which clearly added to the complexity of proceedings. In addition, there had been some doubts surrounding the applicable test to such instances, for such test was that normally applied to ascertain the place of tort for jurisdictional purposes under what used to be Order 11, rule 1(1)(h) of the Rules of the Supreme Court. Regardless of the fact that this rule was abolished and replaced by rule 1(1)(f) in 1987, which no longer requires such a place to be determined, this process had been questioned on the ground that a decision to grant leave to serve a writ out of the jurisdiction was, and still is, discretionary. Whilst an English court might be inclined to decide that a tort had been committed in several places for the purposes of a rule of jurisdiction, it had to insist on one single place of tort for the purposes of choice of law (see Fawcett 1992, pp 552–554).

Such a distinction between English and foreign torts had been justified on the ground that it would not be desirable to hold a person, who acted lawfully in England, liable in this country due to the application of a foreign law. It must be noted, however, that retaining this distinction would have the opposite effect in cases where the law of the UK imposed liability and the law of the relevant foreign country did not.[5] Also retaining the protective effect of this distinction would become derisory where the damage occurred within the European Economic Area. Should the damage occur within that boundary, a plaintiff would be able to bring his action in that country by virtue of Article 5(3) of the Brussels Convention 1968 or the Lugano Convention 1988 on jurisdiction and enforcement of judgments in civil and commercial matters. The courts of that country might well apply its own law under which the defendant would be liable. Were the plaintiff to succeed in his/her action, UK courts would have the obligation to recognise and enforce that judgment in accordance with the provisions of the Conventions.

By way of summary, the state of the common law rules was far from clear. The general rule of double-actionability operated in favour of defendants. The first limb of the rule incorporated a nationalistic attitude. The nature and extent of the exception required further elaboration. The distinction made between English torts and foreign torts promoted complexity, for it necessitated the identification of the place of tort as a first step in the process of determining the applicable law. Hence, well balanced reforms were needed to remedy such shortcomings. Does the new law tackle these shortcomings?

The New Law

Part III (sections 9–15) of the 1995 Act,[6] which largely implements the Law Commissions' draft Bill, extends in application to England and Wales, Scotland and Northern Ireland. Like the common law, it adopts a general rule which identifies the applicable law, and provides for an exception to apply in appropriate circumstances.

1. Scope of Part III

Part III, unlike the common law rule of double-actionability, applies to any action brought in any part of the UK in respect of a tort or delict which has a foreign

5 It is worthy of note that Part III of the Private International Law (Miscellaneous Provisions) Act 1995 declined to incorporate this recommendation, but at the same time excluded the tort of defamation from the ambit of the new rules.

6 Part I of the Act makes provisions in relation to interest on judgment debts and arbitral awards; and Part II makes provisions in relation to the validity of marriages entered into by unmarried persons under a law which permits polygamy.

element. Indeed, the provisions of Part III apply equally to both UK and foreign torts. This is contrary to the Law Commissions' recommendations which had preserved this unfair distinction made under the common law. In their Report No 193, they had recommended that where the conduct constituting a tort or delict takes place in the UK, the law of the relevant part of the UK should apply. This had been justified on the ground that a person who acts in the UK should not, by the application of a foreign law, be held liable in a UK court for consequential injury, loss or damage which occurs elsewhere and would not be recoverable under UK law. The Government, however, declined to implement such a distinction, and rightly so, on the basis that it would reintroduce the nationalistic attitude which the Law Commissions were otherwise seeking to remove.

It can safely be said that Part III of the Act is not a comprehensive piece of legislation. Apart from the tort of defamation which will be examined separately, a further issue was left outside both the ambit of the Law Commissions' draft Bill and that of the 1995 Act. This related to the complex question of the possibility of raising contractual defences in a tort action. The state of the common law rules was, and still is, far from clear in this context (see, eg, *Sayers* v *International Drilling Co* [1971] 1 WLR 1176; and *Coupland* v *Arabian Gulf Petroleum Co* [1983] 1 WLR 1136). Indeed, the Law Commissions admitted so and stated that such defences could be seen 'as exclusively contractual, exclusively tortious', or 'as an issue where choice of law rules in contract and tort have roles to play, but different ones'. In their opinion, this was a difficult question of characterisation which depended on the particular facts of each case as well as on policy considerations. As such, the Law Commissions felt unable to recommend a satisfactory legislative intervention. The end result is that such defences remain to be dealt with as issues of characterisation. By virtue of section 9 of the Act, the common law rules remain applicable in this context.

It must also be noted that other choice of law rules which apply in particular cases, such as torts committed on the high seas, which are governed by the principles of maritime law, are not affected by the Act.

2. Exclusion of defamation

In their Report No 193, the Law Commissions took the view that specific provisions in relation to defamation should be made. This was due to the concerns raised in cases whereby a statement made in the UK which, though not defamatory by UK law, was so in the country where it was published. It was recommended that there should not be any *prima facie* applicable law, since it was believed that such cases would be best dealt with by way of English general rules. However, due to the fact that there was no uniform concept of defamation in the different regimes of private international law, and the fact that the relevant law may impose liability when UK law did not, a protective measure was recommended. Whenever the tort occurred in substance in the UK, the law of the relevant part of the UK would apply. As this would not solve the case of the statement originating in this country and subsequently published abroad, it was further recommended that where the UK was the country of origin of the statement in question, UK law would apply irrespective of where the alleged wrong was subsequently published. Moreover, in order to prevent defendants from obtaining the automatic application of English or Scots law simply by repeating the defamatory statement in the UK, it was also recommended that when a statement was published abroad and simultaneously or previously published in the UK, the applicable law would be that part of the UK where the proceedings were brought.

When the Bill was first introduced into the House of Lords, it discarded the above measures concerning defamation. The Lord Chancellor justified this omission on the ground that the Law Commissions' proposed provision had depended on 'a somewhat simultaneous publication of the same matter in a number of jurisdictions'. It had then proceeded to give priority to UK law which would apply if the publication was made previously or simultaneously in the UK. This, according to the Lord Chancellor, seemed to be based on a similar principle as the double-actionability rule and therefore, should not be incorporated in the new law.

Nevertheless, many arguments against the impact of subjecting defamatory statements to the mercy of the general provisions of the new law have ended, and rightly so, in success. Defamation has been excluded altogether from the scope of the 1995 Act. Such arguments were in terms of the impact the new law would have had on the freedom of expression had the Bill been adopted in its original form as introduced into the House of Lords. For instance, in the words of Lord Brightman quoting from an article in *The Times*, if a British newspaper published truthful but damaging material about an elected politician, and the publication occurred abroad as well as in this country, then if the plaintiff were to bring an action for libel in England, he would fail under the common law because truth would be a defence to publication in UK law. Under the new law, however, the plaintiff would be able to obtain damages or even an injunction in the UK if in the foreign country where the publication occurred truth would not be a defence (SPBC 1994–95, at 51).

Admittedly, such a result would jeopardise the freedom of expression which is considered as an essential human right. Although it was argued at various stages that the provision of displacing the would-be applicable law in such instances on the ground of public policy, would overcome this problem, the absolute need to preserve such freedoms proved paramount and defamation was excluded altogether from the Act. According to section 13, the double-actionability rule remains applicable in this context.

3. The new general rule

In accordance with the Law Commissions' draft Bill, section 10 of the 1995 Act expressly abolishes the long-standing, and much criticised, common law rule of double-actionability and its exception as they applied to any claim in tort or delict, save for defamation claims. This rule has now been replaced by a new revolutionary general rule, stated in section 11, to the effect that a tort or delict with a foreign element will be governed by the *lex loci delicti*, ie the law of the country where the tort was committed. Where, however, the events constituting the tort occur in different countries, an indication as to the applicable law is given in section 11(2) which identifies that law as being, for a cause of action in respect of personal injury or death, that of the country where the individual was when he sustained the injury. For a cause of action in respect of damage to property, the applicable law is that of the place where the property was where it was damaged. In all other cases, it is the law of the country in which the most significant element or elements of those events occurred.

This general rule should identify the most appropriate applicable law in the majority of cases and without recourse to ascertaining the place of tort. It is likely to correspond with the reasonable expectations of the parties involved in the tort or delict. It also accords with the choice of law rules that are applicable in most of the European legal systems. As such, it is expected to promote uniformity and discourage forum shopping.

It is worthy of note that some concern was expressed in relation to the general rule at various stages of the debate. In effect, this rule may lead English courts to hear actions for torts which are unknown to English law, such as privacy, unfair competition or criminal compensation. Such a risk, however, has been circumvented by section 9 of the Act which specifies that the provisions apply to issues which the courts in the UK characterise as issues relating to tort or delict as opposed, for example, to contract or other bases of liability. Hence, if a UK court does not characterise an issue as being one of tort, such court will not hear the action. Alternatively, UK courts may invoke the ground of public policy, as provided by section 14 of the Act, in order to disregard such actions.

4. An exception to the rule

As is the case with every general rule, section 12 provides for a rule of displacement to be applied in any case where, upon comparing the significance of the factors connecting the tort with the country whose law would be applicable under the general rule with that of any factors connecting the tort with another country, it appears to be substantially more appropriate for the applicable law for determining any or all of the issues arising in the case, to be the law of another country.

This exception is likely to operate in favour of the law of the territory in which the tort has the most real and substantial connection, ie a proper law exception. It has the effect of applying another law to any or all of the issues where it would be inappropriate to decide the case according to the law of the place of wrong, as was the case in *Boys* v *Chaplin*. It would be invoked in two situations: (1) where there was no single territory or country in which the most significant elements in the sequence of events occurred, or (2) where it would substantially be more appropriate that another law should apply.

The word *substantially* was emphasised by Lord Mackay, (Hansard, HL, 1994, vol 559(11), col 833) in terms that the exception is not intended to operate every time another applicable law might be appropriate, but only where it would be *substantially* so. But what is meant by *substantially*? When is the exception likely to apply? Section 12(2) attempts to provide some guidance in terms of identifying some particular factors which may be taken into account as connecting a tort with that other country. Those factors may relate to the parties, to any of the events which constitute the tort in question or to any of the circumstances or consequences of those events. Clearly, such an exception attempts to preserve flexibility as opposed to the certainty provided by the general rule. Although it is likely to create interpretation problems, it has answered many of the questions which remained unanswered under the common law. It will certainly apply in cases like *Boys* v *Chaplin* and *Red Sea*. It will certainly apply to the whole case or alternatively to one or more specific issues in the dispute. Whether or not it will cause major interpretation problems remains to be seen.

The remaining provisions ensure that the reforms in this Part do not have retrospective effect. They also save the effect of various procedural rules, the application of the principles of public policy and certain mandatory domestic rules, such as the rule that English courts would not give effect to foreign penal, revenue or other public law, which are regarded as so important that, as a matter of construction or policy, they must apply to any action before UK courts, and even where the claim would otherwise be governed by a foreign law. These are important safeguards for defendants against liabilities and remedies under foreign law. These safeguards may be invoked either where a certain rule of the applicable foreign law contravenes some fundamental provision of UK law, or where such rule embraces penal, revenue or other public law as understood by UK rules of private international law that it would not be tolerable to enforce here. Part III of the Act also excludes the application of renvoi.[7]

Conclusions

Mr Justice Brooke, the Chairman of the English Law Commission, referred to the double-actionability rule as the 'double whammy' in favour of defendants and as being virtually unique in all systems of law which have a European foundation (SPBC 1994–95, pp 10–15). True it provided certainty, but the other side of the coin was reflected in the too uncertain flexibility caused by the exception. By abolishing this rule and introducing a new general rule which identifies the *prima facie* applicable law as being that of the place of injury, damage or death, Part III provides clarity and certainty. Moreover, it will no longer be necessary to apply the substance test to determine the place of tort, especially where the claim relates to a transnational tort. This new general rule may be displaced where appropriate grounds so require. In short, the new rules embrace certainty, simplicity and ease of application and limited flexibility, which are vital qualities in the underlying jurisprudential policy considerations in any desirable choice of law rule (see Fawcett 1984).

The vital question remains however, whether the Act has struck the right balance between certainty and flexibility. Indeed, there is a need for a balance between the certainty which enables one to ascertain what the relevant rules are and to apply them without recourse to lawyers and courts, and a flexibility which gives the courts in difficult cases the freedom to reach a just decision in a given case. This is expressed with the commercial world in mind in cases where, for example, insurance companies have a need to understand and know what the law is. They need, as Dr North put it 'as good a steer as possible as to what the outcome of the case would be' (SPBC 1994–95, at p 36). The new provisions seem to have achieved this aim. They identify a clear and precise general rule which can easily determine the applicable law. This rule may, however, be displaced where upon comparison of the significance of the factors which connect a tort or delict with the country identified under the general rule with the significance of the factors connecting the tort or delict with another country. Admittedly, this may create some interpretation problems, but it is not anticipated to cause the grave injustice the common law rules had occasionally caused.

As for the argument regarding the difficulties created by English courts having to apply a foreign law, this pales into insignificance when one considers that English courts have been repeatedly requested to do so in many areas of Private International Law. Moreover, this is not necessarily fatal since the foreign law has to be pleaded and proven by the parties, otherwise English courts will assume that it is the same as English law.

Whether or not Part III of the Act is the required curative measure for preventing future injustices remains to be seen. However, it can certainly be commended, for the first limb of the double-actionability rule, which had operated as a sword against plaintiffs and as a shield in favour defendants, has been swept away. The boundaries of the exception have been extended and its edges have been trimmed. It clearly is not a bitter pill and it can safely be described as a preventive measure for the reoccurrence of such injustices as those which had been caused by cases similar to *M'Elroy* v *M'Allister*.

---

7 Part IV deals with the commencement of the various Parts of this Act.

Bibliography

Collins, L (1993) *Dicey & Morris on The Conflict of Laws*, 12th ed (London: Sweet & Maxwell).

Fawcett, J J (1984) 'Policy Considerations in Tort Choice of Law' 47 *Modern Law Review* 650.

Fawcett, J J (1992) *Cheshire & North's Private International Law* 12th ed (London: Butterworths).

Law Commission No 124 (1983) *Foreign Money Liabilities* (London: HMSO).

Law Commission No 146 and Scottish Law Commission No 96 (1985) *Polygamous Marriages* (London: HMSO).

Law Commission No 193 and Scottish Law Commission No 129 (1990) *Choice of Law in Tort and Delict* (London: HMSO).

Law Commission Working Paper 87 (1984) *Choice of Law in Tort and Delict* (London: HMSO).

Special Public Bill Committee Report (1994–95) *Private International Law (Miscellaneous Provisions) Bill* HL Paper 36, Session 1994–95.

Stone, P (1995) *The Conflict of Laws* (London: Longman).

OPEN ACCESS, RIGHTS AND LEGISLATION

F. R. Barker, LLB, PhD

Edge & Ellison, Solicitors, Birmingham

and

N. D. M. Parry, LLB

Lecturer in Law, The Law School, University of Hull
<n.d.parry@law.hull.ac.uk>

First Published in Web Journal of Current Legal Issues in association with Blackstone Press Ltd.

SUMMARY

At first sight, Part V (ss 59–83) of the National Parks and Access to the Countryside Act 1949 (hereinafter 'the 1949 Act') is a radical piece of legislation. It provides for members of the public to have open access to specified areas of 'open country'. This is in apparent contrast to the general position in England and Wales, where the prevailing private property regime is essentially founded on rights to exclude the public from land (see Munzer 1990, pp 88–90; Gray 1991, p 294) and any public access that does exist is usually confined to passage along defined routes making up the rights of way network. This article seeks generally to examine the impact and effect of Part V of the 1949 Act, and to evaluate the public access 'rights' for which it makes provision, in particular in the light of some of the recent changes to the law of trespass introduced by the Criminal Justice and Public Order Act 1994.

CONTENTS

'Open Access': The Scheme of the 1949 Act

The 1949 Act provides for arrangements between local planning authorities (ie County Councils, District Councils, Metropolitan District Councils or London Borough Councils (see 1949 Act, s 114(1), the Town and Country Planning Act 1990, ss 1(1), (2)) and persons having an interest in certain land (hereinafter referred to as 'interest holders') to secure, subject to certain restrictions, open access to that land by the public for open air recreation. The land in question must be 'open country', defined as including countryside woodlands (one of several extensions to the definition added by Countryside Act 1968, s 16) and areas consisting 'wholly or predominantly of mountain, moor, heath, down, cliff or foreshore (including any bank, barrier, dune, beach, flat or other land adjacent to the foreshore)' (see 1949 Act, s 59(2)). The open access may be either agreed between interest holder and authority in an access agreement, or imposed by the authority by means of an access order. Any arrangement reached might also be combined with a 'management agreement' under the Wildlife and Countryside Act 1981, s 39(1) between a planning authority (ie the district planning authority or, for land within a National Park, the county planning authority: see Town and Country Planning Act 1990, s 1(1), (2); Wildlife and Countryside Act 1981, s 39(5)) and an interest holder 'for the purpose of conserving or enhancing the natural beauty or amenity of any land . . . or promoting its enjoyment by the public'.

There are a number of issues of significance to note about Part V of the 1949 Act. First, its emphasis on the negotiation and agreement of public open access over land with interest holders may well result in a greater degree of goodwill on the part of the latter towards public access to land than is the case with imposed public access. This, in turn, may have tangible benefits by encouraging those with private interests in land to make improved provision for public access. Although provision is also made in the Act for authorities to make access orders, it seems these were intended as a 'reserve' option, and will presumably only be used where agreements cannot be reached (Countryside Commission/Sports Council 1987, pp 76, 89; see also pp 90–5; Bonyhady 1987, pp 149–50). Second, Part V of the 1949 Act provides for the creation of public access to open country at a regional level through local planning authorities. In this way, local circumstances – such as the nature of the upland terrain, the uses made of it, the likely impact of any access arrangement, and the views of the farming and interest-holding communities and recreational groups – can be considered. Finally, and most significantly, the public access rights to 'open country' secured under the provisions of Part V of the 1949 Act are 'rights to roam' – rights, in other words, to wander freely over such land, unconstrained by the need to follow a network of permissive paths or public rights of way. It can be argued that rights to roam are, more than any restricted rights of access along specified routes, genuinely rights to be *included in* land.

'Rights': Definitions and Nature

The term 'right' is often used indiscriminately and disingenuously in a variety of ways to mean a multitude of different things depending on the prevailing circumstances, and discussions of Part V of the 1949 Act are no exception. Any lack of clarity here, however, is likely to weaken the discussion and, to avoid this problem, the analysis of legal rights set out by W N Hohfeld in his paper, *Fundamental Legal Conceptions as Applied in Judicial Reasoning I* (Hohfeld 1923) is adopted here (see also Becker 1977, pp 7, 11–15; Simmonds 1986, pp 129–135; Wellman 1985, chs 1 and 2; Munzer 1990, pp 17–27). Hohfeld's analysis is exceptional in its rigour and depth and, although not perfect, it provides a useful vocabulary for dissecting complex legal situations and constitutes an indispensable starting point for any analysis of rights.

Hohfeld's concern was to illustrate and criticise the tendency of the judiciary and legal writers to attach the label 'right' generally and indiscriminately to four very distinct legal advantages – claims (or claim-rights), liberties (or privileges), powers and immunities – which one party may have against another (see Hohfeld 1923, pp 35–36). All four conceptions are arguably a 'species of a single genus', and share the common feature of being legal advantages in the sense that 'the law sides with the possessor *vis à vis* some second party in a possible confrontation or conflict of wills' (see Wellman 1985, p 56). It is simply that not all of them are protected by the imposition of a correlative duty on another person (see Munzer 1990, p 20).

A legal claim-right implies that the person against whom it is enforceable owes a correlative legal duty to the right-holder: A has a legal claim-right against B that B do (or not do) X if and only if B owes A a corresponding legal duty to do (or not do) X. Thus to say that A has a legal claim-right to possession of his land against B means that B has a legal duty to stay off (not to trespass on) the land (see Hohfeld 1923, p 38; Wellman 1985, pp 8,13). A legal liberty (or privilege) gives A the freedom to perform an action as against B, and B has a correlative legal 'no-claim' that A shall not perform that action. In other words, A has a legal liberty in the face of B to do (or not do) X if and only if B has no legal claim against A that A refrain from doing (or not doing) X. Thus A, a landowner, has the legal liberty to enter his land despite the protestations of B, his neighbour, because B has no legal claim against A that A refrain from entering (see Hohfeld 1923, pp 38–39; Munzer 1990, p 21). A legal power gives A the ability to alter his relations with B by performing some action such as entering a contract or making a will: if A sells or gives his land to B, B's legal relation of non-ownership is changed to one of ownership. A therefore has a legal power over B if and only if B is under a correlative legal liability to have his legal relation with A changed in some way by A's performance of an action (see Hohfeld 1923, pp 50–52; Wellman 1985, pp 8,13). Finally, a legal immunity is a right enjoyed by A against B where A is not subject to having liabilities imposed upon him by the exercise of B's powers: in other words, A has a legal immunity from B as regards some legal relation of A if and only if B is under a correlative legal disability which prevents him from changing A's legal relation. Thus a landowner, A, is immune from action by B, his neighbour, purporting to sell A's land because B is legally disabled from alienating A's legal ownership of the land in the sense that none of his actions would have legal effect in this regard (see Hohfeld 1923, pp 60–61, Wellman 1985, pp 8, 13, 52).

In the light of Hohfeld's rigorous analysis, one can see how employing simplistic and 'remarkably inarticulate' (Wellman 1985, p 11) expressions like 'A is the (fee-simple) owner of Blackacre' is likely to lead to confusion by obscuring the fact that the property rights making up this 'ownership' will usually be a complex bundle of Hohfeldian legal conceptions (see Honoré 1987, pp 161–192). In particular a landowner will normally have, for example, legal claim-rights to possess and exclude others from his land (entailing correlative duties enforceable against others not to trespass thereon). He will also have, for example, a legal liberty to grow the crop of his choice (entailing a correlative legal 'no-claim' on others that he refrain from doing so), a legal power to sell, bequeath or give away his land (entailing a correlative legal liability on others to be legally affected by the exercise of this power), and a legal immunity against its confiscation by the state (entailing a legal disability on the state from so doing). Similarly, a statement such as 'the public have a right of access to Whiteacre' is unrevealing because it fails to specify which of the Hohfeldian conceptions is involved, and this makes it difficult to comment on the relation or conflict between these rights and the private property claim-rights, powers, liberties and immunities over the land to which access is sought. This article is not directly concerned with those entering land along the network of public rights of way that exists in England and Wales (see further on this Riddall & Trevelyan (1992); Barker & Parry (1995)). Rather, it seeks to examine the position of those entering land by virtue of statutory access to 'open country' pursuant to Part V of the 1949 Act.

Legislation: The 1949 and 1994 Acts

The 1949 Act

At first sight, the approach of Part V appears quite radical, entitling the public to wander freely over upland areas. Upon closer examination, however, it will be seen that it operates negatively rather than positively. Although the title to s 60 refers to the *rights* of the public where an access agreement or order is in force, s 60(1) provides only that, where an access agreement or order has been made, an individual who enters without breaking or damaging any wall or fence, and who complies with the relevant bylaws and the extensive restrictions contained in ss 60(3), 90(1) and 90(3)(a) of the Act, is not to be regarded as a trespasser.

In Hohfeldian terms, this 'right' would seem to be properly classified as an immunity against being treated as a trespasser, rather than a claim-right of access. It entails only a correlative disability on the interest holder precluding him (provided the conditions of access are complied with) from treating a person within the area as a trespasser. Rather than according the public a claim-right of access, enforceable against the interest holder, it seems the 1949 Act grants the public only a basic permission (in the form of a Hohfeldian immunity) to have access on stringent conditions, any breach of which will render the entrant a trespasser.[1]

1 In Wellman's words, '[t]he practical importance of possessing an immunity is the safety it confers upon one's legal position' (p.52). An alternative approach might be to classify a permissive access right to land as a Hohfeldian liberty, entailing a correlative no-claim on the private landowner who created or allowed the rights that the public should not exercise them. There is, however, a potential problem with this approach in that the weak link in the Hohfeldian scheme is arguably the purported legal relation between a liberty and a 'no-claim'. In fact, unlike the other conceptions, liberties appear to be legal advantages which are merely allowed by the law, but on which the law takes no stance in terms of entailing correlative legal disadvantages on others. Hohfeld's attempt to define the correlative of a liberty as a 'no-claim' is open to the criticism that it is 'the absence of things put as things' (see Pound 1959, vol. IV, p.80). Treating a permissive public access right as a liberty may therefore be inappropriate because the owner of a private interest in land *does* appear to stand in a legal relation with a person entering the land since he may bring a legal action for trespass against the entrant, unless the latter is entering pursuant to, and within the conditions of, a permissive public access right which legally disables the owner from so doing.

Although the relevant planning authority could take action in the event of a member or members of the public being denied access (see 1949 Act, s 68), those excluded would seem to have no direct remedy, as the Act stands at present, against the interest holder to enforce their immunity-right of access. There is only a limited duty owed by the interest holder to a person entering 'open country' pursuant to Part V of the 1949 Act in so far as the Occupiers' Liability Act 1984 now affords such entrants the same protection in relation to personal injury as it does to trespassers.[2] Whilst this is an improvement on the position under the Occupiers' Liability Act 1957, which expressly excluded those entering land by virtue of Part V of the 1949 Act from the protection afforded to 'visitors' (see Occupiers' Liability Act 1957, s 1(4)), the duty which the 1984 Act imposes does not appear to be correlative to a claim-right of access in the Hohfeldian sense. It is suggested that the only claim-right which is correlative to and entailed by this duty is the claim-right enjoyed by an entrant under the 1949 Act to be treated, by the interest holder, at least as well a trespasser. This, in itself, sheds no light on the nature of the open access entitlement under Part V of the 1949 Act, but seems to be consistent with its generally negative tenor.[3]

This negative approach suggests strongly that, despite its radical appearance, the 1949 Act protects and reflects private property values to a large degree. A close examination of the provisions of Part V gives the distinct impression that public 'rights to roam' created under its authority are to be regarded as *interferences with* established private property rights, the scope and effect of which must be limited and controlled. In its current form, it tends to perpetuate the emphasis on private property rights, associated inherently with the entitlement of the owner of the land to exclude the public therefrom (classic judicial expositions include those in *Harrison* v *Duke of Rutland* [1893] 1 Q B 142; *Hickman* v *Maisey* [1900] 1 Q B 142 and *AG* v *Antrobus* [1905] 2 Ch 188; and see also Munzer 1990, pp 89–90; Waldron 1988, pp 39–39; Honoré 1987, pp 166–168, 181, 184). The provisions of Part V of the 1949 Act do little to promote and strengthen public rights to roam as legitimate, wider, 'inclusive' property interests, in the sense of entitlements enjoyed by each member of the public to have access to – *not to be excluded from* - land.

The 1994 Act

The stance of the 1949 Act is further strengthened by the changes introduced by Part V of the Criminal Justice and Public Order Act 1994 Act, particularly ss 70 and 71. Whilst these sections have received less publicity than the new criminal offence of aggravated trespass (created by the Criminal Justice and Public Order Act 1994, s 68) and apparently targeted at hunt saboteurs, they are in this context arguably of wider significance. Unlike aggravated trespass, there is no requirement

---

2 Contrast the position of those using the public rights of way network, which consists of public highways, the users of which are not protected by the Occupiers' Liability Act 1984, (see s 1(7) and Barker & Parry 1995).

3 The Law Reform Committee in its report, which preceded the 1957 Act, placed emphasis on the inter-relationship between s 60(1) of the 1949 Act, which provides that entrants under the Act are not to be treated as trespassers, and s 66(2) which, the Committee considered, made it clear that s 60(1) was not intended to increase the legal liability of the occupier of the land to entrants under the 1949 Act (see Law Reform Committee 1954, para 82). The Committee therefore concluded that such entrants should not receive the protection of the 1957 Act. The Law Commission in its later report considered that limited protection should be afforded by analogy with the position of trespassers, whom they recommended should receive the limited protection of the 1984 Act (see Law Commission 1976, para 41).

of having an intention to intimidate persons engaging in lawful activity on land or to obstruct or disrupt that activity, (see s 68(1)).

Ss 70 and 71 of the 1994 Act add new ss 14A, 14B and 14C to the Public Order Act 1986 and confer on local authorities a wide power to make orders prohibiting what are referred to as 'trespassory assemblies' and criminalising certain conduct associated with such assemblies. The Public Order Act 1986 s 14A(1) now confers a discretion on a chief officer of police to apply for such an order, where he reasonably believes that an assembly (meaning twenty or more persons – see s 14A(9)) is intended to be held on land in the open air to which the public has no right of access or only a limited right of access. Section 14A(1) also requires that the officer reasonably believe first, that the assembly is likely to be held without the permission of the occupier of the land or to conduct itself in such a way as to exceed the limits of any such permission or the limits of the public's right of access, and second, that it may result in serious disruption to the life of the community or significant damage to land, or a building or monument on it, of historical, architectural, archaeological or scientific importance (see s 14A(1)). The power to prohibit trespassory assemblies is reinforced by the creation of criminal offences (see the Public Order Act 1986, s 14B inserted by the 1994 Act, s 70) in respect of persons who organise an assembly which they know is prohibited by an order under the Act (see s 14B(1)). Similarly a person who takes part, or incites another to take part, in an assembly which they know is prohibited is also guilty of an offence (see ss 14B(2) and s 14B(3)). There is also a wide power for any uniformed police officer to stop and direct not to proceed any person whom he reasonably believes to be going to a trespassory assembly covered by a prohibition order, which the police officer reasonably believes is likely to be an assembly which is prohibited by that order (see the Public Order Act 1986, s 14C inserted by the 1994 Act, s 71).

As has been pointed out by at least one commentator (Smith 1995, p 24) these provisions raise important questions about the extent to which private property rights in land should be permitted to override rights to freedom of expression in public. They are particularly relevant in the context of public 'rights to roam' created under the 1949 Act because what is now s 14A of the Public Order Act 1986 is drafted so widely that it may catch – and thereby potentially negate – many such rights. Land subject to an open access agreement or order made under the 1949 Act will clearly be 'land to which the public has a limited right of access' within s 14A(1), and there is a real danger that the other requirements for a prohibition order will be satisfied. The definition of an 'assembly' in s 14A is so wide that any group of twenty or more members of the public seeking to exercise their rights to roam will be caught by it. In addition the extensive range of restrictions to which public rights to roam under the 1949 Act are subject (see ss 60(3) 90(1), (3)(a)) may make it relatively easy to argue that such an assembly 'is likely . . . to exceed the limits of the public's right of access' within s 14A(1)(a). Finally it may not be difficult to contend that a group of twenty or more members of the public exercising their rights to roam 'may result in serious disruption to the life of the community', or in significant damage to land of historical or other importance so as to satisfy s 14A(1)(b).

A local authority in England and Wales can only make a prohibition order under the Public Order Act 1986, s 14A with the consent of the Secretary of State (see s 14A(2)). Nevertheless, the power to make such an order reinforces the view that the rights of open access enshrined in the 1949 Act are, in reality, currently treated as interferences with private property rights, rather than as legitimate, wider interests in land.

Changing the Nature of Open Access Rights

It can be argued that, in a society where public, rights-based access to land is an issue of increasing social and legal concern, the negative and restrictive approach of the 1949 Act is outmoded and ripe for change. Evidence of the growing social and legal importance of public access to land comes from a variety of sources, including recent Countryside Commission initiatives (see Countryside Commission 1989, 1992 and 1993), the introduction of the Rights of Way Act in 1990 as specific legislation to protect public rights of way, and a noticeable rise in litigation in which the main issue has been public access to land.[4] If Part V of the 1949 Act is to play any part in addressing the contemporary social and legal concern over public access, it arguably needs to accord a greater degree of legal protection, emphasis and support to the entitlement of the public to have access to 'open country', if necessary at the expense of the traditional exclusive, private property rights currently enjoyed by the 'owners' of such land.

As was mentioned earlier, property can be analysed as a 'bundle of rights' in or over a resource (in this case land) (see Waldron 1987, pp 26–30; Ackerman 1977, pp 26–28; Macpherson 1978, pp 3–4, 6–11), and the argument that ownership is made up of a number of 'essential incidents' is also well known (see Honoré 1987; Ackerman 1977, pp 26–27). Both property and ownership can therefore be seen as relative and relational concepts, particularly as regards land. A landowner can be identified as the person with the strongest link with the particular piece of land in question (his rights over it minus his liabilities) within the complex web of legal relationships existing between persons who are concerned with the land in question in some way. Alternatively, to phrase it another way, he can be described as the person with the weightiest package of incidents in relation to the land and, in particular Honoré's first incident of possession (and thereby exclusion) (see Honoré 1987, p 166–68). The ideas explored here for strengthening Part V of the 1949 Act, and with it the entitlement of the public to have access to open country, would be likely to have the effect of shifting some of the legal emphasis currently attached to the private, exclusive interests of the owners and occupiers of such land, in favour of attaching greater importance to the inclusive entitlements of members of the public to have access – not to be excluded from – it. Such an approach may, in turn, start a process of reformulating the nature of property and the respective weight accorded the rights in the bundle making it up, and result in individual property systems exhibiting a greater balance between private and public rights (for further detail on this 'reformulative' idea see Barker and Parry 1995, and also see *R* v *Doncaster Metropolitan Council ex parte Braim* (1989) 57 P & CR 1 at 15, where a public right to recreation over Doncaster Common was recognised).

If Part V of the 1949 Act is to play a part in strengthening the legal protection, emphasis and support accorded to the entitlement of the public to have access to 'open country', several changes to its essentially negative approach may be necessary. These changes to Part V might well destroy the consensual element inherent within it, and thereby rule out any advantages (mentioned at the start of

4 See, for example, *R* v *Doncaster Metropolitan Borough Council ex parte Braim* (1989) 57 P & CR 1; *Rubinstein* v *Secretary of State for the Environment* (1989) 57 P & CR 111; *Mayhew* v *Secretary of State for the Environment* (1993) 65 P & CR 344; *Christchurch Borough Council* v *Secretary of State for the Environment & Barratt Southampton Ltd* (1994) 68 P & CR 116; *Dunlop* v *Secretary of State for the Environment & Cambridgeshire County Council* (1995) 70 P & CR 307: *R* v *Suffolk County Council ex parte Steed* (1995) 70 P & CR 487; *R* v *Secretary of State for the Environment ex parte Andrews* (1996) 71 P & CR 1.

the article) that can be attributed to it. They are, however, arguably a necessary step in securing more extensive public rights to roam over open country.

i. Public claim-rights of access

A first change to the Act would perhaps entail providing that access arrangements created under its provisions generate public claim-rights of access. Establishing public access rights of comparable strength to those private property claim-rights of possession and exclusion likely to be raised against them might be some recognition of the contemporary importance of public, inclusive rights of access to land. The responsibility for requiring reluctant interest holders (at least) to permit such access could remain, as at present, with the relevant planning authority, but there may also be an argument for allowing members of the public, as bearers of these wider rights of access, to enforce directly the correlative duties entailed on interest holders.[5] The rôle of direct individual enforcement in this context would seem to have a number of advantages. It could help to conserve valuable local authority resources, and may be considerably more efficient than reporting a breach of duty to an authority and waiting for enforcement action. It is significant that 'public spirited', individual action of this kind was seen as such a potentially effective form of enforcement in relation to the new obligations imposed on owners and occupiers of land when the Rights of Way Act 1990 was introduced, that the ability to take such action was deliberately restricted.[6] Although enforcement by individuals is also costly, and the number of actions ending up in court might ultimately be small, the prospect of private action (sometimes with financial support from representative groups such as the Ramblers' Association or the Byways and Bridleways Trust – see, eg *Rubinstein* v *Secretary of State for the Environment* (1989) 57 P & C R 111; *R* v *Secretary of State for the Environment, ex parte Riley* (1990) 59 P & C R 1) could have a significant effect in encouraging interest holders to comply with any duties entailed by access agreements over open country. Leaving it to representative groups alone to police the situation and bring enforcement action on behalf of their members and the public at large is another option, although significant research indicates that this approach may not be effective (see Countryside Commission/Sports Council 1987, pp 14–15, 16–17, 123–130).

ii. Reducing the restrictions accompanying open access arrangements

A second change to Part V of the 1949 Act might be to reduce the number and extent of restrictions accompanying open access arrangements. The immunity against liability for trespass provided by s 60(1) is made subject to a wide range of restrictions set out in Sch 2 of the 1949 Act – including driving vehicles, lighting fires, disturbing or killing livestock and damaging the land – and to any express condition in the access arrangement allowing the exclusion of 'the land or any part thereof' at particular times, thus enabling the closure of the land to public access to allow for shooting (see the 1949 Act, s 60(3)). Provision is also made in the

5 In the case of access agreements, this would constitute a significant modification to the privity of contract principle. Such a modification to the privity principle might be seen as analogous to the modifications which allow easements (*private* rights of access) and restrictive covenants to 'run with land' and be enforced by and against persons who were not privy to the original agreement which created the easement or covenant. The analogy is not, however, a particularly close one and should be treated with caution, given the fundamental differences between such private interests in land and the public access entitlement which is the subject of this article.

6 See Hansard HL ser 5, vol 519, col 1488, Baroness Nicol, 6 June 1990; see also Hansard HC ser 6, vol 167, col 1223 Henry Bellingham, 23 February 1990; vol 171, col 1344, Edward Leigh.

1949 Act for the making of local authority bylaws to govern access arrangements: these may be made for a variety of purposes, including 'the preservation of order', 'the prevention of damage to the land', to secure that persons will 'behave themselves', and 'to prohibit or restrict the use of the land' (see ss 90(1), (3)(a)). Cumulatively, these restrictions may control the exercise of public access granted under the Act to a very large degree and, although the regulation of the public's behaviour may be a legitimate issue of concern for those with private interests in land, it can be argued that the Act is imbalanced in this respect. Reducing the impact and extent of these restrictions would also have the advantage of limiting the potential for the application of the trespassory assembly provisions now in the Public Order Act 1986, since those exercising their right to roam would be less likely to exceed the limits of the public's right of access for the purpose of the 1986 Act, s 14A(1)(a).

In contrast to the range of conditions aimed at protecting private property rights, those provisions of the Act designed to protect the public's rights of access are few and meagre. There is an express stipulation that interest holders must not do any works which would interfere with access (see the 1949 Act, s 66(1)), and a reference to the fact that access agreements and orders may contain additional requirements relating to the making of 'expedient' provision 'for securing that sufficient means of access to the land . . . will be available for the public . . .' (see s 67(1)). This imbalance strengthens the perception of public access immunity-rights created under the Act as interferences with private property rights which must be controlled and restricted.

iii. Strengthening the obligations on local authorities

A third change to the Act might be to strengthen the obligations on local authorities to enter into access arrangements with those holding private interests in open country. At present under the Act, local planning authorities merely have powers to make access agreements and orders, and few appear to use them to any degree (see Shoard 1987, pp 373–383). Each authority was required to carry out within two years of the commencement of the 1949 Act a review of its territory with a view to deciding if access orders or agreements would be in order (see generally ss 61–63). However, the Act does not appear to make any provision for authorities that failed to meet this requirement, and a review conducted around forty years ago would in any case be due for reconsideration today.[7]

One way forward here might be to impose a duty on authorities to make access agreements or orders wherever they consider that the public interest outweighs the individual's interest in excluding the public from the land he or she nominally holds. If an access agreement could not be reached, then, having already decided that an access arrangement of some sort is in the public interest, the authority would be under a duty to create one by means of an access order.[8] The effective discharge of this statutory duty would necessarily require the authority to keep a 'rolling' check on potential terrain within its area which might be or become particularly suitable for access arrangements, and also on social and other factors

7 Compare, for example, the continuing obligations on local planning authorities to review the provision of conservation areas under the Planning (Listed Buildings and Conservation Areas) Act 1990, s 69.

8 If such a duty were created, there might be an issue as to the entitlement to compensation for those whose private property rights in land were adversely affected. It might be argued, however, that paying such compensation would merely reassert the primacy of private property interests in land, an issue which this article seeks to evaluate critically.

which might affect the relative weight of public and private interests in relation to the making of such arrangements.

In considering whether to make access arrangements, authorities would need to reflect a balance between the public and private interest. Individuals may not have too much difficulty representing their own private interests, but it may be less easy to assess and represent 'the public interest' (see in particular Countryside Commission/Sports Council 1987, pp 14–15, 16–17, 123–130). One option might be for authorities to take decisions whether to create particular open access areas on the merits of each case. This would presumably entail their gathering evidence of any public interest, need and desire for such areas by, for example, placing notices in relevant local newspapers and on and around the land concerned. Although local authorities are arguably well placed to monitor and appreciate regional and national trends which may affect the balance between public and private interest, a disadvantage of this approach is that it is likely to be cumbersome, expensive and time-consuming, and might not always accord the public interest sufficient weight. An alternative, although more radical, approach might therefore be to start from a presumption of public interest in favour of the creation of open access areas, based on the contemporary social and legal importance of public access to land. It would then be for those with private interests in open country to convince the relevant local authority of the case for not creating public rights to roam over such land.

Conclusions

The provisions of Part V of the National Parks and Access to the Countryside Act 1949 have the potential for meeting at least some of the current public demand for recreational access to land.[9] As they stand at present, however, reinforced by the trespassory assembly provisions added to the Public Order Act 1986 by the Criminal Justice and Public Order Act 1994, they may be too conservative in their approach.

The application and effect of the provisions of Part V may, therefore, need to be strengthened and, in particular, there may be good arguments for making open access arrangements less dependent upon the consent of those with private interests in open country. A side effect of such an alteration to the statute would be that the consensual element which currently underpins open access would be lost. Although this element may be advantageous in the sense that it generates goodwill towards the idea of public access to land, it is probably not, in itself, a sufficient argument for retaining the provisions of the 1949 Act in their present form. They tend to perpetuate the view that public rights to roam over open country are interferences with property rights, whose scope and effect must be controlled and restricted, rather than legitimate, wider, inclusive interests in land, worthy of more proactive development and protection. The ideas for change explored above could also start a process of reformulating the prevailing conception of private property in England and Wales. In a small way they could affect the respective legal emphasis attached to various rights making up the property 'bundle', by shifting the emphasis away from private, exclusive rights traditionally enjoyed by owners, occupiers and 'interest holders' over land, in favour of attaching greater importance to access rights of a wider, public, inclusive nature (see further Barker & Parry, 1995).

9 For the most recent attempt to extend rights of access to the countryside see the Access to the Countryside Bill – first reading 30th January 1996 (see Hansard HC ser 6, vol 270, col 779–785).

Bibliography

Ackerman, B (1977) *Private Property and the Constitution* (New Haven: Yale University Press).
Barker, F R & Parry N D M (1995) 'Private Property, Public Access and Occupiers' Liability' 15 *Legal Studies* 335.
Becker, L (1977) *Property Rights: Philosophic Foundations* (Boston: Routledge & Kegan Paul).
Bonyhady, T (1987) *The Law of the Countryside: The Rights of the Public* (Abingdon: Professional Books).
Countryside Commission/Sports Council, (1987) *Access to the Countryside for Recreation and Sport* (CCP 217).
Countryside Commission, (1989) *Managing Rights of Way: An Agenda for Action* (CCP 273).
Countryside Commission, (1992) *Rights of Way: An Action Guide* (CCP 375).
Countryside Commission, (1993) *National Target for Rights of Way* (CCP 436).
Gray, K (1991) 'Property in Thin Air' (1991) 50 *Cambridge Law Journal* 252.
Hohfeld, W (1923) *Fundamental Legal Conceptions*, (ed) W Cook, (New Haven: Yale University Press).
Honoré, A M (1987) *Making Law Bind* (Oxford: Oxford University Press).
Law Commission No 75 (1976), *Report on Liability for Damage or Injury to Trespassers and Related Questions of Occupiers' Liability* (London: HMSO) Cmnd 6428.
Law Reform Committee Third Report (1954), *Occupiers' Liability to Invitees, Licensees and Trespassers* (London: HMSO) Cmnd 9305.
Munzer, S (1990) *A Theory of Property* (Cambridge: Cambridge University Press).
Pound, R (1959) *Jurisprudence* (St Paul, Minnesota: West Publishing Company).
Riddall, J & Trevelyan, J (1992) *Rights of Way: A Guide to Law and Practice* (2nd ed) (Ramblers' Association/Open Spaces Society).
Shoard, M (1987)*This Land is Our Land: The Struggle for Britain's Countryside* (London: Paladin, Grafton Books).
Simmonds, N (1986) *Central Issues in Jurisprudence* (London: Sweet & Maxwell).
Smith, A T H (1995) *Criminal Law Review* 19.
Wellman, C (1985) *A Theory of Rights* (Totowa, New Jersey: Rowman & Allenheld).

THE EC DATA PROTECTION DIRECTIVE 1995: AN ANALYSIS

Freddy Kosten and Dr. Chris Pounder

Data Protection News, Hoskyns Group plc
<dp.news@hoskyns.co.uk>

First Published in Web Journal of Current Legal Issues in association with Blackstone Press Ltd.

SUMMARY

This paper explores and analyses the provisions of the EC Data Protection Directive 1995. To assist readers, it is our practice to capitalise terms, relating to natural or legal persons, which are defined in the Directive.

CONTENTS

Chapter I: General Provisions

This Chapter contains Articles 1–4 of the EC Data Protection Directive 1995 (95/46/EC) (the Directive). They are preliminary provisions which describe why the Directive is important, identify what kinds of personal data are covered by its provisions, define the scope of the Directive and specify which national law is to apply.

Article 1 explains the purpose of the Directive: to 'protect the fundamental rights and freedoms of natural persons, and in particular their right to privacy with respect to the processing of personal data'. Such protection 'shall neither restrict nor prohibit the free flow of personal data between Member States'.

Article 2 introduces definitions which differ from those in the Data Protection Act 1984 (the UK Act). For instance:

(a) 'personal data' comprise 'any information relating to an identified or identifiable natural person (''Data Subject'')'. Personal data are, therefore, not limited to information which is processed automatically, nor to information about a 'living individual', nor do they exclude the intentions of the Data User with respect to the Data Subject (the UK Act imposes all three of these restrictions).

(b) 'processing of personal data' describes 'any operation or set of operations which is performed upon personal data, whether or not by automatic means'. Use of the word 'any' clearly emphasises that every conceivable operation on personal data is 'processing' (eg from collection, use, and disclosure, to storage and destruction). Thus, non-automated processing such as the manual manipulation of personal information stored on a micro-fiche would be an 'operation'.

(c) a 'Controller' is the 'natural or legal person' who 'determines the purposes and means of the processing of personal data' (whether 'alone or jointly with others'). This definition is close to that of 'Data User' in the UK Act.

(d) a 'Processor' is the 'natural or legal person' who 'processes personal data on behalf of the Controller'. Since the definition of processing encompasses 'any operation', a 'Processor' includes any person who is instructed by the Controller to manipulate personal data (eg a contractor who destroys printout, organises mailings, or collects completed application forms). In practice, this definition will generally not impact on staff acting on behalf of their employer who is also a Controller.

(e) a 'Third Party' is 'any natural or legal person . . . other than the Data Subject, the Controller, the Processor and the persons who, under the direct authority of the Controller or the Processor, are authorised to process the data'. This elucidates the status of 'Third Party' implicit in the UK Act.

(f) a 'Recipient' is one 'to whom data are disclosed, whether a Third Party or not'. Data Subjects can thus be Recipients of personal data. The definition permits 'authorities which may receive data in the framework of a particular enquiry' not to be regarded as 'Recipients', a qualification which can be seen as introducing the equivalent of some of the non-disclosure exemptions of the UK Act (eg disclosures required by law; Section 34(5)(a)).

(g) 'Data Subject's consent' is 'any freely given specific and informed indication of his wishes by which the Data Subject signifies his agreement to personal data relating to him being processed'. The Directive does not demand express consent in writing, or the keeping of formal consent records; the indication could be a verbal 'yes' or even a 'nod and a wink' although, in some circumstances, the absence of proof that consent had been given could create problems.

(h) 'personal data filing system' comprises 'any structured set of personal data which are accessible according to specific criteria, whether centralised, decentralised or dispersed on a functional or geographical basis'. If personal data can be retrieved through use of an index, or accessed via criteria such as name, reference or policy number, address, vehicle registration mark etc, then these data can be considered as stored in a 'filing system'.

Article 3 limits the scope of the Directive to personal data that are processed wholly or partly by automatic means, and to personal data processed by non-automatic means if these data are, or are intended to be, part of a 'filing system' (eg organised, or intended to be organised, in a structured manual file). In addition, Article 3 stipulates that Member States shall not apply this Directive to the processing of personal data outwith Community competence (eg to policing or to 'purely personal' matters). These exceptions prepare the ground for continuation of the wide exemptions found in Sections 27 (national security) and 33(1) (domestic and recreational affairs) of the UK Act.

Article 4 establishes that each Member State shall apply the Directive:

(a) to any Controller 'established on the territory of the Member State'.

(b) to Controllers who are 'established on the territory of several Member States'. For instance, if a UK company had offices in Paris and Berlin, then the French and German offices would have to comply with the standards of French and German law.

(c) to circumstances under which a specific national law applies because of the application of international public law. For instance, the UK Embassy based in any country is in international law UK territory; any Controller established at this location would be subject to UK data protection law.

(d) to processing carried out, in a Member State, on behalf of a Controller who is not established in the European Union. For instance, a USA company which processes personal data in the UK would need to appoint someone who can be 'nobbled' by the UK's Data Protection Authority. However, if the processing takes place 'only for purposes of transit (of the data) through the territory of the Community' then there is no need to appoint a representative.

Chapter II: General Rules on the Lawfulness of the Processing of Personal Data

This, the longest Chapter of the Directive, contains Articles 5–21. These are the main operative provisions. They list the main obligations placed on Controllers and specify the rights of Data Subjects. All these provisions, together, define what constitutes lawful processing.

Article 5: Lawfulness
This Article permits Member States to 'determine more precisely the conditions under which the processing of personal data is lawful', as long as this is 'within the limits . . . of this Chapter'. The Article can be seen, therefore, as promoting subsidiarity; it provides Member States with the flexibility to implement Articles 6–21 whilst taking into account national, legal and cultural traditions.

Article 6: A Principled Approach
This Article introduces a duty on Member States to ensure that Controllers comply with five 'principles relating to data quality'; some aspects differ significantly from the first six Data Protection Principles of the UK Act. For instance, personal data must be:

(a) 'processed fairly and lawfully'. Since processing, by definition, includes collection (ie obtaining), this obligation incorporates the First Data Protection Principle of the UK Act. Articles 10 and 11 provide more detail as to the information which has to be provided to Data Subjects and to Third Parties, when information is collected about the Data Subjects.

(b) 'collected for specified, explicit and legitimate purposes and not further processed in a way incompatible with those purposes'. This Principle prohibits any 'further processing of personal data if such processing would be incompatible with the purpose(s) of collection. The link to the purpose specified at collection is important; new purposes determined after collection are likely to be in breach of the Principle unless necessary steps are taken by the Controller (eg to seek the consent of the source(s) for the new purpose). This approach is often referred to as the 'Finality Principle'.

(c) 'adequate, relevant and not excessive in relation to the purposes for which they are collected and/or for which they are further processed'. Note that the Directive again links the Controller's purpose(s) at the time of collection and at the time of further processing. The preamble to the Directive states that the latter purpose(s) 'shall not be incompatible with the purposes . . . originally specified'.

(d) 'accurate and, where necessary, kept up to date; every reasonable step must be taken to ensure that data which are inaccurate or incomplete having regard to the purposes for which they were collected or for which they are further processed, are erased or rectified'. The word 'reasonable' provides some flexibility with respect to the obligations imposed by this principle; however, Article 12 does imply that a disclosure log will be necessary.

(e) 'kept in a form which permits identification of Data Subjects for no longer than is necessary for the purposes for which the data were collected or for which they are further processed'. This extends the UK's Sixth Principle by differentiating between the purpose(s) associated with collection and the purpose(s) of further processing. Longer periods can apply if personal data are processed for 'historical, statistical or scientific' purposes and if a Member State imposes 'appropriate safeguards'.

Article 7: When Can You Process?
This Article sets out the only circumstances under which personal data can be processed lawfully (ie at least one such circumstance must apply, otherwise a Controller's processing is unlawful). These circumstances are:

(a) 'the Data Subject has given his consent unambiguously'. Since there must, by definition, be an 'indication' of consent, implied consent (ie when consent is assumed in the absence of an indication) is unlikely to meet this requirement.

(b) 'processing is necessary for the performance of a contract to which the Data Subject is party' (or in order to complete some pre-contractual stage at the request of the Data Subject).

(c) 'processing is necessary for compliance with a legal obligation to which the Controller is subject' (eg statutory duties imposed, by law, on Controllers).

(d) 'processing is necessary in order to protect the vital interests of the Data Subject'. 'Vital interests' should involve some kind of emergency; the preamble to the Directive cites the protection of 'an interest which is essential for the Data Subject's life'.

(e) 'processing is necessary . . . in the public interest'. The phrase 'public interest', as the first Calcutt Report (Cm 1102) noted 'means different things to different people'; in other words, the phrase has uncertain application in the UK.

(f) 'processing is necessary . . . in the exercise of official authority vested in the Controller or in a Third Party to whom the data are disclosed'. This would cover many Controllers and Third Parties who are public bodies, and others whose responsibilities are established and limited by statute.

(g) 'processing is necessary for the purposes of the legitimate interests pursued by the Controller or by the Third Party or Parties to whom the data are disclosed, except where such interests are overridden by the interests or fundamental rights and freedoms of the Data Subject'. The condition sets up a balance between two interests. Thus, if the consequences of the processing are detrimental to a particular Data Subject, and there are no other 'necessary' grounds that would take precedence, then one would expect the Data Subject's interests to override the Controller's interests in the continuation of the processing. One would always expect the Data Subject's interests to prevail if the Controller acted unlawfully (eg did not comply with the provisions of this Directive).

Article 8: Sensitive Personal Data

This Article specifies that the processing of special categories of personal data (ie those described in Section 2(3) of the Data Protection Act, plus 'trade-union membership') is prohibited, unless at least one of the conditions outlined below applies. The conditions which permit such processing comprise:

(a) 'the Data Subject has given his explicit consent to the processing'; however, Member States can enact legislation to prohibit the processing even if such consent has been obtained.

(b) 'processing is necessary for the purpose of carrying out the obligations and specific rights of the Controller in the field of employment law insofar as it is authorised by national law providing for adequate safeguards'. Note that this condition is very narrowly defined.

(c) 'processing is necessary to protect the vital interests of the Data Subject or of another person where the Data Subject is physically or legally incapable of giving his consent'. As mentioned above with respect to Article 7, 'vital interests' is of limited scope.

(d) 'processing is carried out in the course of its legitimate activities with appropriate guarantees by a foundation, association or any other non-profit-seeking body with a political, philosophical, religious or trade-union aim and on condition that the processing relates solely to the members of the body or to persons who have regular contact with it in connection with its purposes and that the data are not disclosed to a Third Party without the consent of the Data Subjects'. The objective is to ensure that organisations like charities (eg in support of certain religious beliefs) are not subject to the need to obtain consent to the processing of sensitive personal data. This exception seems odd since one would expect the 'members' in 'regular contact' to have provided such consent. Cults with 'philosophical' or 'religious' aims which are also suspected of 'brainwashing' their members will presumably have no difficulty in obtaining the necessary consent!

(e) 'processing relates to data which are manifestly made public by the Data Subject' (eg when a person 'comes out', or reveals political loyalties in a letter to a newspaper) or if the processing 'is necessary for the establishment, exercise or defence of legal claims' (eg an insurance company which holds medical data because the Data Subject is suing for negligence).

(f) 'processing of the data is required for the purposes of preventive medicine, medical diagnosis, the provision of care or treatment or the management of health-care services, and where those data are processed by a health professional subject . . . to the obligation of professional secrecy'. The UK Government expressed concern that compliance with earlier drafts of Article 8 would entail a cost of £1 billion to obtain the necessary consent, and would thus interfere with the internal NHS market. This wording should lay these worries to rest.

(g) when processing is sanctioned through legislation. Article 8 provides Member States with considerable flexibility (eg on the grounds of 'substantial public interest', whatever this means; see Article 7) to lay down exemptions in addition to those listed above (eg who is allowed to hold criminal records, or use a Universal Personal Identifier or a PIN); however, such legislation must provide 'suitable safeguards'. The Commission must be notified of the scope of any legislation which permits an exemption which relates to these special categories of personal data.

Article 9: Freedom of Expression

This Article permits Member States to provide exemptions for the specific purposes of journalism, and to protect artistic or literary expression, but only if such exemptions 'are necessary to reconcile the right to privacy with the rules governing freedom of expression'. Since in the UK there are no statutory controls on the media (ie no rules governing freedom of expression), it is difficult to see how the provisions of this Article can be implemented in this case.

Article 10: 'Collection of Data From the Data Subject'

Article 10 imposes procedures similar to those developed through the 'fair obtaining' obligations of the First Principle of the UK Act. The Article stipulates that Controllers 'must provide a Data Subject from whom data relating to himself are collected with at least the following information, except where he already has it:'

(a) 'the identity of the Controller and of his representative, if any'.

(b) 'the purposes of the processing for which the data are intended' (the use of the word 'intended' implies that the Data Subject must be given advance notice of all the Controller's purposes).

(c) and 'any further information . . . insofar as such . . . is necessary, having regard to the specific circumstances in which the data are collected, to guarantee fair processing in respect of the Data Subject'. The Article illustrates the kinds of details which might help 'guarantee fair processing'; these include: 'the Recipients or categories of Recipients of the data', 'whether replies to the questions are obligatory or voluntary', the 'possible consequences of failure to reply', and the existence of the Data Subject's rights of access and rectification.

Article 11: Collection of Data About the Data Subject From a Third Party
This Article requires a Controller to provide the Data Subject with certain information whenever personal data about the Data Subject are obtained from somebody else (eg via a report containing a Third Party's opinion of the Data Subject, or when an employee of a Controller contributes to the personal data held about Data Subjects). This information must be provided either 'at the time of undertaking the recording of personal data' or 'if a disclosure to a Third Party is envisaged, no later than the time when the data are first disclosed'. The details to be provided are similar to those set out in relation to Article 10, except that Article 11 states that it might also be necessary to provide the Data Subject with details of 'the categories of data concerned' (ie a description of the items of data held by the Controller).

There are several exceptions from the need to provide these details; they apply when:

(a) the Data Subject already has the information.

(b) an exemption applies (see Article 13).

(c) 'if recording or disclosure is expressly laid down by law'. So, for instance, the Electoral Registrars in the UK would not have to inform Data Subjects concerning those who had purchased the register, since this disclosure is authorised by statute.

(d) if the provision of information proves impossible. This is a tough condition, and is only likely to apply in rare cases (eg the personal data do not include the Data Subject's address).

(e) if the provision of information involves 'a disproportionate effort'. There are two ways of interpreting the word 'disproportionate'. Firstly, in relation to the effort involved (eg if the obligation would impose unreasonable demands on the Controller) and secondly, in relation to the Directive's prime objective of protecting the Data Subject (eg if the recording or disclosure involved was unlikely to harm or distress the Data Subject, then provision of this information could be claimed to be disproportionate to that aim).

Article 12: Rights of Access
The Directive grants Data Subjects several rights which Controllers have to satisfy; these rights extend beyond those provided in Part III of the Data Protection Act. The complete list in Article 12 is as follows:

(a) to obtain 'confirmation as to whether or not data relating to him are processed', and information concerning (at least) 'the purposes of the processing, the categories of data concerned, and the Recipients or categories of Recipients to whom the data are disclosed'. These requirements resemble those in the UK Act: via part of the Subject Access provisions (Section 21(1)(a)), and the right to inspect any Data User's Register Entry (Section 9).

(b) to obtain 'in an intelligible form . . . the data undergoing processing'. Unlike the UK Act, Article 12 further identifies, as one component of the right of Access, the obligation to provide the Data Subject with 'any available information' as to the source of the data; this information can only be withheld if an exemption applies (Article 13; see next paragraph). By contrast, the UK Act permits an individual, as source, to remain unidentified (except if the source is a social worker or health professional involved in a professional capacity with the Data Subject).

(c) to obtain 'knowledge of the logic involved in any automatic processing of data concerning him at least in the case of the automated decisions referred to in Article 15(1)'. In essence, Member States have to enact legislation so that the broad facts provided to Data Subjects (eg under Article 10) could be augmented, on demand, by details about any automated decision-making process.

(d) to have personal data rectified, erased or blocked if the processing 'does not comply with the provisions of this Directive, in particular because of the incomplete or inaccurate nature of the data'. This could be a very powerful weapon: Controllers could find it difficult to refuse Data Subjects who say 'you have not complied with Article X. Now delete my data'.

(e) to obtain 'notification to Third Parties to whom the data have been disclosed of any rectification, erasure or blocking . . . unless this proves impossible or involves a disproportionate effort'. The Article points, inexorably, towards the implementation of a disclosure log.

Article 13: Exemptions and Restrictions

The Directive provides that Member States can, to 'safeguard' certain aspects, 'adopt legislative measures to restrict the scope of the obligations and rights' in relation to: compliance with the Principles (Article 6) ; the provision of information to Data Subjects (Articles 10 and 11); the rights of Data Subjects (Article 12); and the requirement to publicise the existence of a processing operation (Article 21). Article 13 therefore would, for instance, permit the UK to maintain all the Subject Access and non-disclosure exemptions found in the UK Act. In further detail, exemptions and restrictions may be imposed whenever these are necessary to safeguard:

(a) 'national security' and 'defence' purposes. Note that under Article 3, personal data held for certain purposes (eg national security, public security, policing) are excluded from the scope of the Directive. The exemption is necessary since 'ordinary' Controllers who process personal data for 'normal' purposes might need to disclose such data for these purposes.

(b) 'public security'. In the UK Act, there is no specific exemption for this aspect, but certain personal data could involve the exemptions under Section 28.

(c) 'the prevention, investigation, detection and prosecution of criminal offences, or of breaches of ethics for regulated professions'. In the UK Act, Section 28 permits exemptions for crime prevention purposes and for breaches of ethics which result in crime.

(d) 'an important economic or financial interest of a Member State or of the European Union, including monetary, budgetary and taxation matters'. These interests link to at least three Sections of the UK Act: Section 27 since national security relates to the economic well-being of the UK, Section 28 with respect to the 'collection of any tax or duty', and Section 30 with respect to the finance sector. These last provisions will permit the continuation of some of the Subject Access exemptions found in the Orders made under Section 30 of the UK Act, as modified by Section 190 of the Financial Services Act 1986 (eg pertaining to the regulatory functions of the Bank of England).

(e) 'a monitoring, inspection or regulatory function connected, even occasionally, with the exercise of official authority' (mainly in respect of security and criminal matters). This exemption would cover relevant disclosures of personal data to official bodies (eg as with many disclosures subject to the non-disclosure provisions).

(f) 'the protection of the Data Subject'. This could maintain the Subject Access exemptions to particular health and social work data, if Access to those data could seriously harm the patient or social work client (Section 29 of the UK Act).

(g) 'the rights and freedoms of others'. This could maintain the exemptions associated with legal professional privilege (Section 31(2) of the UK Act) and other restrictions on the right of Access already sanctioned (eg adoption records as in Section 34(2) , or genetic records as in Section 32(8) of the Human Fertilisation and Embryology Act 1990).

(h) research and statistics. The exemption is limited to Article 12 only, and applies to personal data which 'are processed solely for purposes of scientific research' or are kept no longer than 'necessary for the sole purpose of creating statistics', but only if such data are 'subject to adequate legal safeguards'. This would allow the UK to continue with Section 33(6) of the UK Act.

Article 14: The Data Subject's Right to Object

Article 14(a) obliges Member States to grant the Data Subject the right to object 'at least in the cases referred to in Article 7(e) and (f)' and 'at any time' when there are 'compelling legitimate grounds relating to his particular situation to the processing of data relating to him, save where otherwise provided by national legislation'. The words:

(a) 'at least in the cases referred to in Article 7(e) and (f)' allow Member States to legislate with respect to any 'case' whatsoever (ie even beyond those specified in Article 7). However, the minimum scope of such legislation must relate at least to the last two paragraphs of Article 7 (ie if 'processing is necessary . . . in the public interest or in the exercise of official authority . . . or . . . for the purposes of the legitimate interests pursued by the Controller . . . except where such interests are overridden by the interests . . . of the Data Subject').

(b) 'compelling legitimate grounds relating to his particular situation to the processing of data relating to him' place the right to object onto a case-by-case basis, and ensure that, to succeed, Data Subjects would have to show that the consequences of the processing were likely to be strongly detrimental to them.

(c) 'save where otherwise provided by national legislation' permit Member States to enact legislation which would override the right to object in any appropriate circumstance.

The right in Article 14(b) to object with respect to direct marketing is much clearer; it is strengthened by the requirement that 'Member States shall take the necessary measures to ensure that Data Subjects are aware' of this opportunity (eg through appropriate publicity). The options provided are:

(a) for a Data Subject to 'object, on request and free of charge, to the processing of (his) personal data . . . which the Controller anticipates being processed for the purposes of direct marketing', or

(b) if the purposes of the direct marketing involve Third Parties (eg host mailing), the Controller must inform the Data Subject 'before personal data are disclosed for the first time to Third Parties or used on their behalf', and expressly offer 'the right to object free of charge to such disclosures or uses'.

Article 15: Automated Decisions About Individuals
This Article first establishes the right not to be subject to a decision based on automated processing, and follows this with several exceptions; decisions which do not conform with one of these exceptions may be set aside. The detailed obligation on Member States is to 'grant the right to every person not to be subject to a decision which produces legal effects concerning him or significantly affects him and which is based solely on automated processing of data intended to evaluate certain personal aspects relating to him, such as his performance at work, creditworthiness, reliability, conduct etc'. However, the Article accepts the validity of such a decision (and the negating of the Data Subject's right) when the processing:

(a) does not produce a 'legal effect', nor 'significantly' affect the Data Subject, nor concern any 'personal aspect' of the Data Subject.

(b) allows for a review of the decision (eg by staff), since the decision would then not be 'solely' the result of an automated process.

(c) results in a decision which relates to the performance of a contract (or entering into a contract) 'provided that the request (for the processing) by the Data Subject has been satisfied or that there are suitable measures to safeguard his legitimate interests'. The Article provides one example of a safeguard: 'arrangements allowing him to defend his point of view' (ie an appeal against the decision).

(d) 'is authorised by a law which also lays down measures to safeguard the Data Subject's legitimate interests'.

Article 16: Confidentiality of Processing
This Article stipulates that 'any person acting under the authority of the Controller or of the Processor' (eg staff, or a sub-contractor), 'including the Processor himself, who has access to personal data must not process them except on instructions from the Controller, unless he is required to do so by law'. Given that processing, by definition, is 'any operation performed on personal data' (eg collection, transmission, disclosure and destruction), then depending on the processing operations, these instructions might need to be quite detailed.

Article 17: Security of Processing
Controllers and Processors will be obliged, by law, to take 'appropriate technical and organisational measures to protect personal data against accidental or unlawful destruction or accidental loss, alteration, unauthorised disclosure or access, in particular where the processing involves the transmission of data over a network, and against all other unlawful forms of processing'; this, in essence, is a restatement of the Eighth Principle of the UK Act. However, this Article also specifies other security obligations for Controllers. These are:

(a) a requirement to have 'regard to the state of the art' with respect to security measures (ie be aware of new security fandangos);

(b) to see that 'such measures shall ensure a level of security appropriate to the risks represented by the processing and the nature of the data to be protected' (ie carry out some kind of risk analysis), and to take account of 'the cost of their implementation' (ie how cost-effective the new security methods would be);

(c) to 'choose a Processor providing sufficient guarantees in respect of the technical security measures and organisational measures governing the processing to be carried out', and to 'ensure compliance with those measures';

(d) to record the security measures adopted 'in writing or in another equivalent form'. This 'contract or legal act' shall stipulate that 'the Processor shall act only on instructions from the Controller' and that the Processor shall meet the security obligations of this Article.

Articles 18–20: Notification

Articles 18–20 outline a number of options, which range from a Controller having to obtain prior approval of the Data Protection Authority to process personal data, to exemption from the duty to notify. These options are:

(a) full notification. Articles 18(1) and 19 establish a regime very similar to the current UK registration framework (ie Data User identification details and, for each Purpose, a description of Data Subject Types, Data Classes, Sources, Disclosures and Overseas Transfers). Article 19 slightly modifies this list: it omits the obligation to register Sources; it expands Disclosures to include 'Recipients or categories of Recipient', and adds an obligation to notify 'a general description allowing a preliminary assessment to be made of the appropriateness of the measures taken . . . to ensure security of processing'.

(b) simplification of, or exemption from, notification. Article 18(2) allows Member States to determine that certain personal data, whose processing is 'unlikely . . . to affect adversely the rights and freedoms of Data Subjects', can be exempt from notification or be subject to a simplified notification procedure. UK legislation can thus be expected to continue the exemptions from registration found in the current UK Act (eg payroll and accounts; Section 32), where each exemption sets out a list of conditions to which Data Users must conform (otherwise the exemption is invalid). Simplification of the registration process, on the basis of the risks which the processing signifies to Data Subjects, is actively being considered by the UK's Data Protection Registrar.

(c) notification through a designated official. Article 18(2) permits Member States to provide for simplified notification or for exemption from notifying the Data Protection Authority, if national law requires a Controller to appoint 'a data protection official' who is responsible 'for ensuring in an independent manner the internal application of the national provisions taken pursuant to this Directive', and 'for keeping the register of processing operations carried out by the Controller'.

(d) special exemption from notification. Through Article 18(3), Member States can exempt from the notification procedures any 'registers' of personal data which, by statute, have to be made public; in this way, the UK Government can broadly maintain the exemption from registration found in Section 34(1) of the UK Act.

(e) optional notification. Article 18(5) states that 'Member States may stipulate that certain or all non-automatic processing operations involving personal data shall be notified, or provide for these processing operations to be subject to simplified notification'. Given the current UK Government's opposition to the extension of legal safeguards to structured manual records, it would be surprising if it decided to take advantage of this provision.

(f) advance notification. Article 20 permits Member States to define certain processing operations as 'likely to present specific risks to the rights and freedoms of Data Subjects'. If a State takes advantage of this provision, the Data Protection Authority will be obliged to carry out checks prior to permitting a Controller to start processing operations.

Article 21: Publicising of Processing Operation
Member States are obliged to 'take measures to ensure that processing operations are publicised', and to ensure that 'a register of processing operations' is open to public inspection. Thus, there will be a list in the public domain, equivalent to the Register established by the UK Act, of Controllers and their Purposes, categories of Data Subjects, Data Classes, Recipients or categories of Recipients, and Transfers to third countries. However, there is no obligation for this public register to include the notified 'general descriptions' of security arrangements, although States can legislate for this if they so wish. If an exemption or simplified notification applies, then 'Controllers or another body appointed by the Member States' must make available, on request, 'at least' the information that would have been notified if an exemption or simplification did not apply.

Chapter III: Judicial Remedies. Liability and Sanctions

Articles 22–24 link national data protection legislation to the judicial process; they oblige Member States to:

(a) enable any person to have access to the Courts and 'provide for the right of every person to a judicial remedy for any breach of the rights guaranteed him by the national law'. The UK Act establishes such access through Sections 21, 24 and 25.

(b) allow 'any person who has suffered damage as a result of an unlawful processing operation or of any act incompatible with the national provisions' to seek compensation from the Controller. This extends compensation possibilities considerably when compared with those provided by Section 22 (inaccuracy) and Section 23 (inadequate security) of the UK Act. In effect, any breach of Chapter II, if damage arose as a result, could lead to a claim for compensation.

(c) 'lay down sanctions to be imposed in case of infringement of the provisions adopted pursuant to this Directive'. In the UK Act, these find expression through criminal sanctions (eg in Section 5), and through the various Supervisory Notices available to the Registrar (eg the power to enforce compliance with the Principles).

Chapter IV: Transfer of Personal Data to Third Countries

Article 25 stipulates, in essence, that transfer of personal data to Third Countries can take place so long as 'the third country in question ensures an adequate level of protection'.

Article 26 defines derogations from Article 25, and indicates that transfer can occur even though an adequate level of protection cannot be guaranteed, on condition that:

(a) 'the Data Subject has given his consent unambiguously to the proposed transfer'.

(b) 'the transfer is necessary' as part of 'a contract between the Data Subject and the Controller', or for 'the implementation of precontractual measures'.

(c) 'the transfer is necessary for the conclusion or performance of a contract concluded in the interest of the Data Subject between the Controller and a Third

Party'. This is a very flexible condition, and permits the Controller to transfer personal data to any Third Party anywhere in the world (eg for telesales, airline bookings etc).

(d) 'the transfer is necessary or legally required on important public interest grounds, or for the establishment, exercise or defence of legal claims'; as mentioned with respect to Article 7, 'public interest' is a vague term.

(e) 'the transfer is necessary in order to protect the vital interests of the Data Subject' (see Article 7).

(f) 'the transfer is made from a register which according to laws or regulations is intended to provided information to the public'. The logic for this provision seems to be as follows: the personal data are in the public domain, and consequently are insecurely held (ie anybody can access the data). Thus, there are no grounds on which to prohibit the transfer of the data to a very 'insecure' third country, irrespective of what use may then be made of those data.

(g) Controllers are authorised, by Member States, to transfer personal data to countries which offer an inadequate level of protection, if a Controller 'adduces adequate safeguards with respect to the protection of the privacy and fundamental rights and freedoms of individuals' (eg via a contract).

Chapter V: Codes of Conduct

Article 27 allows for Member States and the Commission to 'encourage the drawing up of Codes of Conduct intended to contribute to the proper implementation of the national provisions'; draft Codes can then be submitted 'to the opinion of the national (data protection) authority' which in turn can seek 'the views of Data Subjects or their representatives'. Draft Codes can be submitted to the Working Party (a group of Data Protection Commissioners; see Articles 29 and 30) to determine for instance, whether the Codes would comply with national law. In short, these Community Codes will have the same status as Codes of Practice under the current UK Act; whilst a Code is for 'guidance' only, disregard could trigger sanctions by the professional body which produced that Code, and complaints to the Authority that the processing operations had contravened the legitimate expectations of Data Subjects.

Chapter VI: Supervisory Authority

Article 28 concerns Data Protection Authorities. It requires each Member State to 'provide that one or more public authorities are responsible for monitoring the application within its territory of the provisions (in) this Directive'. Member States with a federal structure can thus have more than one Data Protection Authority (eg one per Land in Germany). From the UK perspective, the Article also establishes a more powerful Authority than the current Office of the Data Protection Registrar, which will be:

(a) endowed with 'investigative powers, such as powers of access to data forming the subject-matter of processing operations (covered by this Directive) and powers to collect all the information necessary for the performance of its supervisory duties'.

(b) equipped with 'effective powers of intervention, such as (that of) ordering the blocking, erasure or destruction of data, of imposing a temporary or definitive ban on processing, of warning or admonishing the Controller, or that of referring the matter to national parliaments or other political institutions'.

(c) involved in the prior checking of certain sensitive processing operations (see Article 20).

(d) consulted when Member States are 'drawing up administrative measures or regulations relating to the protection of individuals' rights and freedoms with regard to the processing of personal data'.

(e) able 'to engage in legal proceedings' when breaches of national legislation occur, subject to appeal through the Courts.

(f) able to 'hear claims lodged by any person, or by an association representing that person, concerning the protection of his rights and freedoms in regard to the processing of personal data'.

(g) able to 'hear claims for checks on the lawfulness of data processing lodged by any person when the national provisions adopted pursuant to Article 13 of this Directive apply'.

(h) expected to produce 'a report on its activities at regular intervals' (eg as per the UK Registrar's reports to Parliament).

(i) expected to liaise with other Data Protection Authorities 'to the extent necessary for the performance of their duties'.

Articles 29–30 establish a Working Party whose members will include one representative of the Data Protection Authority in each Member State (if the State has a federal structure, then a joint representative of all its Authorities has to be found), as well as one representative each from the Commission and from the Community. The Working Party will have 'advisory status and act independently' and will be able to convey, to the Commission, its opinions on various data protection problems (eg on 'Codes of Conduct', divergences between national legislation, data protection problems occurring in third countries, implementation of the Directive by Member States). The Working Party will publish an annual report which will be presented to the European Parliament and the Commission. At first reading this seems a body with little power except to put forward opinions; much will depend on its expertise and the status accorded to it by Member States.

Chapter VII: Community Implementing Measures

Article 31 deals with 'The Committee'. This Committee is, so to speak, the political powerhouse. It comprises representatives of the Member States, is chaired by the representative of the Commission, and makes its decisions through qualified majority voting (which excludes the chair). If there is a data protection problem, the representative from the Commission submits draft measures to be adopted; the Committee then deliberates and delivers its opinion. If the Committee disagrees with the Commission, then the matter is remitted to the Council of Ministers for resolution (at most within 3 months). In this way, initiatives or opinions arising from Working Party concerns can be reported to the Commission, considered by the Committee, and adopted if agreed; once adopted, the measures 'shall apply immediately'. Note that the Committee is not obliged to follow the Working Party's advice, neither is it obliged to inform or even seek the views of the Working Party if it wishes to pursue a data protection matter on its own initiative.

Final Provisions

The Directive, although agreed in July 1995, was not formally adopted until October 24th. Articles 32 and 33 dictate that Member States shall enact the required new legislation within three years of the date of adoption and provide some 'breaking in' flexibility which allows States to:

(a) apply a delay of up to three years, from the date the national legislation comes into force, with respect to personal data whose processing is underway at that time. This means there is no delay with respect to personal data whose processing begins after this time (even if the data are processed in a manual filing system).

(b) apply a nine year delay, from the date the national legislation comes into force, to the application of three Articles with respect to personal data already held in manual filing systems. These Articles are: Article 6 (Principles), Article 7 (Lawfulness of processing), and Article 8 (special personal data). Note that this extension does not include Article 12 (ie the rights of Data Subjects)

(c) provide, subject to suitable safeguards, that 'data kept for the sole purpose of historical research' need never be brought into conformity with Articles 6–8. Note that this derogation is limited; it excludes any other form of research, and leaves such data subject to the other Articles in the Directive.

Finale: Data Protection News

The views expressed are those of the authors and are a condensed and revised version of a 22,000 word analysis of the Directive published in Issue No.21 (Spring 1995) of Data Protection News (a quarterly publication). If you wish to obtain further details about Data Protection News, please contact Dr. Chris Pounder, Data Protection News, Hoskyns Group plc, 190 City Road, City House, London EC1V 2QH. Telephone 0171–814–5738. Email: <dp.news@hoskyns.co.uk>

Bibliography

The EC Data Protection Directive 1995
http://www2.echo.lu/legal/en/dataprot/dataprot.html
The pages of the Legal Advisory Board of the European Commission which contain, amongst other things, the full text of the Directive albeit an unofficial version.

The Journal of Information Law and Technology
http://ltc.law.warwick.ac.uk/elj/jilt/dp/
The first issue of this new UK based electronic journal contains a useful special feature on the EC Data Protection Directive. This feature contains articles on the impact of the Directive from the UK, Danish, Dutch, Irish and Swedish perspectives.

Pounder, C and Kosten, F 'Surfing The Internet – Skating on Thin Ice? published by UK Index. **http://www.ukindex.co.uk/dataprot.html**

The UK Data Protection Registrar **http://www.open.gov.uk/dpr/dprhome.htm**
The home page of the Office of the Registrar which includes a brief outline of the UK Data Protection Act 1984.

THE USE OF PUBLIC INTEREST IMMUNITY CLAIMS IN CRIMINAL CASES

The Earl Grey Memorial Lecture, University of Newcastle upon Tyne, 29 February 1996

The Right Hon. Sir Richard Scott

Vice-Chancellor of the Supreme Court

First Published in Web Journal of Current Legal Issues in association with Blackstone Press Ltd.

CONTENTS

Introduction

I am honoured to have been asked to give this year's Earl Grey Memorial Lecture and was interested to notice Earl Grey's association with Southern Africa. It was he, I suspect, who gave his name to Greytown, a town in Northern Natal not far from my home in Natal, and who gave his name also to at least two leading South

African schools, one in Bloemfontein, the other in East London. So I am particularly pleased to be giving the Earl Grey Lecture.

I hope you will forgive me for having chosen as the subject of the lecture a legal issue. It is not, however, an arcane legal issue. It is an issue which relates to the conduct of criminal trials and the need to ensure that trials are fair.

There would I think be general agreement that criminal trials are not fair if documents or information to which the prosecution have access but the defence do not, and that if disclosed might enable a defendant to prove his innocence, are withheld from him. It is in this context that Public Interest Immunity claims (hereafter PII claims) must be considered.

May I make clear what I mean by PII claims. They are claims made on public interest grounds to withhold documents or information from being produced or given in evidence in Court proceedings. These claims may be made and are frequently made, in civil cases and from time to time in criminal proceedings. The great seminal cases establishing the principles of public interest immunity law have, however, been civil cases not criminal cases. I want to suggest to you this afternoon that the application to criminal trials of PII principles derived from civil cases and designed for application in civil cases has been a mistake and an impediment to the evolution of satisfactory principles for dealing with PII claims in criminal trials.

I make that suggestion with a certain amount of trepidation. I am not a criminal lawyer. I did no criminal work in practice at the Bar and as a judge I have never presided over a criminal trial or taken part in a criminal appeal. My card of entry, however, is the examination I have had to give over the past three years to the PII claims that were made in connection with the *Matrix Churchill* trial and the *Ordtec* trial. I have been educated by submissions explaining and justifying the practice and procedure that attended those claims put before me by a number of government lawyers, by prosecuting counsel in the two cases and by the Attorney-General.

The Matrix Churchill Trial

In the *Matrix Churchill* trial three defendants, directors of Matrix Churchill Ltd., were charged with export control offences. They were charged with exporting to Iraq machine tools capable of being used and intended to be used for the manufacture of munitions – shells, missiles and the like – while dishonestly concealing from the government licensing authorities that the machine tools were intended for that use. They proposed to mount a two-pronged defence – they said, first, that they had been encouraged by Mr Alan Clark, when he was Minister for Trade in 1988, to conceal any intended military production uses of their machine tools and to emphasise the capability of the machine tools to be used for civil production purposes. They said, second, that in any event Government, or sections of Government, had known that their machine tools were intended for military production and that they had nonetheless been granted export licences. One of the problems of this second line defence is to decide what one means by 'Government'. 'Government' consists of many thousands of individuals and many different sections of Government Departments, agencies and the like. It would obviously be of some importance to the defendants to show that the knowledge they alleged was held by as wide and influential a section of Government as possible. To establish this proposed line of defence they needed, therefore, Government documents either showing that the intended use of their machine tools was known or providing a basis from which that knowledge might reasonably be inferred and which could be used to cross-examine Government witnesses.

Accordingly, the defendants applied for Government documents. Government met their application by making PII claims. Ministers signed certificates stating that if the various documents covered by the certificates were disclosed, grave and unquantifiable damage might be done to the public interest. At a hearing before the trial judge counsel for the Crown argued, as he had been instructed to do, that the documents ought not to be disclosed. The trial judge read the documents, concluded that they ought to be disclosed and ordered their disclosure. They provided the basis for a substantial cross-examination of Government witnesses, including Mr Alan Clark, to be mounted by defence counsel. The upshot of this, following Mr Clark's agreement in cross-examination that he did not regard the possible use of the machine tools to manufacture conventional weapons as matter of concern, was the collapse of the prosecution. The rest is history.

The documents covered by the unsuccessful PII claims in the Matrix Churchill case fell broadly into two classes. First, there were documents passing between officials and Ministers in the ordinary Government departments, the Department of Trade and Industry, the Ministry of Defence and the Foreign and Commonwealth Office, regarding the licensing decisions on machine tools exports to Iraq that were being made. Second there were documents mainly emanating from intelligence agencies which disclosed information coming from intelligence sources regarding the use or likely use Iraq might make of these machine tools.

The justification for these PII claims was that the making of PII claims of this character in civil cases was well established and that the same principles were applicable in criminal cases.

The Osman case

The proposition that the PII principles applicable to civil cases were applicable also to criminal cases was based on the judgment of Lord Justice Mann in *R* v *Governor of Brixton Prison, Ex parte Osman* [1991] 1 WLR 281. The case arose out of the proposed extradition of Mr Osman to Hong Kong to face charges of conspiracy, bribery, theft and false accounting. He wanted to resist extradition and sought to rely on certain correspondence passing between the English Magistrates' Court and the Home Office and between the Home Office and the Government of Hong Kong. The Crown claimed PII protection for the correspondence. It is important to notice that the PII claim was made not in a criminal trial but in a habeas corpus application. There were, it was held, reasons which had nothing to do with PII why Mr Osman was not entitled to rely on this correspondence. But on the PII point, Mann LJ posed the question (at p 287): '. . . is public interest immunity claimable in criminal proceedings'?. He answered the question by saying that:-

> '. . .there is no discernible reason why the immunity should not apply in criminal proceedings'.

The decision of Mann LJ in *ex parte Osman* has been taken as justifying the proposition that the principles of PII established in the civil cases to which I will in a moment refer are applicable also to criminal trials.

Are civil PII principles applicable in criminal trials?

Bearing in mind that *ex parte Osman* was not a criminal trial but was a habeas corpus case, I am not sure that this reliance on *ex parte Osman* was ever justified. But, assuming that it was, I want to question the proposition that the PII principles applicable to civil cases are applicable also to criminal trials.

a. Criminal cases

Let me make clear at the outset that there is no doubt and never has been that PII claims of an appropriate character can be and should continue to be made in criminal trials. Documents and evidence relating to informants provide the classic case in point. Documents disclosing the identity of an informant, or disclosing the channels through which information about the offence has been obtained by the prosecuting authority, will not ordinarily be made available to the accused, nor will questions of witnesses designed to reveal this information be allowed, unless, in either case, the disclosure is necessary to prevent a miscarriage of justice.
This principle was well established at least as long ago as 1890. In *Marks* v *Beyfus* (1890) 25 QBD 494, the judge at a criminal trial refused to order a witness to give the name of informants. He was upheld by the Court of Appeal. Lord Esher MR (at p 498) referred to the 'rule clearly established and acted on . . . that in a public prosecution a witness cannot be asked such questions as will disclose the informer. . . .' Lord Esher went on to make clear the limits to this rule. He said (ibid) that:

> 'if . . . the judge should be of opinion that the disclosure of the name of the informant is necessary or right in order to show the prisoner's innocence then one public policy is in conflict with another public policy, and that which says that an innocent man is not to be condemned when his innocence can be proved is the policy that must prevail.'

This limitation is, obviously, of crucial importance. But the point I wish to make is that the propriety of making PII claims in criminal cases has been accepted for a long time. I repeat that there is no doubt that PII claims can be made in criminal trials. The question for consideration is not whether PII claims can be made in criminal cases. They obviously can. The question is, first, what sort of PII claims is it proper to make in criminal cases and second, how should PII claims in criminal cases be dealt with once they are made.

b. Civil cases

The great civil cases in the House of Lords, *Duncan* v *Cammell Laird* [1942] AC 624, *Conway* v *Rimmer* [1968] AC 910, *Burmah Oil* v *Bank of England* [1980] AC 1090 and *Air Canada* v *Secretary of State for Trade (No 2)* [1983] 2 AC 394, established a number of principles of PII law and practice.

Common to all these cases was that PII claims for protection of documents either on a contents basis or on a class basis could be made. A word of explanation may be necessary. The contents of a document may be such that, if disclosed, damage to the public interest would be likely to follow. Documents revealing the names or working practices of members of the SIS provide an obvious example. PII protection for such documents can be claimed on a contents basis. Many documents, however, have nothing in their contents that can be pointed to as being likely, if disclosed, to cause damage to the public interest. But they may nonetheless be documents that, in the opinion of Ministers, ought not, because of the particular class into which they fall, to be disclosed. If such documents are to be protected from disclosure, the protection must be claimed on a class basis. Viscount Simon, in *Duncan* v *Cammell Laird* gave this classic description of the principle underlying PII claims. He said (at p 686):

> 'The principle to be applied in every case is that documents otherwise relevant and liable to production must not be produced if the public interest requires that they should be withheld. This test may be satisfied, either (a) by having regard to the contents of the particular document, or (b) by the fact that the document belongs to a class which on grounds of public interest, must as a class be withheld from production.'

He gave an example of a justifiable class claim (at p 642): 'where the practice of keeping a class of documents secret is necessary for the proper functioning of the public service'. Lord Reid, in *Conway* v *Rimmer*, said (at p 952) that he did not doubt 'that there are certain classes of documents which ought not to be disclosed whatever their content may be'. He instanced 'Cabinet minutes and the like'.

In *Duncan* v *Cammell Laird*, the House of Lords held that it was not open to the court to go behind a Minister's statement that damage to the public interest would be caused by production of the documents in question. The Minister's statement on the matter was held to be conclusive. On this point, but only on this point, the House of Lords in *Conway* v *Rimmer* disagreed. They held it was open to the Court to require the documents in question to be produced for the Court's inspection and then for the Court itself to decide whether or not the requirements of justice in the case overrode the particular public interest invoked by the Minister in claiming immunity from production of the documents. This decision introduced, therefore, the so-called balancing exercise. Pre-*Conway* v *Rimmer* any balance between the requirements of justice on the one hand and the public interest against disclosure on the other hand would have been struck, if it was struck at all, by the Minister. The Minister's certificate that the public interest required the documents to be withheld from production could not be challenged. But post *Conway* v *Rimmer* the final decision as to where, on balance, the public interest lay was with the Court.

But, as I have already said, these were both civil cases. Such references to criminal cases as may be found in the speeches in the two cases do not suggest that the principles being enunciated were thought to apply also to criminal cases. In *Duncan* v *Cammell Laird* Viscount Simon said that (at pp 633–634):

> 'The judgment of the House in the present case is limited to civil actions and the practice, as applied to criminal trials, where an individual's life or liberty may be at stake, is not necessarily the same.'

That seems a clear enough indication.

Viscount Simon cited with approval a passage from the judgment of Eyre CJ in *R* v *Hardy* (1794) 24 St Tr 199, a criminal case:

> '. . . if it can be made to appear that really and truly it is necessary to the investigation of the truth of the case that the name of the person [i.e. the informer] should be disclosed, I should be very unwilling to stop it.'

In 1956 the then Lord Chancellor, Lord Kilmuir, in a statement to the House of Lords said that:

> 'We also propose that if medical documents, or indeed other documents, are relevant to the defence in criminal proceedings Crown privilege should not be claimed'.

Lord Reid referred to this statement in his speech in *Conway* v *Rimmer* and then, in countering the argument that if the documents were not protected from disclosure 'freedom and candour of communication' would be prejudiced, said (at p 942):

> 'So we have the curious result that freedom and candour of communication is supposed not to be inhibited by knowledge of the writer that this report may be disclosed in a criminal case but would still be supposed to be inhibited if he thought that his report might be disclosed in a civil case.'

This remark seems to me to make it clear that Lord Reid did not regard the Crown privilege being claimed in the *Conway* v *Rimmer* malicious prosecution action as being any bar to disclosure of the documents if relevant to a criminal trial.

Lord Pearce, in *Conway* v *Rimmer*, made a remark to the same effect. He said (at p 987):

> 'Moreover if, as at present [the document] may be disclosed in criminal proceedings, then there is already an outside chance of disclosure'.

It seems to me clear enough that in 1968, when *Conway* v *Rimmer* was decided, it was accepted that different principles applied in criminal proceedings. I would refer again to *Marks* v *Beyfus* decided in 1890. Lord Esher made it clear that 'if disclosure . . . is necessary or right in order to show the prisoner's innocence' the information about the informer would have to be disclosed. Lord Justice Bowen, in the same case, said that (at p 500):

> 'The only exception to such a rule [i.e. the rule against disclosure of an informant's name] would be upon a criminal trial, when the judge if he saw that the strict enforcement of the rule would be likely to cause a miscarriage of justice, might relax it (in favorem innocentiae); if he did not do so, there would be a risk of innocent people being convicted'.

Marks v *Beyfus* was decided nearly eighty years before *Conway* v *Rimmer*. But it is plain that the decision whether the information or documents relating to the informer would have to be disclosed was one that would be taken by the judge presiding over the criminal trial. The notion that a Minister's certificate would be conclusive plainly never applied to criminal trials. *Marks* v *Beyfus* was referred to with express approval by Lord Reid in his judgment in *Conway* v *Rimmer*.

But compare those dicta of Lord Esher and Bowen LJ, describing the approach in criminal cases, with Lord Reid's description of the balancing exercise to be carried out in civil cases. Lord Reid said (at p 940):

> 'There is the public interest that harm shall not be done to the nation or the public service by disclosure of certain documents and there is the public interest

> that the administration of justice shall not be frustrated by the withholding of documents which must be produced if justice is to be done.'

He pointed out that (ibid):

> 'There are many cases where the nature of the injury which would or might be done to the nation or the public service is of so grave a character that no other interest, public or private, can be allowed to prevail over it [but] there are many other cases where the possible injury to the public service is much less and there one would think that it would be proper to balance the public interests involved.'

Is the balancing exercise described by Lord Reid in the passages I have just cited, reconcilable with the insistence in *Marks* v *Beyfus* that, if disclosure is necessary to show the innocence of the accused, disclosure must be permitted?

c. The recent criminal cases

The approach in criminal cases described in *Marks* v *Beyfus* has been repeated in more recent cases.

In *R* v *Hallett* [1986] Crim LR 462, Lord Lane CJ referred to the 'rule of exclusion' that barred the disclosure of information that might identify informants and then went on:

> '. . . it is a rule which excludes evidence as to the identity of informants, unless the judge comes to the conclusion that it is necessary to override the rule and to admit the evidence in order to prevent a miscarriage of justice and in order to prevent the possibility that a man may by reason of the exclusion, be deprived of the opportunity of casting doubt on the case against him'.

Lord Lane concluded that 'if the judge does come to the conclusion that the lack of information as the identity of the informer is going to cause a miscarriage of justice, then he is under a duty to admit the evidence'. Is this conclusion consistent with a balancing exercise under which 'the nature of the injury which would or might be done to the nation or the public service [may be] of so grave a character that no other interest, public or private can be allowed to prevail over it'? I do not think so.

In *R v Agar* [1990] 2 All ER 442, Lord Justice Mustill (as he then was) said (at p 448):

> 'There was a strong, and absent any contrary indication, overwhelming public interest, in keeping secret the source of information: but, as the authorities show, there was an even stronger public interest in allowing a defendant to put forward a tenable case in its best light'.

In *R* v *Clowes* [1992] 3 All ER 440, Mr Justice Phillips (as he then was) made the point that I have been endeavouring to make. He said (at p 454):

> 'I do not find easy the concept of a balancing exercise between the nature of the public interest [against production of the documents] on the one hand and the degree and potential consequences of the risk of a miscarriage of justice on the other'.

It is, of course, inherent in the 'balancing exercise' to be carried out in a civil case in which a PII claim has been made that the weight of the public interest factors relied on as justifying the withholding of documents may require that the documents be withheld from the litigant who requires them notwithstanding that they may be crucial to his case. The passage I have cited from Lord Reid's judgment in *Conway* v *Rimmer* makes that clear. But is this ever a possibility in a criminal case? On the authority of *Marks* v *Beyfus*, *R* v *Hallett* and *R* v *Agar*, I would say 'No'.

d. The criteria for upholding PII claims in civil cases
It is instructive in this context, to notice the basis on which, in civil cases, non disclosure of documents on PII grounds has been upheld.

(i) '. . . where disclosure would be injurious to national defence, or to good diplomatic relations, or where the practice of keeping a class of documents secret is necessary for the proper functioning of the public service . . . and the minister feels it is his duty to deny access to material which would otherwise be available, there is no question but that the public interest must be preferred to any private consideration'. (Viscount Simon in *Duncan* v *Cammell Laird* at p 642)

Could that have been said if 'any private consideration' was that of a defendant in a criminal trial? Surely not.

(ii) 'If . . . national security would or might be imperilled by the production and consequent disclosure of certain documents, then the interest of a litigant must give way'. (Lord Morris in *Conway* v *Rimmer* at p 955)

Could that have been said if the 'litigant' were a defendant in a criminal trial. It could not.

(iii) '. . . if the production of a State Paper would be injurious to the public service, the general public interest must be considered paramount to the individual interest of a suitor in a court of justice' (Lord Morris in *Conway* v *Rimmer* at p 963)

A defendant in a criminal trial is not 'a suitor in a Court of justice' but, in any event, the remarks could not possibly have been made with a defendant in a criminal trial in mind.

And, finally,

(iv) '. . . it is for the party seeking discovery to establish clearly that the scale falls decisively in favour of [the public interest in the administration of justice] if he is to succeed in his quest. If he fails, even material clearly 'necessary . . . for disposing fairly of the case or matter must be withheld'. (Lord Wilberforce in *Air Canada* at p 442).

Could Lord Wilberforce have expressed this view if the party seeking discovery were a defendant in a criminal case? I am sure he could not.

The correct approach to PII claims in criminal trials

The passages I have cited make clear that, in a civil case, the public interest in the administration of justice, which underpins, of course, the private interest of the litigant who wants the documents, will sometimes have to give way to the greater weight of the public interest against disclosure. That, as I have said, is inherent in the balancing process.

What has such a balancing process to do with the public interest that a defendant in a criminal trial should have a fair trial and that an innocent man should not be convicted? The suggestion that the public interest would ever have to give way in a balancing exercise is, to my mind, a grotesque one and is, moreover, one that is contradicted by the dicta in the criminal cases to which I have referred.

But, if that is so, what should be the approach to PII claims made in criminal trials?

In answering that question recourse should, I suggest, be had to first principles rather than to principles distilled from the seminal civil cases to which I have referred.

a. The disclosure cases

A PII objection to the disclosure of a document does not, either in civil cases or in a criminal trial, need to be made except, in relation to a document that is, under the rules of discovery applicable to the proceedings, disclosable. The rules governing disclosure of documents in criminal cases have been authoritatively re-stated in some important recent decisions.

In a 1993 case, *R* v *Melvin* (unreported), Mr Justice Jowitt referred to the following passage from the Court of Appeal judgment in *R* v *Ward* [1993] 1 WLR 619 at 642:

> 'The obligation to disclose only arises in relation to evidence which is or may be material in relation to the issues which are expected to arise, or which unexpectedly do arise, in the course of the trial'.

Mr Justice Jowitt drew particular attention to the adjective 'material' and went on to say this:

> 'I would judge to be material in the realm of disclosure that which can be seen on a sensible appraisal by the prosecution: (1) to be relevant or possibly relevant to an issue in the case; (2) to raise or possibly to raise a new issue whose existence is not apparent from the evidence the prosecution proposes to use; (3) to hold out a real (as opposed to fanciful) prospect of providing a lead on evidence which goes to (1) or (2).'

This test of materiality has been expressly approved and adopted in two Court of Appeal cases. In *R* v *Keane* [1994] 1 WLR 746, the Lord Chief Justice, Lord Taylor, said (at p 752) that:

> 'The prosecution must identify the documents and information which are material according to the criteria set out above [i.e. Mr Justice Jowitt's criteria]. Having identified what is material, the prosecution should disclose it unless they wish to maintain that public interest immunity or other sensitivity justifies withholding some or all of it.'

In *R* v *Brown (Winston)* [1994] 1 WLR 1599 Lord Justice Steyn (as he then was) referred to 'The right of every accused to a fair trial' and observed that 'in our adversarial system, in which the police and prosecution control the investigatory process, an accused's right to fair disclosure is an inseparable part of his right to a fair trial'. After citing the passage from Mr Justice Jowitt's judgment in *R* v *Melvin* which had been adopted by the Lord Chief Justice in *R* v *Keane* as correctly stating the test of materiality for disclosure purposes, Lord Justice Steyn continued (at p 1606):

> 'This is a test which we would also adopt. It might be helpful, however, if we added a few comments under two headings. In the first place the phrase 'an issue in the case' must not be construed in the fairly narrow way in which it is used in a civil case. It must be given a broad interpretation'.

The application of Mr Justice Jowitt's criteria, adopted and applied by the Court of Appeal in *R* v *Keane* and *R* v *Brown (Winston)* will identify the documents that, subject to PII claims, must be disclosed to the defence. It is worth reminding oneself of the reason why 'material' documents have to be disclosed. It is in order to avoid the possibility that the defendant may, for want of the documents in question, be unable to pursue, or effectively to pursue, or to decide whether to pursue, a particular issue and that a miscarriage of justice may consequently be caused. But the breadth of the disclosure required by Jowitt J's criteria of 'materiality' makes it at least highly likely that among the 'material' documents will be found some whose potential to provide assistance to the defence will not be apparent. Some, indeed, may be positively harmful to the defence. Relevance is, after all, a strictly neutral concept. Similarly a PII claim may well cover documents with an apparent potential to assist the defence as well as others whose potential to assist the defence is not apparent.

b. Disclosure of documents which might assist the defence

As to documents which appear to have the potential to assist the defence, could a situation ever arise in which disclosure could be refused on PII grounds? This is, to my mind, a fundamental but conceptually simple, question. The answer to it, both on authority and on principle should, in my opinion, be a resounding 'No'. In the context of a criminal trial how can there be a more important public interest than that the defendant should have a fair trial and that documents which might assist him to establish his innocence should not be withheld from him? In civil cases where private interests are in competition, the interests of one party may from time to time have to be subordinated to the greater public good. But there surely cannot be any such subordination of the interests of a defendant in a criminal trial. In civil cases, the weight of the public interest factors against disclosure may justify a refusal to order disclosure notwithstanding that without disclosure an otherwise sound case might fail. But, in a criminal trial the balance must always come down in favour of disclosure if there is any real possibility that the withholding of the documents may cause or contribute to a miscarriage of justice. The public interest factors underlying the PII claim cannot ever, I suggest, have a weight sufficient to outweigh that possibility.

In criminal trials, once it has been decided that a document might be of assistance to the defence, that should be the end of the PII claim. If that is so, there is only one issue for decision when a PII claim is made in a criminal trial in respect of 'material' documents, namely, is there a real possibility (as opposed to a fanciful one) that the documents might be of assistance to the defence.

The present tenor of authority is that a judge adjudicating on a PII claim at a criminal trial does conduct a balancing exercise. In *R* v *Clowes*, Mr Justice Phillips expressed himself to be doing so (at p 454). But he rejected the PII claims. He said (at p 455):

> '. . . the likelihood of the [documents] containing additional material evidence is sufficient to justify upholding the witness summonses in the face of the public interest immunity involved'.

He was not prepared to run the risk that the withholding of the documents might lead to a miscarriage of justice.

In *R* v *Keane*, the Lord Chief Justice said that 'if the disputed material may prove the defendant's innocence or avoid a miscarriage of justice, then the balance comes down resoundingly in favour of disclosing it'.

In *R* v *Brown (Winston)*, Lord Justice Steyn said that (at p 1608) '. . . the judge must always perform a balancing exercise taking into account the public interest and the interests of the defendant', but he went on to cite the passage from Lord Taylor's judgment in *R* v *Keane* that I have just cited.

It does not, perhaps, matter whether or not the process required to be performed by judges in criminal trials when dealing with PII claims is referred to as a balancing exercise. I would not myself so describe it. The reason I would not do so is that the weight of the public interest factors underlying the PII claim cannot, or should not, be allowed to tip the scale. *R* v *Keane* and *R* v *Brown (Winston)* concerned documents which might assist the defence. A document which might be of assistance to the defence would, I think, necessarily be a document that might 'prove the defendant's innocence or avoid a miscarriage of justice.' The dicta of the Lord Chief Justice in *R* v *Keane* and of Lord Justice Steyn in *R* v *Brown (Winston)* suggest that it is not possible to have public interest factors in favour of non-disclosure whose weight can tip the scale against disclosure of such documents. If that is an accurate assessment, then the only question on a PII claim in a criminal case is whether the documents might be of assistance to the defence. If the posing of that question and the reaching of an answer are to be described as carrying out a balancing exercise, so be it. But it is important to recognise that it is a balancing exercise of a very different character from that performed in civil cases.

c. Are 'class' claims ever appropriate in criminal trials?

I want now to return to the matter of class claims. I have, I must confess, serious misgivings as to whether PII class claims should any longer be regarded as acceptable in criminal cases. The reason for this is two-fold. On the one hand it seems to me that genuinely sensitive documents can be protected by PII contents claims. All 'informant' documents can, I would think, be covered by contents claims. Class claims to cover documents emanating from the intelligence and security agencies have in the past been regarded as an example, par excellence, of documents which should be given PII protection because of the class to which they belong and irrespective of their contents. But evidence given to my Inquiry by Mr David Bickford, the Legal Adviser both to the SIS and to the Security Service was to the effect that class claims were not necessary. He said:

> 'To date the Services [i.e. the SIS and the Security Service] have had no real difficulties protecting their sensitive information from disclosure by relying on contents claims.'

He added that 'if any information held by the Services was relevant to the issues in any criminal trial it [would be], in my view, inconceivable that the Court would weigh the balance in favour of a class claim'. I entirely agree.

Later in his evidence, he said:

> 'I am concerned that the use of class claims undermines the credibility of the Services. The Services obtain information in the same way as law enforcement

> agencies (but usually in a more intensive and long term manner). Agents are used, surveillance is deployed, eavesdropping and clandestine searches are made. These matters will not protect something that is relevant to the issues.'

In short, in Mr Bickford's view, which I share, any genuinely sensitive material can be protected by contents claims. Seeking PII protection by means of class claims is not necessary for protecting sensitive material.

The second reason why, in my view, PII class claims should not be made in criminal cases is that experience has shown that the existence of class claims has encouraged Government to seek protection for ever expanding categories of documents.

Lord Upjohn in *Conway* v *Rimmer* referred to (at p 993):

> 'documents which by their very nature fall in a class which require protection such as, only by way of example, Cabinet papers, Foreign Office dispatches, the security of the State, high level interdepartmental minutes and correspondence and documents pertaining to the general administration of the naval, military and air force services.'

Lord Salmon in the *Burmah Oil* case referred to (at p 1121):

> 'Classes of documents which are immune from production because their production would imperil the safety of the state or diplomatic relations, and also classes of documents such as Cabinet minutes and others whose immunity from production is considered necessary for the proper functioning of the public service.'

Lord Wilberforce said in the *Air Canada* case that (at p 437):

> 'the documents now in issue . . . can claim to bear a higher degree of confidentiality than those involved in *Burmah*: they relate directly to the making of decisions as to government policy in a sensitive area, viz. the economic and financial policy of the government . . .'

Whether, in the absence of any sensitive contents that would qualify for PII protection on a contents basis, documents in these classes do require PII protection is a matter for debate and not here in point. What is in point is that the documents contemplated as qualifying for PII protection on a class basis are, broadly speaking, documents relating to matters of high policy. And yet, in both the *Matrix Churchill* case and in the *Ordtec* case (at trial, not at the appeal) PII protection was claimed on a class basis for a number of documents that could not possibly have been described as relating to 'high policy'. The lawyers in the Treasury Solicitor's Department who were responsible for advising on the PII claims took the view that PII class protection should be claimed for any documents relating to advice given by an official to a Minister, whether relating to formulation of policy or to the taking of an executive decision. In oral evidence given at my Inquiry, one of their lawyers expressed the opinion that:

> '. . . it is regarded as damaging for the public interest that any of this process [i.e. the process of advising Ministers and decision making] should be exposed. . . .'

He was asked, 'Is this approach bred of a desire for convenient administration?'
He answered, 'I think so, yes.'
He amplified his answer thus:

> 'It would be very difficult to distinguish between degrees of policy advice, whether it is of a high or medium level, and the tendency is to regard all advice on policy of significant importance as being within the class. As a result, a cautious approach is followed, and all documents of such nature are claimed to be within the class.
>
> The damage to the public interest, if the class did not exist, would be the exposure of the decision making process.'

Is this what the Law Lords who gave the several judgments in the House of Lords cases to which I have referred had in mind in endorsing the making of PII class claims? I do not think so.

Whether judicial authority supports the making of class claims *in civil cases* in respect of government documents of the nature of some of those for which PII protection was sought in the *Matrix Churchill* case, seems to me very doubtful. But even assuming that these PII class claims would have been justifiable in a civil case, they ought not, in any opinion, to have been made at a criminal trial.

I have already observed that, strictly, PII only arises in respect of documents whose relevance to the issues in the case would otherwise require their disclosure. Wide criteria of relevance are now, under the authority of *Keane* and *Brown (Winston)* applied in criminal cases. One of the reasons and justifications for the very wide ambit of disclosure of documents required in criminal cases is, I believe, that the selection of documents that, although relevant to an issue in the case, can safely be withheld from the defence without the risk of a miscarriage of justice is often very difficult. An error in selection, however justifiable it may seem at the time, may later transpire to have been prejudicial to the defence and to the fairness of the trial. So if, in criminal cases, documents are material and prima facie disclosable, they ought, I suggest, to be disclosed unless they have a sensitivity of content that would justify a PII contents claim. Moreover, experience does suggest that if PII class claims continue to be sanctioned in criminal trials, Whitehall departments will inevitably seek to bring within the recognised classes an increasing range of documents. I see no realistic reason to suppose that the instinctive Whitehall reaction to seek to withhold Government documents from public inspection is likely to change.

In my opinion, whatever the justification and authority for PII class claims in civil cases, PII claims in criminal trials should be confined to contents claims. Class claims should not be allowed.

There is a further point which distinguishes PII claims in civil cases from those in criminal trials. In a civil case (including a habeas corpus application of the *ex parte Osman* variety), if an order for disclosure of documents is made the case will continue on foot with the material in question disclosed to the parties. In a criminal case, on the other hand, an order for disclosure will not necessarily lead to the disclosure of the documents. The prosecuting authority will have the option of discontinuing the prosecution in order to safeguard the material from disclosure. In a civil case between private litigants, the government, the police or other public authority seeking to resist disclosure will, once the PII claim has been rejected, have no means of avoiding disclosure. The option of discontinuing the case will not be available.

Conclusion

In summary, there are substantial differences between the operation of PII in civil cases and the operation of PII in criminal cases. The most significant of these differences is, I suggest, that in criminal cases there is no fine balance to be struck between, on the one hand, the public interest underlying the PII claim and, on the other hand, the public interest in the administration of justice. This balance must always be struck in a civil case and the weight of the former may often tip the scale. In criminal cases the only question is, or should be, whether the documents in question may assist the defendant in proving his innocence. This is not just a difference in the weight to be placed in the scale in favour of disclosure. It involves a quite different approach to the issue of disclosure. The notion that PII law and practice are applicable in the same way both to PII claims in civil cases is, in my view, wrong and has served to hinder and distort a sensible development of the law and practice in this field.

LEGAL PRACTICE COURSE RESEARCH SKILLS: TEACHING COMPETENCE OR RAISING AWARENESS?

Hugh Brayne

Professor of Law and Head of Kingston Law School, formerly Director of Professional Legal Education, University of Northumbria at Newcastle <h.brayne@kingston.ac.uk>

and

Peter Breakey

Senior Lecturer and Course Leader of the Part-Time Legal Practice Course, University of Northumbria at Newcastle c/o <Kelly.Wallace@unn.ac.uk>

First Published in Web Journal of Current Legal Issues in association with Blackstone Press Ltd.

SUMMARY

This article considers the changes that need to be made by both staff and students in order to achieve the standards set by the Law Society for the Legal Practice Course[1] skill of Legal Research. It describes a research awareness exercise conducted this year at the University of Northumbria which was designed to raise awareness and to promote competence in legal research. (Although the article

1 The Legal Practice Course is a nine month course which must be completed by all those who wish to qualify as solicitors in England and Wales. Students on the course will have usually have completed either a three year law degree or a degree in a different discipline followed by the nine month CPE. On completing the LPC most students will enter a two year training contract. Introduced in 1994, the LPC requires students to cover the four 'core' subjects of Business Law and Practice, Conveyancing, Litigation and Wills Probate and Administration, together with two options. As well as passing a number of assessments in these subjects (which incorporate the pervasive themes of Financial Services, European Law, Professional Practice and Revenue Law) students must demonstrate competence in five legal skills, drafting, advocacy, interviewing, negotiation, and legal research. The standard required to pass the course as a whole is one of readiness to enter a training contract.

relates primarily to the Legal Practice Course (LPC), what we did and why we did it should be of relevance to all readers interested in student legal research.)

CONTENTS

What prior research experience do LPC students have?

LPC students usually arrive with either three or one year's study of law under their belts. In our view legal research ought to have been the common element underpinning their CPE or undergraduate studies and we hope that the review of legal education by the Lord Chancellor's Advisory Committee will lead to changes in this direction. At present however the research experience of LPC students is very variable and with many students it is best to assume no previous experience.

Should research be taught anyway?

Perhaps the idea of teaching the skill of research is a contradiction in terms. Perhaps the experience of previous generations, who taught themselves whilst in practice how to look things up, was good enough. As articled clerks and, before that, as students on the Part II and the Law Society Final courses respectively, we were both given little or no guidance on legal research. Perhaps it was assumed that we had learned these skills at the academic stage. Perhaps no thought was given to the subject at all. In any event, what we learned was self-taught. We tended to learn by trial and error and by watching others, copying their strengths but repeating their weaknesses.

Do poor research skills pervade the profession?

Neither of us is surprised, in the light of our own legal education and training, by the findings reported by the Consumers' Association in the October 1995 issue of Which? magazine, that 19 out of 20 solicitors failed to give best advice on a commonplace consumer problem These solicitors appear, according to the findings, to have been willing to give advice without researching it adequately. The Law Society's President described the findings as 'simply a publicity opportunity . . . rather than a serious attempt to look at service given by solicitors.' (Ames 1995). Regardless of whether or not he is right about the quality of the research findings, we think there may be a deeper problem which needs to be acknowledged. Is it surprising that practitioners have difficulty with research when, until the advent of the LPC, it had been unnecessary to demonstrate research skills before qualification? What was learned was at undergraduate level, generally in a non-practical context, or not at all.

Progress?

But here is the good news. The profession has, in theory, committed itself to the highest standards in legal research training for the next generation. Students on the LPC are required to demonstrate competence in legal research before obtaining the diploma which entitles them to start a training contract. On paper the requirements for competence are very high. The Law Society's written standards for research require that:

> 'The student should understand the need for thorough investigation of factual and legal issues and should understand the need for preparation and the best way to undertake it.
>
> The student should be able to:—
>
> (a) determine the objectives of the employer or client;
> (b) identify and analyse factual material;
> (c) identify the legal context in which factual issues arise;
> (d) identify sources for investigating relevant facts;
> (e) determine whether further facts are required;
> (f) identify and analyse legal issues;
> (g) apply relevant legal issues to facts;
> (h) relate the central legal and factual issues to each other;
> (i) identify the legal, factual and other issues presented by documents;
> (j) analyse a client's instructions and be able to identify the legal, factual and other issues presented by them;
> (k) present the results of research in a clear, useful and reliable form.
>
> The student should be able to demonstrate an understanding of:—
>
> (i) the use of primary and secondary texts;

(ii) the methods of locating cases and statutes;
(iii) the use of treatises, periodicals, digests, and standard practitioner texts;
(iv) the uses of indexes and citators;
(v) the use of computerised research.'

Has the LPC improved research skills?

It has been suggested however that the first two years' LPC students entering practice have not reached the high standard set. In 1995 Richard King, Chair of the Legal Education and Training Group, presented a paper on the subject to a Law Society workshop (1994). He reported that the profession, which recruits from the LPC, is finding three overall weaknesses in trainees:

'1. Trainees are weak at appreciating the need to convert the results of their legal research into practical solutions for clients. . . .
2. They do not exercise a degree of creativity in solving problems . . . Trainees too often display 'straight line thinking' which leads them into a blind alley. The development of lateral thinking, and more confident use of available materials, is a necessity.[2]
3. Occasionally, trainees do not get their research right. This is due to two failings:—

(a) The poor use of materials. . . .
(b) Trainees occasionally fail to appreciate the importance of getting things right to a very high degree of specificity and detail.' (King 1994)

King was speaking explicitly of students who had completed the LPC, students who had satisfied an examination board of their competence in the research standards set by the Law Society. Similarly Helena Twist of Nabarro Nathanson told an LPC conference in 1994 that she had found no difference between students coming into practice with an LPC qualification and their predecessors who had taken the Law Society Final examination. On this account students who had not been required to look anything up from one end of the course to the other (since the LSF gave students printed notes on all subjects) were no worse than those who had been taught and assessed in legal research. At the conference to which Helena Twist spoke one of the authors challenged the LPC teachers present to state whether any student had been excluded from passing the course because of a failure in any of the five legal skills. No such students could be identified. Are the high standards being met by all students?

The authors do not claim, at least in this paper, to know how to solve these perceived problems. High threshold standards in research have been set, and yet students who have passed the course have apparently arrived in practice without the skills which those standards aim at. Why might this be? Can anything be done? In *Professional Skills for Lawyers* (Brayne & Grimes, 1994) one of the authors of this article attempts to set out a research methodology for students to follow. This book does not however address the question of how students who do not follow

2 It can be argued that 'creative' problem solving is not only difficult to 'teach' but also is a skill which should be cultivated by 'experts' rather than the relative 'novices' undertaking the LPC. See Ericsson & Smith (eds) *Toward a general theory of expertise*, Cambridge, 1991.

this, or any other methodology, can be taught and inspired to take research seriously.

Teaching skills is difficult

Such problems are not confined to law-teaching. The following quotations are from Graham Gibbs, of the Oxford Centre for Staff Development, addressing the teaching and assessment of skills in Higher Education generally (Gibbs, 1995). Our additions in brackets after each quotation are no doubt somewhat cynical and facetious, but we believe they at least partially reflect underlying attitudes within parts of the profession of law teachers:

> 'Because assessing skills is so time consuming and because the development of skills requires frequent practice accompanied by formative feedback, tutors can rarely cope with the volume of work involved.'

(Sorry, we don't have time to do the job properly).

> 'Some institutions teach and assess skills largely independently of course content and content-based assignments. One of the main problems facing transferable skills is how poorly they transfer.'

(Sorry, we can only treat research seriously for certain designated research exercises.)

> 'It is . . . common for students to be assessed on skills they do not have and which they have been given no assistance to develop.'

(But we don't apologise because you pass anyway.)

> 'The quality of products can give a very misleading impression of the quality of the processes through which they were produced.'

(We can't fail you if you get the right result.)

> 'Assessing personal skills is not something most lecturers have done before; they often lack the skills themselves.'

(We're hardly going to admit that one!)

How should we approach the teaching of research?

On the Northumbria University LPC this year we tried to address some of the concerns we share with Graham Gibbs. We believed that we should focus on the attitude problems indicated above. Perhaps they can be used as yardsticks to what we did. Did we move towards a course ethos capable of:

giving the research work sufficient time?
giving the students explicit help in developing the skill?

integrating the research teaching across subject areas?
developing staff confidence in carrying out the same work? and
ensuring that the process of researching is recognised, not just the answers?

Of these concerns, we admit that changing ourselves and our own attitude to research, in practice and teaching, were the most significant. We too cut corners, think along tramlines, fail to document our research properly, rely on out of date or secondary sources. We wanted to change our own ethos and influence key members of the team in the same way. To achieve this it was essential that:

The task of teaching research should not be ghetto-ised – i.e. left to those with a bee in their bonnet. The work had to be designed and carried out at least across the LPC course team. We therefore cajoled members of each of the four core subject teams to join us.

An open minded approach from the teachers should be adopted. Therefore research tasks should ideally not be devised where we already knew the answers. In that way we could try to see the task from a student perspective.

The tasks should lead to the student having to use a wide range of legal research tools: from texts, through encyclopedias, to computer databases.

The students should end up finding things in their research that are in themselves interesting and useful. In this way we planned to assist them in addressing potential knowledge gaps in the core subject areas.

How could we inculcate a research culture?

We knew the profession was not yet satisfied with the abilities of new trainees to carry out legal research, and we had decided to beef up the research element on our course, but, as Graham Gibbs had pointed out, developing and assessing skills is time consuming. Our discussions started in early summer; the shortage of time meant that we would only be able to take a small step in time for the beginning of this year's course. This would therefore be a pilot programme on which we would build.[3]

We decided that practical research should be a major theme of our introductory programme, in the belief that the style of learning emphasised at the start of the course would make a strong impression on students. Pushing, at the start of the course, the importance of research would focus students' minds sharply on their research abilities (or, as many students candidly reported, lack of them).

The challenge, after this opening research blitz, would be to ensure that the message was not forgotten in the following weeks, as the grind of ploughing through the core subject material, and the regular diet of assessments -all LPC students face a minimum of 17 assessments within nine months- took its toll on student enthusiasm.

The move at Northumbria, in line with national trends, away from lectures in the core subjects and towards transaction-based student-centred workshop learning, was intended to reinforce the importance of students finding things out for themselves. In addition to this, specific research exercises were set in each optional subject that the students took.

3 Whilst writing this article the authors have become aware of Steve Nathanson's work in this field (Nathanson, 1989) and this will no doubt influence future programmes.

The Introductory programme

Our Introductory Programme research 'blitz' began with a ninety minute lecture/workshop. This was followed by a ten day period in which students spent a substantial part of their time working on a set of twenty research questions which had been distributed in their introductory block manuals. The introductory programme culminated in an hour long seminar in which some of the questions, research methods and answers were discussed.

The lecture

The lecture session was split into three themes:

1. Not researching is not good enough (raising the level of anxiety).
Our lecture began by referring to the feedback from the profession on recent graduates. We emphasized that it seemed clear that the most successful and progressive firms increasingly saw competence in research as a valuable commodity. Incompetent research was clearly dangerous both to the firm and to the job prospects of the individual.

2. Some basic tools (showing the way).
We distributed a list of the major sources of legal information together with a guide to how to decide which source to use (taken from Stott, *Legal Research*, Cavendish, 1993). We stressed that it was not possible to learn research simply by attending a lecture on the subject – even this one. Like most other skills, after receiving initial instructions and guidance, practice and feedback would be essential to improve the skill. We suggested that as students on the LPC, they were fortunate in being able to practise their skills for nine months in an almost entirely risk free environment. Privately however we wondered if they would carry on practising any research once the timetabled exercises were completed? How many of them would be sufficiently efficient and self-disciplined to devote time to such non-assessed activity? (We look at this again below.)

3. A case study (showing research skills in context).
This part of the lecture examined a real life problem that had arisen in our Student Law Office (where undergraduate students represent actual clients). Students were shown the brief file note outlining the problem; they were then asked to work in groups to generate questions and research strategies. As the case study exemplifies the approach we wanted students to adopt, much of this lecture material is reproduced as Appendix 1. It was also handed to students at the end of the lecture.

The research questions

Duly inspired and/or intimidated (ideally perhaps both) by the introductory lecture the students then had some 7 to 10 days in which to prepare their answers to the research questions. At the end of this period the questions and answers were then considered in one hour seminar sessions attended by the tutors who had set the questions and groups of around 12 students.

Not knowing how long the exercise would take nor how adequate our library resources would be, we had given only general instructions to the students. They had been asked to do as many questions as they were able to, in whichever order they wanted.

The outcomes varied widely. Some students with prior experience of legal practice seemed to relish the challenge that the exercise presented and answered all 20 questions. The majority of students attempted around 10 of the 20 questions. Many of these said that they would have liked to have attempted more but felt they had been given insufficient time to complete the exercise.

The research tasks

Where had the research tasks come from? In the summer we had asked members of each of the core subject teams to produce a set of four research questions of varying difficulty associated with their subject area. (Civil and Criminal litigation were treated as separate subjects for this exercise.) The questions produced varied widely from the relatively straightforward to the specialised, from the general to the practical.

The following is an example of the straightforward type of question:

> 'Which sections of which Acts (and/or statutory instruments) govern the following matters:
>
> (a) the formal validity of a will;
> (b) the distribution of the estate of someone who dies without leaving a valid will;
> (c) the procedure for obtaining a grant of representation to enable an estate to be wound up?'

This sort of question ought not to have caused a law graduate too many problems. The subject matter was likely to be familiar, precise answers could be found by taking a few relatively simple steps and the question was purely academic. Unlike a typical real life legal problem, there were no facts in dispute, the precise question which needed to be answered had already been formulated and it would have been fairly clear when a satisfactory answer had been found. In short, there was no practical context to consider.

Similarly,

> 'Which sections of the Companies Act 1989 have not yet been brought into force?'

demanded no great intellectual ability. A long list of sections which are in force can quickly be located in *Is it in force?*

Nevertheless this question seemed to serve a useful purpose. Those students (and there were several) who had not noted down their list correctly could be reminded of the importance of accuracy to which Richard King had referred. Those who had failed to use the Noter Up, and therefore missed the fact that two sections of the Act had been brought into force in July 1995, had discovered the need to update. Those unfortunate few who had trawled through *Halsbury's Statutory Instruments* looking at all the references since 1989 to the Companies Act 1989 will, we hope, never again forget the existence of *Is it in force?*

As well as such academic questions, questions on case law and on proposed changes in the law, several questions were set in a more practical context : An example is set out below:

> 'As a solicitor attending a client at the police station, you are under a duty to protect your client's interests. If your intervention during an interview is such that the police would like to throw you out of the interview, can they do so?'

Many students chose to answer these practical questions. Whether this was because they liked the practical context or because of an interest in the legal subject matter was impossible to tell.

The most practical question of all could only be answered by a site visit. The question asked students to research exactly what protection a pedestrian had at a particular junction, and the catch in the question was that although the crossing had light signals for pedestrians, it was not, when the rules were applied to that junction, a pelican crossing. This could only be worked out by going out (only 100 yards away from the Law building) and seeing if there were wavy lines on the approach to the crossing. This was too practical – not one student reported going and looking.

Tutor answers to these two sample questions are given in Appendix 2. These answers were not handed to students, however.

Should tutors have to teach outside their own subject area?

There had been some debate amongst staff about whether each seminar tutor should discuss only the questions which he or she had set or should attempt to cover the whole range of questions. We left this decision to individual members of staff and decided to evaluate after the event how it had gone.

In the end only one of the five tutors decided to confine the seminar to questions with which he was familiar. In retrospect it is clear that this 'specialist' approach had both advantages and disadvantages. On the negative side it is difficult for a tutor discussing a subject with which he or she is extremely familiar to truly understand the difficulties faced by students considering it for the very first time. On the other hand, the specialist tutor should more easily be able to see where mistakes have been made, to explain any conceptual difficulties which arise and to advise on the best research materials available in that subject area.

Students in the groups taught by the 'specialist' tutor had been instructed to focus their research work primarily on the questions in the tutor's subject area. This meant that although they explored only a relatively narrow area of law, all of them, unlike students in other groups, had started with a task which they could be expected to complete. These students were probably therefore more actively engaged, or at least, interested in, all of the discussions which took place in their seminars. In other groups the disparate coverage of questions by students meant that some students would lose interest in the seminar if the question being discussed was not one which they had covered. It seems sensible to try to avoid this problem in future, but equally it is clear it is not directly related to the adoption or otherwise of the 'specialist' tutor approach. In future to ensure that all the students have covered the same questions we shall set fewer questions per seminar and make them all compulsory.

A rolling programme of research exercises covering different areas of law could address the problem of tutor specialisation – although it may be that narrowness of subject matter is irrelevant, at least to the student, in an exercise designed to practise the skill of research. And if we really want to address the staff research culture, allowing lecturers to specialise could mean they do not need to engage in the kind of research from first principles that we are asking the students to undertake.

The difficulties in relying on answers prepared by one's colleagues!

We had agreed that each tutor who had set questions for the exercise would prepare a detailed answer, including the research steps taken, which would be circulated to the rest of the team. This could cause obvious difficulties when one tutor was relying on his or her colleague's written answer and had not attempted to research the question him or herself. The temptation to 'pass the buck', leaving an enquiring student understandably frustrated, is strong.

Problems can also arise when the tutor has researched the question in his or her colleague's specialist subject area. We all know that even the finest legal minds can disagree on a point of law, so it is hardly surprising that we should sometimes disagree with our colleagues. Students however, particularly on the LPC, crave certainty and no matter how much one explains to oneself and one's students that disagreement is to be expected, it usually seems to leave a bad feeling and to detract from the 'credibility' of members of staff.

A partial solution (which would have really tested our team commitment to the desired research culture) would have been for every member of staff involved in the seminar to research all questions, and not rely on the written advice of colleagues more familiar with the territory as to how they researched that question.

It proved impossible to discuss answers to all 20 questions in a one hour session, so some students probably felt frustrated at not covering questions to which they had prepared answers.

The different tutors adopted different approaches to this seminar although all of us attempted to establish an understanding of the research process and any answers found.

Evaluation of the programme – an initial questionnaire

At the end of our introductory programme around 40 students completed a questionnaire which included a section on the Research lecture and seminars. This was only a quarter of the students who had been through the Introductory Programme. Although there were a number of criticisms, primarily relating to the way in which we had structured the programme (students felt they had been given too much to do in too short a time) it was clear that most students were now conscious of their own weakness in carrying out practical legal research and had been very pleased to be given an opportunity to improve their skills. Roughly three quarters said they had found the lectures 'useful' or 'very useful' and over three quarters felt that the written lecture material was 'useful' or 'very useful'. The seminar exercises were particularly well received with almost a third of the students saying that they found them 'very useful'. Many volunteered enthusiastic comments. We feel that the combination of this enthusiasm and a more carefully designed and more extensive programme could produce very satisfactory results in future years.

An outcome we value is that at least some of the previous complacency about legal research was dislodged. Most students who volunteered feedback after the seminars suggested that they had moved from being unknowingly incompetent at research to becoming knowingly and painfully aware of their deficiencies. So the question now is: what use did the students then put this ignorance to? Did they consciously try to get better, or merely continue to 'get by' as many must have done in their previous studies?

Evaluation of the programme — a follow-up questionnaire

Twelve weeks later, towards the end of a demanding first term, we distributed a second questionnaire to 45 full time students attending a revision lecture. Relating specifically to research, this questionnaire was designed to gauge what longer term effect, if any, the students felt that the introductory programme had had.

We asked students to tell us which research sources they had been using in their study of the core subjects. Almost all had relied heavily on their subject manuals. Roughly a third said that they 'often' referred to other textbooks. Around 10% said that they 'often' referred to primary sources and over 50% said that they were consulting primary sources 'sometimes' in both Litigation and Business Law and Practice. But this still leaves nearly half relying entirely on secondary sources.

Almost none of our students were using legal databases regularly but this may have been at least partially because of a lack of easy access to facilities which are in the process of being upgraded.

We were encouraged that over 70% of respondents felt that their research skills had improved since the beginning of the course. As a public relations exercise on behalf of research awareness our programme had been successful. The same 70% (who had by now passed their assessed research exercise) felt that they were indeed competent in legal research. To label a student as 'competent' may encourage complacency, but it is a requirement of the Legal Practice Course. A better description would be to describe the student as 'familiar with basic research techniques'. It would be helpful to know if their future employers share this view of their competence. We are currently surveying the views of local trainees and their supervisors on how useful the LPC was, and have asked for comments on research skills. We also await with interest the results of similar research commissioned by the Law Society.

It was also encouraging to see that 60% of the respondents said that they were devoting at least three hours per week to legal research tasks other than directed reading. The same percentage said that they had applied the problem solving techniques described in the research lecture and set out in Appendix 1. Less encouraging was that fewer than 40% said that they intended to practise their legal research skills as far as possible in the future, the majority being content to practise their skills where directed to specific tasks. Of course, this response may relate only to their intentions while studying for the LPC.

Judged by the yardsticks for a successful programme which we identified above, i.e.:

giving the research work sufficient time;
giving the students explicit help in developing the skill;
integrating the research teaching across subject areas;
developing staff confidence in carrying out the same work; and
ensuring that the process of researching is recognised, not just the answers;
we had only partially succeeded in our objectives.

We had given more time to research but most students indicated they would have preferred more time still. We had tried to give students explicit help in developing the skill but only on a group and not on an individual basis. Research was now included across subject areas but we could still not claim that it was fully integrated.

Cultural change is bound to be slow: but there is evidence to suggest it is happening. When our colleagues from the LLB (Exempting) team discovered what we were doing, they invited us to deliver the same programme to that course; a four year degree which incorporates all LPC elements, unique to the University of Northumbria. A group of students who accidentally missed out (because they take a year in France as part of the Exempting Degree some of their programme is rearranged) clamoured to be given this research programme.

Conclusion

It is now clear that what was intended to be a 'blitz' was no more than a taster. Students wanted more time, more guidance, and more seminars. Despite encouraging noises about the time spent on research activities since the programme, they are not turning in significant numbers to primary sources. They are still largely relying on pre-digested information. Almost all report an increase in awareness and ability. This is perhaps a start.

But the main beneficiaries, we now realise, have been the two authors. We are now taking legal research more seriously, and this will continue to influence our own teaching, publishing and practice.

Epilogue

A keen student, caught up in the research work, failed to get a ticket in advance for the big football match at St James' Park that Saturday. On the day of the match he found a tout selling tickets outside the ground at £40 a piece. However as soon as he handed over the money the police swooped, arrested the tout and confiscated the student's ticket. Silently protesting 'that's not fair, you can't do that', the student decided to apply the research techniques he had just learned and concluded that he could sue the police for the price of the ticket. He recounted the story to us with some pride, but his courage failed him when it came to taking action. Perhaps discretion is the better part of research as well as valour, – certainly it was in this case – as he later discovered he had got the answer wrong!

Appendix 1

Extracts and comments on the lecture material.

1. The ethos

Firstly we desired to wrench students away from the habit, learned at the academic stage, of thinking of legal problems as coming with given and unalterable facts. The following quote, from a psychologist, was used to illustrate the need for a different approach:

> 'In the adversary (sic) system the lawyers have identified their particular versions of the issues, facts and relevant law. The judge's job is to choose between them and not to conclude, however much it may coincide with common parlance, that the truth may lie somewhere in between. Judges' written decisions read as perfectly sensible and many may wonder why there was all the fuss, why the case was taken so far. But the judge, in his or her decision, has the advantage of deciding the "true facts" and editing out the controversy' (Carson D. 1988)

2. The case study

Here is the case study file note for which the research strategy was required. (The file note is from a real case.)

> 'The new house that [client] has moved into with family has been found to have faulty wiring (despite chartered surveyors' report and electricians' search of property).

She wants to know whether she can sue:

(1) the electricians who had recently said it had been rewired, before they bought house or
(2) estate agents who recommended the electrician?'

3. Generating questions before answers

Students were then asked to attempt to generate questions which would need to be answered before advising this client. These could be factual or legal questions. A brainstorming rather than a critical approach to generating questions was encouraged.

When students had generated a reasonably large number of questions, they were asked to evaluate them and if necessary to reformulate them. We told them to break down questions into elements that were capable of an answer. For example:

Has my client got a good case? (This question cannot be answered without answering many other questions, and is therefore unhelpful.)
Can I prove negligence? (This question is capable of answer, but is still very broad.)
Is there a duty of care owed by the estate agent in selecting an electrician for the purchaser? (Here, we suggested, is a question which can be researched, and is probably sufficiently narrow for the researcher to know if the answer has been found.)

We suggested that stage 1 is to ask questions, stage 2 is to address the issue of how to answer them, and stage 3 is to attempt the research. After the students had spent some time trying to formulate questions, we gave them the following list of suggestions. We made it clear that they were not intended to be perfect or exhaustive, because refining the questions is part of the strategy. We had put ourselves through the same process as the students when we tried to answer the questions, and from the research described in answer to questions 1 and 6, we show that the questions were reformulated as the process took place.

1. Who is my client?
2. What is the cost of putting the work right?
3. What is wrong with the wiring?
4. Should a competent electrician have spotted the problem?
5. What is the appropriate compensation?
6. What duty is owed by the estate agent?
7. What duty is owed by the electrician?
8. What is the likely cost of pursuing a claim?
9. Is the client eligible for help?
10. Is the house safe at present? Is any action urgently needed now? Who can pay for this? Will remedial action affect later legal action?
11. What does the client really want? Money? Justice? An end to the hassle?
12. Who is the electrician? Is he or she insured? Professionally qualified? What accreditation schemes exist for electricians?
13. What is the relationship between the electrician and the client?

Strategies for research

The development of research strategies, and the next stage, the attempts at answers to two sample questions, are set out below together to avoid repetition. However, the process suggested was to attempt to define research strategies for all questions before starting to answer particular ones. In this way the size of the task, and the priorities, could be identified.

What is set out below is the document handed to students at the end of the lecture, and it contained the following caveat:

> 'The strategies below do not purport to give textbook answers to the questions. Some of the questions I formulated turned out to be unanswerable – in breach of my own guidance, they were too vague and needed reformulating as I went along. Sometimes there is no definitive answer and I have to rely on extrapolation and reasoning, the very essence of lawyering. Sometimes further questions are thrown up, which I have not attempted to address – but you will need to if you are not confident of the answers to such questions.'

1. Who is my client?

Research strategy planned

1. Check rules that apply in *Professional Conduct Guide*.
2. Ask Mrs G. If she wants husband to be included, ask him.
3. Who will pay? Can legal aid be granted jointly? Check regulations in *LA Handbook*.

Research carried out

(NB The law stated in this appendix and in Appendix 2 is what we found in September 1995.)

1. I started by looking up 'client' in the *Guide to the Professional Conduct of Solicitors* (6th Ed 1993) – always make a note of exactly what source you have used, because you or someone else may need to retrace your steps – hoping that

the index would reveal something like 'acting for more than one', or 'joint clients'. It did not. Several areas of potential relevance, such as confidentiality and conflict of interest occurred under that heading.

I tried 'instructions' (page 216–222) but this did not cover the question of identification of the client(s).

The guide contains a chapter on 'Relationship with the client'. Again, however, there is nothing there on the issue of who is my client.

Under 'retainer' duties to the client are described – the need to apply a 'proper standard of work'.

It seems there is nothing in the guide directly on the question as asked. Research does not necessarily, or at least immediately, reveal answers to questions as phrased.

If I rephrase the question: 'Is there anything known to me that could cause a conflict of interest to arise if I were to act for both wife and husband?' and 'Who is my client at present?' I can begin to seek further factual and legal information. I need to go to the next stage of asking Mrs G (the current client) about ownership, payment etc., before identifying if it is the husband or the wife or both who have the interest in this matter.

If both, how do I make them both my client? If only one, that person has to instruct me.

The guide does not answer this explicitly, as I can find nothing on the point under the above index entries. Can I start again from first principles? Under 'Client – instructions' (pp. 284–5) there is a statement which starts 'when confirming the clients' instructions in writing' – so this is presumably a part of the duty. It implies that there has been a statement on instructions earlier in the guide, and I flick back through principle 13. 13.02 and 13.03 talk of what to tell the client – but not how to be instructed. 13.04 talks of what to do when taking instructions in relation to costs. I go back to 'Retainer'; and find under 12.05 guidance on what to do if the instructions are obtained from a third party not the client. If the husband is to be a client, then the wife is a third party in my relationship with him. He must instruct me directly – the guidance says see him or obtain written instructions – and under 12.04 check whether there is any reason to suspect undue influence (not apparent in this kind of case).

3. (Assuming both instruct me and nothing is revealed which could cause a conflict of interest, and limiting the research to civil legal aid issues.)

1995 Handbook: nothing under 'client', so try 'applicant'. Page 57–63 for civil legal aid. This takes us to the Notes for Guidance. These talk of the applicant as an individual – implicitly answering the question about a joint application. But notes are not law. The notes refer to statute and regulations. Part IV of the 1988 Legal Aid Act can be found, via the contents list of the Act, to deal with civil legal aid. Legal Aid is available (s.15) to 'any person' who satisfies the tests described (not researched at present). S.15 refers to regulations, and the contents page takes us to p. 260. Reg. 10 again talks of applications being made by 'any person'. Reg. 32 (identified by flicking through the regs) talks of proceedings in which another person has an interest, but fails to identify what happens if that other person is also applying for legal aid.

The question needs refining, perhaps. Is the issue one of financial eligibility and contributions? Try: If wife and husband both apply for legal aid, how are the resources assessed?

Resources in the index takes us to the Civil Legal Aid Assessment of Resources Regulations 1989. Reg. 4 sets out how income and capital are calculated, but reg

7 states that the income of a spouse is treated as that of the applicant. If each makes an application do they end up paying two sets of contributions? Unfair as it seems, this appears to be the answer, so do we advise Mrs G (or Mr G) to pursue the application on his own? This would raise yet another question, whether one person can recover the other's share of the damages without being party to the action. But perhaps we need to delve into the Schedules referred to in reg. 4 on computation of income and capital. Nothing comes up here. Intuition drives me not to give up yet.

Try looking up contributions. The index sends us to page 48 for 'waiver of'. Here we find a statement under Notes for Guidance, Note 4. This cites no authority, but states: 'When a person (including spouses or cohabitees) has more than one certificate in force, those certificates will be linked and only one contribution will be sought.'

Do we have an answer? Could the answer have been obtained simply by ringing the Board? Yes, but as a lawyer you should be in a position to challenge the Board if you don't agree with their interpretation, so check what they tell you if you have any reason to doubt the answer received.

2. What is the cost of putting the work right?

Research strategy planned:

1. Does client know? Ask.
2. Obtain estimate. Who will instruct? What will it cost?
3. What is wrong with the wiring?

Research strategy planned:

1. Does client know?
2. Obtain expert report.
3. Who will pay? If legal aid granted, will LAB? What procedure? How soon? Check in *LA Handbook*.
4. How will we find an expert? Is there a register? A central body for electricians? Anyone I know who I can trust to advise on this?

4. Should a competent electrician have spotted the problem?

1. Ask expert to advise specifically on this.

5. What is the appropriate compensation?

Research strategy planned:

1. How does the law decide the measure of loss to the client(s)? Assuming this is a question of tort, look at up to date text book on tort.

6. What duty is owed by the estate agent?

Research strategy planned:

1. Decide if this is a contractual relationship, or one of tort. Look in up to date text books, especially any text on professional negligence.
2. Look up similar cases and articles: try *Current Law* (key words estate agent, duty of care); try journal index; try Lawtel, Lexis.
3. Is there any statute law on estate agents? Index to *Halsbury's Statutes*.

Research carried out:

Assuming that research has led me to conclude that I am primarily interested in liability in tort, and also assuming that my factual research has led me to believe that pursuing the electrician is going to be unproductive because he has no assets or insurance, then it becomes crucial to know whether there is a duty on the agents.

What would the duty consist of? To take care in selecting the electrician they recommend to carry out the wiring check.

I started with *Clerk and Lindsell on Tort,* 16th Ed, backed up by the third cumulative supplement. Under estate agent there was no entry in the index. There was a lot under professional negligence, but again not for this profession. It was time to browse, so I went to chapter 11 on professional negligence. At 11.02 I found a helpful general statement from the case of *Lamphier* v *Phipos* (1838) 8 C & P 475 that: Every person who enters into a learned profession undertakes to bring to the exercise of it a reasonable degree of care and skill.

But I also found shortly after a statement that a third party (i.e. non client) will recover for purely financial loss only exceptionally. For example in *Harris* v *Wyre Forest DC* [1989] 2 WLR 790 there is a general statement that there is no duty to persons other than the client to warrant the quality of buildings – there must be evidence that the professional undertook a duty. The case is now 6 years old, but worth looking up, which I did. In the actual case the duty was owed by a building society valuer to a mortgagor.

The cumulative supplement refers to *Caparo* v *Dickman* [1990] 2 WLR 358. This case held that there is a duty to a third party for statements made if there is a known recipient relying on it (in the actual case the auditors of a company's accounts were not in that situation, and owed no duty to the plaintiffs who in reliance on the statements acquired a company at above value).

It seemed to me at this point that *Caparo* is an important case. We can argue from it that the particular degree of proximity required to establish a duty is found. We need to talk to the client and establish exactly what recommendation was given to use this electrician, and then in relation to the breach of the duty, to establish whether there is any reason to believe the estate agents should have known he was not to be relied on. But in the meanwhile, given that this is a fluid area of law, has *Caparo* been approved subsequently, overturned, distinguished etc.? There are several ways forward here. Lexis would throw up citations of the case just by using *Caparo* as the search keyword. *Current Law Case Citator* could identify those cases where it has been mentioned. A journal search is likely to indicate any important case law in the area, since this is a very important topic both professionally and academically.

I used Lexis and the journal index, both available on the same computer terminal on floor 4 [of Northumbria's Library]. Without citing every article and case which resulted, I found repeated references to a case *McCullagh* v *Lane Fox and Partners Ltd* QBD 14 January 1994 [1994] 08 EG 118 and [1994] EGLR 48. This essentially repeats the principles of *Caparo*. An estate agent misrepresented to the purchaser that the property was an acre whereas it was only a quarter acre. It was held that there was sufficient proximity, a duty of care was owed (but as the price paid had been a reasonable price for the property there was no loss to the plaintiff).

The question that now needs to be answered is what happened, will we be able to establish sufficient proximity, and a breach? (As it happened the agent had not only recommended the electrician but had also directly instructed him; and it turned out that the electrician was not accredited with the professional body, so on both counts the facts supported a duty and breach.)

7. What duty is owed by the electrician?

Research strategy planned:

1. Define the relationship between clients and electrician. Who actually commissioned the inspection? who paid for it? ask clients. Obtain any written instructions and report.

2. Assuming the answer is that the estate agents handled this and there are no written instructions – is this a contractual relationship? Is it one of agency? Look in text book for principles.

8. What is the likely cost of pursuing a claim?
Research strategy planned:
1. Identify stages at which case may be resolved.
2. Ask more experienced litigator.

9. Is the client eligible for help?
Research strategy planned:
1. Which client?
2. Check regulations for green form and for civil legal aid, ascertain capital and income requirements; allowances; obtain financial information from each client.

10. Is the house safe at present? Is any action urgently needed? Who can pay for this? Will remedial action affect later legal action?
Research strategy planned:
1. Ask clients? Obtain expert opinion on safety.
2. If action urgently needed, will destruction of evidence affect case? Try text on civil litigation. Ask experienced litigator.
3. Can any money be obtained in advance of a trial? Check civil litigation procedure – e.g. County Court Practice.

11. What does the client really want? Money? Justice? An end to the hassle?
Research strategy planned:
1. Ask – but do not pressurise for decision.

12. Who is the electrician? Is he or she insured? Professionally qualified? What accreditation schemes exist for electricians?
Research strategy planned:
1. Obtain name and address from client; from estate agent; phone or visit; check letterhead if available; talk to expert currently instructed.
2. Look in electrical press.

13. What is the relationship between the electrician and the client?
Research strategy anticipated:
Question already tackled above.
The handout contained the raw research carried out and written up, to show a process and not a result. Not all questions were answered and we did not wish to suggest we were yet in a position to advise the client. The handout therefore ended with the following question:

> 'Has the formulation of these questions and research strategies led to the need to ask any more? e.g. Is there anyone else who might be sued? What is the position if one is liable and the other not? If both are liable, who pays the damages?'

Appendix 2

Seminar research questions and sample answers
Research question:

'As a solicitor attending a client at the police station, you are under a duty to protect your client's interests. If your intervention during an interview is such that the police would like to throw you out of the interview, can they do so?'

Tutor answer
'Starting point – the problem seems to be about police procedures. I looked up the microfiche of books in the library and found a large number of books on the Police and Criminal Evidence Act, mostly quite old. I decided to look at the Act itself (but it is hard to know whether a student would actually appreciate that this Act is relevant just from the title – in which case, a short circuit would be to look in a book they already have, Osborne, index: police powers – detention – legal advice during, to get onto the same pathway).

I looked up 'police' in *Halsbury's Statutes*, but parts of the Act were omitted and to be found in volumes 12 (Criminal Law) or 17 (Evidence).

Looking at vol. 12 police – detention – legal advice got me to p. 906 and s. 58 of PACE. This shows that a detainee has the right to consult a solicitor at any time, with exceptions under s. 58(8) where the exercise of the right would (inter alia) lead to interference or harm to the evidence. Reasons for delaying this right must be given in the custody record.

This does not really answer the question – at least directly, since it is the right of the detainee, not a description of procedures at the time of its exercise. For safety I checked in the cumulative supplement, and the section has not been amended. I also looked in the Noter Up, and for PACE I found reference to the Codes of Practice (Number 3) Order SI 1995/450. On floor 4 [Northumbria Library] the SIs are not that recent, but it was available at Official Publications. The SI states that version 3 of the codes is to replace the previous version, and the Code, being a publication of HMSO, is available from the Librarian, and stated as being in force from April 1995.

From there it is downhill. Code C deals with detention, and section 6 the Right to Legal Advice, 6.9 states

> 'The solicitor may only be required to leave the interview if his conduct is such that the investigating officer is unable properly to put questions to the suspect'.

Note 6D clarifies that solicitors should intervene to protect their clients including advising not to answer certain questions. It says that examples of improper interventions include answering questions on behalf of the detainee or providing written replies.
6.10 states:

> 'If the investigating officer considers that a solicitor is acting in such a way, he will stop the interview and consult an officer not below the rank of superintend-ent. . . . [to make the decision]'

Copies of the code could have been found in *Blackstones Criminal Practice 1995* (but is it up to date to April 1995? No), Brayne's LPC Criminal Litigation case study (P.3) [provided to our students, Blackstone 1995], Stones (1996, not yet published) and a number of up to date publications on PACE. Old publications on PACE however are no use because they will not show that the codes have been replaced.

Other ways of finding the information would have included a journal search on say police detention, or just an index search in *Criminal Law Journal*, since detention and police are topics likely to be written about a lot.
Research question:

'There is a light controlled junction on John Dobson Street, beside the YWCA. What protection does the green person signal afford a pedestrian crossing the road?'

Tutor answer:
The purpose of asking this question is to remind students of the dangers of making assumptions and of the need to cross check the legal research with the factual situation. I fell into the trap myself when I first looked up this point. Students may think the lights at John Dobson Street (if anyone actually went and looked – they should because the [Northumbria LPC] Civil Litigation case study will be based on this) are a pelican crossing and therefore look at the protection given in the Pelican Crossing regulations. But the definition in those regulations of a pelican crossing includes the presence of wavy lines on the road. At John Dobson Street there are no such lines. Nevertheless pedestrian signals exist, and it turns out that all they do is indicate to the pedestrian when it is safe to cross. They do not accord precedence to the pedestrian, and so any pedestrian claim or criminal prosecution would be based on other principles: negligence for a civil claim (as evidenced by driving through a light that was red for the driver) or contravention of the regulations requiring a driver to stop at the red light for a criminal case.

How to go about researching this: I went straight to the *Highways Encyclopedia*. There are pelican crossing regulations, which do not apply, and Traffic Signs Regulations and General Directions SI 1981/1859, which describe at reg. 35 under the heading 'Light Signals for Pedestrians' what is 'the period during which in the interests of safety pedestrians should not cross' (i.e. when the red person is showing). That seems to be the full extent of any statutory protection available to the pedestrian from these signals.

Bibliography

Ames, J (1995) 'Consumer report slates poor work' 35 *Law Society Gazette* 64.
Brayne, H and Grimes, R (1994) *Professional Skills for Lawyers* (London: Butterworths).
Carson, D (1988) 'Psychologists should be wary of involvement with lawyers' in Van Koppen, PJ, Hessing, DJ and Van den Heuvel, G (eds) *Lawyers on Psychology and Psychologists on Lawyers.*
Gibbs, G (1995) *Assessing student centred courses* (Oxford Centre for Staff Development).
King, R (1994) 'The Profession's Viewpoint' presented to a Legal Research workshop at Redditch, 21 July 1994.
Nathanson, S (1989) 'The role of problem solving in legal education' 39 *Journal of Legal Education* 167.

LOOK WHO'S STALKING: SEEKING A SOLUTION TO THE PROBLEM OF STALKING

Michael J. Allen

Professor of Law, Newcastle Law School
Mike.Allen@newcastle.ac.uk

First Published in Web Journal of Current Legal Issues in association with Blackstone Press Ltd.

SUMMARY

This article examines the phenomenon of stalking and considers the approaches being adopted to deal with it by victims, prosecutors and the courts in England and Wales. The adequacy of the current civil remedies and criminal offences which are available to deal with the problem is examined. The recent proposals by Government to legislate for a statutory tort of harassment and new criminal offences to deal with the problem are also critically analysed. The author concludes with an analysis of the issues to be considered in drafting any future legislation.

CONTENTS

Introduction

The Royal Family are much in the news, but recently two members have played a part, albeit passive and unwilling, in a current debate taxing politicians and lawyers – do we need a law against stalking? In January, Bernard Quinn was arrested for conduct likely to cause a breach of the peace arising from his stalking of the Princess Royal (magistrates subsequently dismissed the charge) while Klaus Wagner was arrested for obstructing the highway outside the gym where the Princess of Wales kept fit – the CPS dropped the charges due to insufficient evidence. The Government's response to this problem has been the publication on July 11, 1996, of a Consultation Paper by the Home Office and Lord Chancellor's Department, *Stalking: The Solutions* (Home Office, 1996). Responses were required by September 9, 1996, which hardly gives much time for careful reflection particularly when the consultation period coincides with the peak domestic holiday period. While deer may be to the fore in signing petitions in favour of a law against stalking, we humans perhaps need to consider more carefully whether such an offence is required or whether offences (and civil remedies) which already exist adequately cover this behaviour.

Stalking is a course of conduct which harasses, threatens, intimidates, molests, alarms or causes distress to an individual and which is carried out either for that purpose or for the purpose of compelling that person to do or refrain from doing anything which that person has a right to refrain from doing or to do.[1] Often the purpose of the stalker is to compel the victim to engage in, or re-engage in, a relationship with the stalker (Goode 1995) but there are other motivations such as persecutory delusional disorders or schizophrenia (see Harmon et al 1995; Mullen and Pathe 1994). The conduct involved is generally persistent comprising following that individual, surveillance of their home or place of work, entry on to their property, telephone calls (including faxes), and the sending of letters (or email messages) or other articles. Occasionally it can involve damage to property and in extreme cases may lead to physical assault. Sometimes the conduct is directed not at the person with whom the stalker wishes to establish a relationship or with whom he is aggrieved but towards others associated with that person.

---

1 See Goode (1995) who states that the essence of stalking is 'intentionally harassing, threatening, and/or intimidating a person by following them about, sending them letters or articles, telephoning them, waiting outside their place of abode and the like'. The Home Office definition is more limited: 'Stalking . . . can be broadly described as a series of acts which are intended to, or in fact, cause harassment to another person' (Home Office 1996, para 1.2).

Stalking is not a recent phenomenon[2] but pressure for a law against stalking has been growing over a number of years and NASH, the National Anti-Stalking and Harassment Campaign and Support Association has been at the forefront of the campaign for an offence of stalking. A private member's bill introduced in the House of Commons by Janet Anderson MP failed on 10 May to receive a second reading but assurances were given by the Home Office that the problem was currently under consideration.[3] In the meantime action in the criminal courts is being taken against 'stalkers' and it raises serious questions about the current state of the law in relation to non-fatal offences against the person generally and the role of the judiciary in developing the law in this sphere.

1. The nature of the problem

A major problem in the debate about stalking is the lack of hard data. As stalking is not an offence per se it does not feature in the criminal statistics. Most of the pressure for a change in the law in the United Kingdom has come from the tabloid press highlighting particular instances of behaviour classed as stalking. The tabloids, however, are hardly the most reliable source for an objective assessment of the problem. NASH has begun to collate information through its telephone crisis line enquiries (Von Heussen 1996). In a two year period from January 1994 to January 1996, 6,072 victims of stalking contacted the crisis line for advice. NASH also notes that 17 stalking related deaths of victims took place in 1994 and 1995. This information is a useful starting point tending to indicate the scale of the problem but it is not comprehensive. It is, however, the only information cited in the consultation paper (Home Office 1996, para 1.8). More recently research into the extent of stalking by Maria Wallis, Assistant Chief Constable of Hampshire, on behalf of the Association of Chief Police Officers, found that out of 44 forces asked about differing types of behaviour which would constitute stalking, only four were unable to give examples (see *The Times*, September 3, 1996). In the United States a survey concluded that as many as 200,000 people are stalked each year and five per cent of all American women are likely to be the victims of stalking during their lifetime.[4] A number of high profile personalities in the United States have been stalked including Madonna, Janet Jackson, Johnny Carson and Rebecca Schaeffer, the latter finally being murdered in July 1989 by her stalker, an obsessed fan, after he had pursued her for two years (see also Lardner 1995). The response in the US has been rapid with almost all states enacting anti-stalking laws designed to 'criminalize the repeated following or harassing of another person when combined with a credible threat of serious violence' (see Faulkner and Hsiao 1994;

2 See e.g. *Davis* v *Lane* 87 Eng Rep 887 (QB 1704); *King* v *Nettle* 1 Hawkins, *Pleas of the Crown* (6th ed 1787) 254 n 2; *R* v *Dunn* 113 Eng Rep 939 (QB 1840).

3 See HC Deb vol 263, col 345w. Home Office Minister David Maclean announced that 'proposals to combat the menace of stalkers will be published by the Government at the earliest opportunity' Home Office Press Notice 140/96 9 May 1996. When the Criminal Justice and Public Order Bill was going through its committee stages an attempt was made to introduce an offence of stalking which would carry the same penalties as the Public Order Act 1986 s 5. The offence would have been made out on proof that the accused had repeatedly molested, pestered or followed another and so behaved within the hearing and sight of such person that such person was likely to be caused harassment, alarm, distress or fear for personal safety. The amendment was rejected.

4 *Anti-stalking Legislation: Hearing on S. 2922 Before the Senate Committee on the Judiciary*, 102d Cong, 2d Sess (1992), cited in Strikis (1993). See also the National Victim Centre, **http://www.nvc.org/ddir/info43.htm**

National Victim Centre). A number have been the subject of constitutional challenges (see Faulkner and Hsiao 1994; Sohn 1994; Boychuk 1994) while their efficacy in protecting victims to any greater extent than existing laws had done is in doubt (see Sohn 1994; McAnaney et al 1993).

It is dangerous to draw direct comparisons from one jurisdiction to another as there are so many differences between the societies and legal systems in the USA and the UK but clearly the research being carried out in the US is relevant to the current debate. One crucial question to be answered before legislation is considered here is who are the stalkers? Unless there is information as to the kinds of people who engage in stalking one cannot determine whether legislation to create a new offence of stalking might be effective or whether other measures may be more effective or whether a combination of approaches would be the most appropriate response. Even if this is determined and it is decided that a law against stalking could serve a beneficial purpose other factors such as the willingness of the police to enforce such a law and prosecutors to bring prosecutions under it will play a significant part in practice in determining whether the law will be effective in dealing with the problem.

McAnaney *et al* state (McAnaney et al 1993, pp 821–823):

> 'Stalkers can be obsessed fans, divorced or separated spouses, ex lovers, rejected suitors, neighbours, co-workers, classmates, gang members, former employees, disgruntled defendants, as well as complete strangers.'

They identify from psychological, psychiatric, and forensic literature four different categories of stalkers whose motives and behaviours may differ while, in addition, the potential for violence may differ between individuals within categories. The four categories are (ibid pp 832–834):[5]

1. Erotomania: this is a delusional disorder in which the erotomanic believes himself to be loved by the object of his delusions even though that person may not even be aware of his existence.[6] Celebrities are often the objects of such delusional fantasies. Both males and females are affected by this disorder but males are more prone to become aggressive when their affections are not reciprocated.

2. 'Borderline Erotomania': this covers individuals who develop intense emotional feelings for someone whom they know does not reciprocate their feelings. Usually there is a history of some contact between the stalker and the victim which has triggered the development of this condition. Such individuals have usually suffered serious disturbances of bonding or attachment in childhood giving rise to difficulties in relationships as adults. They are also prone to intense fury referred to in the psychological literature as either 'Narcissistic Rage' or 'abandonment rage' when facing in adulthood the inevitability of abandonment.[7]

3. 'Former Intimate' Stalkers: these are individuals who have had an intimate relationship with the victim whether as spouse or lover and refuse to be rejected

5 The Los Angeles Police Department Threat Management Unit's files formed the basis of a study by researchers who developed a slightly different typology of stalkers: (i) simple obsessional (equivalent to 'Former Intimate' Stalkers); (ii) love obsessional (equivalent to 'Borderline Erotomania'); (iii) erotomania; and (iv) false victimisation syndrome (no equivalent). See Zona et al 1993.

6 Kurt states (1995 p 223):

> 'This condition has been recognized as a pathological form of love since ancient times. Descriptions of it can be found in the writing of Hippocrates, Plutarch, Galen and others.'

See further Enoch and Trethowan 1979.

7 LAPD estimates 48% of stalkers fall into this category.

after the relationship has ended.[8] In many cases these stalkers have a prior history of abusive relationships.[9] These are highly emotionally dependent individuals who experience rejection as abandonment. The victim of the stalker may be the former spouse or lover or that person's current spouse or lover. An ending of the relationship will not bring to an end the risk of violence where it was an abusive relationship and it may herald an increased risk of violence where there was no prior overt manifestation of violence.

4. Sociopathic stalkers: serial rapists and serial murderers characteristically stalk their victims but not from the point of view of seeking to initiate or maintain a relationship but rather to seek victims that fit the characteristics of an 'ideal victim' and then to facilitate their attack.

NASH has not engaged in a typology of stalking but has sought to identify the relationship of the stalkers to their victims. Of the 6,072 victims who contacted their crisis line 80% had suffered 'post relationship stalking', 15% 'casual contact stalking' (this may equate to borderline erotomania but further information would be necessary before such a conclusion could be drawn), and 5% had been stalked by strangers. The Wallis research for ACPO analysed 151 cases of stalking. Of these 25 stalkers were 'domestic' stalkers (ex-partners or husbands), 24 were known to the victim through work, 40 were known casually, 30 had some other relationship with the stalker and 32 were unknown. What these NASH and ACPO figures do not reveal is what percentage of stalkers suffer from mental illnesses, psychological or personality disorders. The figures do display a need for further investigation particularly of the link between domestic violence and stalking (see also Kurt 1995).

While a typology is useful in helping develop understanding of the different motivations stalkers may have it does not provide a solution to the problem. Indeed, in light of the differences between stalkers and their differing social, psychological and psychiatric problems a range of solutions is required. Victims perhaps naturally look to the law and in particular the criminal justice system to provide a solution. There are limits, however, to what the criminal justice system can do to protect victims. The remainder of this article will examine the range of offences which may be used against stalkers, the civil remedies which are available and the question whether further legislation is required.

2. Criminal Offences

While a specific offence of stalking has not been enacted the criminal law is being used against stalkers. Recourse has been had by prosecutors to existing offences in the form of offences against the person and public nuisance. Is this an appropriate use of these offences? Are there other offences which could be used? Is further legislation necessary?

---

8 LAPD estimates that 47% of stalkers fall into this category.

9 The 1990 FBI *Supplemental Homicide Report* reveals that 4% of male homicide victims in 1990 were killed by their wives or girlfriends but 30% of female homicide victims were killed by husbands or boyfriends. In the United Kingdom for the years between 1982 and 1987 38%–49% of female victims, but only 5%–7% of male victims, were killed by their partners: see *Hansard* (HC), 12 May 1989, Vol 152 cols 565–566, cited in Law Com No 207, para 2.2. In describing the nature of domestic violence the Law Commission include a range of behaviours which would fall within the definition of stalking: see para. 2.8.

a. Non-fatal offences against the person and stalking

While stalking embraces a range of conduct its impact on the victim is often to cause distress and fear. Obviously if the stalking behaviour leads to physical attack upon the victim a prosecution for the appropriate offence against the person will be appropriate. In several recent cases involving persistent stalking behaviour, however, prosecutions for offences against the person have been brought on the basis that the stalking behaviour has impaired the victims' health. Such prosecutions provide the courts with opportunities to impose fairly severe prison sentences. The unreformed[10] state of the law in this area also lends itself to manipulation to encompass stalking activity.

'Inflicting' grievous bodily harm

In *Gelder* (news item, *The Times*, 16 December 1994) the Court of Appeal quashed a conviction for inflicting GBH contrary to the Offences Against the Person Act 1861 s 20 arising from obscene telephone calls to the victim which had resulted in psychiatric illness. The trial judge had directed the jury to consider what a normal person would feel would be the effects of the calls on the recipient. The conviction was quashed on this basis as the *mens rea* of the offence requires either intention to cause physical harm or recklessness thereto. Lord Taylor CJ stated:

> 'The defendant was entitled to have the jury consider whether he foresaw that there was any risk of harm to this woman by making the calls. It may well be that the jury might have come to the same conclusion even if the judge gave them the correct direction. But we cannot be sure of it.'

The Court declined to consider the separate ground of appeal in which the appellant claimed that it was impossible to inflict GBH over the telephone. A consideration of this issue would have been welcome as the Court would have had to address the question of the meaning of 'inflict' in s 20. In *Wilson* [1984] AC 242 the House of Lords had reason to examine the meaning of 'inflict'.[11] Lord Roskill (with whom the remainder of their Lordships agreed) concluded that 'there can be an infliction of grievous bodily harm contrary to section 20 without an assault being committed'.[12] It was clear, however, that what was required was force

---

10 In *Parmenter* (1991) 92 Cr App R 68 before the Court of Appeal, Mustill LJ lamented that the law after 129 years was 'so impenetrable'. In *Savage* [1992] AC 699 at p 752 Lord Ackner referred to the 1861 Act as 'a rag-bag of offences brought together from a wide range of sources with no attempt, a the draftsman frankly acknowledged, to introduce consistency as to substance or as to form'. The CLRC 14th Report, para. 3. states that the Act of 1861 'is overdue for replacement'. In Law Com. No 218 the Law Commission stated:

> 'Law that is muddled, irrational, unclear, or simply difficult of access, is almost certain to produce injustice. . . . the present law of offences against the person suffers from all those defects.'

11 The issue before the House was whether under s. 6(3) of the Criminal Law Act 1967 a conviction of the lesser offence of assault occasioning actual bodily harm could be returned on a trial of a single count of inflicting grievous bodily harm. The House held that such a conviction could be returned where the allegations impliedly, if not expressly, include an allegation of assault. The House reaffirmed this point in *Savage and Parmenter* [1992] 1 AC 299.

12 His Lordship cited with approval the reasoning of the Supreme Court of Victoria in *Salisbury* [1976] VR 452:

> '[A]lthough the word 'inflicts' does not have as wide a meaning as the word 'causes' . . . the word 'inflicts' does have a wider meaning than it would have if it were construed so that inflicting grievous bodily harm always involved assaulting the victim. In our opinion, grievous bodily harm may be inflicted . . .either where the accused has directly and violently 'inflicted' it by assaulting the victim, or where the accused has 'inflicted' it by doing something, intentionally, which, though it is not itself a direct application of force to the body of the victim, does directly result in force being applied violently to the body of the victim, so that he suffers grievous bodily harm.'

being applied to the body of the victim either directly by the accused or by doing something which directly results in force being applied as where, e.g. D sets a trap for the victim by digging a hole into which he falls. This view was affirmed by Lord Mustill in *Mandair* [1995] 1 AC 208, 229[13] who stated that ''inflict'' conveys the idea of a direct and immediate doing of harm'.[14] These dicta, however, have not prevented the Crown Court at Reading from convicting the accused in *Burstow* [1996] Crim LR 331 of inflicting GBH contrary to s 20 on the basis of a campaign of silent telephone calls to V, 'hate' mail, theft of clothing from her washing line and scattering of condoms in her garden. V suffered severe depression which the defence conceded amounted to grievous bodily harm and the Crown conceded that there was no assault or battery – i.e. no force was directly applied to the body of the victim. Judge Lait ruled that the House of Lords in *Wilson* had gone no further than accepting that there can be an 'infliction' without an assault and had not accepted the *Salisbury* judgment in full. Consequently there was no reason for giving 'inflict' a narrow or restrictive meaning. In effect, as the prosecution argued, 'inflict' meant 'impose upon'. In response to this ruling the accused changed his plea to guilty. This decision was affirmed by the Court of Appeal, *The Times*, 30 July 1996. Lord Bingham of Cornhill CJ considered that the decision in *Chan-Fook* [1994] 1 WLR 689 that actual bodily harm was capable of including psychiatric injury was fatal to the appellant's case as there could be no meaningful distinction in this respect between actual bodily harm and grievous bodily harm. Judge Lait and the Court of Appeal, however, are guilty of playing fast and loose with authority. They may choose to dispense with dicta in *Wilson* as being obiter but they cannot dispense with the ratio decidendi of *Clarence* (1888) 22 QBD 23, a decision of the Court for Crown Cases Reserved (as modified but not overruled by *Wilson*) where there was no 'infliction' even though there was direct physical contact. This can only be because the presence of consent to sexual intercourse in this case meant that the physical contact involved did not constitute force (see Smith and Hogan 1993, p 426; Smith 1996, pp 333–334). It is submitted that the application of force physically to the body of the victim is a prerequisite for a conviction under s 20 on the basis of inflicting GBH. Any dilution of this requirement runs contrary to the authorities, namely, the ratio of *Clarence* and the obiter dictum of Lord Roskill in *Wilson* which has been approved by the House of Lords in both *Savage* and *Mandair*.

Assault

The Court of Appeal has also seen fit to rework the meaning of 'assault' to ensure the conviction of a stalker. In *Ireland*, *The Times*, 22 May 1996 it held that a telephone call or series of calls followed by silence could constitute an assault, affirming the conviction of the appellant of assault occasioning actual bodily harm. In this case the three victims suffered, according to psychiatric evidence, 'significant psychological symptoms which included palpitations, difficulty in breathing, cold sweats, anxiety, inability to sleep, dizziness and stress'.

---

13 Here the issue was whether a verdict of guilty of 'causing' GBH contrary to the Offences Against the Person Act 1861 s 20 could be returned on an indictment charging causing GBH with intent contrary to s 18. The Court of Appeal had quashed the conviction on the basis that the offence was one unknown to the law as the statute used the word 'inflict'. The House of Lords restored the conviction on the basis that the jury's verdict could only mean causing GBH on another person under that section, i.e. in a manner required by the section.

14 Lord Mustill dissented on the main issue in the case but he was the only one of their Lordships to examine the meaning of 'inflict'.

Although assault is now regarded as a statutory offence[15] the offence is not defined in any statute but at common law. Assault, in its technical or 'psychic' sense (see Law Com No 218, para 18.1; Williams 1983, p 173), is 'any act by which D intentionally or recklessly causes P to apprehend immediate and unlawful personal violence' (see Smith and Hogan 1993, p 398; *Fagan* v *Metropolitan Police Commissioner* [1969] 1 QB 349; *Venna* [1976] QB 421; *Savage* [1992] 1 AC 699, 740) – i.e. it is the apprehension of a battery and a battery is the application of unlawful force to another. In none of these cases did the courts agonise over the *actus reus* of assault as they took it to be widely understood as entailing the apprehension of a battery.[16]

The level of violence need not be very great and will be satisfied by any unlawful touching of the victim.[17] The accepted definition of assault in the criminal law also correlates with that in the law of tort (see Brazier, ed, 1995, para 12–12). The main doubts which have existed have been as to the *mens rea* and as to whether words alone, unaccompanied by action, can constitute an assault (see Williams 1957).

In light of this background, there are a number of problems with the decision in *Ireland* but two in particular merit mention.[18] Firstly, the Court has engaged in a subtle reconstruction of the word 'violence'. All previous decisions characterise violence in the context of assault as the use of force on the body of the victim or the apprehension of a battery. In this case the Court deduces violence from the fact of harm, Swinton Thomas LJ stating:

> 'In most cases an assault is likely to involve direct physical violence to the body. However, the fact that the violence is inflicted indirectly causing psychological harm does not render the act to be any less an act of violence. . . . In our judgment repetitious telephone calls of this nature are likely to cause the victims to apprehend immediate and unlawful violence.'[19]

Swinton Thomas LJ has confused and reformulated several concepts. In his first sentence he refers to assault in the sense of battery. He then proceeds to talk about 'violence . . . inflicted indirectly'. He appears implicitly to be adopting the same

15 See *DPP* v *Little* [1992] QB 645 where it was held that assault and battery were separate offences contrary to Criminal Justice Act 1988 s 39 and that they had been statutory offences since the enactment of the Offences Against the Person Act 1861 s 47.

16 This seems to have been settled for a long time as East, *A Treatise of the Pleas of the Crown* Vol 1 (1803) 406, defined assault and battery as follows:

> 'An assault is any attempt or offer with force and violence to do a corporal hurt to another, whether from malice or wantonness; as by striking at him, or even by holding up one's fist at him in a threatening or insulting manner, or with such other circumstances as denote at the time an intention, coupled with a present ability of using actual violence against his person; as by a pointing a weapon at him within the reach of it. Where the injury is actually inflicted, it amounts to a battery, (which includes an assault;) and this, however small it may be. . . .'.

See also Hawkins, *A Treatise of the Pleas of the Crown* Vol 1 (1716) 133.

17 See *Thomas* (1985) 81 Cr App R 331 and Blackstone, *Commentaries*, iii, 120 states:

> '[T]he law cannot draw the line between different degrees of violence, and therefore prohibits the first and lowest stage of it; every man's person being sacred, and no other having a right to meddle with it, in any the slightest manner.'

18 One which will not be explored is whether words alone can constitute an assault and if so, can the absence of words do so.

19 Doubtless the editor of the Oxford English Dictionary will be interested in this use of the word 'violence' which the Shorter OED defines as:

> 'the exercise of physical force so as to cause injury or damage to a person; physically violent behaviour or treatment.'

reasoning as Judge Lait in *Burstow* and seems to consider that battery may be committed indirectly. Even if one accepts this re-reading of *Wilson* one is left asking what is the indirect application of force to the body of the victim which is apprehended in the instant case? It is clear that Swinton Thomas LJ is not merely redefining battery to include indirect applications of violence but that he is then proceeding to redefine violence. As all the previous authorities on battery had defined the offence to require proof of a physical touching of the body of the victim (and for assault the apprehension of such) the basis for this radical reconstruction of 'violence' is highly suspect.

Undoubtedly 'violence' may be reconstructed, perhaps needs to be reconstructed, and it has been in other spheres (see Fawcett *et al* 1996, esp. chap. 2). This has been a feature of the debate on battered women who kill. Apart from highlighting gender bias in the criminal law in the way in which it constructs the defences of self-defence and provocation, this debate has reconceptualised violence to include 'emotional violence' (see Nicolson and Sanghvi 1993) and 'emotional battering' (see Wells 1994). In the context of domestic violence generally the House of Commons Home Affairs Committee accepted that 'domestic violence' includes 'any form of physical, sexual or emotional abuse which takes place within the context of a close relationship'.[20]

Swinton Thomas LJ has adopted this wider definition which incorporates molestation or harassment. Undoubtedly suffering was inflicted upon the victims but that is not a sufficient basis for finding an assault, in its generic sense, had been committed or, failing that, for redefining assault to include the appellant's conduct. There are dangers in treating assault as a general catch all offence covering multifarious forms of violence, molestation and harassment. Indeed, had the Court of Appeal cast its net wider in seeking guidance on constructing violence it may have found some in its own decisions under the Criminal Justice Act 1991, s. 31(1) helpful. This section defines a 'violent offence' for the purpose of imposing a longer sentence for reasons of public protection as one 'which leads, or is intended or likely to lead, to a person's death or to physical injury to a person. . . .' An offence resulting in psychological harm does not fall within this definition (see *Robinson* (1992) 14 Cr App R (S) 448; Murphy, ed, 1996, para E1.10). Had the trial judge sought to impose a custodial sentence under the Criminal Justice Act 1991 s 1(2)(b) the Court of Appeal would have had to strike it down as the authorities indicate that either physical injury must have resulted or been intended before an offence can fall within this definition.[21] It is somewhat paradoxical to find the Court of Appeal redefining violence in a way which runs contrary to the closest analogous statutory definition of that concept and one which is of such recent origin. It is hardly conducive to clarity or justice for there to be two such divergent notions of violence.

---

20 Third Report 1992–93, *Domestic Violence* HC 241–1, para. 5 adopting the definition suggested by the Domestic Violence Intervention Project. The Law Commission in Law Com 207, recognised the pressure to widen the meaning of violence (para 2.3):

> 'The term 'violence' itself is often used in two senses. In its narrower meaning it describes the use [or] threat of physical force against a victim in the form of an assault or battery. But in the context of the family, there is also a wider meaning which extends to abuse beyond the more typical instances of physical assaults to include any form of physical, sexual or psychological molestation or harassment which has a serious detrimental effect upon the health and well-being of the victim, albeit that there is no 'violence' involved in the sense of physical force.'

21 See *Palin* (1995) 16 Cr App R (S) 888; *Richart* (1995) 16 Cr App R (S) 977; *Ragg* [1995] Crim LR 664. In *Richart* Court of Appeal criticised the definition of 'violent offence' for being unduly narrow but it only recommended amendment of the statutory definition to include 'an offence which would lead to a reasonable apprehension of violence' in the sense of physical injury.

Swinton Thomas LJ has altered the focus from one which concentrates on the conduct of the accused in determining whether an assault has been committed to one which concentrates on the consequences of that conduct. The false logic in which the Court of Appeal engaged is evident in the following dictum:

> 'In our judgment, if the Crown can prove that the victims have sustained actual bodily harm, in this case psychological harm, and that the accused must have intended the victims to sustain such harm, or have been reckless as to whether they did sustain such harm, and that harm resulted from an act or acts of the appellant, namely telephone calls followed by silence, it is open to the jury to find that he had committed an assault.'

Ignoring the misstatement of the *mens rea* for assault occasioning actual bodily harm,[22] the fact that the appellant's conduct caused harm to the victims is not a sufficient condition for conviction. Swinton Thomas LJ has engaged in the age-old judicial habit of 'result-pulled reasoning' (see Ashworth 1995, p 437; MacCormick 1978, Chap VI) which ensures that an undeserving appellant who has engaged in anti-social conduct of a serious kind is convicted but at what cost to the principle of legality.

Secondly, there is the problem of immediacy. If force cannot be applied to the victim immediately, how can there be an assault? Clearly it is not possible to apply force over the telephone. The Court appears to have satisfied itself that causing immediate fear is sufficient – Swinton Thomas LJ stating:

> 'As to immediacy, by using the telephone the appellant put himself in immediate contact with the victims, and when the victims lifted the telephone they were placed in immediate fear and suffered the consequences to which reference has been made.'

This gives rise to the prospect of long-distance assaults. Undoubtedly the victims were caused fear and distress but it is stretching the definition of assault to bring this behaviour within its bounds. Assault is not an offence designed to deal with the creation of fear in general. Its sphere of operation is quite narrow, namely, the creation of a fear (as in the sense of an apprehension) of being subjected immediately, i.e. then and there, to a battery by the assailant. Swinton-Thomas LJ, however, reasoned thus:

> '[O]nce the fear and the damage are established, then when a telephone call is made by the appellant and the victim lifts the telephone and then knows that the man is telephoning them yet again, they will be apprehensive of suffering the very psychological damage from which they did suffer.'

This reveals that he was reasoning backwards from the fact of psychological harm to construe an assault. Where was the apprehended battery?

Swinton Thomas LJ sought to support his reasoning by reference to the case of *Smith* v *Chief Superintendent of Woking Police Station* (1983) 76 Cr App R 234

22 In *Savage* [1992] 1 AC 699, 742, Lord Ackner stated:
'The verdict of assault occasioning actual bodily harm may be returned upon proof of an assault together with proof of the fact that actual bodily harm was occasioned by the assault. The prosecution are not obliged to prove that the defendant intended to cause some actual bodily harm or was reckless as to whether such harm would be caused.'

which he considered 'bore some similarity to the present case'. This was a decision of the Divisional Court affirming the defendant's conviction under the Vagrancy Act 1824 s 4 which provided:

> 'Every person being found . . . in any enclosed . . . garden for any unlawful purpose shall be deemed rogue and a vagabond.'

The issue was whether there was evidence upon which the magistrates could conclude that the defendant, when he peered through the victim's downstairs bedroom window causing her fright, had an unlawful purpose namely to assault the victim. The Divisional Court accepted the definition of assault in *Archbold* (41st ed) para 20–114 as being 'any act which intentionally – or recklessly – causes another to apprehend immediate and unlawful violence'. Kerr LJ concluded (at p 238):

> '. . . it was wholly open to the justices to infer that her state of mind was not only that of terror . . . but terror of some immediate violence. In those circumstances, it seems to me that they were perfectly entitled to convict the defendant who had gone there . . . with the intention of frightening her and causing her to fear some act of immediate violence, and therefore with the intention of committing an assault upon her.'

It is difficult to see any similarity to the present case. The victim and the defendant were in close proximity and the apprehension was that he would attack her physically then and there. In the instant case there was no physical proximity and no suggestion that the victims apprehended personal physical violence being done to them by the appellant at that time. The fact that, in the words of Swinton Thomas LJ, '[f]ear could be instilled as readily over the telephone as it could through the window' is not the point; a fear of anything other than an immediate battery is not sufficient.

The only authority which Swinton Thomas LJ could find to support this major redefinition of psychic assault was one first instance decision in a civil action partly based on assault in the Supreme Court of New South Wales, *Barton* v *Armstrong* [1969] 2 NSWR 451, in which Taylor J held that a threat made over the telephone was capable of amounting to an assault in the specific circumstances of the case.[23] That a first instance decision in an Australian tort case, which is not even cited in *Halsbury's Laws*, *The Digest* or *Clerk and Lindsell on Tort*, could provide the support for such a radical development in English criminal law is, to say the least, surprising. The case, however, is not fully analogous to *Ireland* as the threats made were verbal and specifically threatened physical violence to the plaintiff. Australian tort law maintains the requirement that for assault there must be a 'direct threat by the defendant which places the plaintiff in reasonable apprehension of an imminent contact with his person either by the defendant or by some person or thing within the defendant's control' (Trindale and Cane 1993, p 42). Australian tort law crucially requires the threats to create an apprehension of an imminent battery. It has not yet accepted that silent telephone calls can constitute an assault nor has it dispensed with the requirement that the victim apprehend an imminent battery. So

23 These circumstances included prior threats by the defendant to kill or have killed the plaintiff and the defendant had engaged hired men to carry out these threats who had followed the plaintiff. Accordingly, while the defendant made the threats over the telephone the plaintiff feared immediate violence at the hands of the defendant's hired men who might be in a position to carry them out.

even this tenuous antipodean authority provides little support for the Court of Appeal's decision.

There has been a huge change in the law in this case although Swinton-Thomas LJ expressed the surprising view that 'the conduct complained of falls squarely within the recognised definition of the offence'. Undoubtedly the Court of Appeal found Ireland to be an undeserving appellant but that is not a sufficient reason for stretching the law to ensure his conviction. In their keenness to confirm Ireland's conviction the Court forgot the strong admonition against judicial law-making given by Lord Lowry in *C* v *DPP* [1995] 2 WLR 383, 392 who having reviewed earlier admonitions in previous decisions of their Lordships stated:

> '(1) If the solution is doubtful, the judges should beware of imposing their own remedy. (2) Caution should prevail if Parliament has rejected opportunities of clearing up a known difficulty, or has legislated, while leaving the difficulty untouched . . . (4) Fundamental legal doctrines should not be lightly set aside. (5) Judges should not make a change unless they can achieve finality and certainty.'[24]

The Court of Appeal has extended the ambit of the law of assault in an unquantifiable way placing the requirement that the victim apprehend immediate personal violence in doubt. As the Court of Appeal reasoned backwards from the fact of harm to conclude that there had been an assault, one is left to speculate whether they would have found an assault in the absence of harm. What does 'immediate' now mean? Rather than clarifying the law of assault the Court of Appeal has created more doubt. For example, could indecent suggestions made over the telephone amount to an indecent assault or could threats made over the telephone to a police officer on duty amount to assault on a constable in the execution of his duty?

The decision in *Ireland* is all the more surprising in light of recent analyses of offences against the person and Parliamentary activity or inactivity. The Criminal Law Revision Committee considered that the law relating to assault was sufficiently well understood not to require statutory definition (CLRC 14th Report, paras 159 & 160). The Law Commission suggested a definition for assault to resolve some uncertainties, particularly relating to trivial touchings, and also because as a matter of principle they considered that the 'substance of a criminal offence of violence' ought to be defined but their definition, however, largely codifies the common law (Law Com No 218, paras 18.1–18.7). Parliament has not sought to legislate to place the definition of assault on a statutory basis although it has had ample opportunity to do so, in particular when it enacted the Criminal Justice Act 1988 ss 39 and 40, not to mention the numerous Criminal Justice Acts of the succeeding years. At the same time it has created a number of offences which deal with threatening words or behaviour and nuisance telephone calls (see below). The Court of Appeal should have refrained from stretching the ambit of the s 47 offence of assault occasioning actual bodily harm to cover situations which Parliament had already covered by other offences albeit that the penalties available under these offences are much greater than is available under s 47. If, however, the penalty Parliament has imposed under the laws which exist is inadequate it is for Parliament to rectify that fault not for the courts to stretch the boundaries of other more serious offences in unnatural ways to rectify this deficiency.

24 It is interesting to note that Lord Lowry was in the panels which decided both *R* v *R* and *R* v *Brown*!

Finally, a fundamental principle which the Court set aside is the non-retroactivity principle. This is stated in Article 7 of the European Convention of Human Rights:

> 'No one shall be held guilty of any offence on account of any act or omission which did not constitute a criminal offence under national or international law at the time when it was committed.'

While the decision in *Ireland* does not involve the creation of a new offence by the Court of Appeal it does involve an implicit redefinition of the offence of assault to include conduct which would hitherto not have been covered by that offence. New ways of committing old crimes will undoubtedly arise and courts will be faced with the task of determining whether the new facts fit within the existing statutory or common law definition of the offence. This is an appropriate judicial function. The problem arises, however, when the court discerns that the new antisocial behaviour does not fit within the accepted definition of the offence and then is tempted to redefine the offence to catch this behaviour. This is what the House of Lords did in *R* v *R* [1992] 1 AC 599 when it removed a husband's immunity from liability for raping his wife (see further Giles 1992; Ashworth 1995, p 340). It did so because of changed social circumstances.

In determining whether this latest Court of Appeal decision does breach the non-retroactivity principle some guidance is available in Convention case law (see further Harris et al 1995, Chap 7). The European Court of Human Rights indicated the general scope of Article 7(1) in *Kokkinakis* v *Greece* A 260-A (1993) para 52:

> 'Article 7(1) of the Convention is not confined to prohibiting the retrospective application of the criminal law to an accused's disadvantage. It also embodies, more generally, the principle that only the law can define a crime and prescribe a penalty (*nullum crimen, nulla poena sine lege*) and the principle that the criminal law must not be extensively construed to an accused's detriment, for instance by analogy; it follows from this that an offence must be clearly defined in law. This condition is satisfied where the individual can know from the wording of the relevant provision and, if need be, with the assistance of the courts' interpretation of it, what act and omission will make him liable.'

Inevitably the law requires interpretation and perfect clarity is not achievable. This has been recognised by the Commission in *X Ltd and Y* v *UK No 8719/79*, 28 DR 77 at p 81 where they stated that what is prohibited is the extension of existing offences 'to cover facts which previously clearly did not constitute a criminal offence' but that 'it is not objectionable that the existing elements of the offence are clarified and adapted to new circumstances which can reasonably be brought under the original conception of the offence'. What is required, according to the Court in *S W* v *United Kingdom No 47/1994/494/576* and *C R* v *United Kingdom No 48/1994/495/577*, is the adaptation of existing principles, 'consistent with the essence of the offence' in a reasonably foreseeable way. In the context of marital rape the Court concluded:

> 'The decisions of the Court of Appeal and then the House of Lords did no more than continue a perceptible line of case law development dismantling the immunity of a husband from prosecution for rape upon his wife. . . . Moreover, there was an evident evolution, which was consistent with the very essence of

> the offence, of the criminal law through judicial interpretation towards treating such conduct generally as within the scope of the offence of rape. That evolution had reached a stage where judicial recognition of the absence of immunity had become a reasonably foreseeable development of the law.'

Without wishing to express support for the judicial reasoning in *R* v *R* or the outcome before the European Court, it can be said that in the case of marital rape the common law had been developing, the marital exception had been eroded by a number of cases, social attitudes to marriage, female autonomy and sexual behaviour had been changing, and the behaviour involved would not necessarily fall within the definition of other offences. By contrast the law on assault prior to *Ireland* could be determined with a fair degree of certainty from a number of previous decisions. All would have indicated that a battery required physical contact and an assault, in its psychic sense, required the apprehension of an immediate battery. There is no perceptible line of cases in which a new definition of these offences has been evolving. On that basis Ireland's behaviour could not amount to an assault. The decision of the Court of Appeal to the contrary is not a reasonably foreseeable evolutionary step but a huge unanticipated judicial leap based on misconceived social defence considerations. Furthermore his antisocial behaviour was already covered by section 43 of the Telecommunications Act 1984 and Parliament had as recently as 1988 chosen not to redefine assault. Undoubtedly the Court of Appeal's decision is open to challenge under the Convention and would be found to be in breach of Article 7(1) under the case law as it currently stands.

b. Other Offences under which stalkers may be prosecuted

Parliament has legislated in a way which covers much of the activity in which stalkers engage.

i. The Telecommunications Act 1984

Section 43 of the Telecommunications Act 1984 creates the offence of improper use of a public telecommunication system. This offence may be committed, *inter alia*, by a person who (a) makes calls of a 'grossly offensive or of an indecent, obscene or menacing character' or who (b) makes persistent calls 'for the purpose of causing annoyance, inconvenience or needless anxiety to another'. This is a summary offence but there is no requirement of proof of purpose where (a) applies. Ireland's activities came within (a) and probably also within (b) but presumably the prosecution were not satisfied with a summary offence even though Parliament had increased the penalty to a maximum fine at level 5 and/or imprisonment for a maximum term of six months. Again obsessional stalkers who make persistent calls may lack the requisite purpose prescribed in the Act.

ii. The Malicious Communications Act 1988

Section 1 of the Malicious Communications Act 1988 creates an offence of sending letters which convey, *inter alia*, threats with the purpose of causing distress or anxiety. This, however, is only a summary offence. It also requires proof of purpose which will fail to catch some stalkers.

iii. The Trade Union and Labour Relations (Consolidation) Act 1992

One statutory offence which derives from a strange source is Trade Union and Labour Relations (Consolidation) Act 1992 s 241 which provides:

(1) A person commits an offence who, with a view to compelling another person to abstain from doing or to do any act which that person has a legal right to do or abstain from doing, wrongfully and without legal authority -

(a) uses violence to or intimidates that person or his wife or children, or injures his property,
(b) persistently follows that person about from place to place,. . .
(d) watches or besets the house or other place where that person resides, works, carries on business or happens to be, or the approach to any such house or place. . . .'

This offence also calls for proof of purpose; this may cover the obsessional stalker who is seeking to compel the victim to give him attention or the former intimate stalker who is seeking to compel the victim to recommence a prior relationship with him. Proof of compulsion may be difficult where there has been no contact between the victim and the stalker. An additional element which must be proved is that of wrongfulness. This requires that the conduct be tortious (see *Thomas* v *National Union of Mineworkers (South Wales Area)* [1986] Ch 20). In light of the decision in *Khorasandjian* (below) such behaviour would be a nuisance. Again, however, the offence is only summary.

iv. Public Nuisance

An offence which has recently been utilised in a case of stalking is that of public nuisance. In *R* v *Johnson (Anthony Thomas)*, *The Times*, May 14, 1996, the same panel of the Court of Appeal affirmed the conviction of the appellant of public nuisance based on his numerous obscene telephone calls over a period of five and a half years to thirteen different women in the South Cumbria area. The Court accepted the definition of public nuisance in *A-G* v *PYA Quarries Ltd* [1957] 2 QB 169. In that case Romer LJ stated (at p 184):

'[A]ny nuisance is "public" which materially affects the reasonable comfort and convenience of life of a class of Her Majesty's subjects. The sphere of the nuisance may be described generally as "the neighbourhood"; but the question whether the local community within that sphere comprises a sufficient number of persons to constitute a class of the public is a question of fact in every case. It is not necessary . . . to prove that every member of the class has been injuriously affected; it is sufficient to show that a representative cross-section of the class has been so affected for an injunction to issue.'

Denning LJ stated (at pp 190–191):

'I prefer to look to the reason of the thing and to say that a public nuisance is a nuisance which is so widespread in its range or so indiscriminate in its effect that it would not be reasonable to expect one person to take proceedings on his own responsibility to put a stop to it, but that it should be taken on the responsibility of the community at large.'

The defence had contended that each of the telephone calls was a single isolated act to an individual person which could have amounted to a private nuisance but it would be wrong to treat them cumulatively to construct a public nuisance. The Court, however, decided that it was permissible to look at the cumulative effect of the calls and concluded that this amounted to conduct which:

'materially affected the reasonable comfort and convenience of a class of Her Majesty's subjects and was a nuisance so widespread in its range or so indiscriminate in its effect that it would not be reasonable to expect one person to take proceedings on her own responsibility.'

This represents a novel use of the offence of public nuisance. The factor common to activities which had been held to amount to public nuisances prior to this case was their indiscriminate impact on members of the public (see Smith and Hogan 1993, pp 762–763). The impact of the appellant's telephone calls was not indiscriminate; they were calls targeted at particular individuals whom he had either met socially or through carrying out work at their homes. A call to any one victim had no impact, nor risk of impact, on any other person, remaining private as between the appellant and the victim. If one follows through with the reasoning of the Court of Appeal, if the appellant had chosen to dump rubbish in each of their gardens rather than telephoning them, this too would have amounted to a public nuisance rather than a private nuisance. Such a conclusion would come as a surprise to tort lawyers.

Secondly, in what way did the calls materially affect the 'reasonable comfort and convenience of life of a class of . . . subjects'? Again the nature of the activity does not impinge on public health, comfort or enjoyment of public amenities in the way in which noise, smells, pollutions, or obstructions of the highway do. It is difficult to find an analogous case to link to this activity and its effects. In *Madden* [1975] 3 All ER 155, eight security officers affected by a telephoned hoax bomb warning at the factory where they worked were held not to constitute a class of the public. Furthermore, while it is true that it is a question of fact whether a sufficient number of persons are affected to constitute a class of the public, the nuisance in this case was neither widespread nor indiscriminate. It was not a case of the appellant doing an act which had any potential to affect an indeterminate range of people in the way that noise, pollution or obstruction of the highway may so do. The question has to be asked, at the time each call was made who were the persons who potentially might be affected? Furthermore, at what point did the public nuisance materialise? Was it when the thirteenth victim had been contacted or was it when each had been contacted a certain number of times? The reason for asking this question is that at some point the appellant's actions moved over from being a private matter to being a public matter and the prosecution would have to establish that at that point he knew or ought to have known that a public nuisance would be the result of his actions (see *Shorrock* [1994] QB 279).

Thirdly, why would it not be reasonable to expect one person to take proceedings on her own responsibility? Public nuisance is useful where no one person suffers particular damage which could form the basis for a private action in tort. While the victims in this case would probably have been unable to sue for private nuisance they did have a remedy through making a complaint to the police of an offence under the Telecommunications Act 1984 s 43. Why did the Court of Appeal consider that it would not be reasonable to expect the victim of an offence to complain to the police. This seems to be a strange message to communicate that victims cannot reasonably be expected to complain to the police. Add to this the fact that the complainant in a criminal case does not bear the cost of the proceedings one is left incredulous at this statement.

There was no need to stretch public nuisance to cover Johnson's actions as they were already covered by the statutory offence. As Johnson's calls were obscene there was no more difficult *mens rea* requirement under s 43 than under the common law. The only reason for proceeding with a prosecution for the offence of public nuisance in the circumstance was the possibility of a heavier sentence. In fact the trial court imposed a sentence which could have been imposed for the s 43 offence. Again, by extending the criminal law in novel ways, the Court seems to be undermining the legislative authority of Parliament.

v. The Public Order Act 1986

Where a person stalks someone in public there are several offences under the Public Order Act 1986 which could be utilised. Under s 4 a person is guilty of an offence if, *inter alia*, he 'uses towards another person threatening, abusive or insulting words or behaviour . . . with intent to cause that person to believe that immediate unlawful violence will be used against him, . . . or whereby that person is likely to believe that such violence will be used' and under s 6(3) he 'intends his words or behaviour . . . to be threatening,[25] abusive or insulting, or is aware that it may be threatening, abusive or insulting'.[26] Thus it would have to be proved that the stalker (1) intended his behaviour to be threatening, or was reckless thereto, and (2) either (a) intended thereby to cause the victim to fear immediate violence or (b) it must have been likely that the victim would have believed such violence would be used. The first part of intent to threaten would require proof of a purpose in the words of Lush J 'of intimidating or overcoming the will of the person to whom it is addressed' (see *Wood* v *Bowron* (1866) LR 2 QB 21 at p 30). In the case of the obsessional stalker his purpose may be to compel the victim to do or abstain from doing something while in the case of those who stalk following the breakdown of a relationship the purpose often is to compel the victim to return to that relationship; in both cases this element of the offence could potentially be established. In the case of (2)(a) it may be easier to establish this intent where there has been a previous relationship which has involved abuse but this is not crucial as (2)(b) is obviously objective in nature and a jury may readily find that it was likely that the person stalked would fear immediate violence. As the point of focus here is the person threatened (see *Loade* v *DPP* [1990] 1 QB 1052), the more timorous that person is the easier it will be for the prosecution to establish that s/he was likely to believe violence would be used.

Under s. 4A (inserted by the Criminal Justice and Public Order Act 1994 s 154) a person is guilty of an offence 'if, with intent to cause a person harassment, alarm or distress, he – (a) uses threatening, abusive or insulting words or behaviour, or disorderly behaviour . . . thereby causing that or another person harassment, alarm or distress.' Persistent stalking, of the kind to which the Princess Royal was subjected, could amount to this offence but proof of intent may be difficult.[27] However, section 5 provides that 'a person is guilty of an offence if he – (a) uses threatening, abusive or insulting words or behaviour, or disorderly behaviour . . .

---

25 If threats are made to a person to kill that person or a third party this may be an offence under the Offences Against the Person Act 1861 s 16. In this case the threat must be made without lawful excuse and with the intention that the person to whom it is made will fear that it would be carried out. In the case of many former intimate stalkers such threats may be made.

26 If words (and silence) could constitute an assault why would Parliament enact this provision? ATH Smith considers that this provision has created a statutory form of assault (Smith 1987, p 101). Note also the Home Office mistakenly believe that intention only will suffice for this offence (Home Office 1996, para 3.4).

27 This is a problem with many of those who may engage in stalking as they may be suffering from an obsessional or delusional condition. McAnaney et al state:

> '[The requirement of intention] may mean that anti-stalking statutes will not reach people who, because they are delusional or otherwise, are not capable of forming the intent. The delusional offender may be acting out of 'love' for the victim, or out of a belief that [he or] she is, or is meant to be, bonded to the victim.' (McAnaney et al 1993, p 907)

within the hearing or sight of a person likely to be caused harassment, alarm or distress thereby' and under s 6(4) he 'intends his words or behaviour . . . to be threatening, abusive or insulting, or is aware that it may be threatening, abusive or insulting'. The test of recklessness here, by comparison to s 4, is subjective in nature. Again in the case of the obsessional stalker it may be difficult to establish either intent or subjective recklessness although in the case of recklessness this may be established where the victim has indicated to the stalker that s/he finds his/her actions threatening and wishes the behaviour to stop.

In the case of each of the above offences under the Public Order Act Parliament has determined that there would be no offence where the accused was within a dwelling and the victim was within that or another dwelling. In respect of the s 4 offence the immediacy requirement would largely have the same effect where the threats are issued by a person in one dwelling to the victim in another. This would also rule out telephone threats where the victim and caller are in dwellings. Of course anomalies are created in that the same call from a public telephone could fall within the statutory definition if, in respect of s 4, the immediacy requirement was satisfied. In respect of harassment, alarm or distress it is clear that Parliament is only seeking to catch behaviour which has a public aspect to it. Most forms of stalking cause harassment, alarm or distress and many involve a public element arising from following the victim or besetting the victim's house. The situation in *Ireland* could amount to one of these offences if the telephone used by the appellant had not been in a dwelling or if the victims did not receive the calls in a dwelling.

Further legislation could remove the need to prove intent for the above offences but whether this is desirable is another matter. The behaviour involved in stalking which might constitute the *actus reus* in the above offences is not wrongful in itself. It should only become a concern of the criminal courts when it is accompanied by an intention as specified above. If there were to be no *mens rea* requirement people could end up inadvertently committing the offence because, for example, their behaviour objectively appeared to be threatening and rendered it likely that the victim would either fear violence (s 4) or be caused harassment, alarm or distress (s 5). If the victim is neurotic, this likelihood would be all the greater. In addition, in the absence of a fault requirement rational sentencing which is based on the level of the offender's culpability is not possible. But perhaps the main reason for counselling against any tinkering with the Public Order offences is that they are not the appropriate vehicle to be used to deal with stalking. Stalking comprises a range of actions in which the stalker may engage over a period of time. Stalking is really concerned with a course of conduct rather than a particular incident which may fall under one of the above offences. The real evil to be addressed is this persistent conduct as it is this which has such devastating effects on the lives of victims and which needs to be reflected in sentencing.

3. *Stalking and civil remedies*

a. Domestic Violence

The problem of stalking has received a partial solution where it arises in the context of a domestic relationship where injunctions may be available under the Domestic Violence and Matrimonial Proceedings Act 1976.[28] The Family Law Act

28 See also Domestic Proceedings and Magistrates' Courts Act 1978 s 16.

1996 will replace the current provisions with a new procedure whereby non-molestation orders may be obtained. The provisions in the Act largely replicate the provisions contained in the Draft Bill appended to Law Com No 207. The Act widens the range of people who may be protected by a non-molestation order covering persons 'associated with the respondent' and 'relevant' children. An 'associated person' is a spouse or former spouse, a cohabitant or former cohabitant (which is confined to heterosexual relationships, s 58(1)), a person who lives or has lived in the same household,[29] a relative, persons who have agreed to marry one another, parties to the same family proceedings, and, in relation to any child, persons who are the parents of the child or who have or have had parental responsibility for the child.[30] A court in deciding whether to make a non-molestation order (and in determining its terms) shall have regard to all the circumstances including the need to secure the health, safety and well-being of the applicant and any relevant child. 'Molestation' is not defined but will cover violence or the threat thereof as well as 'any form of serious pestering or harassment' (Law Com No 207, para 3.1). Any of the activities which might fall within stalking, such as following a person, watching their home or place of work, telephoning them, interfering with their property, sending them offensive letters or other material, would fall within the ambit of molestation. In those situations covered by the Act, therefore, instances of such behaviour could found a non-molestation order. If the respondent has used or threatened violence against the applicant or a relevant child the court shall attach a power of arrest to one or more provisions of the order unless satisfied that in all the circumstances this is not necessary (see s 44). Orders may be made ex parte where it is just and convenient to do so having regard to all the circumstances including the risk of significant harm to the applicant or a relevant child (see s 42). A court may attach a power of arrest to such an order again where violence has been used or threatened and there is a risk of significant harm if such a power is not attached.

Non-molestation orders will hopefully provide greater protection to those who are the victims of stalkers and who fall within the relevant categories of persons entitled to apply for them. It is disappointing, however, that the Law Commission first, and then Parliament decided to limit the class of persons who could apply for such orders. While the statistics deriving from NASH reveal that 80% of stalking victims are stalked by a person with whom they have had a relationship, this statistic does not reveal whether all those relationships would fall within the definition of 'associated person'. One can speculate that many will have had relationships which have not led to marriage, cohabitation, agreements to marry, or living in the same household but that following their breakdown have resulted in stalking. If the purpose of non-molestation orders is to 'secure the health, safety and well-being' of victims of molestation, one is left wondering what the significance of a prior relationship is as a condition for such protection. Is a person's health, safety and well-being less at risk where they either do not know or have not lived with their molester than where they do or have? The Law Commission was aware of legislation in a number of Australian states which placed no limitation on the range of applicants (Law Com No 207, para 3.9) but declined to support such a wideranging power stating:

29 Otherwise than merely by reason of one of them being the other's employee, tenant, lodger or boarder. This provision could cover a gay or lesbian relationship where domestic violence is not unknown (see Stanko 1993; Lockhart et al 1994).

30 The Law Commission included an additional category of associated persons namely, persons who have or have had a sexual relationship with each other (see Law Com No 207, Draft Bill cl 2(f)).

> 'We do not think it is appropriate that this jurisdiction should be available to resolve issues such as disputes between neighbours, harassment of tenants by landlords or cases of sexual harassment in the workplace. Here there is no domestic or family relationship to justify special remedies or procedures and resort should properly be had to the remedies provided under property or employment law.' (Law Com No 207, para 3.19)

It is clear that the Law Commission were not considering 'stalking' as a specific problem and their sweeping generalisation should not be taken as a reason to prevent reconsideration of this issue. While there may be a potential overlap with some legislation this could have been dealt with expressly. Most stalkers will not be neighbours, landlords, employers or fellow employees and thus the potential for overlap is limited. Indeed, the nature of the problem is different from that covered by such legislation. For example, if A, a student, shares a flat with B which they rent from a landlord, and they share chores, meals etc they would be living in the same household. If following the completion of their studies they move to separate accommodation but B, having developed an obsessional fixation on A, begins to stalk her, A could apply for a non-molestation order. By contrast, if A had owned the flat and let a room in it to B, even though they had shared chores, meals etc, she would be unable to pursue this remedy. Property law would not provide her with any more appropriate remedy. The Law Commission, however, did not wish to create 'something approaching a new tort of harassment or molestation' (Law Com No 207, para 3.8) (although since they wrote their report such a tort appears to be developing). The problem with this is that they also recognised that:

> 'behaviour which does not necessarily amount to a tort or a threatened tort can be prohibited under the domestic violence legislation, which can deal with any form of behaviour which has an effect upon the victim sufficiently severe to warrant the intervention of the court.' (Law Com No 207, para 3.15)

Why should those who do not fall within the prescribed relationships be left to pursue remedies in tort which the Law Commission itself recognised are slower, more complex and less appropriate for cases of emergency protection? The case for confining non-molestation orders to defined relationships is flawed.[31] A removal of these limitations may provide one of the most useful means of affording some protection to a large number of victims of stalking. This, however, is ruled out by the Consultation Paper which states:

> '[T]o extend the Family Law Act [would not be] an adequate solution because it would not cover cases of stalking which lack a sufficient domestic nature to come within the scope of the courts' family law jurisdiction.' (Home Office 1996, para 5.4)

This appears to ignore the fact that the jurisdiction to make non-molestation orders is not confined to family proceedings and any limitations of jurisdiction which exist will be as a result of orders by the Lord Chancellor.

31 A victim of stalking may complain to the Magistrates' Court and seek to have his/her stalker bound over to keep the peace or be of good behaviour: Magistrates' Courts Act 1980 s 115. The order may name the complainant as the person for whose protection it is made (see *Wilson* v *Skeock* (1949) 65 TLR 418) but there is no power to insert any other specific conditions such as could be inserted in a non-molestation order (see *Randall* (1986) 8 Cr App R (S) 433).

b. Tort

For those who fall outwith the Family Law Act provisions, limited remedies in tort law are emerging. In *Burnett* v *George* [1992] 1 FLR 525 the plaintiff had been subjected to a series of assaults, unwanted visits, damage to her house, telephone threats and telephone calls at unsocial hours. The Court of Appeal granted an injunction prohibiting the defendant from entering her property and from assaulting, molesting or interfering with her by acts calculated to impair her health. (see also *Pidduck* v *Molloy* [1992] 2 FLR 202). In *Khorasandjian* v *Bush* [1993] 3 WLR 476 the tort of nuisance was utilised to grant the plaintiff an injunction against the defendant who had previously been convicted of threatening and abusive behaviour and subsequently of threatening to kill but who continued to pester her by following her and by phoning her.[32] In *Burris* v *Azadani* [1995] 1 WLR 1372 the law was further developed when the Court of Appeal affirmed the power of a court to include an 'exclusion zone order' in an injunction which restrained the defendant from, *inter alia*, '(a) assaulting, molesting, harassing, threatening, pestering or otherwise interfering with the plaintiff by doing acts to cause her harm whether directly or indirectly . . . : (b) making any communication to the plaintiff . . . whether in writing or orally . . . ; (c) from coming or remaining within 250 yards of the plaintiff's home address. . . .' (for comment see Lawson-Cruttenden 1995). The Court both affirmed that the plaintiff had a cause of action in nuisance and, in addition, under the tort of harassment as the plaintiff had a 'legitimate interest' in receiving protection from behaviour 'which might be highly stressful and disturbing'. Of course civil remedies are costly and it is necessary to know who the stalker is to be able to institute proceedings. In addition a power of arrest for breach of an injunction in such cases does not exist so further action on the part of the victim is necessary to institute contempt proceedings. These developments in tort also have the effect of undermining whatever the rationale is for limiting the class of persons who can apply for non-molestation orders.

4. Legislating for stalking

i. Civil Law

In its Consultation Paper (Home Office 1996, para 5.5) the Government proposes a new statutory tort of molestation leaving it to the courts to define. As they have been, and will continue to be, doing so in the context of domestic violence, clarity will emerge while the absence of a statutory definition allows for a degree of flexibility to cover any new forms which molestation may take. A defendant will be liable if he intended to cause harassment or distress or realised or should have realised that his conduct would do so (para 5.6). The existing practice of tailoring injunctions to meet the needs of particular cases would apply. It is important, however, that any such statutory tort provides a defence of lawful excuse so that legitimate activities are not caught.[33] This is provided for by the proposal that it

32 The Court of Appeal also stated that harassment which caused physical or psychiatric illness to the recipient was actionable and that where there was a risk that the cumulative effect of harassment might cause such illness it could be restrained on a quia timet basis. (See for comment Bridgeman and Jones 1994; R. Townshend-Smith 1995).

33 The obtaining of an interlocutory injunction on 15 August 1996 by the Princess of Wales against the photographer Martin Stenning has raised concerns about press freedom being restricted. The order banned Stenning from 'approaching within 300 yards of her, communicating with her, and harassing or interfering with her safety, security or well-being'.

be a defence for the 'person to show that he was acting reasonably in the course of his profession, trade, business or other lawful activity' (para 7.5). In a novel proposal the Government suggests that rather than relying solely on the law of contempt to deal with the breach of an injunction, breach of an injunction in the case of stalking should be a criminal offence punishable with up to five years' imprisonment. Such a penalty means that it would be an arrestable offence counteracting one of the weaknesses of contempt proceedings for breach of an injunction. As the standard of proof for obtaining an injunction is the civil standard, it is suggested that to make breach of such an injunction a criminal offence should be eschewed. Rather breach of an injunction should be an aggravating factor in respect of the commission of a 'stalking' offence (see below).

ii. An offence of stalking?

Criminalization of behaviour which falls within the ambit of stalking, remains an option. The offences which may be used at present to deal with this problem have not been designed with that purpose in view. It is important to recognise that stalking is a course of conduct which may combine a range of actions each of which on its own may not appear serious but when combined over a period have a serious impact on the victim causing harassment, distress, alarm, inconvenience and often more serious impairment of the victim's psychological well-being. Current offences under the Public Order, Telecommunications and Malicious Communications Acts address only particular aspects of stalking and do not provide the opportunity for a sentencer to fully reflect the gravity of the conduct in the sentence. Repeat offenders do not face the prospect of more severe sentences. While the offence under the Trade Union and Labour Relations (Consolidation) Act 1992 covers a wider range of activity it is only a summary offence and was designed to deal with intimidation in the context of strikes rather than the problem of stalking. The innovative use of the Offences Against the Person Act and public nuisance by prosecutors, upheld by the courts, reflects, perhaps, judicial frustration at being unable to adequately punish serious behaviour. Where the victim suffers harm recourse to the former statute may be understandable. This again, however, is not a solution although the enactment of the Law Commission's Criminal Law Bill (see Law Com No. 218) would cover behaviour such as that in *Ireland* and *Burstow*. This does not appear to have been considered as an option by the Government possibly because such a piece of legislation would take more parliamentary time and would not create the same PR opportunities which a short and pithy statute on stalking would provide. More piecemeal legislation, however, is not desirable; a complete overhaul of offences against the person is long overdue with stalking being treated as an aspect of that problem.

The Government, however, proposes to 'develop the existing law relating to harassment and to eliminate the difficulties which have led to its ineffectiveness in dealing with the conduct of stalkers' (Home Office 1996, para 5.17). It proposes two offences[34] which are developments of the offences under sections 4 and 4A of the Public Order Act 1986. The first offence which would be punishable with up to five years' imprisonment and/or an unlimited fine would require:

> 'the persistent use of words or behaviour, which either intentionally leads a person to believe, or which occurs in circumstances where a reasonable person

34 For both offences it would be a defence for the 'person to show that he was acting reasonably in the course of his profession, trade, business or other lawful activity.' (para 7.5)

> should have realised that a person would believe, that violence would be used against him or that he is likely to believe that violence would be used against him.' (para 7.3)

This appears to be a variation of the offence of assault (as understood before the decision in *Ireland*) except the belief need not be that violence would be used immediately. The *mens rea* is a form of '*Caldwell*' recklessness. The element of persistence, however, is what sets this apart from assault. The problem with this proposal, however, is the requirement of a belief that violence will be used.[35] The nature of the obsessional harassing conduct engaged in by many stalkers may not be such as to give rise to such a belief even though it may cause distress to the victim and lead to psychiatric injury. In such cases, where harm ensues, resort would have to be made to s 47 or s 20 of the Offences Against the Person Act 1861 as extended in *Ireland* and *Burstow* but the new offence would not be made out if harm did not ensue.

The second proposed offence for which the maximum penalty would be six months imprisonment and/or a fine at level 5 of the standard scale, would require:

> 'the persistent use of words or behaviour which either intentionally causes a person to be harassed, alarmed or distressed, or which occurs in circumstances where a reasonable person should have realised that this would be the effect.' (para 7.3)

This offence will obviously catch all the stalking behaviours identified above and will catch both the malicious stalker and the obsessional stalker. However, it will not provide an adequate response to serious persistent behaviour which does not fall within the first offence.

The problem with both the current distortions of the law to cover individual cases and the Government's precipitate proposals for the future is that they create a danger that victims will be denied justice. It is a mistake to regard stalking as serious only where there are threats of violence or where violence is used or anticipated or where harm ensues. Many stalkers have no intention to use violence nor will their behaviour necessarily amount to a threat but it can cause harassment, alarm or distress to the victim nonetheless. The behaviour involved can be serious in its impact on the victim's freedom and their quality of life. The fact that a resilient victim does not suffer psychological harm or anticipate violence should not be the basis for denying them protection.

Legislation does exist in other countries from which lessons may be learned. It is outside the remit of this article to engage in close textual analysis of the various state offences of stalking in the United States[36] or the Criminal Law Consolidation (Stalking) Amendment Act 1994 (No 7) which operates in South Australia. However, a few points will be made which legislators in the United Kingdom should take into account.

The purpose of an anti-stalking law must be to provide protection to victims[37] from behaviour which seriously impairs their quality of life. The essence of this

---

35 It is assumed that the Government is using the term 'violence' as it is generally understood and not in the novel way in which it was used by the Court of Appeal in *Ireland*.

36 For this and a useful model statute see Faulkner and Hsiao 1994; Lingg 1993; see also National Victims Centre for a collection of State Statutes.

37 The legislation should include within the definition of 'victim' members of the victim's family or household or others in an intimate relationship with the victim as they may become targets for the stalker's threats or conduct.

behaviour is not that it threatens violence or will lead to violence (although it generally creates a fear of violence on the part of the victim) but rather that it constitutes an enforced form of contact between the victim and the stalker which the victim does not want and which the stalker pursues either for the purpose of compelling the victim to do or abstain from doing that which the victim has a right to abstain from doing or to do, or simply for the purpose of causing harassment, alarm or distress to the victim That many victims are put in fear, or suffer harm, are aggravating factors but these should not be seen as prerequisites to establishing an offence.

It must also be recognised that stalkers differ in (1) their motivations, (2) the psychiatric, psychological and personality disorders from which they may suffer, (3) their predilection to violence (see McAnaney et al 1993), and (4) their amenability to deterrence by means of criminal sanctions. Any response to stalking, therefore, must seek to provide protection from all such stalkers. Where stalkers fall into the erotomanic category, their criminal liability may be doubtful as they may fit the M'Naghten insanity criteria. An insanity verdict does, of course, provide the opportunity for the court to subject the stalker to a treatment regime whether in an institution or in the community but the defence may seek to avoid the question of insanity and simply challenge the prosecution evidence of intent. If the offence of stalking is framed solely to require an intention to harass, intimidate, threaten the victim or cause the victim to fear violence, a prosecution of such a stalker may fail. In the case of stalkers in the borderline erotomania category the same difficulty with intent arises and such stalkers would fall outwith the M'Naghten criteria. It is crucial, therefore, that the basic offence focus on the conduct and the underlying purpose of coercion which is common to many stalkers (apart from the sociopathic in category 4 who present an entirely different problem) while providing an alternative form to cover those whose intent is to harass etc or who due to their disturbed mind do not form the intent.

In many ways an offence of stalking should seek to provide a means of early intervention and provide a graduated response to reflect the gravity of the offending behaviour. The conduct which stalkers engage in would not constitute an attempt to commit a substantive offence. Even if the stalker is disposed to violence, letters, telephone calls, following of the victim and surveillance of his/her home would, at best, amount to merely preparatory acts. Intervention, however, is justified to prevent the risk of violence and/or serious distress or psychological harm to the victim.

As many of the activities (following, watching, telephoning, sending letters etc) which fall within the concept of stalking may be carried out with no illegitimate purpose in mind, it is important that an anti-stalking law does not unduly restrict the rights of citizens to engage in these activities. The performance of one action by a person should not be sufficient to amount to this offence (although it may amount to one of the existing offences outlined above). The feature which distinguishes stalking from many other forms of offending is that the stalker engages in a course of conduct in respect of the victim. To establish an offence of stalking there should be a requirement that the stalker engage in a course of conduct comprising at least two separate incidents of unwanted contact. An additional requirement that the conduct be engaged in without lawful excuse would provide protection for those who may contact the victim for a legitimate purpose, albeit unwanted by him or her, for example, debt collectors or journalists.

In legislating, however, the mistake would be to create an offence unconnected to the other remedies which may be available. On conviction of an offence of stalking a court should be empowered to make a non-molestation order. The Government have proposed, however, that the victim should be free to apply to the civil courts for an injunction following a conviction. Apart from giving rise to a duplication of judicial effort this would be an additional burden on the victim both in emotional and financial terms. The more sensible solution is for sentencers to have the power to make such orders. Generally, stalking committed while such an order is in force (whether made in civil or criminal proceedings) could amount to an aggravated form of the offence. The existence of the aggravated form of the offence would also act as an incentive to victims to apply for non-molestation orders at an early stage whether or not complaint had been made to the police. This would also provide a means of protection to the victim where, perhaps, the police had not treated the victim's complaint seriously. The aggravated form of the offence could also cover stalking where the intention is to cause fear of serious violence or where harm, either physical or psychological, is caused by the offence, or where damage is caused to the victim's property. Similarly, possession of an offensive weapon on an occasion to which a charge relates, should amount to an aggravating factor as it evidences a risk of violence which the activity on its own may not evince.

A further purpose which the legislation must serve is that of providing a framework within which sentencers are enabled to impose appropriate, graded, sentences which reflect the gravity of the offending. Conviction of the basic offence should be a sufficient basis for the imposition of a non-molestation order. Sentencers should also be aware of their powers to impose appropriate orders, for example, probation with a treatment requirement (see Powers of Criminal Courts Act 1973, sch 1A, para 5) or a hospital order (see Mental Health Act 1983 s 37). Because of the unusual nature of this type of behaviour it may even be appropriate to impose a requirement that all those convicted of stalking be remanded for psychiatric reports if such were not obtained prior to trial. If the aggravated form of the offence is made indictable only the sentencer would have the additional power under s. 41 of the Mental Health Act 1983 to make a restriction order. As it is inevitable that many stalkers may not be amenable to deterrence or rehabilitation and will reoffend, and probably do so in respect of the same victim, repeat offences should either be regarded as aggravated forms of the offence or, alternatively, be triable only on indictment to enable courts to impose sentences which afford greater protection. To this end it is important that any offence of stalking is treated as an offence of violence as defined in the Criminal Justice Act 1991 s 31 to permit sentencers either to impose a custodial sentence under s 1(2)(b) or a longer custodial sentence under s 2(2)(b).

Conclusion

It would be foolish to think that an anti-stalking law will resolve the problem of stalking. The psychology of many stalkers may not be amenable to change and thus their behaviour may continue regardless of the punishment imposed on them. In addition, whatever, is done in relation to stalking it will probably have limited impact on thc sociopathic stalker. Providing protection from such individuals is, essentially, a policing problem but one which is unlikely to offer up any effective solution. What is clear, however, is that more information is necessary on the incidence of stalking and the psychology of stalkers to ensure that the most effective means are adopted to deal with the problem. There is a problem and it is not being addressed adequately by current legislation or by the hamfisted attempts by the courts to bring the offending behaviour within the ambit of other offences. An anti-stalking law is necessary to recognise and deal with this conduct rather than the haphazard pieces of legislation and common law which may be used to deal with particular aspects of the problem. Such legislation, however, requires careful drafting and a grading of offences and penalties. It also needs to be tied in to other processes, in particular non-molestation orders, to enable early intervention to take place before the conduct and its consequences become serious. In addition, there must be recognition that police, courts and prisons are not the only means to achieving a solution to the problem. Probation officers, social workers and mental health practitioners may all have a role to play. The danger in the Government's proposals is that they are a precipitate response to the problem resulting from recent media attention. The proposed offences and tort, if enacted, would not provide an adequate solution to the problem although a quick response may enhance the Government's 'law and order' credentials and provide a few extra votes for them at the next election. The problem with precipitate legislation, however, is that its deficiencies come home to roost later as the history of the Aggravated Vehicle Taking Act 1992 and Dangerous Dogs Act 1991 show only too clearly.

Bibliography

Ashworth, A (1991) 'Interpreting Criminal Statutes: a Crisis of Legality?' 107 *Law Quarterly Review* 419.

Ashworth, A (1995) *Principles of Criminal Law* (Oxford: Oxford University Press).

Boychuk, MK (1994) 'Are Stalking Laws Unconstitutionally Vague or Overbroad?' 88 *Northwestern University Law Review* 769.

Bridgeman, J and Jones, M (1994) 'Harassing conduct and outrageous acts: a cause of action for intentionally inflicted mental distress' 14 *Legal Studies* 180.

Brazier, M, ed (1995) *Clerk and Lindsell on Torts* (17th ed) (London: Sweet and Maxwell).

Criminal Law Revision Committee, Fourteenth Report (1980) *Offences Against the Person* (London: HMSO) Cmnd 7844.

Enoch, MD & Trethowan, WH (1979) *Uncommon Psychiatric Syndromes*, 2nd ed, (Chicago: Year Book Medical Publishers).

Faulkner, RP & Hsiao, DH (1994) 'And Where You Go I'll Follow: the Constitutionality of Anti-stalking Laws and Proposed Model Legislation' 31 *Harvard Journal of Legislation* 1.

Fawcett, B, Featherstone, B, Hearn, J & Toft, C (1996) *Violence and Gender Relations: Theories and Interventions* (London: Sage).

Giles, M (1992) 'Judicial Law-Making in the Criminal Court' *Criminal Law Review* 407.

Goode, M (1995) 'Stalking: Crime of the Nineties' 19 *Criminal Law Journal* 21.

Harmon, RB, Rosner, R & Owens, H (1995) 'Obsessional Harassment and Erotomania in a Criminal Court Population' *Journal of Forensic Science* 188.

Harris, DJ, O'Boyle, M & Warbrick, C (1995) *Law of the European Convention on Human Rights* (London: Butterworths).

Home Office and Lord Chancellor's Department Consultation Paper, *Stalking: the Solutions* (Home Office 1996) **http://www.open.gov.uk/home–off/lh1426a.htm**

House of Commons Home Affairs Committee (1992–93) Third Report, *Domestic Violence* HC 241–1.

Kurt, JL (1995) 'Stalking as a Variant of Domestic Violence' 23 *Bulletin of American Academy of Psychiatry and Law* 219.
Lardner, G (1995) *The Stalking of Kristin: a Father Investigates the Murder of His Daughter* (Grove Atlantic Inc).
Law Commission No 207 (1992) *Family Law: Domestic Violence and Occupation of the Family Home* (London: HMSO).
Law Commission No 218 (1993) *Legislating the Criminal Code: Offences Against the Person and General Principles* (London: HMSO) Cm 2370.
Lawson-Cruttenden, T (1995) 'The Final Emergence of the Tort of Harassment?' *Family Law* 625.
Lingg, R (1993) 'Stopping Stalkers: a Critical Examination of Anti-Stalking Statutes' 67 *St John's Law Review* 347.
Lockhart, LL, White, BW, Causby, V & Isaac, A (1994) 'Letting Out the Secret – Violence in Lesbian Relationships' 9 *Journal of Interpersonal Violence* 469.
MacCormick, DN (1978) *Legal Reasoning and Legal Theory* (Oxford: Clarendon Press).
McAnaney, KG, Curliss, LA & Abeyta-Price, AE (1993) 'From Imprudence to Crime: Anti-Stalking Laws' 68 *Notre Dame Law Review* 819.
Mullen, PE & Pathe, M (1994) 'Stalking and the Pathologies of Love' 28 *Australian and New Zealand Journal of Psychiatry* 469.
Murphy, P, ed (1996) *Blackstone's Criminal Practice* (London: Blackstone Press Ltd).
National Victim Centre: State Anti-Stalking Laws **http://www.nvc.org/hdir/statestk.htm**
Nicolson, D and Sanghvi, R (1993) 'Battered Women and Provocation: The Implications of *R.* v. *Ahluwalia*' *Criminal Law Review* 728.
Smith, ATH (1987) *Offences Against Public Order* (London: Sweet and Maxwell).
Smith, JC and Hogan, B (1993) *Criminal Law*, 7th ed (London: Butterworths).
Smith, JC (1996) '*Burstow*: Commentary' *Criminal Law Review* 333.
Sohn, EF (1994) 'Anti-stalking Statutes: Do They Actually Protect Victims?' 30 Criminal Law Bulletin 203.
Stanko, B (1993) 'Men Who Beat the Men Who Love Them – Battered Gay Men and Domestic Violence' 33 *British Journal of Criminology* 449.
Strikis, S (1993) 'Stopping Stalking' 81 *Georgetown Law Journal* 2771.
Townshend-Smith, R (1995) 'Harassment as a Tort in English and American Law: the Boundaries of *Wilkinson* v *Downton*' 24 *Anglo-American Law Review* 299.
Trindale, F and Cane, P (1993) *The Law of Torts in Australia*, 2nd ed (Melbourne: Oxford University Press Australia).
Von Heussen, E (1996) *Facts About Stalking* (NASH).
Wells, C (1994) 'Battered woman syndrome and defences to homicide: where now?' 14 *Legal Studies* 266.
Williams G (1957) 'Assault and Words' *Criminal Law Review 219.*
Williams, G (1983) *Textbook of Criminal Law*, 2nd ed (London: Stevens).
Zona, Sharma & Lane (1993) 'A Comparative Study of Erotomanic and Obsessional Subjects in a Forensic Sample' *Journal of Forensic Science* 894.

COMPUTER-GENERATED DISPLAYS IN THE COURTROOM: FOR BETTER OR WORSE?

Declan O'Flaherty B.A.

Postgraduate Student, The Queen's University of Belfast, Northern Ireland <P9580786@Queens-Belfast.ac.uk>

First Published in Web Journal of Current Legal Issues in association with Blackstone Press Ltd.

SUMMARY

Much has been written about computer-generated evidence in the courtroom and most of it has focused on the admissibility of such evidence. However, in this article the intention is to shift the emphasis towards more practical aspects of the topic. Accordingly, a distinction will be drawn between the main types of computer-generated displays in use today. This is followed by a brief analysis of the processes involved in the production of these displays. Next, the benefits and drawbacks of using the technology will be considered. Finally, a number of practical steps are proposed which could be taken to make the use of computer-generated displays more equitable.

CONTENTS

Introduction

Picture this scene. In a moment of high drama in a complex case arising out of a road traffic accident, the jury are instructed to don specially designed helmets and gloves. Then, an expert witness takes the participants through a computer-generated simulation of what he believes took place at the accident scene. The expert controls the progression of the simulation, while enabling the jury to gain their own perspectives on such factors as the quality and character of the road, the position and velocity of the vehicles, the existence of any warnings and the prevailing weather conditions (Gore 1993, p 477). In effect, the jury experiences a re-creation of the actual event in fully interactive three-dimensional (3-D) graphics. Does it sound far-fetched? Perhaps not, and indeed in the near future in the United States, at least, the likelihood of such a scenario being played out in courtrooms all over the country is more of a probability than a possibility.

Computer applications in the courtroom are nothing new. Early uses consisted primarily of organisational tools to help lawyers and judges store and retrieve data quickly (see Leith 1991, pp 139–148). More recently, major advances in technology have meant that computer-generated displays have been unleashed in the courtroom in an attempt to aid jury understanding of complex events and fact patterns. The scenario depicted above is but an extension of that involving the use of Virtual Reality[1] which its proponents believe possesses the potential to alter dramatically the face of litigation (Gore 1993, p 460).

The use of computer-generated displays is almost commonplace in US litigation where they have been widely praised for their ability to aid jury comprehension. They have also been heralded for their inherent power of jury persuasion in an era where jurors are more than comfortable with the idea of receiving and retaining information via television. Furthermore, computer-generated displays offer significant benefits in terms of presentation of evidence. However, lawyers on this side of the Atlantic have been more cautious in their approach to the use of these displays.[2] Indeed, in this instance it may be proper to err on the side of caution because convincing arguments have been made against the use of the technology in the courtroom. One leading commentator has suggested that every advantage of a computer-generated display 'carries with it a concomitant potential for abuse or unintentional misuse that could manipulate a juror's impression of a simulated event' (Berkoff 1994, p 849).

Much has been written about computer-generated evidence in the courtroom and most of it has highlighted the admissibility of such evidence.[3] However, I propose to shift the emphasis towards more practical aspects of the topic. Accordingly, in

1 'The term ''virtual'' describes a reality that is not a conventional, genuine reality but rather something that exists in contrast to reality, yet operates as if it were actual reality' (Gore 1993, p 460).
2 It has been reported that the first instance of computer-generated graphics being used in a British court took place at Oxford Crown Court in September 1994: *R* v *Wharton* (Horten 1994, p 1289) The use of the technology had already been well-established in US litigation by that time.
3 For example, see Bainbridge 1996, ch. 28, pp 270–276; Ormerod 1995, pp 22–24. For an Irish perspective on the subject, see Fennell 1995, pp 316–320.

the next section, a distinction is drawn between the main types of computer-generated displays in use today. This is followed by a brief analysis of the processes involved in the production of these displays. I will then highlight both the benefits of using the technology and the potential disadvantages. Finally, a number of practical steps are proposed which could be taken to if not eradicate the abuses, at least make the use of computer-generated displays more equitable.

1. Types of Displays and Production Techniques

It is important at the outset to draw a critical distinction between the three main types of computer-generated displays currently in use. They are computer animations, simulations and the most recent development, Virtual Reality. In this section, a brief account of the processes involved in the production of these displays is also given.

a. Animation, Simulation or Virtual Reality?

A computer animation is an actual series of computer-generated images or pictures. Each image in the series is altered slightly frame by frame in order to mimic actual movement, and that which is displayed on the screen is the totality of the exhibit. By contrast, a computer simulation involves the input on many sophisticated rules of physics and mathematics which form the parameters within which the facts of the particular scenario operate. The exhibit that is presented to the jury, therefore, involves infinitely more than the simple image displayed on the screen (Berkoff 1994, p 830). The essential difference between a computer simulation and animation is that 'the computer simulation, verified by an expert as being scientifically sound and based on scientific knowledge and physical laws, should demonstrate not what ''might'' have happened or what ''could'' have happened but what actually did happen' (Hoenig 1993, p 5). However, as Muir (1992, p 4) points out the simulation and animation need not be mutually exclusive. They are sometimes contained in one large program. However, the best computer simulation programs do not usually contain the best quality graphics or animation and vice versa.

Virtual Reality (VR) proceeds one step further than computer simulations and animations by breathing real life into them. VR takes its viewers beyond passive observation of computer-generated displays to the next realm of interactive 3-D simulations. As Gore (1993, p 475) puts it, 'while a picture may be worth a thousand words, the power of actually experiencing an event inevitably surpasses that of viewing a picture.' VR also takes computer-generated displays even further by making its environment suitable for multi-person participation. VR effectively permits events to be relived. Thus, a multi-person VR approach to litigation could permit the entire jury, experts and lawyers to be within the scene and experience the occurrence. To borrow the words of Gore (1993, p 476) again: 'VR empowers its participants to surpass their immediate identities and encounter events from diverse viewpoints with very little expenditure of effort and time.'

b. Production of Computer-Generated Displays

The production of a basic computer animation is a five-step process (Muir 1992, p 5). The first step is the collection of any pertinent data including drawings, sketches, police or accident reports, depositions of eye witnesses, photographs etc. The second step is creating a storyboard, sketching out key events and adding words to the still images to describe the motion that is to be animated. The third step is creating the computer models. Here the input data describing the various objects in the animation are actually built on the computer. The fourth step is composing the motion script. Data or the positions of an object with respect to time are put into the computer to control the motions of the object during the animation. The fifth step is rendering. The computer takes all input data (i.e. lighting, texture and composition of the materials that make up the objects) to determine what the object will look like and renders or calculates a still frame containing the image.

Berkoff (1994, p 831) takes the example of a car accident to explain the production of a computer simulation. The first step is inputting the co-ordinates of the objects that were present at the accident scene. The next step involves calculation of the motions of each object that played a significant role in the accident. The testimony of eye-witnesses and accident witnesses are also taken into account. Berkoff (1994, p 831) notes that:

> 'While the laws of science provide the rules by which the evidence of the specific incident must abide, the computer provides the best fit within these rules for the complex data handed to it.'

Once the basic computer animation or simulation has been produced, the final step is to record the product on either videotape or on CD-ROM or Laser Disc format. While a videotape production takes less time and is significantly less expensive, CD-ROM's and Laser Disc technology are becoming increasingly widespread and offer many advantages, not least of which is the storage capacity they offer. For example, one laser-disc side holds 54,000 pictures, charts and graphs or 30 minutes of moving video, offering greater speed, flexibility and clarity than the usual videotape presentation. Entire depositions, treatises and other materials can be stored on a single disc. (Marcotte 1989, p 54)

VR takes 3-D computer displays a stage further by enabling participants to explore an audio-visual representation of the world where objects can be handled and manipulated in real time and real space. A master computer and software, which create the environment and command the movements of the objects within the scene, are required to achieve VR. Sensors, mounted in a helmet and glove worn by the participant, monitor his/her movements and alter the artificially created environment in harmony with the graphic 3-D objects. The effect of this can be quite staggering:

> 'Used together, these tools allow complete immersion into a computer-created, human dictated world. Objects are touched, their resistance to movement sensed, and the scene altered at will by the participant.' (Gore, 1993, p 467)

2. Advantages of Computer-Generated Displays in Litigation

This section involves a detailed analysis of the perceived benefits of using computer-generated displays in the courtroom. They are that such displays:

(i) aid jury understanding;
(ii) persuade juries of the correctness of the evidence shown in the display; and
(iii) provide important benefits to an advocate in the presentation of his/her arguments before the court.

Each will now be analysed in turn.

a. Aid to Jury Comprehension

> 'Communication is at the heart of litigation; everything else is secondary. Evidence is meaningless if it cannot be transmitted effectively to the fact finder, and from the perspective of the litigator, evidence may be valueless if it is not transmitted persuasively.' (Lederer 1994, p 1113)

Computer-generated animations, simulations and virtual reality provide an effective means of conveying evidence to a jury, particularly in complex or technical trials. Berkoff (1994, p 845) recognises the difficulties facing those parties presenting evidence in such trials:

> 'As the complexity of the issues presented to a jury increases, the amount of interest, comprehension, and retention will decrease. For a party presenting such complex issues to a jury, the object is to present them in the most comprehensible, succinct, and attention-getting method possible.'

In a recent survey on jury comprehension the American Bar Association found that the trier of fact is often confused, bored, frustrated and/or overwhelmed by technical issues or complex fact patterns (Gore 1993, p 478). It is often the responsibility of an expert witness to explain such issues to a jury and in this context, computer-generated displays provide a wonderful tool. As Muir (1992, p 4) puts it:

> 'They offer a bridge for the technical community to communicate complex issues to a lay audience.'

b. Tool of Jury Persuasion

It is also evident that visual displays have a greater psychological impact on juries than purely verbal presentations. Surveys have shown that humans are essentially visual learners. We retain 87% of the information which is presented to us visually while we retain only 10% of what we hear (Borelli 1996, p 453). To quote Berkoff (1994, p 846), it is clear that 'visual presentation is more effective than verbal communication, and that verbal communication is most effective when coupled with a visual presentation.' From a litigator's point of view, the persuasive value of computer-generated displays is undeniable and an invaluable weapon in his arsenal.

A brief look at a number of the cases in which computer-generated displays were utilised demonstrates the powerful and persuasive effect the technology can have on those who view it. The first use of a computer simulation at trial was entitled 'Hexane Explosion' and was utilised in Kentucky case in which a gas leak triggered multiple explosions in Louisville (Berkoff 1994, p 846). If a computer simulation had not been used, the jury would have had to digest cumbersome traditional forms of demonstrative evidence needed to make the same points: diagrams of the chemical plant, maps of the city sewer system, eyewitness accounts of the explosion, and expert testimony on gas technology. Instead, with the use of computer simulations, the jury was ostensibly able to 'see' what happened. Two days after the jury was shown the computer simulations, the defendants settled the case.

In a 1989 Florida personal injury case, computer-generated displays persuaded the jury to award seven million dollars to the plaintiff (Gore 1983, p 473). The jury failed to believe thc defendant's version of the facts that the plaintiff lost control of her car; instead, the computer re-enactment indicated that the defendant's vehicle had collided with the rear of the plaintiff's car thereby causing the accident. In the criminal case of *People* v *McHugh* (476 NYS 2d 721 (Sup Ct 1984)), the defence used a computer-generated display to show that the prosecutor's version of events could not possibly have happened (Bardelli 1994, p 1358). In that case, a computer simulation of a car accident revealed the accident's unavoidability due to an uncovered manhole on the road and thus, persuaded the jury to acquit the man on trial for manslaughter and drunk driving.

c. Presentation of Arguments

The use of laser-discs and CD-ROM's for storage allows computer-generated graphics, animations and simulations to be seamlessly integrated into the overall presentation with no interference in the trial process (Walsh 1995, p 29). Put graphically, 10 foot tall stacks of paper and evidence can easily be reduced to 2 or 3 pocket-sized CD-ROM's. One of the most famous cases involving the use of computer-generated evidence was that arising out of the Delta 191 crash at Dallas/Fort Worth Airport in 1985.[4] The crash led to a fierce legal battle between the airline and the US government. Government lawyers in the case were among the first to adapt laser-disc technology for courtroom use. One of the government's lawyers stated the advantage of using the technology to be:

> 'You don't have to rummage through 30 boxes looking for documents. . . [Laser discs] allow you to effectively integrate video and documentary evidence.' (Marcotte 1989, p 54)

Furthermore, by swiping barcodes, counsel has the ability to instantly retrieve an exhibit. As Kissane-Gaisford (1995, p 473) has written:

> 'During an oral presentation, the speaker can gracefully intersperse oration with the graphical presentation of evidence, simply by scanning the bar-code mid-sentence. This technique can be used to display the evidence nearly instantaneously, timed to correspond with the end of the talented orator's point for maximum impact.'

Once the evidence is displayed, computers can also provide tremendous presentation advantages such as stop-action, varied perspectives and slow-motion. It is also possible to enlarge, highlight, duplicate or compare evidence. This flexibility of computer-generated displays adds greatly to its explanatory power:

> 'Not only can it go places that are physically impossible to get to in other ways, but once an accident or an event is animated or stored in the computer, the viewpoint can be easily moved to another vantage point, whether it be that of a witness, the pilot of a plane or simply one that gives the viewer a better understanding of what happened.' (Muir 1992, p 5)

4 In *Re Air Crash at Dallas/Fort Worth Airport on Aug. 2, 1985*, 720 F Supp 1258 (ND Tex 1989), aff'd, 919 F2d 1079 (5th Cir 1991), cert denied sub nom *Connors* v *United States*, 112 S Ct 276 (1991).

3. Potential for Misuse

There is no doubt that computer-generated displays are a powerful tool of persuasion in the armoury of any technologically adept litigator who is prepared to use them. Nevertheless, some commentators have expressed considerable unease about the use of such technology in the courtroom. The consequences of misuse of computer-generated displays cannot be underestimated particularly in the context of a criminal trial where as one writer has noted:

> 'Rather than an award or loss of money judgement, the defendant in a criminal prosecution is subject to a loss of liberty' (Bardelli 1994, p 1358)

These are not the rantings of Luddite technophobes who prefer the quill-pen to the light-pen but rather represent measured and coherent criticisms of the technology and its use in modern litigation. As such they merit serious consideration and in this section I hope to explore some of those criticisms.

a. 'Seeing is Believing . . .'

Critics argue that the persuasive power of computer-generated displays is also their greatest disadvantage. Computer-generated displays invariably leave a strong impression on jurors. Indeed, they tend to mesmerise factseekers and relax their natural critical natures (Jenkins 1976, p 600). The tendency on the part of the jury is to think 'I saw it on TV, therefore it must be true'. Such a conclusion may of course be far from the truth and essentially removes from the jury their fact-finding function:

> 'The fear is that the highly communicative nature of computer graphics and the myth of the infallible computer will take the decision out of the jury's hands. The old adage ''seeing is believing'' may gain extra force in this setting' (Borelli 1996, p 455).

The US case of *People* v *Mitchell* (Cal App First Dist Div 2, Marin County Superior Court No. SC–12462-A (1994)) provides an apt illustration of the dangers of adopting such a view. In that case, the defendant, James Mitchell, was accused of the murder of his brother, Artie Mitchell. The defendant claimed he acted in self-defence. The prosecution used computer animation to show that because of Artie's location behind a wall, James could not have seen any threatening gestures made by Artie. Following objections by defence counsel, the judge ordered that the human-like figure representing Artie be replaced by a geometric shape to avoid the risk that the jury might assume as proven fact the position of Artie's hands in the animation. The case highlights the point that computer animations do not always present factual information, rather as Ellenbogen (1993, p 1120) has remarked:

> '[They] are simply artfully planned and staged presentations promoting one party's unproven theory.'

b. Prejudicial Effects of Not Using The Technology

The persuasive influence of computer-generated displays on jurors is compounded when an opposing party does not use the technology at trial (Selbak 1994, p 361). A party opting to present a traditional case will often be prejudiced by the use of computer-generated evidence by the other side. The available statistics would seem to support such a view. By 1992, it was estimated that computer-generated displays had been used in 858 cases in the US where litigation took place between major companies. In these, all except 15 settled out of court and in all the 15 cases which went to trial, the side using computer-generated displays was successful (McKeone 1992, p 6).

It would appear that cost is the main reason parties forgo the use of computer-generated displays. Such displays can prove to be very expensive indeed. For example, the exhibits in the Delta Airlines case cost the US government between $100,000 and $150,000 to produce. The cost might have been two or three times that figure adding in time and travel of outside experts (Marcotte 1989, p 56). Clearly, such exorbitant costs would be far beyond the resources of the average litigator. The high cost particularly favours prosecutors in criminal cases who will have the state's resources at their disposal against usually less wealthy clients. A related concern alluded to by Selbak (1994, p 361) is that litigants with limited budgets may feel compelled to settle rather than seek a trial on the merits when facing opponents who are able to afford animated graphics.

c. Potential For Tampering With The Evidence

There is a great deal of scope for tampering with the evidence in computer-generated displays. This possibility was recognised in the dissenting judgement of Justice Van Graafeiland in the US case of *Perma Research & Development* v *Singer* (542 F 2d 111 (2d Cir) cert denied, 429 US 987 (1974)). The learned judge stated that although a computer has tremendous potential for generating more meaningful evidence, 'it presents a real danger of being the vehicle for introducing erroneous, misleading or unreliable evidence.' While computer-generated displays offer apparent advantages in jury presentation such as varying perspectives, slow-motion and stop-action, such facilities can also be used to manipulate the events being shown. As Marcotte (1989, p 56) explains:

> 'Just as a writer uses punctuation, the selective use of a zoom, close-up and fadeout can accent different points. A constantly moving object can appear to change speed or direction by merely changing the point where it is viewed. While the animation may be technically correct, it can be misleading. The medium shapes the message.'

The infamous Rodney King trial provides an analogous illustration of the manipulative use of stop-action in a video-tape. The focal piece of evidence in the case was a video-tape showing the police officers involved beating Rodney King. The defendants' lawyers were able to use stop-motion very effectively 'to de-emphasise the brutality of the event, slowing real time to a snail's pace and demonstrating the supposedly calculated safety precautions taken by the officers' (Berkoff 1994, p 851).

Even where there is no deliberate attempt to tamper with the evidence, computer-generated displays can be unintentionally misleading. Computer animations in particular rely a great deal upon data collection, human judgement and speculation at each step of the animation process. Since a computer is no better than the human using it, and no human is perfect, it follows that computer-generated displays are also prone to error. This is known at the 'Garbage In, Garbage Out' (GIGO) principle. Hoenig (1994, p 6) points out the danger posed by such human fallibility:

'If an expert plugs 'garbage' into the computer, i.e. date, information or principles that are false, erroneous or misleading, the computer-generated result constitutes 'garbage' unworthy of going to the jury. When the GIGO principle is violated, the jury is not being given scientific evidence that is correct and, therefore, it obviously is not helpful in the search for the truth.'

Conclusion: Some Specific Suggestions

The foregoing discussion has shown that computer-generated displays are a powerful tool for the presentation and explanation of arguments at a trial. However, powerful objections to the use of the technology threaten to outweigh its probative value. In order to avoid this undesirable development, steps need to be taken to eradicate the abuses and ensure the continued growth and development of the use of computer-generated displays in the courtroom. Several commentators have focused on the need to formulate a stringent set of criteria through which computer-generated displays must pass before being admitted in evidence (see e.g. Ellenbogen, 1993, pp 1102–1119; Bardelli 1994, pp 1360–1376). However, rather than re-treading this path, I propose to highlight more practical steps which can be taken by both judge and advocate to avoid misuse of the technology. Firstly, counsel must be vigilant to the ever-present danger of misuse. That means advance preparation, diligent discovery and analysis of the underlying data behind any animated simulations or graphics. During the trial itself, vigorous cross-examination of the expert witness testifying alongside the evidence is necessary to ensure that the display is what it purports to be. As one writer remarked: 'They [Counsel] must look upon computer simulations as tools, but tools that require extremely fine tuning.' (Berkoff 1994, p 853).

Judges also have an important role to play in avoiding juror complacency about the accuracy of what they are presented with in evidence. Borelli (1996, p 458) points out that the trial judge has almost unlimited discretion especially in summation, to disallow displays that might be so 'realistic' or emotion-provoking as to unfairly prejudice one side. However, it is arguable that this may not be sufficient. Since juries are strongly affected by visual evidence, the prejudicial effect of an improper viewpoint shown live in the courtroom cannot be undone. In these instances, a limiting instruction by the judge, instructing the jury to disregard the highly-prejudicial image would be largely ineffective (Selbak 1994, p 365). A better approach would be for judges to forewarn jurors of the potentially biased nature of the computer evidence before it is shown in court. The cry in this instance would seem to be: 'forewarned is forearmed.'

The issue of prejudicial cost remains. This is likely to be less of a problem in the future as technological advances and increased demand are already resulting in lower costs.[5] In the meantime, steps should be taken to ensure that if one side is utilising computer-generated displays, the opposing side should also have access to such a resource. McKeone (1994, p 6) suggests that legal aid should be granted to facilitate this where necessary. Such an approach has found favour among some in the US where for example, the court in *US* v *Stifel* (11 433 F 2d 431 (6th Cir 1970), cert denied, 401 US 944 (1971)) stated that

5 'What might have cost $1million five years ago would cost $250,000 today' (Marcotte 1989, p 56). Moreover, by purchasing a program such as AutoDesk 3D Studio relatively cheaply, many law firms can do the work in-house and save even more money (Selbak 1994, p 342).

'if the government sees fit to use this time consuming, expensive means of fact-finding, it must allow time for a defendant to make a similar tests, and in the instance of an indigent defendant, a means to provide for payment of same.'

Granting legal aid in these circumstances would help to ensure a more equitable playing field as far as computer-generated displays are concerned.

As a tool, computer-generated displays have revolutionised much of today's litigation in complex trials. The development of virtual reality and decreasing costs of the technology means that this trend is likely to continue. However, all those concerned with a trial involving the use of computer-generated displays need to be aware of the potential for misuse associated with the technology and proceed accordingly. The steps outlined above, if implemented, may not eliminate the potential for misuse, but they will certainly help to alleviate the problem to a large extent. Justice and fairness cannot be sacrificed in the pursuit of gains in efficiency. If this happens, 'the result could well be "verdict by cartoon" instead of verdict according to scientific truths' (Hoenig 1993, p 5).

Bibliography

Bainbridge, D (1996) *An Introduction to Computer Law*, 3rd ed (London: Pitman Publishing).
Bardelli, E J (1994) 'The Use of Computer Simulations in Criminal Prosecutions' 40 *Wayne Law Review* 1356.
Berkoff, A T (1994) 'Computer Simulations in Litigation: Are Television Generation Jurors Being Misled?' 77 *Marquette Law Review* 829.
Borelli, M (1996) 'The Computer as Advocate: An Approach to Computer-Generated Displays in the Courtroom' 71 *Indiana Law Journal* 439.
Ellenbogen, M A (1993) 'Lights, Camera, Action: Computer-Animated Evidence gets its Day in Court' 34 *Boston College Law Review* 1087.
Fennell, C (1995) 'Admission of Proof of Computer-Generated Evidence' 89 *Law Society of Ireland Gazette* 316.
Gore, R A (1993) 'Reality of Virtual Reality? The Use of Interactive, Three-Dimensional Computer Simulations at Trial' 19 *Rutgers Computer & Technology Law Journal* 459.
Hoenig, M (1993) 'Computer Simulations and Other Weapons' *New York Law Journal* 3.
Horten, M (1994) 'Graphic Evidence' *Solicitors Journal* 1289.
Jenkins, M M (1976) 'Computer-Generated Evidence Specially Prepared for Use at Trial' 52 *Chicago-Kent Law Review* 600.
Kissane-Gaisford, J D (1995) ' The Case for Disc-Based Litigation: Technology and the Cyber Courtroom' 8 *Harvard Journal of Law and Technology* 4716.
Lederer, F I (1994) 'Symposium: Changing Litigation with Science and Technology: Technology comes to the Courtroom, and. . ..' 43 *Emory Law Journal* 1095.
Leith, P (1991) *The Computerised Lawyer* (London: Springer Verlag).
McKeone, M (1992) 'Making or breaking the case: computers in court' *Law Society Gazette* 29.
Marcotte, P (1989) 'Animated Evidence: Delta 191 crash re-created through computer simulations at trial' *ABA Journal*, December, 52.
Muir, D (1992) 'Computer Graphics – Debunking the Myths' *Michigan Lawyers Weekly*, 30 March, p S3B (Supplement).

Ormerod, D (1995) 'Proposals for the Admissibility of Computer-Generated Evidence' 6 *Computers and Law* 22.
Selbak, J (1994) 'Digital Litigation: The Prejudicial Effects of Computer-Generated Animation in the Courtroom' 9 *High Technology Law Journal* 337.
Walsh, A (1995) 'Demonstrative Evidence: 'A Picture Paints a Thousand Words'' 6 *Computers and Law* 28.

PREVENTION OF TERRORISM (ADDITIONAL POWERS) ACT 1996

Kiron Reid*

Lecturer in Law, University of Liverpool
<K.J.C.Reid@liverpool.ac.uk>

First Published in Web Journal of Current Legal Issues in association with Blackstone Press Ltd.

**Thanks to Philip Jones in the office of Simon Hughes MP, and to Paul Simpson for help in obtaining sources.*

SUMMARY

On Tuesday 2 April the Prevention of Terrorism (Additional Powers) Act was rushed through Parliament in a single day. In the House of Commons, the Second Reading of the Bill took place at 10.10 pm, and the Third Reading at 1.21 am on Wednesday morning, and the Bill completed its passage through the House of Lords at 4.30 pm that day. The Opposition acquiesced in the Bill's rapid progress onto the statute book. The legislation allows the police to search clothing following the exercise of random stop and search powers, for which no reasonable grounds are required, and provides for searches of non-residential premises on a warrant issued by a justice of the peace. It also permits searches of any goods on accompanied or unaccompanied vehicles entering or leaving Great Britain or Northern Ireland, and provides a power to impose a police cordon, and for the application of parking prohibitions and restrictions. This article will first examine the reasons why the Bill was considered so hastily by Parliament, then consider the content of the legislation, looking at historical parallels for the purposes of legal analysis, and conclude with an exposition of some of the theoretical and practical objections to emergency laws passed in haste. The article will concentrate on the stop and search powers, as potentially involving the greatest interference with individual liberty.

CONTENTS

---

1. The Guillotine

Due to a timetable (guillotine) motion only clause 1 of the Bill was considered by the House of Commons in Committee. Concerns over the passage of emergency legislation in haste will be outlined below. To begin with, it may be informative to consider the reasons for the speed in this case. The Home Secretary explained that the additional powers had to be enacted very quickly, before the Easter recess (HC Deb vol 275, cols 35–7, April 1, 1996). This announcement followed fears of a spectacular terrorist attack to mark the 80th anniversary of the Irish Republican Easter Rising in Dublin in 1916 (For one response, see Earl Russell, HL Deb vol 571 col 282 April 3, 1996). The significance of the date as particularly evocative seems a little implausible, given that in fact the 75th anniversary of the Rising was much more widely commemorated. However, the argument may be lent some credence by the explosion of a Provisional IRA bomb underneath the Hammersmith Bridge, on Wednesday 24 April – the anniversary of the Rising (This incident will be considered in relation to the efficacy of the legislation, below). And the anniversary was certainly significant, coming so soon after the IRA cease-fire was ended with a bomb attack at Canary Wharf in London on 9 February, when two people were killed and over 100 injured. Before the legislation and timetable had been announced, the Opposition Home Affairs spokesman, Jack Straw, was one of those consulted, in his capacity as a Privy Councillor.

In the House of Commons, the Home Secretary denied claims that the police had been lobbying for the new powers before the end of the cease-fire (see the responses to Alan Beith, Simon Hughes, Andrew Mackinlay and Kevin McNamara, HC Deb vol 275, cols 198–200, April 2, 1996). However, newspaper reports appear to suggest that the Home Secretary's answer was incorrect. *The Observer*, 7 April 1996, reported that the Association of Chief Police Officers had been requesting such powers since 1992 (at p 15). This has since been confirmed by the Commissioner of the City of London Police, William Taylor. Speaking at the Annual Conference of the Howard League for Penal Reform, on 11 September, Mr Taylor (speaking of the new power to search pedestrians) stated, 'We had tried to get that power in the original Act but that had not been supported.' A longer debate in Parliament may have allowed the truth of the matter to emerge. A similar picture emerges from the passage of the original Prevention of Terrorism Act in 1974. The then Labour Home Secretary, Roy Jenkins, revealed in his autobiography that the original legislation was actually envisaged, and partly prepared by civil servants, some time in advance of its actual implementation following the Birmingham pub bombings (Jenkins 1991, pp 393–7).

The timing of the introduction of these new powers is particularly curious, given that additional anti-terrorist stop and search measures had been included in the

Criminal Justice and Public Order Act 1994 (less than a year and a half earlier), and that the Prevention of Terrorism Act had been renewed itself only three weeks earlier. Therefore the most plausible explanation for the timing of the new powers is that suggesting party political motivation. The Government was able to try and embarrass the leadership of the Labour Party twice in three weeks by providing two opportunities for backbenchers to rebel against their party leadership's new policy of abstaining on these measures (The Parliamentary Labour Party had previously opposed the renewal of the Prevention of Terrorism legislation). To adopt the reasoning of Owen Lomas when considering earlier legislation (the Prevention of Violence Act 1939), 'a criticism of the executive's approach to . . . legislation' – is 'the absence of any consideration of the intrinsic value of . . . civil liberties.' (Lomas 1980, p 22).

2. *The Power To Stop And Search Pedestrians*

The legislation builds on previous anti-terrorist measures. In particular, it complements the power contained in the Criminal Justice and Public Order Act 1994 s 81 (which inserted a new s 13A into the Prevention of Terrorism (Temporary Provisions) Act 1989). This section gave a police officer of or above the rank of Commander of the Metropolitan Police, or assistant chief constable outside of London, the power to authorise the exercise of extensive stop and search powers, for a period not exceeding 28 days, if 'expedient to do so in order to prevent acts of terrorism.' (Terrorism is defined in the 1989 Act, s 20(1), as 'the use of violence for political ends' and includes 'any use of violence for the purpose of putting the public or any section of the public in fear.') Section 13A(3) conferred on a constable in uniform the power:

> '(a) to stop any vehicle;
> (b) to search any vehicle, its driver or any passenger for articles of a kind which could be used for a purpose connected with the commission, preparation or instigation of acts of terrorism . . . ;
> (c) to stop any pedestrian and search any thing carried by him for articles of a kind which could be used for a purpose connected with the commission, preparation or instigation of acts of terrorism.'

This power could be exercised in the complete absence of any reasonable grounds for suspicion. Previously the police would have had available only the power under the Police and Criminal Evidence Act 1984 (PACE) s 1 to stop and search for stolen or prohibited articles, or the power to establish road checks under s 4, which had to relate either to a specific criminal offence, or to a person unlawfully at large. Both required reasonable grounds for suspicion. Otherwise the police would have had to resort to their power of arrest under s 14 of the Prevention of Terrorism (Temporary Provisions) Act 1989 which required, for example, reasonable grounds for suspecting a person to be guilty of an offence (14(1)(a)), or concerned in the commission, preparation or instigation of an act of terrorism (14(1)(b)), or the supplementary power of search under s 15(3) which still required reasonable suspicion (for the suggested limitations of which, and concerns over the deficiencies of these provisions see Walker 1992, p 195). Under the original s 13A (in the Metropolitan police areas, and excluding Heathrow airport) 1,746 vehicles have been stopped, and there have been 1,695 searches of vehicles and 2,373 searches of occupants since the Criminal Justice and Public Order Act 1994. This has led to only two arrests under the PTA but 66 other arrests (HC Deb vol 275, col 210, April 2, 1996). Despite repeated requests on both 1 May and 2 May, the Home Secretary failed to provide appropriate figures for Northern Ireland. Seamus Mallon (SDLP MP for Newry and South Armagh) (as well as some Labour MPs who voted against the measures) expressed particular concern that stop and search powers would be used in a discriminatory fashion against young people (HC Deb vol 275, col 273, April 2, 1996).

Section 1 of the new Act repeals subsection (3)(c) above, and inserts a new s 13B after s 13A. Section 13B extends the previous power to allow the person to be searched, as well as anything carried by him or her. This extension is aimed particularly at searching for incendiary devices (Sir Michael Shersby, Michael Howard, HC Deb vol 275, col 41, April 1, 1996). The new power to search pedestrians has to be authorised separately from the power contained in 13A, but authorisation can be given orally (13B(7)) and then must be confirmed in writing as soon as reasonably practicable. There are two safeguards in the new section. First, the Secretary of State must be informed as soon as reasonably practicable, may cancel the authorisation or curtail the length of time for which it applies, and must in any event confirm it within 48 hours (13B(8)-(9)). Second, the extent of a search in public by a constable is limited (13B(4)). A constable may only require a person to remove in public his 'headgear, footwear, outer coat, jacket or gloves.' This limitation is additionally inserted into s 13A for the first time – a useful revision. This brings this power of search more closely into line with the limitations contained in PACE s 2(9), although marginally wider in permitting the removal of headgear and footwear (Kevin McNamara observed that the former could create problems in relations with the Sikh community, HC Deb vol 275, col 169, April 2, 1996. The Act is not limited to Irish terrorism). It is presumed that s 13A applies to bicycles, (see *Garner* v *Burr* [1951] 1 KB 31, DC, at 33, *per* Lord Goddard CJ), although the section does refer to the 'driver' of the vehicle.

Despite the absence of any requirement of reasonable grounds, the power must presumably only be used by a constable for *bona fide* anti-terrorist purposes. If abuses such as those under the old 'sus laws' become apparent, for example use of the stop and search powers in a racially prejudiced way, then this practice could be the subject of an action for judicial review, or of a civil action against the police for false imprisonment. The existing powers and new power are subject to the PACE Code of Practice on stopping and searching, Code A, which should mitigate against abuse (The City of London Police Commissioner has suggested (above) that stops under the original s 13A have been accepted precisely because they are random – as this has removed any stigma being attached to a stop). A pedestrian (or the driver of a vehicle) stopped has the right to obtain a written statement that he (or the vehicle) was stopped under the above section if he applies for one within twelve months (ss 13A(9) and 13B(10)). There must presumably be a corresponding duty on the constable to thus make a record of the search. However, it is not explicitly stated that the constable must inform the subject of this right – unlike the requirement to make this clear for the exercise of the stop and search powers under PACE (see ss 2 and 3). Even with records of searches, though, it may be difficult to exercise any effective scrutiny over the use of discretion by the individual constable. On the other hand, there is an additional safeguard in that the consent of the Director of Public Prosecutions is required for a prosecution for an offence under 13B (failing to stop when required to do so, or wilfully obstructing a constable in the exercise of these powers).

The recent bomb that partially exploded under Hammersmith Bridge, on 24 April, may be claimed by the Provisional IRA as a victory over these new measures. On the other hand, the Government may be able to point to the success of their counter-terrorist strategy. Political concern focused on another high profile attack in the City of London, or Docklands, and it is in the City that the new powers were straight away brought into effect by the police. The Home Secretary noted that the existing powers under s 13A have been invoked only in the City and in the Metropolitan police district after the explosion at South Quay in February (for more than one period of 28 days in the City, and for 7–10 days, on more than one occasion, in the Metropolitan police district, HC Deb vol 275 col 36 April 1, 1996). The fact that the terrorists had to move their attention to West London, for the anniversary of the Easter Rising, possibly with more risk of civilian casualties (damaging public relations), may be claimed as showing that the new powers are working.

However, there are many comparisons with previous legal measures (apart from the figures for s 13A, above), that suggest that the increased powers will be of only limited efficacy. One example is the notorious Metropolitan Police Special Patrol Group operation, 'SWAMP '81'. Despite being a planned crackdown on street robberies, this use of arbitrary roadblocks and stopping and searching led to 943 stops, 118 arrests, and 75 charges – but only one of the charges was for robbery (Scarman 1981, p 57). Post-PACE the situation does not appear to have greatly improved. Walker and Starmer suggest that stop and search powers are not an effective use of police resources (Walker and Starmer 1994, p 32–3):

> 'If supervision cannot be secured, the radical alternative is the abolition of most stop and search powers. After all, most police forces existed without them before 1986, and the charging rate under PACE (which has never exceeded 17 per cent, compared to about 70 per cent charging or cautioning following arrest) suggests that excessive police resources are being diverted into this exercise to no good purpose.'

A similar point, though less damning, can be made in relation to police roadblocks (s 3 of PACE). Uglow notes that:

> 'Between 1986–90 the police mounted 1,545 road blocks, detaining several hundred thousand people. This produced 331 arrests, 158 (48 per cent) of which were unconnected with the reasons for setting up the road block.' (Uglow 1995, p 76.)

Furthermore, the exercise of specific anti-terrorism powers has been equally unsuccessful. Of the 7,202 people detained under the Prevention of Terrorism Acts between 1974 and 1990, only 652 were charged after detention (Walker 1992, Table 6, p 176. See further, Hillyard 1993). However, supporters of clause 1 emphasised the deterrent effect of anti-terrorist measures, which they suggested was far more valuable than shown by bare figures for arrests and charges. Also, the harm caused by terrorist atrocities is so great that it could be argued that the interference with liberty is justified by the fact that 10 per cent of those detained are subsequently charged. And it may be argued that improving intelligence, with the increased co-operation between MI5 and the police, will lead to more effective use of these new powers.

The European Convention On Human Rights

The exercise of stop and search powers does not appear to fall within any of the exceptions to Article 5 of the European Convention on Human Rights, which enshrines the right to liberty and security of persons. It is unclear whether a stop of very short duration is included in the category of detention (although any search would appear to infringe security of the person). It has been asserted that:

> 'a person who is made to believe that he is obliged to remain when stopped on the street . . . by the police for the purpose of being questioned, searched or subjected to a test in the administration of the criminal law should be protected by Article 5.' (Harris et al 1995, p 100.)

There is no general power of preventive detention under the second limb of Article 5(1)(c) (*Lawless*, 1 July 1961, Series A, no 3). However, even if any infringement of Article 5 was inherent in the extension of the stop and search powers, this would certainly be permitted by a derogation under Article 15, which allows derogation in 'time of war or other public emergency.' (See generally Harris 1995, chap 16.) Freedom of movement itself is protected by Article 2 of the Fourth Protocol, which has not been ratified by the United Kingdom. Derogation would presumably be permitted, though, under the proviso in Article 2(3) permitting restrictions 'in the interests of national security or public safety.'

3. The Remaining Content of the Legislation

a. Search Of Non-Residential Premises

Section 2 of the Prevention of Terrorism (Additional Powers) Act 1996 amends Schedule 7 to the Prevention of Terrorism (Temporary Provisions) Act 1989 in relation to search of non-residential premises (inserting paragraph 2A). This enables the police to apply for a magistrates' warrant to search a list of non-residential premises, and not just particular premises as at present.

> 'The new power would enable the police to respond to intelligence that, for example, a bomb was stored in a lock-up garage or lorry park in a particular area.' (Michael Howard, HC Deb vol 275 col 36 April 1, 1996.)

Paragraph 2 of the Schedule provides the police in terrorist investigations with a very similar power of search to that under PACE s 8 (See generally Feldman 1993, chap 9). Under the latter a justice of the peace may grant a search warrant, on application by a constable, if satisfied that a serious arrestable offence has been committed and various other conditions are satisfied as to the impracticability of obtaining access to the material with consent. The key difference with the former is that the justice of the peace must be satisfied that there are reasonable grounds for believing that material on the premises will be of substantial value to the terrorist investigation. In both these provisions 'reasonable grounds for believing' are required – a more stringent requirement than the 'reasonable grounds for suspicion' found frequently elsewhere in PACE.

The new paragraph 2A inserts a separate power, relating only to search of non-residential premises, which requires an application by an officer of the rank of superintendent or above. The other requirements (above) are absent, but the authorisation has to be requested by a more senior officer, and the warrant must be executed within 24 hours, a safeguard not present in the other provisions mentioned. However, as in paragraph 2, a superintendent may authorise a search in cases of great emergency (paragraph 7), and this applies also to searches for material that would under PACE be categorised as excluded or special procedure material (for example personal records or journalistic material). Under PACE (and in normal anti-terrorist investigations) more onerous conditions apply for obtaining a search warrant for access to the latter kinds of material.

b. Powers To Search Goods

Schedule 5 to the 1989 Act is amended by s 3 of the new Act – which inserts a s 4A. This states that:

> '(1) For the purpose of determining whether they are or have been involved in the commission, preparation or instigation of acts of terrorism . . ., an examining officer may search any goods which have arrived in or are about to leave Great Britain or Northern Ireland.'

This gives a new and perhaps sensible power to search unaccompanied baggage and goods. It is the only one of the new powers that is not already available in Northern Ireland, and is thus applied to the whole of the United Kingdom and not only to Great Britain. However, it is far too broadly phrased in one or two important respects. Anything found during the search can be detained for up to seven days for examination (s 4A(6)) and if the person carrying out the search 'is of the opinion that it may be needed for use as evidence in criminal proceedings he may detain it until he is satisfied that it will not be so needed' (s 4A(7)). There is nothing in the section to limit the application of the power to anti-terrorist criminal proceedings (what is the position, for example, if illegal drugs are found?), and there is nothing to impose any obligation to examine the goods expeditiously or, for instance, as soon as reasonably practicable. Unless these limitations can be implied, the provision should be amended certainly to include the latter. As to the former, the legislation will need to be carefully monitored to see if any abuses of the power become apparent. And a requirement of 'reasonable belief' should replace mere 'opinion' – otherwise, at present, as in relation to the power to stop and search, the only possible legal challenge would appear to be on the basis that the examining officer was not acting in good faith. The attitude of the Home Secretary does not bode well in alleviating concerns over the normalisation of special powers (see below), given this regrettable exchange in the House of Commons (HC Deb vol 275, col 39, April 1, 1996):

> **Mr Michael Jopling:** 'Will he give an undertaking that if, in the use of these new powers, drugs, stolen property, offensive weapons or other smuggled materials are discovered that are nothing to do with terrorism, those discoveries will be followed by prosecutions where that is possible?'
> **Mr Howard:** 'I can indeed give my right hon. Friend the undertaking that he seeks.'

If such widespread, and potentially general, powers are to be given to the police it is submitted they should be conferred explicitly rather than implicitly.

c. Police Cordons, Parking Prohibitions and Restrictions

The final sections of the Act give the police a power to impose a police cordon (s 5 inserting s 16C) and power to impose parking prohibitions and restrictions (s 16D). The Act, in providing, for the first time, a clear legal basis for the imposition of police cordons, was demonstrated to be unfortunately timely due to the IRA bombing in Manchester on Saturday 15 June. The use of a cordon in Manchester played a key part in protecting the public and avoiding any fatal casualties from the explosion there. Over 75,000 people were safely evacuated from the busy shopping centre of the city (*The Observer*, 16 June 1996, p 1).

A superintendent, or lower ranking officer if a matter of great urgency, may authorise a cordon. An oral authorisation must be confirmed in writing as soon as reasonably practicable, and an authorisation by a constable must be either confirmed or cancelled by a superintendent (Schedule 6A). The period for which a cordon is in force must not exceed 14 days. By Schedule 6A the police are given very wide powers to order individuals to leave and to move vehicles, and a constable may remove or move any vehicle. Presumably they may use reasonable force to do this, but the Schedule is silent on the matter of compensation if damage is caused. The only remedy would appear to be an ordinary action for negligence, if any duty of care is owed, or possibly an action for trespass to goods.[1] Paragraph 7 of Schedule 6A provides for very widespread powers of search of premises, and persons found on those premises, within cordoned areas, similar to those outlined above in ss 2A and 13B.

In contrast to a police cordon, which can be imposed if 'expedient to do so in connection with an investigation into the commission, preparation or instigation of an act of terrorism' (for example to search for a bomb or forensic evidence), the parking prohibitions and restrictions can only be authorised 'in order to prevent acts of terrorism' (such as a car bomb attack on a Government building or royal residence: HC Deb vol 275, col 37, April 1, 1996) and can only be authorised by a Commander of the Metropolitan Police, or assistant chief constable outside of London.[2] Under 16D(7) a person is guilty of an offence 'if he leaves a vehicle, or permits a vehicle to remain at rest, on a road' in contravention of a prohibition or restriction imposed. Presumably *mens rea* is required for this offence, so that a person would not be guilty if he did not know of the restriction or prohibition (*Gammon (Hong Kong) Ltd* v *A-G of Hong Kong* [1985] AC 1, PC). Alternatively, this may be covered by the defence of reasonable excuse contained in subsection (8). Also the consent of the DPP is required for a prosecution for any breach of s 16D or Schedule 6A.

4. *Emergency Law Passed in Haste*

The concerns arising from emergency legislation passed in haste are considered in detail elsewhere (Reid and Walker, forthcoming) so this section will merely review some of the major issues that arise. In the United Kingdom criticism has been

1 On the reluctance of the courts to accept a duty of care in such circumstances, see *Hill* v *Chief Constable of West Yorkshire* [1988] 2 All ER 238, HL, cf *Swinney* v *Chief Constable of Northumbria Police*, (1996) *The Times*, 29 March, and *Rigby* v *Chief Constable of Northamptonshire* [1985] 2 All ER 985, which show that, despite public policy objections, a duty of care may be found on the facts of a particular case.

2 In the House of Lords, Baroness Blatch gave the further examples of financial centres and major transport facilities, as potential targets: HL Deb vol 571, col 293, April 3, 1996.

particularly acute in relation, for example, to the Official Secrets Act 1911, and the Prevention of Terrorism (Temporary Provisions) Act 1974. To consider the latter, two particular concerns arise: one regarding the hurried initial enactment; and one regarding the excessive reliance on what was proposed as specialised 'emergency legislation'. Many criticisms of the legislation might have been avoided if there had been a chance for detailed scrutiny by Parliament rather than the Bill being rushed through in a panic for political reasons (Walker 1992, pp 31–3). In relation to the new powers, these points were echoed by Alan Beith, for the Liberal Democrats (opposing the timetable but not the content of the Bill, HC Deb vol 275, col 39, April 1, 1996. See also the comments of Lord Rodgers, HL Deb vol 571, col 280, April 3, 1996).

Further, the use of special powers may be described as 'excessive' in two senses: excessive in the sense that special powers are invoked when 'normal' powers would suffice to deal with a particular aspect of the emergency; and excessive in the sense that special powers are applied to 'normal' situations which are not part of the emergency (see Hillyard 1987).[3] Part of the problem again arises from the shortcomings of panic legislation passed at the time of the emergency, which is likely to be badly structured and inadequately based on clear principles (HL Deb vol 571, col 336–7, and col 338, April 3, 1996, for the examples given by Lord Annan, and Lord McIntosh of Haringey respectively). Similar observations may be made in relation to legislation passed by a Government in order 'to be seen' to be doing something about a matter of concern. (For one example see Walker and Reid, 1993). By contrast, in the United States, anti-terrorism legislation in response to the Oklahoma City bomb has just been passed a year later (Antiterrorism Act 1996) – although President Clinton was highly critical of the length of time taken by Congress to pass the legislation as proposed. (*Electronic Telegraph* 16 April 1996; Statement by the President, April 24, 1996).

In its *Final Report on Emergencies* (NZLC 1991) the New Zealand Law Commission recommended that when emergency powers are required they should be conferred in 'sectoral legislation' – legislation deliberated upon and designed in advance of an emergency and tailored strictly to the needs of each particular kind of emergency (NZLC 1991, p x). This approach was felt to be preferable to last-minute emergency legislation (NZLC 1991, para 4.12):

> 'The choice will be between legislation carefully prepared in advance, conforming to the principles and safeguards . . . and hastily drafted legislation conferring wider powers than are necessary and omitting appropriate protections against abuse. Moreover, New Zealand and overseas experience suggests that emergency legislation passed in haste is likely to remain on the statute book long after its immediate purpose has been served.'

This call has been echoed in Britain by academic and other commentators such as Greer (1983) and Evelegh (1978). With the ending of the IRA cease-fire, it may

3 An example of the latter might be that, as well as the anti-terrorist stop and search powers, the Criminal Justice and Public Order Act 1994 also contained a new power to stop and search in anticipation of violence (s 60), which is very similar to the anti-terrorist measures in that it is of temporary duration, in a specified area, and no grounds are required. This provision is aimed at countering specific anticipation of violence, for instance at the time of football matches, but is widely phrased. Home Office Minister of State, David Maclean, explained that the Government 'was persuaded that the need to meet the tests of reasonable suspicion seriously inhibits effective preventive action by the police when they believe that violence is likely to break out'. HC Deb vol 241, col 69, April 12, 1994. See further Bailey et al, 1995.

now have been too late to prevent the enactment of hurried counter-measures to terrorism, but the lesson still needs to be learnt for the future that consideration of the issues in advance gives time for proper scrutiny. Lord Lloyd's current Inquiry into Legislation Against Terrorism is one place to begin the work. (For an analysis of the current position, see Walker, 1996). Although that Inquiry, by Lord Lloyd and Sir Brian Kerr, was established by the Government in January 1996 'to consider the future need for specific counter-terrorism legislation' on the basis of a continuing Provisional IRA cease-fire, review of the new powers is still certainly within its remit.

Bibliography

Bailey, S, Harris, D and Jones, B (1995) *Civil Liberties: Cases and Materials*, 4th ed (London: Butterworths).

Evelegh, R (1978) *Peacekeeping in a Democratic Society* (London: Hurst).

Electronic Telegraph (1996) Issue 363, 16 April 1996.

Feldman, D (1993) *Civil Liberties and Human Rights in England and Wales* (Oxford: OUP).

Greer, S (1983) 'Military Intervention in Civil Disturbances' [1983] *Public Law* 573.

Harris, D, O'Boyle, M and Warbrick, C (1995) *Law of the European Convention on Human Rights* (London: Butterworths).

Hillyard, P (1987) 'The Normalisation of Special Powers' in Scraton, P (ed) *Law, Order and the Authoritarian State* (Milton Keynes: Open University Press).

Hillyard, P (1993) *Suspect Community*, (London: Pluto Press).

Jenkins, R (1991) *A Life at the Centre* (London: Macmillan).

Lomas, O (1980) 'The Executive and the Anti-Terrorist Legislation of 1939' [1980] *Public Law* 16.

New Zealand Law Commission Report No 22 (1991), *Final Report on Emergencies*, (Wellington, New Zealand).

Reid, K and Walker, C 'Military Aid in Civil Emergencies: Lessons from New Zealand' (forthcoming).

Scarman, L (1981) *The Brixton Disorders 10–12 April 1981: Report of an Inquiry by the Rt Hon Lord Scarman OBE* (London: HMSO) Cmnd. 8427.

Uglow, S (1995) *Criminal Justice* (London: Sweet & Maxwell).

Walker, C (1992) *The Prevention of Terrorism in British Law*, 2nd ed (Manchester: Manchester University Press).

Walker, C (1996) 'Anti-terrorism laws for the future' 146 *New Law Journal* 586.

Walker, C and Reid, K (1993) 'The Offence of Directing Terrorist Organisations' [1993] *Criminal Law Review* 669.

Walker, C and Starmer, K (1994) (eds) *Justice in Error* (London: Blackstone).

THE UK CHILD SUPPORT AGENCY: A STEP TOWARDS EU CO-OPERATION IN THE FIELD OF FAMILY LAW

Claire Archbold (LLB)

Lecturer in Law, The Queen's University of Belfast

and

Helen Xanthaki (LLB, M.Jur.)

Lecturer in Law, The Queen's University of Belfast

First Published in Web Journal of Current Legal Issues in association with Blackstone Press Ltd.

SUMMARY

Increasingly, European Union (EU) member states are having to wrestle with the dilemma of absent parents who do not discharge their obligation to maintain their children, leaving them to be supported by state social welfare payments. The implementation of the free movement of persons creates a further transnational dimension to this problem. The authors suggest that a common solution should be introduced throughout the EU and consider whether the introduction of the innovative Child Support Agency (CSA) in the United Kingdom (UK) could serve as such a solution. For this purpose, the authors present the legal framework of the CSA and assess its suitability for implementation within the two main civil law jurisdictions of France and Germany. The authors conclude that the CSA in its present form would contravene the well established constitutional principles of the separation of powers and of the independent judiciary but suggest that the incorporation of certain elements of the CSA, located within the traditional judicial child maintenance system, would provide the best way forward for the further co-operation of member states in the field of family law.

CONTENTS

Introduction

The furtherance of the welfare of the child/ren, especially during and after a painful divorce, seems to be the main common aim of most national family and divorce regulations, both within Europe and elsewhere, and the protection of the child/ren's financial interests is vital to this aim. However, despite the repeated and persistent attempts of most modern judicial systems to provide the child/ren, both within and outside marriage, with an effective procedural and substantive remedy for the payment of child maintenance by the debtor parent/s, an effective judicial route guaranteeing payment of child maintenance, at least in the majority of cases, is yet to be discovered.

The recent attempt of the UK government to meet this need took the form of a 'Next Steps' agency, the Child Support Agency (CSA), whose main aim is to ensure full and prompt payment of maintenance for all children. Within the UK the introduction of the CSA received mixed responses from both academics and journalists. However, it is now accepted that, despite some persistent administrative problems, the CSA constitutes a positive step towards the solution of the problem of parents who fail to fulfil their child maintenance obligations. The question arising at this point is whether, in an era of increasing co-operation amongst EU member states, the CSA could be adopted as a long-term policy in the field of child maintenance by all member states.

The adoption of a common position presents numerous benefits. In an era where EU nationals take advantage of economic, as well as political and legal, integration through the increasingly frequent intra-EU family migration, mixed nationality marriages and changes in the work or domicile locations of one or both parents, the prevalence of a common formula of child maintenance evaluation and payment could facilitate the member states in their commitment to effectively tackle the problem of late or non-payment of child maintenance, irrespective of the nationality and place of residence of parent/s and/or child/ren. Such is the importance awarded to the EU member states' co-operation in the field of Justice and Home Affairs, that the Treaty on European Union (the Maastricht Treaty) in Art K 1(6) has expressly provided for the judicial co-operation of member states in civil matters. This would clearly cover any court co-operation in the enforcement of orders of child maintenance. However, mere judicial co-operation has not proven adequate so far. The need for further collaboration, on a legislative and/or administrative basis, is becoming gradually more evident, as the problem of child maintenance becomes more wide-spread.

Having established the necessity of further co-operation in the field of child maintenance payment, the authors will attempt to explore the possibility of using the CSA formula as a common starting point for collaboration amongst Member States. In order to achieve this aim, the authors will begin with a brief presentation of the CSA as introduced in the UK. Particular emphasis will be given to the structure of the CSA, its procedures and types of decisions, as well as to the review of the CSA decisions by the courts. The authors will proceed to explore the possible reception of the CSA within continental jurisdictions. For this purpose, reference will be made to the constitutional principles of the separation of powers and of the independent judiciary as these are implemented in continental constitutional theory and practice. The authors will also present alternative solutions to the problem of child maintenance provided by some continental jurisdictions. Thus, it will briefly refer to the relevant legislation in two countries with long civil law traditions, whose legal provisions have greatly influenced most other European civil law jurisdictions: France and Germany. This reference will also lead to an assessment of the existence of a common position on child maintenance payment amongst the Continental EU member states. If such a common position already exists within the Continent, the CSA, despite its accomplishments in the UK, will stand alone and be impossible to emulate within the EU.

A. The UK approach to child maintenance

Background to the Child Support Act 1991

Prior to the introduction of the CSA, in the UK the obligation to maintain children was thought of as suitable for enforcement by the courts (Domestic Proceedings and Magistrates' Courts Act 1978, s 2; Matrimonial Causes Act 1973, ss 22–24; Children Act 1989, schedule 1, para 1). Application for child maintenance was made to the court by the parent with custody of the child. Where the parents were unmarried, the circumstances in which maintenance could be claimed and its amount were limited. Where the parents were married, however, the financial provision available was potentially unlimited (Matrimonial Causes Act 1973, ss 22–24A), and the court had to consider an impressive array of factual matters before reaching a decision (Matrimonial Causes Act 1973, s 25, as amended by Matrimonial and Family Proceedings Act 1984, s 18). The value of a system based on such great judicial flexibility was recognised to be that it allowed the court to take into account the infinite variety of circumstances which might occur in a case without forcing judges into a statutory straitjacket.

In addition to being a perceived advantage, however, this was also one of the anomalies of the old system – that although decisions on child maintenance are taken by a court, they may be argued to be not in their nature judicial decisions, based on the application of legal rules; but, as the statutes in question require a decision which takes into account all the circumstances of the case, to be essentially discretionary and therefore more akin to administrative decisions (Domestic Proceedings and Magistrates' Courts Act 1978; Matrimonial Causes Act 1973).

Structure and location of the CSA

The new UK solution, by contrast, may be argued to be a mechanism by which an administrative body takes a judicial decision. The idea of enforcing and collecting child maintenance by administrative rather than judicial means had been mooted in the UK as long ago as 1974, when the Labour Government considered (but did not implement) it as a way, along with guaranteed maintenance allowances and day care facilities, of assisting one parent families (*Report of the Committee on One Parent Families,* Cmnd 5627). However, for the Conservative government under Mrs Thatcher, the proposal was not seen as part of a wider system to assist the unfortunate, but as a way to 'make [absent parents] accept their financial obligations' (Smith 1991, p 644). The Child Support Act was designed to privatise responsibility for children, and in particular to ensure that parents and not the State bore the financial burden of raising them. In Parliament, Mrs Thatcher made it clear that the UK Government was not going to follow other European countries by payment of maintenance advance or by subsidising child care to allow single parents to go out to work (Eekelaar, 1991, pp 15–21).

The relocation of child support enforcement mechanisms in the executive came at a time when the government was restructuring the Civil Service into a large number of decentralised, semi-autonomous agencies, and it was this form which was chosen for the new CSA. Introducing the Child Support Act in Parliament, the Lord Chancellor said:

> '. . . a CSA will be established as a next steps agency under the authority of the Secretary of State for Social Security. The agency will trace absent parents, investigate the parents' means and assess, collect and enforce payments of child maintenance . . . As a next steps agency, the agency will have no independent existence in statute. The powers that it will need to do its work are, therefore, expressed as powers of . . . the Secretary of State for Social Security.' (HL Deb vol 526, col 770, 25 February 1991)

From 1988, the Conservative government in the UK has changed the unified civil service which had until then carried out the business of government to a new system in which policy has been made by government departments, supported by a very small central civil service, but implemented by so-called 'Next Steps Agencies'.[1] These small, decentralised bodies are run at arm's length from government, with the watchwords of better management and efficiency. Bodies ranging from the Companies Registry to the Inland Revenue have become agencies, with each local office responsible for its own operations. Traditional methods of constitutional accountability such as parliamentary questions to Ministers do not operate meaningfully within this framework (Bradley and Ewing 1993, pp 217–218). Although the powers of parliamentary Select Committees (Bradley and Ewing 1993, pp 220–223) too are limited in respect of Next Steps Agencies, the CSA has shown that with Agency co-operation, the Select Committee mechanism can still have some effect. It was the Social Security Select Committee's 1994 report on the Agency (*Social Security Committee 5th Report*), which was directly responsible for the publication of the 1995 White Paper *Improving Child Support*.

1 The idea of Next Steps Agencies came from a report to the Prime Minister's Efficiency Unit (Jenkins, Caines and Jackson, 1988) which aimed to '. . . identify institutional, administrative, political and managerial obstacles to better management and efficiency that still remain; and to report to the Prime Minister on what further measures should be taken' (p 33). See also Drewery 1988 and Hennessy 1991.

The CSA's Chief Executive's evidence to the Social Security Select Committee, however, reflects the shift in Parliamentary and executive thinking in the UK away from traditional mechanisms of constitutional accountability towards private sector ideas of efficient management and market control:

> 'I think that Child Support Agencies . . . are rather unusual in that they are not like business and are also not like the public sector, they are not like social services, they are dealing with private debt but they also have a very strong customer focus. . . .' (*Social Security Committee 5th Report*, p xi.)

Procedure of the CSA

Under the Child Support Act it is the Secretary of State for Social Security who has the duty to collect and enforce child maintenance (Child Support Act 1991, s 4). He is obliged to refer applications for maintenance to a child support officer a civil servant whose delegated powers are specified in his/her instrument of appointment (Child Support Act 1991, ss 11 and 13(2). Similarly, appeals from the Child Support Officer's assessment are to the Secretary of State who delegates his function to, in the first instance, a child support officer not involved in the original decision, and then to a Child Support Appeal Tribunal which also acts as part of the Agency. (Child Support Act 1991, ss 18(7) and 20–25). Only if there is a point of law will the case be brought into the court system and even then only at the final appeal stage.

Replacing previous statutory enactments for qualifying children, the Child Support Act, the founding statute of the Agency, sets out the duty of all parents, married or unmarried to maintain children under sixteen (Child Support Act 1991, ss 1(1) and 54). A parent with care of a child discharges the duty by caring for the child. An absent parent discharges the duty by making maintenance payments for the child through the CSA.

Regardless of how much the absent parent is willing to pay, the Agency makes a maintenance assessment according to a formula set out in Schedule 1 of the Act. The formula is based on Income Support rates for the child, the parent with care and the absent parent together with any of his other dependants. Originally the formula was rigid and took into account only limited circumstances. There was no discretion in either the courts or the Agency to depart from it in even the most blatantly unfair circumstances. The Child Support Act 1995, introduced following the White Paper *Improving Child Support* amends the formula and gives a child support officer discretion to make a departure direction in certain narrowly prescribed circumstances, but the principle that the formula should be applied uniformly remains.

When a child support officer has jurisdiction to make a maintenance assessment, a court cannot make a maintenance order in respect of that child (Child Support Act 1991, s 8). During the transitional period the Agency will administer only new cases. Existing cases will continue to be varied and enforced by the courts until the end of that period. After that the Agency will 'take over' collection, variation and enforcement of prior court orders. As all Agency assessments are subject to a biennial review, court orders will have been effectively annexed by the Agency within two years of take-on.

A parent who is not on benefit may choose to seek maintenance through the Agency or make a private agreement. This latter, however, may only be enforced through the normal contractual enforcement procedures. In order to take advantage of the expedited enforcement procedures for family financial provision, s/he must proceed through the Agency. A parent with care on means tested benefit has no choice but to apply for child support (Child Support Act 1991, s 6). If the child support assessment is sufficient to take her/him outside the benefit system, but the absent parent fails to pay, the parent with care will have to reapply for benefit and wait for several weeks, without income, until the claim is reprocessed. If, however, s/he fails to disclose known details of the absent parent's identity to the Agency, deductions will be made from her/his benefit for up to one year (Child Support Act 1991, s 46 and Child Support (Maintenance Assessment and Special Cases) Regulations 1992 part IX). The only circumstances in which this rule will be waived are those in which the person with care or the child would be at risk of harm for example by rape, incest or violence from the absent parent (HL Debs vol 527, col 386, 14 March 1991).

Classification of Agency decisions

It will already be apparent that there are difficulties in locating the CSA within the traditional mechanisms of constitutional accountability in the UK. Another difficulty which has been mentioned in passing is the classification of decisions as judicial or administrative in UK law. Perhaps the classic definition of a judicial decision was given in 1932 by the Donoughmore Committee, which defined a truly judicial decision as one in which, after the parties present their cases, including evidence of any facts in dispute and arguments on any legal points in dispute, a decision is made:

> 'which disposes of the whole matter by a finding upon the facts in dispute and an application of the law of the land to the facts so found, including, where required a ruling upon any disputed questions of law.' (Donoughmore Committee 1932, p 73.)

Administrative decisions, by contrast, normally taken by the executive, are policy-based, and contain an element of discretion. The Donoughmore Committee concluded that it did not matter whether a decision was taken by a court or a Minister – if it met the criteria set out above, it was a judicial decision (Hadfield, 1996, pp 261–262).

Ironically, the UK has moved from a child support system in which a judicial body was arguably taking an administrative decision, to one in which an administrative body is taking a judicial decision. Although the decision of the CSA is made using a computer, the formula is set out in law, and although ancillary decisions such as whether to deduct benefit from a non-co-operative parent with care, or to make a departure order, involve an element of discretion, the primary decision could fairly be categorised as judicial, although essentially mechanical.

This being so, one might ask what protections there are in UK law for the citizen coming before such an administrative tribunal. The Franks Committee, which reported in 1957, was set up to answer this very question, and it suggested that the criteria by which such a body should be judged are those of 'openness, fairness and accountability'. Its words are worth setting out in full:

> '. . . openness appears to us to require the publicity of proceedings and knowledge of the essential reasoning underlying the decisions; fairness to require the adoption of a clear procedure which enables the parties to know their rights, to present their case fully and to know the case which they have to meet; and impartiality to require the freedom of tribunals from the influence, real or

apparent, of departments concerned with the subject-matter of their decisions.' (Franks Report 1957, para 42).

The last criterion in particular may cause unease in the case of the CSA, and one wonders whether the ability to present the case fully and to have all factors taken into account is really present in a computerised decision, but arguably any defect in the initial procedure may be cured by the provision of an adequate appeal.

Appeal and Review of Agency decisions by the courts

In the Child Support Act as originally conceived there was no provision for review of the substantive merits of the formula assessment in an individual case. In the revised system following *Improving Child Support*, limited review is available in two ways. Firstly, 'broad brush' amendments to the formula take into account exceptional travel-to-work expenses and certain previous capital settlements for the benefit of the children in question and secondly discretionary departure directions may be made, allowing departure from the formula where it works injustice in certain closely defined circumstances (Child Support Act 1995). In other jurisdictions with Child Support Agencies, and in particular in Australia, departure directions, made by the courts, are an integral part of the system, allowing the administrative system to be overridden where justice demands it (see Parker 1990 and Harrison 1990). In the UK, a departure direction is made by a child support officer, and the internal nature of this procedure may give cause for concern. A pragmatist might argue that locating the review procedure within the Agency will prevent the courts being flooded with meritless applications by aggrieved parents, but a cynic might argue that it is another way of preventing the courts from interfering with the Agency.

Although the courts are given some role in the appeals procedure, it is minimal. As already mentioned, an assessment is reviewed by a Child Support Officer and then appealed to a Child Support Appeal Tribunal which is still part of the Agency. Only if there is a point of law will there be a final appeal to the courts. Neither the Tribunal nor the court has any jurisdiction over the merits of the case; the question is merely whether the formula was applied correctly. Similarly where courts are used on appeal in the enforcement procedure, their powers are limited in such a way as to allow them only to rubber-stamp procedurally correct decisions of the executive, allowing them no jurisdiction over the question of whether the enforcement procedure chosen is appropriate, or to look further into the circumstances of the case. Appeal of the Child Support Officer's discretionary decision to impose a deduction from earnings order is to the Magistrates' Court, but only on the ground that the order is defective or that the moneys in question are not earnings. It is not possible to question whether the order is appropriate. Appeal of a distress order – an order for seizure and sale of a person's goods – is only possible on the ground that the 'levy was irregular' (procedurally incorrect). The Secretary of State may apply to the magistrates' court for a liability order as part of the enforcement procedure, but once the court finds that arrears exist, it has no discretion and must make the order. Only at the last stage of enforcement, where proceedings are brought by the Agency to imprison the absent parent for his/her debt, may the court make a full inquiry into his/her means and determine whether his/her failure to pay is due to some default or neglect on his/her part. Only if it is, may he be imprisoned (Child Support Act 1991, ss 32–35).

The other way by which the courts might be able to exercise control over the Agency is by the supervisory mechanism of judicial review, a process by which the court declares the purported exercise of power by an administrative body to be lawful or unlawful; as being either within or outside its actual powers. Judicial review is only available when all other avenues of redress have been tried, and is not a review on the merits, instead asking only whether a decision is validly taken. It will only be available in respect of the discretionary decisions taken by the Secretary of State or his Child Support Officers (Burrows 1993, para 9.45–9.47). This may be one reason for the dearth of applications to date. Another reason may be that the Act is still relatively new (only coming into effect in April 1994), and so any meritorious applicants may not yet have exhausted their other remedies. Whatever the reason, judicial review, available only in a limited number of circumstances in child support cases, has been little used to date.[2]

B. The CSA in the light of civil constitutional theory

Having presented the structure, functioning and types of decisions of the CSA the authors concluded that the resolution of child maintenance disputes by any authority other than the courts would be unconstitutional within these countries. We will proceed with the examination of the possibility of a transfer of the CSA, or a similar formula, within other EU member states. Such analysis can only begin with the evaluation of the legality of the CSA in the light of modern civil constitutional theory and practice. The issue is of particular importance for the evolution of this paper, as, in the event that the CSA proves unconstitutional within civil Continental jurisdictions, its adoption as a common EU solution to the issue of the enforcement of child maintenance obligations would be impossible.

The first point to be questioned by the civil lawyer is the legality of this apparent exclusion of the courts' jurisdiction in cases of child maintenance. In the civil law system the judgement on disputes between natural and legal persons falls within the exclusive jurisdiction of the national courts, which are the exclusive judicial organs of the State (Spiliotopoulos 1991, p 7). The courts are the only organs that have the power to remove any doubt concerning the compliance with the current national law, applicable in the particular dispute, of acts of natural legal persons or the state (Tsatsos 1992, p 141; Fleiner 1963, pp 12–13). Organs of any other nature (legislative or administrative) lack the authority to judge on any such dispute, since their constitutive acts awarding them judicial power would be considered to have been issued 'in violation of authority'. Thus, these organs would lack legal personality, any acts issued by them would be 'non-existent' from an administrative law point of view and any actions of any persons based on such acts would lack legal value.[3]

The principle of the separation of powers

The rationale behind this way of legal thinking lies with an old principle of the constitutional law of most civil law countries: the principle of the separation of

---

2 The two reported cases to date, *R* v *Secretary of State for Social Security, ex parte Biggin* [1995] 1 FLR 851, and *R* v *Secretary of State for Social Security, ex parte Lloyd* [1995] 1 FLR 856, were respectively described in the judgments as 'inappropriate' and 'fanciful and unrealistic'.

3 See decisions 206–209/1929, 365/30 and 531/1971 of the Greek Council of the State (the Greek supreme administrative court). This category of acts exists in the theory and practice of French and German administrative law as *actes inexistentes or Nichtakte* respectively. Dagtoglou considers such administrative acts as acts that are existent but can be nullified by the respective administrative courts (see Dagtoglou 1984, pp 80–81).

powers. The principle of *Separations des pouvoirs, Gewaltenteilung, Diakrisi Exousion* in French, German and Greek respectively stems from the liberal ideas of Locke, Blackstone, de Lolme, the philosophy of the English parliamentarianism of the 17th century and the ideas of Montesquieu as expressed in Art 16 of the 1789 French Declaration. According to it the state – in order to avoid despotism and guarantee the liberty of its citizens – must 'distribute its power to more than one, independent and different from one another organs, in such a way as to guarantee that only a part of its power is exercised by each of the respective organs' (Manesis 1980, p 25; Burdeau, Hamom and Troper 1993, p 105). The principle distinguishes between three powers or functions:

1. the legislative function that passes, modifies, authentically interprets and abolishes legal provisions through constitutionally established procedures;
2. the executive function (divided into governmental power and pure administration) which, through administrative acts, deals with the execution of the legal provisions passed by the legislative function; and
3. the judicial function which, through judicial decisions, deals with the punishment of criminal offences and the settlement of legal disputes arising during the application of the law.

The rationale behind this distinction lies in the idea that the power of the state is one and indivisible. This indivisible power is realised through three different functions: the executive, the legislative and the judicial function (Kuenster 1949, p 401; Raikos 1989, p 213). According to the principle itself these three functions must be independent from one another. Thus, the organs exercising each function should not have the power to influence the way in which the other two functions are exercised and each of these organs must be specialised in the exercise of one of the three functions only. Thus, through the limitation and control of each of the three powers by the other two, the principle of the separation of powers guarantees the citizens' political freedom and the state's democratic functioning.

From the analysis of the principle so far it has become clear that in civil law countries the existence of an agency with the current powers of the CSA would be illegal. Since the courts have the exclusive jurisdiction to decide on civil disputes (which include child maintenance disputes) any legal or administrative act awarding an agency the power to judge on such disputes would be non-existent. Such an agency, even if it was set up under the constitutionally established procedures, would lack legal personality and its acts or decisions would lack legal value. Any person (employee of the agency or any other citizen) enforcing the decisions or acts of the agency or acting under the agency's directions would be acting illegally and – in some jurisdictions – could be committing a criminal offence. It follows that in civil law jurisdictions the CSA would not be able to resolve civil disputes or issue decisions on matters concerning child maintenance, since this activity – as part of the judicial function – is exclusively conducted by the national courts. Thus, the existence of the CSA with its current powers and competence would be unconstitutional (and therefore illegal) on the grounds that they directly clash with the principle of the separation of powers in its classical interpretation.

It should be noted, however, that the theory of the separation of powers in its classical sense no longer prevails in modern constitutional theories. Indeed some authors argue that the principle of the separation of powers in its classical sense was never implemented in practice (Manesis, 1980 p 29). In spite of the simplicity and clarity of the principle itself, in practice the separation of functions and the distinction between them is a complicated issue. The matter becomes even more complicated if one takes into account the inability of modern constitutional lawyers to classify some of the basic phenomena of modern parliamentary life. Indeed, in modern parliamentarianism there are functions that do not fall within any of the three traditional powers, such as the constitutional control of the government, the existence and functioning of political parties and pressure groups or even the existence and functioning of the opposition. It is therefore argued that the separation of powers *stricto sensu* is not the aim of the principle in its modern interpretation. In view of modern constitutional reality, the principle in its modern sense aims to achieve balance and co-ordination between the three functions, while at the same time accepting that in some cases the three functions can not possibly be independent from one another.

The question arising at this point is whether in the light of modern constitutional practice the principle of the separation of powers, in its modern interpretation, would classify the existence of the CSA with its current powers as a case of acceptable interference of one function (the executive) with another (the judicial). The answer to this question seems to be negative. The principle of the separation of powers is still considered one of the basic guarantees of political freedom and its exceptions must be expressly regulated by the constitution and narrowly interpreted by constitutional lawyers.

The principle of the independence of the judiciary

Despite the limited application of the principle on the relationship between the executive and the legislative functions in the modern state, the principle of the separation of powers is still *stricto sensu* applicable to the relationship between the judicial and the other two functions. According to T. Renouix in France the legislative function is clearly stronger than the other two, since the executive function is a mere executive organ of the decisions taken by the legislative function, whereas the judicial function has power (Renouix 1991, p A–26). Thus, even in the modern interpretation of the principle, the judicial function still remains independent from the other two. In its positive sense, this means that the organs of the other two functions must recognise and respect the acts issued by the judicial organs of the state, whereas in its negative sense this means that all non-judicial organs must abstain from any actions that fall within the competence of the judicial organs. Such is the importance awarded to the independence of the judicial function in modern constitutional theory, that the independence of the judiciary now forms a separate principle of constitutional law. These provisions regulate that the national judges – as the natural persons physically conducting the judicial function of the state, in the execution of their duty have 'independent judgement' which should comply with the constitution and the laws of the state only (Manesis 1980, p 36). It seems therefore that the CSA with its current powers would be unconstitutional in modern civil law jurisdictions, since it clashes with the principle of the separation of powers in its classical and modern interpretation as well as with the principle of the independence of the judiciary.

In fact, the content of this latter principle in its positive sense (that all other organs should recognise and respect the acts of judicial organs) seems to indicate that the main course of action awarded to the CSA by its constitutive legislative act (namely the effective retrospective abolition of the courts' decisions on child maintenance) is also unconstitutional. It should be noted here that the abolition of courts' decisions through legislative acts is an established course of action, albeit rare, when the legislative function disagrees with the decisions of the judicial organs of the state. In spite of the profound clash of this course of action with the principles of the separation of powers and the independence of the judiciary, some constitutional specialists argue that – in some cases and in view of the modern interpretation of the principle of the separation of powers – this course of action can be acceptable. In fact, the abolition of courts' decisions by the legislative function is often presented as the only way under which these functions can adapt to the changing conditions of modern life (Georgiadis and Pavlopoulos 1988, p 705). However, F. Fleiner argues that the act that abolishes courts' decisions would lack legal value, as 'the legality of every act of the state depends on the competence of the respective issuing organ'. Since the courts themselves are the only organs that have the competence to modify or abolish courts' precedents, the administrative act in question would lack legal value (Fleiner 1963, pp 26–27; Balis 1961, p 28). Even these specialists, however, argue that the direct retrospective abolition of courts' decisions through legislative acts is unconstitutional (Keramefs 1983, p 100). The condition under which indirect retrospective abolition of courts' decisions could be considered legal is the general and abstract nature of the act in question, indicating the aim of the legislator to apply the principle of equality to a set of legal relationships. In other words, the act in question should aim to the application of the principle of equality, thus subjecting older legal relationships already regulated by the courts to the legal status that governs the modern similar cases.

From the analysis of the effective retrospective abolition of the courts' decisions on older cases of child maintenance it seems that this course of action could be considered legal in civil law jurisdictions. If one looks deeper into the matter, however, things change dramatically, especially if one takes into account the unconstitutionality of the CSA and the consequent 'existence' of all the acts issued by it. Since the regulation of modern child maintenance cases from the CSA has not legally taken place, the legal status of modern cases of child maintenance has not changed. Thus, the regulation of old cases through the effective retrospective abolition of courts' decisions is not based on the application of the principle of equality and should therefore be considered unconstitutional, since it clashes with the principles of the separation of powers and equality.

From our reference to the CSA, in the light of the administrative and constitutional law of modern civil law jurisdictions, it appears that in these legal systems the existence of the CSA, its powers and its main course of action would be considered unconstitutional. Additional flaws in the functioning of the CSA could possibly be found, but they remain outside the scope of an article of this length. Thus, in the search for a common position, which would further co-operation amongst EU member states in the field of child maintenance, one should turn to alternative formulas. It is for this purpose that in its third part the authors will attempt to present the relevant legal provisions within Germany and France, two countries whose civil legislation has influenced almost all Continental jurisdictions. Through this presentation it will be attempted to assess whether a common position on the issue of child maintenance does already exist within the Continent.

C. Child maintenance in France and Germany

Child maintenance in Germany

In the unified FRG child maintenance and support both inside and outside marriage are the parents natural rights and obligations, whose execution is supervised by the community[4] (Art 6, para 2 GG). Under Art 1602 BGB maintenance is owed only to children unable to support themselves by their parents, who must use all their resources equally for the maintenance of themselves and their children from their present and other marriages (Art 1609 BGB). These resources include income from additional secondary work, bonuses, State benefits, or money paid by third persons for the support of their own personal needs (Pages-Cabanel 1985, p 36; Schlueter 1995, p 166). The lack of personal income on the part of the father does not affect his obligation to financially support the children of a previous marriage. The content of the parents' child maintenance obligation includes 'the costs of all needs', namely cost of food, clothes, home, medical insurance, as well as the cost of the child's spiritual, musical and professional development. The parents pay either *in natura* (i.e. by offering the child housing and care) or by compensation (i.e. a sum of money). There are two types of child maintenance by compensation: The *Individualunterhalt* (calculated according to the financial situation of the parent and the way of life of the child) and the *Regelunterhalt*, (regulated under Art 1615 BGB by a government decree and increased every second year so as to adapt to the increase in the average cost of living. The *Regelunterhalt* is usually recommended by the respective executive authority (the *Jugendamt),* which is considered the *ad hoc* tutor of the child. If the income of the parents changes after the divorce, the level of life that the child would have had changes as well; thus, the child maintenance owed by the parents changes dramatically (Graba 1994, p 479).

As far as the enforcement of child maintenance obligation is concerned, there are three systems of protection for the child: the contractual, the judicial and the administrative system. The child may opt for a contractual agreement on maintenance, thus receiving the dual protection offered by the notary before whom the agreement is signed (Art 1934 BGB) and by the court confirming the agreement (Art 1615 BGB). The judicial system offers the child protection in the form of a court decision which can be directly executed against the parent. The administrative system offers the child protection in the form of benefits or compensation due to the parent's death at war, due to nazism or during the parent's military service.

As far as the execution of the obligation is concerned, the child may opt for the acquisition of a court decision allowing it to liquidate the parent's fortune and keep the amount of money owed together with interest (291, 288 BGB). Moreover, the child may choose to obtain a court decision permitting her/him to acquire a detailed report of the parent's sources of income and ordering direct payment from the parent's employer[5] or debtor. A third, indirect option concerns the child's right

4 For an analysis of the problems caused by the unification of Germany on family law cases and especially cases of child maintenance, see Horst Heiner Rotax, '*indesunterhalt in Mecklenburg-Vorpommern*' in (1993) 40 *FamRZ (Zeitschrift fuer das gesamte Familienrecht)* at pp 143–1150. For an analysis of the German status of child support, see P. Finger *Familienrecht mit familiensoziologischen und familienpolitischen Schwerpunkten* (Athenaeum Verlag, 1979) at pp 95–409.

Children within and children outside marriage now have equal rights under para 5 of art 6 of the GG. It should be noted that modern family law does no longer use the terms 'legitimate' and 'illegitimate' when referring to the status of children born within or outside marriage respectively. As far as German law is concerned, the terms *ehrliche* and *unehrliche Kinder* is now being used. Parents are not only the natural parents of a child born within marriage, but also the mother of a child born outside marriage. See B. Schmidt-Bleibtreu and F. Klein, *Komentar zum Grundgesetz fuer die Bundesrepublik Deutschland* (Hermann-Luchterhand Verlag, 1973), at p 206.

The positive obligation of the state is to respect the individuality and 'self-responsibility' of the family, whereas the negative obligation of the state is to abstain from any actions that would unjustifiably harm the family. See *ibid.*, p 205.

5 See Arts 834 ZPO; 829, 166–168 and 835 CPC. As part of the protection offered to the parent, the transfer of the whole salary of the parent is illegal. See L. Pages-Cabanel, *op.cit.*, at pp 116–119.

to pursue payment under threat of a criminal procedure under Art 170 of the Penal Code, according to which failure to pay maintenance constitutes a criminal offence. If the child chooses this route, he/she may pursue the civil execution of the parent's obligation during the criminal trial.

Child maintenance in France

In France one of the obligations arising from marriage is the mutual, non-transferrable and non-reciprocal obligation of both spouses to provide for the biological, financial, moral and educational development of their children (Art 203 CC). This includes the provision of food, shelter, general expenses and medical insurance/expenses. It goes without saying that the parental obligation of child maintenance is extended so as to cover children born outside marriage, or even adopted children (Carbonnier 1991, p 557). The parental obligation for child maintenance is, in contrast to the German legal system, non-transferable. Thus, in case of death of one of the parents the obligation ceases to exist and the heirs of the deceased have no obligation to continue paying child maintenance (TGI Bayonne, 2 Oct. 1973, J.C.P. 1974, 1117604). The obligation covers everything that is considered necessary for the well-being of the child (Ass.plen. 20 juill. 1979, Bull.Civ. No 6; Gaz. FW. 1979, 2.545, note Viatte). For the calculation of the sum owed as child maintenance the judge considers the child's needs and the resources of the parent. In fact, what is taken into account is the amount of money that the parent would have earned, had s/he used all the possible sources of income at his/her disposal (Civ. 2e, 17 dec. 1965, D. 1966. 465, note R. Savatier; 21 janv. 1976, *Bull. Civ.* 11, no 17). Obligations from other marriages are also taken into consideration (Civ. Ire, 17 mars 1964, *Gaz. Pal.*, 1964, 2.56). Only when payment *in natura* is impossible, is the child offered money as a monthly allowance. The obligation of the parent to pay child maintenance and the precise sum owed to the child must be either declared by a court or agreed by the parties and signed in a contract before a notary (30 juin 1982, *Gaz.Pal,* 1982, 2. 440, note Brazier; also see Versailles, 16 dec. 1980, J.C.P. 1982. 11. 19716, note Lincoln).

French law offers the child a set of five protective legal routes provided that the child has obtained a *title executoire*[6] from the *tribunal d'instance:*

(a) Since the court's order for payment of child maintenance is covered by a judicial real security, the child may liquidate the parent's immobile fortune (houses, estates, car).

(b) The child can pursue the 'direct payment of maintenance instalments', thus acquiring a court decision allowing him/her to be paid directly by the parents' employer, debtor or even the bank with which the parent has an account.

(c) The child may opt for payment by public organisations, which – after the court decision determining the parent's obligation to pay and the amount owed to the child – have the power to fine the parent and enforce the court's decisions on behalf of the child. The advantage of this procedure regulated by Art 293 of the law of 22.12.1984 (as amended by decree 86–1073 of 30.9.1986) lies in its simplicity, since the only actions required on behalf of the child are the acquisition of a court decision and the presentation of the case to the respective public authority. All subsequent legal actions leading to the regular payment of child maintenance are conducted administratively without any further requirement (financial or other) from the child him/herself.

6 This is any document that under the provisions of the Code of Civil Procedure can be used as an order to the bailiffs for the execution of the obligation in question.

(d) The child may opt for payment through the *Tresor Public* after the relevant order from the public prosecutor of the *tribunal de grande instance* within whose district the child is domiciled. The *Tresor Public* has the power to pursue on behalf of the child all maintenance debtors after the acquisition of a final court decision provided that the child has already used in vain the first two legal routes. The procedure is free for the child. The Treasury is paid by the parent a salary of 10% over the debt (*JO, Deb. Senat, p* 2162, col. 1).

(e) The child has an indirect way to enforce the court's decision on child maintenance: to threaten the parent who has failed to pay for two consecutive months that he/she will be brought before the criminal courts with the charge of 'family abandonment' (Art 357–2 Penal Code).

Does a common position on the issue of child maintenance already exist within the EU?

This brief reference to the two main Continental civil law systems, the German and French, leads to the assessment that a common formula for the enforcement of child maintenance obligations does already exist in Continental EU member states, not as a result of a conscious decision to harmonise, but by virtue of the proximity of these legal systems. In these countries the resolution of child maintenance disputes, namely the determination of the debtor/s and beneficiaries of child maintenance in each case, the determination of the nature of child maintenance owed and the evaluation of the sum owed in view of the particular circumstances surrounding each case, is left to the civil courts, which have the exclusive jurisdiction to judge on such issues.

The common legal mechanisms set to ensure the payment of child maintenance in the EU Continental legal systems include the child/ren's rights to acquire a detailed report of the parents' income (which may be juxtaposed with the parents' inland revenue declaration), to demand the judicial liquidation of this income, to achieve payment directly through the parents' employer and, last but not least, to bring the parent/s who fails or omits to pay before the criminal courts.

These profound similarities amongst Continental EU member states both in the basic concept of exclusive judicial jurisdiction for the settlement of all child maintenance disputes and in the legal framework for the attainment of its payment have created an excellent collaborative environment in these states' efforts to ensure the payment of child maintenance. The intra-EU judicial co-operation in civil and criminal matters under Art K1 (6) and (7) of the Maastricht Treaty contributes to the final result, which is a theoretically flawless legal framework for the protection of the child/ren and the effective enforcement of child maintenance obligations, even in the multi-nationality and multi-residence family environment of this current era.

Within this collaborative environment the introduction of the CSA, which signifies the creation of a new, radically different, administrative formula for the enforcement of child maintenance obligations, seems to be out of step with the rest of the EU. The question arising at this point is whether the UK should get in line with its EU counterparts and abolish the CSA. In answering this question, one must take into account that in practice the Continental system is not without its imperfections. Perhaps the most obvious one of those is the limited legal aid available to children who, in making use of the exclusively judicial mechanisms for the settlement of child maintenance disputes, wish to bring their case before the civil and/or criminal courts.

It is in view of this undoubted contradiction between the exclusive judicial mechanisms for the achievement of child maintenance on the one hand and the restrictions in legal aid for the use of these mechanisms on the other, that the administrative CSA formula could be used as a refreshing conciliatory tool for the 'fine tuning' of the already existing common child maintenance payment system within the EU.

Such a formula could accommodate both tendencies within Europe, namely the judicial solution favoured by civil law countries, as well as the administrative solution suggested by the UK. A compromise along these lines does not seem impossible, since at present administrative agencies do play a role in the enforcement of child maintenance obligations in the civil law countries, either as aids to the child for the completion of the necessary judicial procedure for the acquisition of child maintenance in France, or as initial assessors of child maintenance, should the child so require, in Germany. Such a formula would have the advantage of being enforceable within the whole of the EU against all debtor parents, irrespective of their nationality and the place of residence of themselves or their beneficiaries at any given time.

Conclusions

The authors' primary intention was to explore the possibility of a common EU solution to the problems surrounding child maintenance payment. It is clear that in an era of increasing movement of persons and capital within the EU, both on a family and on an individual basis, further collaboration amongst member states on the enforcement of child maintenance obligations is necessary. The authors considered the innovative child support system now in place in the UK, which is favoured as a solution to the problem of non payment of maintenance in many common law jurisdictions. The administrative formula-based CSA procedure was then assessed from a civil law perspective in order to evaluate the possibility of successfully transplanting it into the legal systems of the other EU member states. It was concluded that the resolution of child maintenance disputes by any authority other than the courts would be unconstitutional within these countries in view of the basic constitutional principles of the separation of powers and of the independent judiciary as implemented in Continental constitutional theory and practice.

Having rejected the CSA as a viable starting point for the co-operation of EU member states on the issue of child maintenance, the authors looked to the alternative legal routes prevailing in the two main civil law systems, whose provisions have greatly influenced the overwhelming majority of Continental civil law countries: France and Germany. The authors observed that a common solution does exist within the Continent, whose basic feature is a combination of civil and criminal judicial protection to the child/ren that suffer damages due to the failure of their parent/s to pay for their maintenance. This common solution is the result of the common civil law tradition rather than of a conscious decision amongst the states in question to harmonise the child maintenance provisions and seems to be excellent in theory. However, it has not been proven equally successful in practice.

An effective common EU solution would therefore seem to include elements of both the traditional judicial mechanism and the UK's new administrative one. In the initiation and development of the relevant negotiations, the role of the UK can be positive, active and creative. With its innovative and radically different ideas on the resolution of the issue of child maintenance the UK can lead the EU to the discovery of an effective rapprochement between the judicial and administrative formulas for the payment of child maintenance, something that can only benefit European children.

Bibliography

Balis, G (1961) *General Principles* (Athens: Sakkoulas).
Bradley, AW and Ewing, K (1993) *Constitutional and Administrative Law*, 11th ed, (London: Longman).
Burdeau, G, Hamom, F and Troper, M (1993) *Manuel de Droit Constitutionnel, Librairie General de Droit et de Jurisprudence* (Paris).
Burrows, D (1993) *The Child Support Act 1991 – a Practitioner's Guide* (London: Butterworths).
Carbonnier, J (1991) *Droit Civil – La Famille, Presses Universitaires de France* (Paris).
Dagtoglou, P (1984) *General Administrative Law* (Athens: Sakkoulas).
Donoughmore Committee (1932) *Report of the Committee on Ministers' Powers* (London: HMSO) Cmnd 4060.
Drewery, G (1988) 'Forward from FMI' *Public Law* 505.
Eekelaar, J (1991) 'A Child Support Scheme for the UK' *Family Law* 15–21.
Fleiner, F (1963) *Institutionen des Deutschen Verwaltungsrechts* (Aalen: Scientia Verlag).
Franks Report (1957) *Report of the Committee on Tribunals and Inquiries* (1957) (London: HMSO) Cmnd 218.
Georgiadis, A and Pavlopoulos, P (1988) 'The principle of the separation of powers' 14 *To Syntagma* 705.
Graba, HU (1994) 'Die Entwicklung des Unterhaltsrechts nach der Rechtsprechung des BGH im Jahr 1993' 41 FAMRZ 479.
Hadfield, B, (1996) *Judicial Review, A Thematic Approach* (London and Dublin: Gill and Macmillan).
Harrison M (1990) 'Child Maintenance in Australia: the New Era' in Weitzman, L and Maclean, M (eds) *Economic Consequences of Divorce – the International Perspective* (Oxford: Clarendon), pp. 219–232.
Hennessy, P (1991) 'The Last Retreat of Fame, Mrs Thatcher as History' *Modern Law Review* 492.
Jenkins, K, Caines, K and Jackson, A (1988) *Improving management in government – The next steps* (London: HMSO).
Keramefs, K (1983) *Civil Procedural Law* (Athens: Sakkoulas).
Kuenster, O (1949) '*Das Gewaltenproblem in modernen Staat*' 75 *Archiv des Oeffentlichen Rechts* 401.
Manesis, A (1980) *Constitutional Theory and Practice* (Athens: Sakkoulas).
Pages-Cabanel, L (1985) *L'Obligation Alimentaire de Droit Compare, Institut de Reserches Juridiques* (Paris).
Parker S (1990) 'The Australian Child Support Scheme' *Family Law* 210.
Raikos, A (1989) *Constitutional Law* (Athens: Sakkoulas).
Renouix, T (1991) 'L'apport du Conseil constitutionnel a l'application de la theorie de la separation des pouvoirs en France' *Receuil Dalloz Sirey de doctrine de jurisprudence et de legislation.*
Report of the Committee on One Parent Families (1974) (London: HMSO) Cmnd 5627.
Schlueter, W (1995) *BGB Familienrecht,* (C.F. Mueller-Juristischer Verlag).
Schmidt-Bleibtreu, B. and Klein, F. (1973) *Komentar zum Grundgesetz fuer die Bundesrepublik Deutschland* (Muenchen: Hermann-Luchterhand Verlag).
Smith, R. (1991) 'Who Benefits' 141 *New Law Journal* 644.

Social Security Committee 5th Report, H.C. 1993–94, No. 470.
Spiliotopoulos, E (1991) *Textbook of Administrative Law* (Athens: Sakkoulas).
Tsatsos, D (1992) *Constitutional Law,* Volume B (Athens: Sakkoulas).
Weitzman, L and Maclean, M (1990) *Economic Consequences of Divorce – the International Perspective* (Oxford: Clarendon).
White Paper (1995) *Improving Child Support* (London: HMSO) Cmnd 2745.

IS THE LEGAL PRACTICE COURSE TRAINING FUTURE SOLICITORS TO AVOID PROFESSIONAL NEGLIGENCE?

Mark R. Davies

Lecturer in Law, University of Sussex

First Published in Web Journal of Current Legal Issues in association with Blackstone Press Ltd.

SUMMARY

In 1993 the Law Society for England and Wales introduced the Legal Practice Course as the final major taught and examined stage of solicitors' training replacing the previous Law Society Finals Course. In this article it is argued that many of the occurrences of solicitors' negligence result not from a lack of legal knowledge but from poor working practices. The article considers whether the LPC meets the challenge of better preparing future solicitors for a modern and changing practice environment. It will be argued that the consideration of solicitors' negligence has an important contribution to make to the current debate about the measurement of the quality of professional services. From this consideration will be given to the question whether the LPC, coupled with some current perceptions of the quality of the training contract, is the best way of minimising solicitors' negligence in the future.

CONTENTS

Introduction

The Legal Practice Course (LPC) was introduced by the Law Society for England and Wales in 1993 as the final major taught and examined stage of solicitors' training. The new course has been described as 'the foundation for the most profound changes in terms of training for solicitor[s] . . .' (Sherr, 1992, p 164). The LPC follows in a series of attempts to re-design the vocational stage of training for solicitors. The previous attempt occurred in 1980 with the introduction of a revised Law Society Finals Course (LSF). Despite the desire to make the course relevant to the needs of trainees entering practice it was still dominated by dictation style lectures providing 'black letter' law and the description of procedures required for practice. The course was assessed at the end of ten months by means of closed book examinations which relied heavily upon the memorising and regurgitation of course material. No material was required other than that provided by lecture notes and so students were not even required to develop research skills, let alone other skills required of a solicitor. In addition, the course syllabus, consisting of conveyancing, wills and probate, family law, consumer and employment law, company law, criminal and civil litigation and solicitors' accounts seemed to have in mind the relatively small high street practice specialising in private client work, as the major destination for students (Sherr, 1992, p 164). Sherr suggests that in reality, by the end of the course in 1992 some 70 per cent of trainees were entering large city practices whose income predominantly resulted from commercial work (Sherr, 1992, p 164).

Following the lead of the Bar, which in 1989 had introduced a more skills oriented Bar Finals Course, the Law Society reconsidered the final stage of solicitors' training. Criticism was expressed that the LSF did little to prepare students for the realities of practice and that the law and procedure which was learned would quickly become out of date (Sherr, 1992, p 164). In fact, because of the need to publish a syllabus and set examinations nationally, on occasions law and procedure was taught and examined even though it was already outdated. It was in this light that the LPC was devised. The aim was to focus to a much greater extent on the acquiring of skills in order that not only could law and procedure be experienced in a context designed to reflect a practice environment, but the development of research skills should ensure that knowledge and skills could be updated throughout a practitioners' career. As Sherr states:

> 'Although experience is the best teacher, unmonitored experience can be a very poor teacher . . . Only the 'hands on' work of the [training contract] can give [trainee solicitors] the real foundation for the work they will have to perform, but an introduction in a well taught way . . . should cement good practice into the experience of the real world. It should also, if it works properly, teach them how best to learn from that experience.' (Sherr, 1992, p 166)

Central to the training of solicitors is an attempt to ensure that they can carry out their professional duties competently. One of the most striking indicators of incompetence is the cost to the profession of payments for solicitors' negligence. I will argue in this paper that many of the occurrences of solicitors' negligence result not from a lack of legal knowledge but from poor working practices. I will consider whether the LPC meets the challenge of better preparing future solicitors for a modern and changing practice environment. I will also argue that the consideration of solicitors' negligence has an important contribution to make to the current debate about the measurement of the quality of professional services. From this I will consider whether the LPC, coupled with some current perceptions of the quality of the training contract, is the best way of minimising solicitors' negligence in the future.

The Problem of Solicitors' Negligence

The cost to the solicitors' profession of solicitors' negligence has been rising rapidly over the past twenty years. Between 1976 and 1986 the gross annual premium requirement for the insurance of solicitors through the Master Policy Scheme[1] rose from £7 million to £52.3 million (Law Society Gazette 1986 p 3047). From 1st September 1987 to 31st August 1994 a further £395 million was paid out by the Solicitors Indemnity Fund[2] for solicitors' negligence claims and the dishonesty of partners within solicitors' firms. A further £1,520 million was held in reserve by the Fund for pending claims (Solicitors Indemnity Fund 1994, p 11). In the period from 1st September 1987 to 31st August 1994 claims reported to the Solicitors Indemnity Fund have risen by an average of 18.5 per cent per year (Solicitors Indemnity Fund 1994, calculated from the information p 6). The average payment per claim in this period was approximately £15,000 (Solicitors Indemnity Fund 1994, p 8) In addition to the overall amounts paid out by the Indemnity Fund, the individual firm of solicitors involved has to pay the first part of a successful negligence claim in the form of a self insured excess. At present this can range from £3,000 to £150,000 depending upon the annual gross fees of the firm. It can be seen, therefore, that negligence is an expensive problem for the solicitors profession, both in terms of financial expense and the damaging effect successful claims have upon the reputation of the profession as a whole.

1 The Master Policy Scheme was implemented by the Law Society in November 1975 to fulfil the insurance requirements laid down in section 37 of the Solicitors Act 1974.

2 The Solicitors Indemnity Fund Limited replaced the Master Policy Scheme in 1987, as the Law Society's means of insuring solicitors' negligence in accordance with the Solicitors Act 1974.

The Training of Solicitors

The usual training method employed to qualify as a solicitor is to read for a qualifying law degree, or other degree plus the one year Common Professional Examination (CPE). This is followed by the one year vocational stage of training, currently consisting of the LPC. Finally, a two year training contract is undertaken with a firm of solicitors authorised by the Law Society to take trainees. Beyond this, solicitors are required to undertake Continuing Professional Development (CPD) throughout their career. The academic law degree or CPE does not generally provide students with formal practical training in skills which they may require if they subsequently enter practice as a solicitor[3] Rather, the academic stage is usually seen as being intended to ground students in the academic study and appreciation of law in a range of contexts, for example by means of a critical and socio-legal approach as well as the more traditional 'black letter' analysis of legal rules. The academic stage should therefore provide the student with a rounded education as well as providing pre-requisites for entry into the legal professions.

Given the nature of the law degree or CPE, if by the time a future solicitor enters legal practice he or she is to have had exposure to the problems encountered in practice which lead to negligence, this will usually have to have occurred at the LPC stage of training or in the training contract.

Contents of the Legal Practice Course

The LPC consists of four compulsory 'core' subjects: Business Law and Practice, Civil and Criminal Litigation, Wills, Probate and Administration and Conveyancing. In addition, students must also study five skills considered to be central to solicitors' practice: Drafting, Research, Advocacy, Interviewing and Negotiation. The only aspect of the LPC from which the student has a choice is that of two option subjects, chosen from a variety on offer by the LPC provider. Providers are guided by provisions laid down by the Law Society in a set of Legal Practice Course Board Written Standards (the written standards). In considering whether the LPC adequately addresses the problem of solicitors' negligence, I will concentrate on the compulsory elements of the course, the 'core' subjects and the skills.

The Aims of the Legal Practice Course

The LPC should '(i) prepare the student for general practice; (ii) provide a general foundation for subsequent practice' (Written Standards 1995). The student should, inter alia, be able to complete a transaction in a manner which effectively achieves the client's objectives. The student should be able to identify any difficulties which may arise, and also be able to demonstrate an awareness of the limits to his or her own competence and therefore know when to ask for assistance. The written standards therefore recognise that students and trainee solicitors are not to be expected to perform to the same level of competence as a fully qualified and

3 There are some exceptions to this. For example, the Staffordshire University LLB requires students to undertake compulsory courses in interviewing, negotiation and advocacy. However, when viewed in the context of the whole course, such skill elements still play a relatively minor role and are not integrated into the teaching of substantive law subjects.

experienced solicitor. The assumption is made that the trainee will be supervised and should have the opportunity to ask for assistance. However, I will argue that in order for the trainee to know when to seek assistance, or when to take particular care, the substantive elements of the LPC must identify to the student the most common mistakes made by solicitors and where possible the likely reasons for such mistakes.

The Quality Debate

A general interest in the measurement of the quality of professional services, coupled with specific debates raised by developments such as Legal Aid Franchising, has led to much consideration recently about the measurement of quality and the teaching and assessment of skills. I will explore some of the key arguments in order to consider whether 'solicitors' negligence' deserves a place in the array of devices used to measure 'quality'.

'Quality' is not easy to define. Paterson et al suggest that it can range from the striving for excellence at one end of the spectrum, to fitness for purpose and the meeting of client needs and expectations at the other end (Paterson et al 1994, p 139). Goriely suggests that most British studies have focused upon one or two of the following factors: the client orientation of the service, client satisfaction, the accurateness of advice, the efficiency and effectiveness of the service. This reinforces the proposition that process or output measures are likely to be more directly indicative of quality than input or structural measures. Measurements of output can be obtained from a variety of sources, including clients, other lawyers and the lawyer's own perception (Sherr et al, 1994, p 142). All such sources of measurement have their difficulties. Clients, in particular one shot private clients rather than business clients who make regular use of solicitors, are unlikely to be in a position to assess quality. The private client focus may be more on image than substance. In the case of other lawyers, they may have their own agenda for determining quality. For example, a 'radical' criminal practitioner may view the more 'mainstream' practitioner as being too co-operative with the police, and so judge the quality of work undertaken as poor. This may contrast with the view of another 'mainstream' solicitor who sees the same work as being of high quality (see Travers 1994, p 173). Self assessment may well require the solicitor to balance the possibly conflicting issues of quality and income (Sherr et al 1994, pp 139–155). Travers suggests that given the difficulty of achieving any objective measure of quality, a better course would be to move away from the search and to 'encourage professionals to become more reflective about their own activities' (Travers 1994, p 179). This may be effective if such self reflection allowed quality to increase alongside income or, alternatively, if it encouraged the professional to fully consider the wider range of professional identity beyond income.

Consideration of solicitors' negligence claims can add to the quality debate. Determination by the courts of whether a solicitor has been negligent provides an insight by an independent knowledgeable third party into the quality of a solicitor's practice. Consideration of negligence overcomes the difficulties of relying upon the untrained view of an lay client or the pre-determined agenda of another lawyer. However, as with other quality measures, the shortcomings of the negligence approach must also be recognised. In order for a negligence claim to be brought the problem must have been spotted by the plaintiff (usually but not always the client of the solicitor) and this must have been accompanied by the financial ability and personal resolve to bring a claim against a professional adviser. Of the claims which are brought only a small percentage will reach trial and an even smaller percentage the pages of the law reports. The study of reported cases therefore represents a small sub-group of solicitors' negligence matters. These difficulties can be overcome to an extent by widening the scope of research to include settled cases. This, however, raises its own difficulties. These include the ethical considerations of researching case files (see Davies 1994), and the fact that cases settled on the advice of the lawyers involved in the litigation do not have the benefit of the full evidential and judicial consideration. Negligence can also be something of a blunt instrument in terms of measuring quality. The solicitor falls on one side or other of the line of negligent/not negligent. It could be said that this difficulty is shared by other measures of quality, for example, clients and other lawyers are giving a subjective yes or no consideration of whether the work of the lawyer in question was of sufficient quality. Beyond this, greater analysis of the arguments of the judiciary in negligence cases or the opinions of clients or other lawyers commenting upon the quality of a lawyer's work, can only give a general idea of how negligent the solicitor was or how high or low the quality of the work. Such measures of 'threshold competence' may seem less sophisticated than, say, the five grade quality continuum suggested by Paterson et al (1994, p 142). However, it may be less of a difference when in the practice of grading, agreement has to be reached upon which grade a matter should be given, and the dangers of subjectivity and opinion once again emerge. Sherr comments that:

> '. . . quality standards are always proxies for the true quality of service . . . developing a plurality of systems is likely to be important to the further development and refinement of the notions of legal competence. . . .'

It may be advocated that the consideration of negligence has an important place within this plurality.

Quality and the LPC

In terms of educational theory 'capability' may be a more appropriate term than 'competence' to describe what the LPC is striving towards. Stephenson et al describe capability in terms of confidence in one's knowledge, skills, self esteem and values. In particular:

> 'Capable people have confidence in their ability to (1) take effective and appropriate action, (2) explain what they are about, (3) live and work effectively with others and (4) continue to learn from their experiences. . . .' (Stephenson et al 1992, p 2).

Capability is part of specialist expertise, allowing the application of skills and knowledge to varied and changing situations, and providing for continuing personal development beyond formal education. It is further suggested that because ability to adapt and update requires confidence and judgement students should develop this by being directly involved in deciding what they learn and how they learn it.

The guiding ethos behind the LPC appears to be one of developing 'capability'. However, in this paper I use the term 'competence' in discussing the standards to be achieved to avoid negligence. This is justified in part on the grounds previously discussed that ultimately negligence is a yes/no question, a question as to whether the 'threshold competence' has been achieved. A second and perhaps more important reason is that the Law Society in discussions about the development of the LPC and subsequently have used the term 'competence'. Nicholas Saunders, Head of Legal Education with the Law Society at the time of introduction of the LPC defines 'competence' as:

> 'Knowledge plus skill . . . [including] the ability to perform certain basic tasks required by the trainee . . . [and] the ability to move efficiently and quickly into a completely new area and absorb the subject.' (Saunders 1993, p 111).

This definition in many ways closely resembles Stepenson's 'capability'. Jessop also uses 'competence' in a manner similar to Stephenson's use of 'capability' when he states that:

> '. . . competent performance at work . . . requires employees to think, plan, make decisions and communicate, all of which call upon . . . knowledge, principals, rules, procedures and so on.' (Stephenson 1990. p 39)

The choice of term therefore becomes one of semantic preference. I shall generally use the term 'competence' in this paper to include not only the 'threshold competence' required to avoid a successful negligence action but also to consider whether the LPC effectively develops in students the ability to adapt to the variety of unusual and changing circumstances likely to be encountered by a solicitor in practice.

Skills within the LPC

The Law Society was influenced in the planning stages of the LPC by the National Council for Vocational Qualifications' (NCVQ) approach to competence. Central to the NCVQ approach is the description of a job in terms of outputs and the standard of performance needed to satisfactorily achieve these (Maughan et al 1995, p 262). In this context the written standards describe in broad terms the skills required to practise competently (Maughan et al 1995, p 264). One potential difficulty with the NCVQ and Law Society approach is that the syllabus and requisite standards are set centrally. This can offer greater scope for ideology to creep in and for suggestions for change from outside to be undervalued. Jones illustrates this by pointing out that despite the strong evidence at the time the LPC was being planned that the majority of trainees entered commercially oriented practice, the Law Society still focused upon the symbolic status of domestic conveyancing and wills & probate as being central to the LPC syllabus (1993). The output measure of competence may also hide other serious deficiencies. An obvious example is that a person may, by adopting a surface approach to training, produce what appears to be a competent result, for example by appearing to make effective use of a checklist during an interview, but lack the underlying understanding of the skill and so have difficulty in adapting the skill from a classroom environment to the unpredictability of practice. It is considered to be particularly difficult to devise criteria which satisfactorily assess both process and performance (Maughan et al 1995, p 269). The inevitability of a mass production feel to the current LPC is likely to exacerbate the difficulties of distinguishing process and performance.

Another question mark over the current LPC is its separation of skills from substantive law. Thc assumption appears to be that legal practice consists primarily of 'the manipulation of a given base of knowledge by a ''tool kit'' of techniques and skills' Maughan et al 1995, p 273). This conflicts with recent thinking which considers professional practice to involve the interaction of knowledge with values, attitudes and behaviours and that skills need to be developed in the context of feedback which can then be used to continue the development of each of these factors (Maughan et al 1995, p 272). In effect the teaching and practice of skills best able to develop capability. Brayne encapsulates the problem when saying that:

> 'The trouble is, on the LPC, that short exercises assessed on any checklist tend to reveal superficial manifestations of skills, and are poor at diagnosing underlying habits. . . .' (Brayne 1994, p 236).

Also of concern is that, as with the LSF, assessment dominates the LPC, and so the primary question for the student remains not, 'will I be a good lawyer?', but, 'will I pass the test?' (Brayne 1994, p 227). Even though skills are assessed separately from substantive knowledge, the written standards do provide for skills competence to be demonstrated in a practical context and to show correct application of law and procedure. This does, however, have its practical difficulties when the assessor has to decide the extent to which a skill can be demonstrated poorly yet still be competent and also how a skill can be competently demonstrated when up to 50 per cent of the substantive law and procedure underlying it is incorrect (Brayne 1994, p 235). This position is supported by the author's own experience of Law Society Assessment visits of an LPC course. The assessors appeared to be of the opinion that as it was 'skills' rather than substantive knowledge being assessed, reasonable leeway should be allowed for errors in substantive knowledge. However, it appeared to be accepted that no method was readily available to say just how this should be done and as a result a large degree of intuitive opinion as to whether a skill 'looked' to be competently demonstrated came to the fore. In the context of solicitors' negligence the appearance of a well developed skill, for example an impressive looking draft of a document, a confident negotiation stance or a sympathetic and well structured interview is far more likely to result in negligence if underlain by important errors of law and procedure than the opposite position where the outward manifestations of the skill are relatively unrefined but the underlying requirements to perform the task competently are essentially sound. Because skills assessment on the LPC is carried out in isolation and an apparently high level of substantive error does not preclude being assessed competent, Brayne suggests that almost no one will fail the skills assessment (Brayne 1994, p 235). Also, this approach to skills assessment may encourage a surface rather than a deep approach to learning (Macfarlane 1992). The alternative approach of fully integrating skills with the acquisition of substantive knowledge is not without its difficulties. In particular the difficulty of genuine integration and avoidance of the danger of substantive knowledge excessively dominating. Skills education should 'value the accumulation of experience at least equally with the acquisition of facts' (Macfarlane 1992). An effective integration of substantive knowledge and skills should however produce a more effective approach and achieve one of Macfarlane's aims that:

'In skills education the acquisition of knowledge is exemplified by the "active" change in patterns of thinking brought about by experiential problem solving situations.' (Macfarlane 1992, p 303).

A possible danger with the current state of the LPC is that whilst individual law schools are guided by the written standards on how to teach and assess skills, and each LPC has to pass the initial validation and annual monitoring by the Law Society, the question arises as to whether the theoretical tools are available to do this. It may be argued that skills teaching merely entrenches another form of doctrine which goes largely unquestioned (Macfarlane 1992, p 303). Macfarlane concludes that the theory relating to the teaching of skills is very much in its infancy. LPC course design and the validation and monitoring process could therefore be said to have taken place in a theoretical vacuum, and that practices may become the accepted norm without being subject to serious challenge (Macfarlane 1992, p 313)

The Core subjects within the LPC

In order to consider whether the LPC adequately prepares students to avoid future professional negligence, I will consider the substantive knowledge and skills requirements laid down by the written standards in relation to the four core subjects. By comparing these provisions with what appear to be common causes of solicitors' negligence, consideration can be given to whether the LPC addresses the requirements of negligence as a measure of quality. I have already suggested that it is a difficult task to obtain a sufficiently broad base of information to confidently identify common causes of solicitors' negligence. For the purposes of this paper reported cases are used as the major source of such information, supplemented by generalised commentary from those closely involved in the field (primarily the Solicitors Indemnity Fund and solicitors acting in the litigation of claims) to support the patterns of negligence deduced from the cases. It was not practical in terms of the time available for all of the cases in the area to be considered. Because the information required was of a factual nature, 'what went wrong and why?', cases were identified by carrying out keyword searches on LEXIS. Using subject specific words such as 'conveyancing' in combination with words such as 'negligence', 'mistake' and 'error' provided sufficient cases to work with. One noticeable fact about these cases is that they range across a relatively broad time span. This raises the concern that the older cases may have involved different working practices than those employed today. An obvious example would be the comparison of unregistered conveyancing before the widespread availability of photocopying with registered conveyancing in today's computerised environment. In order to address this, an attempt was made to restrict the cases identified by the search to within the last 20 years, but this limited the numbers excessively. On balance it was therefore considered that the underlying skills requirements of solicitors had not changed to such an extent, and that older cases could still provide useful information about the general nature of mistakes constituting negligence.

Conveyancing

The conveyancing element of the LPC allows the student to build upon academic knowledge of land law, in order to acquire the skills to carry out the range of property work undertaken by solicitors in practice. In the period 1st September 1987 to 31st August 1994 conveyancing has accounted for the highest proportion of negligence claims against solicitors, representing approximately 51 per cent of such claims in terms of the amount paid to claimants (Solicitors Indemnity Fund 1994, p 13). The cost to the profession of conveyancing negligence over this period was close to £200 million. Consideration of the causes of conveyancing negligence, and the provision within the LPC to reduce these may be seen as very important if the costs of solicitors' negligence are to be reduced.

The Conveyancing Syllabus in the Legal Practice Course

The written standards provide, inter alia, that the student should be able to: identify the client's goals, identify and investigate the relevant facts, research and identify the relevant legal issues, advise the client on the legal consequences of his or her proposals, draft documentation to effect the transaction and recognise the potential for a conflict of interest and act within the solicitors' professional conduct rules (Written Standards 1995). The written standards go on to further sub-divide and detail the knowledge and skills which the student should gain. On the procedural side, the student should be able to: carry out pre-contract and pre-completion searches, identify any difficulties arising from the searches and enquiries, identify any planning considerations, advise the client on the legal affects of the results of searches and enquiries and decide what further action may need to be taken. The student should also consider how the conveyancing transaction is being financed. If the solicitor is acting for a mortgage lender as well as the purchaser, the needs of this mortgagee must also be addressed. The written standards assume that the student will have a sound grasp of the contract and property law which underpin conveyancing transactions.

Do these written standards address the most common problems of conveyancing negligence in practice?

Common Problems leading to Conveyancing Negligence

One of the most striking factors which arises from a consideration of solicitors' negligence cases in the area of conveyancing is the number of such cases which involve the commission of very basic errors. The cases identified in Appendix 1 list a catalogue of errors many of which could have been avoided if simple precautions were implemented into conveyancing practice. For example, the use of a systematic diary system with backup provisions to ensure that time limits are not missed. Ensuring that the solicitor's work load is not so high as to prevent documents, whether they are simple search results or complex business leases, being read thoroughly. Only rarely do errors appear to result from a significant lack of knowledge by the solicitor. Domestic conveyancing in particular has become a high volume, low fee area of work, having to be carried out quickly if it is to be profitable. To achieve this it may be necessary to employ methods which increase the risk of errors being made, or necessitate the omission of safeguards. In light of such pressure, the requirement, for example, to carry out certain searches and enquiries can become one of routinely requesting the searches and making the standard enquiries and then when the replies are received placing these on the file without ever giving them proper consideration. It has been suggested that there is effectively a price war amongst the providers of conveyancing services. This leads to work being carried out at a price where it would be extremely difficult to both take the care necessary to minimise the risk of error and at the same time to make a profit. Some firms have been able to make use of staffing structures and technology to allow high volume domestic conveyancing to be carried out both profitably and efficiently. Other firms, however, may have been unable to afford to take this route and in order to compete are forced to take on too many cases and to cut corners in carrying out the work.[4] It may also be suggested that if, increasingly, high volume conveyancing practice is carried out by para-legal staff rather than qualified solicitors, consideration of whether the LPC prepares students for conveyancing practice diminishes in importance. It may, however, be argued that the contrary applies. Non-qualified staff have to be adequately overseen by a solicitor (failure to do so may result in disciplinary action before the Solicitors Disciplinary Tribunal, see for example decision 4824), and in setting up, training staff and monitoring a high volume conveyancing operation the 'skills' required for conveyancing will have to be employed. Any lack of competence by such a solicitor could therefore be imparted into the whole operation and magnified accordingly.

The written standards appear to anticipate many of the errors common to conveyancing. Some of those errors which are not addressed within the LPC may be considered too advanced for trainee solicitors. For example, the interpretation of complex clauses in leases may fall within this category, although it is probably the case that once in practice some trainees are given a full caseload and may be left much to their own devices, including dealing with complex or unusual matters. If consideration of more complex matters is not within the scope of the LPC, thought should be given to whether such issues should be addressed by means of formal training post LPC and post qualification as a solicitor. As previously stated, solicitors are required to undertake CPD each year as a condition of being allowed to practise. However, the solicitor can choose from a wide range of courses offered by commercial providers. The courses chosen need not reflect any particular problem area the solicitor may be facing and, in the current economic climate, many solicitors may simply choose courses which are relatively cheap and close at hand, rather than choosing those which would provide the best educational benefit. Also, CPD has traditionally concentrated on updating knowledge rather than upon enhancing skills or developing learning strategies, although some CPD providers may be moving slowly in the direction of skills development (Webb 1995, p 3). A counter pressure to this move comes from the increasing concern with the cost of CPD. One response from the Law Society is to allow greater flexibility in obtaining CPD, including allowing solicitors to undertake self-managed reading from authorised sources. If such reading is largely 'black letter' in nature then this moves CPD even further away from skills development. One re-design of CPD suggested by Webb is to move to the concept of 'action research'. This would provide for individualised learning and the capacity for continuing assessment of professional behaviour, responsibilities, assumptions and values. It would encourage practitioners to be habitually conscious of various conditions of practice (Webb 1995, p 9). This would be achieved by practitioners, either alone or in collaboration with academic researchers, engaging in a systematic attempt to understand and change practice by reflection upon their own actions. In this way practice skills and knowledge would be systematically refined (Webb

4 For further discussion see Sean Webster, *The Times*, 3 August 1993, p 28.

1995, p 8). However, the present position is that in the absence of change to the CPD structure and ethos, CPD is unlikely to be a reliable mechanism for addressing serious inadequacies in the LPC or training contract.

A noticeable omission from the written standards is any reference to the cut price 'production line' nature of much conveyancing in practice. A student successfully completing the LPC may enter a training contract having the legal and procedural knowledge needed to carry out a range of conveyancing tasks, but totally unprepared for the volume of work faced in the practice environment. If the training firm happens to cut corners in order to deal with a high volume of work, the trainee may quickly forget the good practices taught on the LPC and adopt these more risky practices. The Law Society could target the new entrants to the profession and help them to resist being indoctrinated into unsatisfactory practices. LPC students should become familiar with handling a high volume of cases and with good file management. The requirement that the LPC student knows his or her own limitations and when to ask for help, should be extended to emphasise the future solicitors' personal liability under the professional conduct rules and in professional negligence if he or she simply takes on unsatisfactory practices used in the employing firm.[5] In this way trainee and junior solicitors should be supported by the Law Society in resisting taking on a workload beyond their competence or in undertaking work in a manner they know to be undesirable.

A further source of potential problems not fully addressed by the written standards is the need to cross reference certain information between different specialist disciplines. Cases such as *Bell* v *Peter Browne* [1990] 3 All ER 124 illustrate this. The solicitor in this case was primarily concerned with the client's divorce, but negligence arose because of the conveyancing matters which came about as an aspect of the property division between the husband and wife. As solicitors increasingly specialise they need to be trained to spot issues which may fall outside of their specialist areas in order that they can pass on this aspect of the matter to another department within the firm or carry out updating research in order to competently deal with the matter themselves.

Wills, Probate and Administration

In the period 1st September 1987 to 31st August 1994 trust and probate matters, including inheritance tax and taxation, accounted for approximately six per cent of solicitors' negligence claims in terms of amounts paid to claimants (Solicitors Indemnity Fund 1994, p 13). Whilst this represents a much smaller problem than that of conveyancing negligence, these cases have nevertheless cost the solicitors profession around £21 million over the period of existence of the Indemnity Fund (Solicitors Indemnity Fund 1994, calculated from pp 11 and 13).

---

5 It is not strictly true to say that an employed solicitor is liable in professional negligence. The firm is the indemnified party under the Solicitors Indemnity Fund scheme and it is against the firm a complainant will bring an action. There are, however, reports of employed solicitors being sued by their employing firm for losses not met by the Indemnity fund, for example, the self insured excess and any increase in contributions to the Fund. I know of no reported case yet in this area. If such a case did reach the stage of trial it would be interesting to see how the court would deal with an argument by the solicitor that the mistake occurred because he or she was forced by the firm, through volume of work, to employ shoddy practices and to cut corners.

The Wills, Probate and Administration Syllabus of the Legal Practice Course

On completion of the wills unit 'the student should be able to advise a client on testamentary dispositions and intestate succession, draft a will and conduct the administration of an estate, including obtaining a grant of representation. . . .' (Written Standards 1995). Specific aspects of this area of work with which the student should become familiar include: identification of relevant facts, researching legal issues, advising the client of the legal consequences of his or her proposals, and understanding the appropriate tax implications. In order to achieve these aims the student should be able to: 'select and modify appropriate precedents, express testamentary wishes clearly and unambiguously, and make appropriate arrangements for the execution and attestation of the will'.

Common problems leading to negligence in wills and probate cases

A similar picture emerges to that concerning conveyancing. A significant number of the cases result from simple errors and the failure to progress matters quickly and efficiently. The cases given in Appendix 2 illustrate the types of error which occur. Not surprisingly, given that the Indemnity Fund statistics show a far lower occurrence of wills and probate negligence compared with conveyancing, the list of reported cases involving wills and probate negligence is shorter. Another reason for the relative lack of reported cases is the nature of the prospective claimant. If a solicitor is negligent in the preparation of a will the error will often not come to light until after the death of the client. The potential claimants, usually intended beneficiaries, are third parties with no contractual rights against the solicitor. Only in the 1980 case of *Ross* v *Caunters* did the courts fully begin to come to terms with the right of such third parties to bring an action in tort against the solicitor. Therefore, prior to this many potential claims by disappointed beneficiaries will not have been litigated. Many of the errors simply involve the failure to act sufficiently quickly in taking and dealing with instructions or inadequate diary and safety mechanisms to ensure that time limits are adhered to. Some of the cases could result from a lack of knowledge, for example the solicitor being unaware of the effect of marriage on a will, the restrictions on who should witness a will or the subtleties of drafting or interpreting a trust document. However, some of these errors can equally be attributable to the solicitor failing to adequately communicate information to the client or the failure to connect certain knowledge, such as the likelihood that the clients will marry, to the matter at hand.

The relatively simple nature of many of the errors suggest once again that it is not sufficient for the LPC student to be taught the legal and procedural aspects of a wills and probate matter, but that this knowledge should then be put to the test in the context of a heavy caseload and the need to work quickly on a range of different files and different matters.

Business Law and practice

In the period 1st September 1987 and 31st August 1994 Commercial law accounted for approximately six per cent in number and almost thirteen per cent in terms of the sums paid of solicitors' negligence claims (Solicitors Indemnity Fund 1994, p 13). These figures suggest that whilst the total number of claims is relatively low, the average cost per claim is particularly high. This probably reflects the high value of the average commercial transaction, and illustrates the particular danger in terms of cost of a mistake being made within this field.

The Business Law Syllabus of the Legal Practice Course

The written standards provide that on completion of the business law unit the student 'should understand the nature and structure of the different business media . . . should be able to select an appropriate medium and structure to meet the client's commercial requirements, and should be able to advise on the legal and taxation implications of, and procedures required in, common form transactions and developments arising during the life and development of the business' (Written Standards 1995). These requirements are sub-divided into a wide range of issues involving the identification of client goals, research, drafting, advising the various parties involved in sole trader, partnership and corporate forms of business. These requirements would include, inter alia, the taxation implications of setting up, running and disposing of a business, drafting partnership agreements and various company documents and the dissolution of a business.

The most striking factor about the business law syllabus is its breadth. The student is expected to come to grips with the major subjects of partnership law, company law, business taxation, bankruptcy and insolvency. This may be designed to give the student a wide introduction to business law which may then be built upon in practice. However, it may be argued that skimming the surface of such a wide range of subjects does not even provide the student with a basic level of competence. The danger of this is that firms providing training contracts may assume more competence from the student than the LPC actually provides. One solution would be the development of an alternative specialist LPC in business law. This, however, could have the effect of allowing large commercial firms to dictate to a large extent the future training of solicitors and lead to the emergence at the training stage of a two tier profession.

Common problems leading to negligence in business law

There can be a very wide range of work undertaken within the commercial department of a typical solicitors' firm. The choice of solicitors' negligence cases chosen to illustrate typical errors within the field of business law is bound to be somewhat arbitrary. Examples of illustrative cases of solicitors' negligence within the business law field include: failure to register a charge which would have secured the company debts and so would have prevented the need for the creditors to pursue the guarantors *Re Foster* (1986) 2 PN 193; lack of awareness that a company may be restricted by statute from purchasing its own shares *Central Trust Co* v *Rafuse* (1986) 31 DLR (4th) 481. Examples of mistakes which overlap between business law and other areas of solicitors' practice include: a solicitor negligently advising the client to purchase a lease of residential property in the name of a company but failing to address the fact that the client would be unable to obtain a statutory tenancy when the lease expired *Murray* v *Lloyd* [1989] 1 WLR 1060; failure to identify that the lease of a business premises prevented the use to which the client intended to put the building *Transportation Agency Ltd* v *Jenkins*

(1972) 223 E.G. 1101. Errors may also occur when the solicitor is retained on a matter where other professionals, for example accountants, are involved. The solicitor should ensure that his or her retainer clearly identifies the scope of each profession's responsibility where there is scope for overlap, for example in the context of tax advice. This ensures that the solicitor does not omit to do something simply because it was assumed that the other profession would deal with it. Other errors can occur in business transactions when the solicitor does not have sufficient knowledge of regulations associated with the business in question. For example, various businesses require licences in the field of transport, consumer credit or food safety. Such matters are not addressed by the written standards. It may also be more likely for solicitors to have to prepare unusual one off documents in the business law field than in other areas, putting the solicitors' legal research and drafting skills to greater test.

Unlike conveyancing and wills and probate work, errors in the field of business law are far more likely to result from a lack of knowledge than more simple clerical and file management errors. This may be because of the very wide range of business law work, resulting in a much greater capacity for unfamiliar areas to be encountered. The written standards may be attempting to deal with this by introducing the student to a wide range of business law subjects. However, as has already been discussed, this may be at the expense of the student gaining in depth knowledge or understanding of any of these areas. The student may therefore enter practice with the belief that he or she has detailed business law knowledge, when in fact the surface has hardly been scratched. The training firm may also look at the business law syllabus and assume that it provides far more detail than it actually does. Even large specialist commercial firms may have difficulty, within the context of the training contract, in giving a trainee solicitor a solid grounding in business law. This is illustrated by the following quote from a trainee solicitor in a large City practice:

> '. . . I have been feeling more pressure to complete a great deal of work in a short time and consequently I have not learnt as much as I should from this work. I also feel that . . . I do not have the specialist knowledge of a corporate lawyer . . . and this is often not taken into consideration when given deadlines.' (Moorhead et al 1995, p 43)

Litigation and Advocacy

Negligence involving litigation, including personal injury litigation, accounted for approximately 22 per cent of claims against solicitors in the period 1st September 1987 to 31st August 1994. The cost to the profession for these claims was close to £87 million (Solicitors Indemnity Fund 1994, p 13). Litigation is therefore second only to conveyancing as the largest subject area in which negligence occurs.

The Litigation and Advocacy Syllabus of the Legal Practice Course

The written standards for litigation and advocacy cover both civil and criminal work and are fairly wide ranging. On a general level they provide that 'the student should have an appreciation of the nature of civil and criminal litigation, should be able to identify the critical steps in the process . . . and should have gained experience through practice of some or all of the stages of litigation' (Written Standards 1995). This specifically includes the student gaining the ability to identify the relevant factual and legal issues, identification of the alternative means of achieving the client's goals and advising the client of the legal consequences of the proposals. The student should then progress to the identification of the overall nature of the transaction and dealing with the matter through the litigation process, including the drafting of requisite documents. The student should gain the ability to advise the client on the cost options in order to finance the matter, including making application for legal aid. The written standards assume that the student will have prior knowledge of the court structure and the common law offences which provide the basis for the litigation process.

Problems Leading to Litigation Negligence

There are a wide range of matters which may involve aspects of the litigation process. This means that similar problems to those discussed in the context of business law are encountered when attempting to identify reported cases of solicitors' negligence in the litigation area. The written standards take a broad approach to the subject, but within the LPC as a whole there is scope for specialist aspects of litigation such as personal injury, commercial litigation and matrimonial work to form the basis of separate option subjects. In reviewing the case law for litigation negligence the position has been adopted that the litigation and advocacy head of the LPC is aimed at providing the basis for all litigation, including more specialist areas, and as such any case which indicates a failure in litigation knowledge or procedure is potentially worthy of note.

A more serious problem in searching for cases involving litigation negligence is the possible distortion caused by the advocates' immunity. Advocates are immune from suit for claims in negligence based upon an alleged failure in the manner in which a case was conducted in court, or the way in which a case was handled in pre-trial work closely connected with the presentation of the case in court.[6] It is not within the scope of this article to consider the merits or otherwise of the advocates' immunity. It may be argued that because an advocate cannot be held negligent then such errors are not of concern. This should not be the case. Just because there cannot be a finding of negligence should not mean that the Law Society and the solicitors' profession should not be concerned with promoting the highest quality in the preparation for and conduct of a trial. As competition for the provision of legal services continues to increase, poor quality of work in any area may result in adverse publicity and an associated loss of income for the profession. It is also of note that the courts do have the power to award costs against, inter alia, a solicitor if it considers that such costs have been wasted as a result of an 'improper, unreasonable, or negligent act or omission. . . .' (Courts and Legal Services Act 1990 ss 4, 111, 112).

Bearing in mind the absence of cases involving negligence in relation to advocacy, examples of errors made by solicitors in the field of litigation are given in Appendix 3. When considering these it should be noted that the scope of a

6 See *Rondel* v *Worsley* [1969] 1 AC 191 and *Saif Ali* v *Sidney Mitchell & Co* [1980] AC 198 and also Courts and Legal Services Act 1990, s 62(1). For a more detailed discussion of this subject see Jackson and Powell 1992.

solicitor's duty may well be a changing one as the distinction between barristers and solicitors increasingly narrows, for example with the extension of solicitors' rights of audience. It is usually accepted that a solicitor acting upon the advice of suitable counsel will have a valid defence to a claim in negligence. However, this will not always be the case. A solicitor should not uncritically act upon the advice of counsel where the solicitor would reasonably be expected to question the accuracy of this advice *Davy-Chiesman* v *Davy-Chiesman* [1984] Fam 48.

Errors in litigation on the whole do not appear to result from any serious lack of knowledge by solicitors. Rather, they seem to result from the lack of use of basic management and diary systems to ensure that time limits are met and that the progress and preparation for trial of cases is handled correctly. Solicitors may also fail to use the litigation process sufficiently forcefully, delaying the issue of proceedings whilst attempting to negotiate a settlement, resulting in the failure to meet a limitation period. The failure to issue proceedings promptly may also hide serious delays in the time it takes to settle cases and the resulting delay in the client receiving damages. This type of poor work is unlikely to lead to a negligence claim and so will not appear in the Solicitors Indemnity Fund statistics. Possible solutions to such problems include a system which requires the regular review of files by the solicitor, and possibly review by other members of the firm. Problems could stem from a lack of knowledge if the solicitor assumes to too great an extent that any matter of difficulty can be passed on to the counsel and counsel's advice relied upon without question.

The written standards attempt to ensure that the student reaches a level of ability which will enable him or her to deal competently with a typical litigation matter. However, once in practice, the student will be faced with a large volume of cases and will need suitable case management techniques to ensure that these can be handled competently. Other factors, such as the choice of expert witness, are seen to lead to negligence but consideration of these aspects of the litigation process are lacking from the written standards.

Will the deficiencies of the Legal Practice Course be remedied in the training contract?

Throughout this paper there has often been the implicit assumption that omission from the LPC will be made up at the training contract stage. Furthermore, the LPC can be seen as having the purpose of preparing the student for the training contract stage only and not for immediate qualified practice. This should not, however, excuse any inadequacies within LPC if research suggests that the training contract stage does not in fact meet this need. Since 1 July 1994 any firm employing trainee solicitors has to be authorised by the Law Society and must abide by a Training Code. This code requires that trainees be given experience to enable them to reach recommended standards of performance or competence in practical and administrative skills by the end of the two year training period (Stebbings 1994, p 98). One recent research project on behalf of the Trainee Solicitors Group, the 'Quality of Life Survey' (Moorhead et al 1995), provides some important insights into considerations about the actual quality of some training contracts. The following findings from this research have relevance to the current study.

An indicator of the pressure trainee solicitors are under, and the workload they are faced with, is the average number of hours worked per week. Approximately

36 per cent of respondents worked between 46 and 80 hours (Moorhead et al 1995, pp 16 and 44). When surveyed about the quality of formal training they received 21 per cent of respondents expressed dissatisfaction and a further 24.5 per cent were unwilling to positively recommend their training (Moorhead et al 1995, p 18). Similar responses applied to informal training, with over 22 per cent claiming dissatisfaction and a further 21 per cent being unwilling to express satisfaction (Moorhead et al 1995, p 19). Thirty-six per cent of respondents were dissatisfied or neutral when asked whether they considered that their training gave them a 'strong basis for qualification'. Interestingly, those respondents who were newly qualified solicitors, and so probably in the strongest position to answer this question were the most critical (Moorhead et al 1995, p 24). In order to counter the possible subjectivity of the respondents' perceptions as to the quality of their training contract, the survey also asked for the amount of time the respondent's firm devoted to training. A fifth or less of the average trainee's working time was spent on training or supervised work. Newly qualified solicitors devoted less than one tenth of their time to being trained or supervised. The vast majority of trainee and newly qualified solicitors' working time therefore appeared to consist of working unsupervised. Newly qualified solicitors expressed the concern that their firm often expected a totally unjustified increase in competence once they formally qualified. This manifested itself in an increased workload and a marked reduction in supervision (Moorhead et al 1995, p 31). More striking still are the findings that 45 per cent of respondents claim to have received no formal training (Moorhead et al 1995, p 25). If the LPC written standards assume that firms providing training will continue to add to the trainees' knowledge post LPC, these statistics draw this assumption seriously into question. Quotes from respondents in both small and large firms suggest that some trainees consider that post LPC they have to learn everything for themselves. In expecting the adjustment to the volume and quality of work required from trainees, some firms were seen as adopting a 'sink or swim' approach. Whilst it is reasonable for future solicitors to develop self reliance in their work, the comments indicated that this was being applied at too extreme a level and too early. In some firms, respondents felt that not only were they not being supervised, but often there was no one available to give help even when it was asked for (Moorhead et al 1995, p 32). Even when supervision was available, some respondents felt that their errors were corrected without adequate explanation, so they were not really learning how to get things right the next time the problem arose (Moorhead et al 1995, p 35).

It should be noted that in the case of many questions, the above survey received a positive response from the majority of respondents. However, in the case of a number of matters which reflect upon the competence of the solicitors' profession, a significant minority of responses were negative. Such findings cannot be ignored when considering the omission of certain elements of training from the LPC written standards.

An alternative to the current training model

This paper has suggested that consideration of solicitors' negligence should be included as a measure of 'quality' within the current debate as to the meaning of that term. Using this measure it has been suggested that the LPC falls short in terms of providing the skills required of solicitors to best avoid negligence. It has further been argued that such deficiencies within the LPC are not guaranteed to be remedied at the training contract or CPD stage. The immediate, and arguably justified, reaction of LPC providers may be that they cannot be held responsible for deficiencies at the later stages of a solicitor's training. However, the passing of responsibility from one stage to the next does not resolve the problem if at the end of the process the competence of solicitors is not maximized. The introduction of a strong skills element into the LPC appears to be a significant improvement over the LSF in terms of preparing students for future practice, although the current limited state of theory relating to the teaching and assessment of skills does draw into question whether the current skills provision on the LPC is being used to best effect. However, I consider that simply tampering with the current LPC to take into account skills theory will not sufficiently address the issue. Moorhead et al show that serious questions can be raised as to the quality of training contracts and that as long as the LPC stage and the training contract stage are separate each provider can blame the other for gaps in training provision.

Consideration of solicitors' negligence suggests that training is required which incorporates skills within the context of the real environment of practice. The teaching of skills purely within the artificial environment of the classroom not only poses the threat of students adopting an uncritical and surface approach to their learning but also fails to impart the file management skills, the lack of which seems to account for a high proportion of solicitors' negligence. In order to address these issues I would advocate the current one year LPC plus two years' training contract be replaced with a three year integrated apprenticeship. Instead of providing a take it or leave it course, LPC providers would work much more closely with each firm employing trainees in order to tailor a course to fit far more closely the needs of each individual trainee. Such a course would still contain a large degree of common elements which all trainees would undertake on either a distance learning basis or a block/day release basis. This would lay the foundation of basic skills and substantive knowledge in a similar manner to the current LPC, although integrated much more into the day to day experience of practice. The basic knowledge and skills provision would be developed by means of practical case management provided by the firm coupled with a more theoretical input by the LPC provider. By means of a close working relationship LPC teachers would gain a practical and ongoing insight into the requirements of practice (whilst many LPC teachers currently maintain links with practice the LPC does not require this, and such links are usually maintained to ensure up to date knowledge of practice rather than to directly interface between the LPC and training contract experience). Firms would benefit from the overseeing of their training by academics developing an understanding of skills at a more theoretical level. Such an approach would not be such a radical departure. It could be said to be combining the best of the old non-graduate five year apprenticeship model of training solicitors with the current graduate entry route. By combining current teaching methods with an apprenticeship model many of the difficulties of teaching skills purely within the classroom could be reduced. It could also serve as a useful adaptation of skills teaching methods used in other countries, for example the highly simulated practice environment used in Australia (Jones 1993, p 100).

The major drawback in attempting to implement such a change is likely to be resistance, or at least inertia, from the current providers in the training sphere. Whilst many firms offering training contracts take training very seriously, the study by Moorhead et al strongly suggests that some firms see trainee solicitors as relatively cheap fee earners who can best learn by means of a sink or swim approach. This latter type of firm is unlikely to welcome scrutiny of its activities by academics, nor possibly to release trainees from fee earning work on a regular basis. From the LPC provider's viewpoint such a change is almost certainly going to be more difficult to organise than the current LPC. The current LPC has the benefit of neatness. LPC providers can devise their courses without reference to the firms to whom their students will subsequently go. An apprenticeship model would require much greater adaptability within courses and a high degree of co-ordination between academic institutions and solicitors' firms, almost certainly involving a greater workload for both. The assumption that only students with training contracts could undertake the final stage of training would constitute a double edged sword. On the one hand it would address the current concerns about oversupply of LPC qualifiers compared with the number of training contracts available. On the other hand, concerns about certain members of society being prejudiced in the search for training contracts would be exacerbated if obtaining a training contract was a integral part of the LPC. A move to an apprenticeship model of training for solicitors would be a radical departure from the direction which the training has taken in the last 20 years. However, it is a model which is employed widely and apparently successfully in many other fields of both graduate and non-graduate employment.

Conclusion

The written standards conclude that 'students should learn from the experience provided by the Legal Practice Course and be able to learn from experience in practice'. This paper has considered whether or not the LPC can provide students with the key knowledge and skills required to avoid the most common causes of solicitors' negligence, and if not whether omissions from the LPC will be remedied once the students have embarked upon the training contract. It has been suggested that many of the causes of solicitors' negligence result not from a lack of legal or procedural knowledge, but from simple clerical, administrative and file management errors. Many of these errors may result from the pressure of work and the number of cases a solicitor is expected to handle at any one time. Whilst the LPC written standards may provide for students to learn how to deal with a variety of matters in the context of individual cases, there is no specific provision for students then to learn how to handle such cases in volume or to develop case management skills for this purpose. It may be considered that such case management skills should properly be learned at the training contract stage. However, the Trainee Solicitors Group study into the quality of training contracts suggests that any omissions of important aspects of solicitors' training from the LPC, on the assumption that they will be covered in the training contract, may be seriously flawed. Some incidences of solicitors' negligence, notably in the area of business law, do arise from deficiencies of knowledge. The written standards for business law appear to attempt to maximise breadth of knowledge, but this may be at the expense of depth of knowledge. Again, any assumption that this will be remedied in the training contract is subject to serious misgivings.

The future training of solicitors should therefore combine the developing theoretical underpinning of how skills may best be learned with the real experience of case management in practice. This can best be done by working with both aspects together, classroom knowledge being applied in practice and then this experience related back to further development in the classroom. In this way a progressive cycle of self evaluation leading to further guided development can be established. The broader aspects of solicitors' training and the quality of solicitors' skills may also be improved by the two way sharing of expertise between lawyers in practice and those in academia envisaged by the apprenticeship model.

Appendix 1

Common errors leading to conveyancing negligence

The failure to register an option *Midland Bank Trust Co Ltd* v *Hett, Stubbs and Kemp (a firm)* [1978] 3 WLR 167; failure to consider the client's position before the execution of the mortgage deed *Forster* v *Outred & Co (a firm)* [1982] 1 WLR 86; failure to search the commons register *G & K Ladenbau (UK) Ltd* v *Crawley and de Reya (a firm)* [1978] 1 WLR 266; failure to warn the building society client that the solicitor had reason to doubt the bona fides of the purchaser *Anglia Hastings and Thanet Building Society* v *House & Son* (1981) 260 E.G. 1128; failure to warn the client that there was no right of way over the property *Piper* v *Daybell, Court-Cooper & Co* (1969) E.G. 1047; failure to warn the client that the property did not have planning permission *Lake* v *Bushby* [1949] 2 All ER 964; failure to check the tenancy rights of tenants occupying property *Goody* v *Baring* [1956] 1 WLR 448; failure to warn the client of the risks involved in carrying out repairs to property prior to the exchange of contracts *Allard* v *Samson* (1966) 110 SJ 229; failure to warn the client of the risks involved on exchanging contracts on a purchase before exchanging on the sale *Morris* v *Duke-Cohan & Co* (1975) 119 SJ 826; failure to consider in detail the content of a sub-lease *CW Dixey & Son Ltd* v *Parsons* (1964) 192 E.G. 197; failure to warn the client of the dangers of exchanging contracts on a purchase prior to the arrangement of a mortgage *Buckland* v *Mackesy* (1986) 112 SJ 841; sending the draft contract to the wrong client *Frank* v *Seifert, Sedley & Co* (1964) 108 SJ 523; failure to obtain the head landlord's licence to assign and permission for change of user *Creech* v *Mayorcas* (1966) 198 EG 1091; failure to spot a defect in title *Pilkington* v *Wood* [1953] Ch 770; failure to ensure that there was a right of way across the only convenient access to property *Hayes* v *Dodd (James & Charles) (a firm)* [1990] 2 All ER 815; failure to notice that a lease of business premises restricted the user intended by the client *Transportation Agency Ltd* v *Jenkins* (1972) 223 EG 1101; dealing with a divorce matter where property is being transferred into the sole name of the wife, failing to protect the husband client's interest in the property *Bell* v *Peter Browne & Co (a firm)* [1990] 3 All ER 124.

Appendix 2

Common errors leading to negligence in the area of Wills & Probate

The failure by the solicitor to return sufficiently promptly to take full instructions to draft a will, resulting in the client dying intestate *Smith* v *Haynes & Co* (*The Times* 3 September 1991); failure to check the position regarding settled property and to advise the client appropriately *Otter* v *Church, Adams, Tatham & Co* [1953] Ch 280; failure to advise on the effects marriage would have upon a will *Hall* v *Meyrick* [1957] 2 QB 455 (11); failure to correctly advise the client as to who should not witness the will *Ross* v *Caunters* [1980] Ch 297; failure to correctly draft a document akin to a trust *Hemmens* v *Wilson Browne (a firm)* [1993] 4 All ER 826; a solicitor accepting the provision in a will for a gift to himself without advising the client to seek independent legal advice.

Appendix 3

Common errors leading to negligence in litigation

Failure to advise the client that the case probably had no merit *Orchard* v *South Eastern Electricity Board* [1987] 1 QB 565; failure to take reasonable steps to trace potential witnesses *Holden & Co* v *CPS* [1990] 2 QB 261; failure to take proofs of evidence from witnesses who were likely to be called to give evidence at trial *Hatch* v *Lewis* (1861) 2 F&F 467; failure to give due consideration to instructing the most suitable expert witness *Mercer* v *King* (1859) 1 F&F 490; failure to advise on the possible alternative sources of funds. The duty of the solicitor extends to considering legal aid and other sources, for example insurance, and applies to the initial contact even before the person formally becomes a client *Grossman* v *Ward Bracewell & Co* (1989) 5 PN 103; failure to attend court or to make arrangements for the attendance of witnesses *Dunn* v *Halton* (1861) 2 F&F 642; failure to issue proceedings within the statutory limitation period, or an unreasonable delay in the conduct of a case leading to its being struck out for want of prosecution *Fitzpatrick* v *Balger & Co Ltd* [1967] 2 WLR 706.

Bibliography

Bennion, F (1994) 'Teaching Law Management', in Birks, P (ed) *Reviewing Legal Education* (Oxford: Oxford University Press).

Bradney, A (1995) 'Raising the Drawbridge: Defending University Law Schools' 1 *Web Journal of Current Legal Issues*.

Brayne, H (1994) 'LPC Skills Assessment – A Year's Experience' 28 *The Law Teacher* 227.

Davies, M (1994) 'Solicitors' negligence: research methodology and the problem of research ethics' 1 *International Journal of the Legal Profession* 387.

Dean, R (1993) 'The College of Law and the Legal Practice Course', in Birks, P (ed) *Examining the Law Syllabus – Beyond the Core* (Oxford: Oxford University Press).

Dugdale, AM, and Stanton, KM (1989) *Professional Negligence* 2nd ed. (London: Butterworths).

Grimes, R (1995) 'Legal Skills and Clinical Legal Education' 2 *Web Journal of Current Legal Issues*.

Goriely, T (1994) 'Debating the quality of legal services: differing models of the good lawyer' 1 *International Journal of the Legal Profession* 159.

Iya, PF (1994) 'Educating lawyers for practice – clinical experience as an integral part of education in the BOLESWA countries of Southern Africa' 1 *International Journal of the Legal Profession* 315.

Jackson & Powell (1992) *Professional Negligence*, 3rd ed. (London: Sweet & Maxwell).

Jones, PA (1993) 'Skills Teaching in Legal Education – The Legal Practice Course and Beyond', in Birks, P, (ed) *Examining the Law Syllabus – Beyond the Core* (Oxford: Oxford University Press).

Law Society Gazette, 16 October 1986.

Legal Practice Course Board (1995), 'Written Standards'.

MacFarlane, J (1992) 'Look before you leap: knowledge and learning in Legal Skills Education', 19 *Journal of Law and Society* 293.

Maughan, C, Maughan, M, Webb, J (1995)' Sharpening the Mind or Narrowing it? The Limitations of Outcome and Performance Measures in Legal Education' 29 *The Law Teacher* 255.
Moorhead, R, Boyle, F, Micallef, H (1995) 'Trainee Solicitors Group Quality of Life Survey'.
Moorhead, R, Sherr, A, Paterson, A (1994) 'Judging on results: quality, strategy and the search for objectivity' 1 *International Journal of the Legal Profession* 191.
Paterson, A (1994) 'The re-negotiation of professionalism' 1 *International Journal of the Legal Profession* 131.
Reuston, K (1994) 'Disillusion in the classroom' *Legal Action* July, 8
Saunders, N (1993) 'The Teaching and Assessment of Skills in the Vocational Stage: The Law Society's View', in Birks, P (ed) *Examining the Law Syllabus – Beyond the Core* (Oxford: Oxford University Press).
Solicitors Indemnity Fund (1994) *Seventh Annual Report.*
Stebbings, AM (1994) 'Implementing a competence system in the professions: from theory to practice. The Law Society Skills Standards' 1 *International Journal of the Legal Profession* 97.
Stephenson, J, Weil, S (eds) (1992) *Quality in Learning – A Capability Approach in Higher Education* (London: Kogan Page).
Taylor, M (1995) 'Pioneering legal skills training' *Legal Action,* April 96–97.
Travers, M (1994) 'Measurement and reality: quality assurance and the work of a firm of criminal defence lawyers in Northern England' 1 *International Journal of the Legal Profession* 173.
Tull, JA (1994) 'Assessing quality and effectiveness in legal services for the poor' 1 *International Journal of the Legal Profession* 211.
Webb, J (1995) 'Extending the Theory – Practice Spiral: Action Research as a Mechanism for crossing the Academic/Professional Divide' 2 *Web Journal of Current Legal Issues.*
Zander, M (1989) *A Matter of Justice* (Oxford: Oxford University Press).

THE COUNCIL OF EUROPE'S FRAMEWORK CONVENTION ON NATIONAL MINORITIES

Steven Wheatley, LLB, LLM

Lecturer, University of Central Lancashire
<s.wheatley@uclan.ac.uk>

First Published in Web Journal of Current Legal Issues in association with Blackstone Press Ltd.

SUMMARY

This article considers the measures adopted by the Council of Europe in response to the perceived 'problem' of national minority groups, in particular the opening for signature, on the 1st of February, of the framework Convention for the Protection of National Minorities in 1995 and previous measures adopted under the European Convention on Human Rights. The article considers the detailed provisions in the framework Convention on the rights of members of national minority groups to non-discrimination and positive rights in the field of culture, education and language. The approach of the framework Convention is contrasted with developments in the work of the Organisation for Security and Co-Operation in Europe and in particular its High Commissioner on National Minorities scheme which has indicated a need to incorporate the demands and aspirations of national minority groups within the decision making processes of the State. The article questions whether the absence of such a scheme within the framework Convention will prove fatal to its successful operation.

CONTENTS

Introduction

The 'problem' of national minorities is most clearly evidenced in the break up of the former Yugoslavia, armed conflict in Chechnya,[1] conflict between the neighbouring Azerbaijan and Armenia States and tensions between the central authorities and national minorities in the Baltic States and in Slovakia. The Council of Europe has recognised that the

> 'upheavals of European history have shown that the protection of national minorities is essential to stability, democratic security and peace in [Europe]' and considered that, 'a pluralist and genuinely democratic society should not only respect the ethnic, cultural, linguistic and religious identity of each person belonging to a national minority, but also create appropriate conditions enabling them to express, preserve and develop this identity . . .' in a 'climate of tolerance and dialogue.' (*Preamble,* framework Convention for the Protection of National Minorities.)

Whilst the international legal community provides for a prohibition on discrimination against some minority groups in Article 27 of the International Covenant on Civil and Political Rights 1966 (999 UNTS 171, UKTS (1977) 6, Cmnd 6702);[2] this article (and the framework Convention) is concerned with the legal protection afforded to a specific minority group, that is the *national minority*, a group, 'which differs from [the majority] in race, language and [/or] religion [and desires] the possibility of living peaceably alongside the population and co-operating amicably with it, while at the same time preserving the characteristics which distinguish them from the majority.' (*Minority Schools in Albania Case* (1935) PCIJ Ser A/B. No. 64, 17). National minority groups are an integral component of the modern State, indigenous to the areas in which they live but designated minorities by the arbitrary imposition of territorial boundaries without reference to the ethnic composition of the political unit. This article will now consider the provisions

---

1 Which Russia fears will become a more generalised conflict between Russians and Muslims on its southern border, notably in conflict with Kazakhstan, Uzbekistan, Kirghizia, and Azerbaijan.

2 'In those States in which ethnic, religious or linguistic minorities exist, persons belonging to such minorities shall not be denied the right, in community with the other members of the group, to enjoy their own culture, to profess and practise their own religion, or to use their own language.'

adopted by the Council of Europe in the protection of the rights of individuals belonging to national minority groups.

The Council of Europe and National Minorities

The traditional focus for the guarantee of human rights in Europe has been the Council of Europe and in particular the European Convention on Human Rights [1950] (ETS (1950) 5, UKTS (1950) 7). The Convention has no specific provisions on minority rights although the range of provisions, on individual rights and non-discrimination, connect closely with traditional concerns of minorities. In addition minority groups will be recognised as having standing in cases of violations of the rights of members of the group (Article 25(1)). Of particular significance to national minority groups are provisions on the rights to freedom of thought and conscience (Article 9), freedom of expression (Article 10), of assembly and association (Article 11) and the right to education (Article 2 of Protocol 1). Moreover, the European Commission on Human Rights has concluded that, 'a minority group is, in principle, entitled to claim the right to respect for the particular lifestyle it may lead as being "private life", "family life" or "home" [under Article 8(1)]' (*G&E* v *Norway* Apps Nos. 9278 and 9415/81, (1983) 35 DR 30, 35 – 36). To advance such a claim the national minority is required to demonstrate that its needs and requirements outweigh those of the general population. This balancing of minority and majority claims whilst allowing the State to discriminate in favour of the national minority (*Liberal Party et al* v *UK* App. No. 8765/79, (1982) 4 EHRR 106, 123) places the minority group in a vulnerable position in any balancing of interests with the majority group.

The substantive provisions of the ECHR are complemented by Article 14 which provides that the rights in the Convention are to be enjoyed, 'without discrimination . . . on any ground such as sex, race, colour, language, religion, political or other opinion, national or social origin, *association with a national minority*, property, birth or other status' (*emphasis added*). The European Court of Human Rights has indicated that Article 14 prohibits any difference in treatment where that distinction has no 'objective and reasonable justification . . . assessed in relation to the aim and effects of the measures under consideration . . . [and] proportionality between the means employed and the aim sought to be realised' (*Belgian Linguistics Case* [1969], Judgement of 23 July, 1968, Series A, No. 6, 34) and the applicant is able to demonstrate some detriment from that distinction in treatment (App. No. 10210/82, 35 DR (1983) 203, 207 *K* v *France*). Whilst of clear value, in theory, in the protection of the rights of persons belonging to national minorities the insistence that Article 14 may only be alleged in conjunction with specific rights in the Convention (i.e. to assembly, expression, etc.) prevents it being utilised to advance claims based on rights which are not found in the European Convention on Human Rights including traditional national minority demands for language rights or linguistic freedom in public (*Clarfayt and Legros* v *Belgium*, App. No. 10650/83, (1985) 42 DR 212), separate schooling – funded by the State – (*Belgium Linguistics Case*), respect of the separate national minority culture (App. No 7823 and 7824/77, *Kalderas Gypsies* v *FRG and the Netherlands* (1977) 11 DR 221) and the right of the group to political autonomy (*Matthieu-Mohin & Clerfayt* v *Belgium*, Judgement of March 2, 1987, Ser A, No 113. 10 EHRR 1).

The Council of Europe in recognising the deficiencies in its provisions relating to the rights of individuals belonging to national minority groups decided to adopt a Framework Convention for the Protection of National Minorities [1995],[3] the first legally binding multilateral instrument devoted specifically to the protection of national minorities. Apart from the preamble, the Framework convention is split into four main operative parts:

Section I contains the fundamental principles which underpin the convention and may serve to elucidate the substantive provisions
Section II contains the specific principles to be implemented by participating States into their national legislation
Section III contains provisions relating to interpretation and application of the framework Convention
Section IV contains the provisions on monitoring.

This article will now consider each of the sections in turn in an attempt to examine the potential impact of the framework Convention on the effective protection of the rights of members of national minority groups and in the protection of the cultural identity of the group itself.

Section I – Fundamental Principles

The framework Convention in identifying the protection of national minorities and the rights and fundamental freedoms of persons belonging to minorities, as, 'an integral part of the international protection of human rights . . . [falling] within the scope of international co-operation' (Article 1), removes any claims of exclusive domestic jurisdiction to the national minorities question by the State parties and recognises a need to deal with such issues on the basis of internationally agreed human rights provisions and in accordance with the principle of good neighbourliness, friendly relations and co-operation between States (Article 2).

The rights within the framework Convention are to be accorded to members of national minority groups, that is members of a group that is numerically less than half of the population with some ethnic, cultural, linguistic or religious cohesion. However, not all cultural, religious and ethnic differences create national minorities and the framework Convention provides no definition of 'national minority', leaving the identification (or not) of the status of 'national minority' group to the State concerned, reflecting both the difficulties inherent in any definition and the failure of the participating States to agree one. Whilst the drafters of the framework Convention, and all other international legal instruments on the issue, have avoided providing a definition of a national minority group, in the operation of the framework Convention a jurisprudence will develop as States establish criteria for the recognition of those groups who may be termed 'national minority' groups for

3 34 ILM 351 [1995]; The Framework Convention is open to signature by any member state of the Council of Europe and any state invited to become party by the Committee of Ministers [of the Council of Europe] (Article 27) and will come into force on the first day of the month after the date on which *twelve members of the Council of Europe* have expressed their consent to be bound (Article 28(1) *emphasis added*) Any Party may denounce the framework Convention by means of a notification to the Secretary General of the Council of Europe. The denunciation becomes effective following a period of six months (Article 31). As of 31st October 1996, 33 States had signed the Framework Convention (including the United Kingdom), but only Cyprus, Hungary, Romania,the Slovak Republic and Spain had actually ratified the instrument. (My thanks to the Treaty Section of the Foreign and Commonwealth Office, London, for the figures).

the purpose of according rights with such criteria required to be consistent with existing accepted principles on the issue.

Defining the 'National Minority'

At the most basic level, a 'national minority' group must encompass less than half of the population of the State (i.e. be a 'minority'), and members of the group must be nationals of the State (i.e. a 'national' minority), sharing some ethnic, linguistic or cultural factor which distinguishes them from the majority. As the framework Convention requires States promote such conditions as are necessary for national minorities to 'maintain and develop their culture, and to preserve the essential elements of their identity, namely their religion, language, traditions and cultural heritage' (Article 5(1)), it is suggested that a national minority group be defined – in the absence of a more generally agreed definition – in accordance with that proposed by Deshenes (Deshenes 1985, p 30) of a

> '. . . group of citizens of a State, consisting of a numerical minority and in non-dominant position in that State, endowed with ethnic, religious or linguistic characteristics which differ from those of the majority of the population, having a sense of solidarity with one another, motivated, if only implicitly, by a collective will to survive and whose aim is to achieve equality with the majority in fact and in law.'

This 'recognition' of a group as a 'national minority' will involve the self-identification by the group itself that it is a minority with a national or ethnic, cultural, religious and linguistic identity; that distinction between the majority and minority having some 'objective' basis in fact. Secondly, as the purpose of advancing a claim of national minority status is to demand a preferential or proportionate claim on the political, economic and social resources of the State, the relevant national government must be involved in the process of recognition, granting much discretion to the State, although that decision must be consistent with the practice and provisions of international law and does not allow the State to arbitrarily deny the existence of national minority groups within its territory.[4] Once the State has identified the appropriate national minority groups within its territory, the framework Convention provides a number of principles which the participating States must apply in their dealings with members of the group which will now be considered.

Section II – The Principles

As a framework Convention, creating general principles and not directly applicable without enactment into domestic law, implementation is the prerogative of the State. The Convention allows a large margin of appreciation to the State in the application of many of the provisions (particularly those on education and language rights) and, moreover, permits the State to impose, 'such restrictions or derogations which are provided for in international legal instruments, in particular the

4 Cf. France's Reservation to Article 27 of the International Covenant on Civil and Political Rights to the effect that, 'France is a country in which there are no minorities' quoted in Alfredsson and de Zayas, *Minority Rights Protection by the United Nations* [1993] 14 HRLJ 1, 7.

Convention for the Protection of Human Rights and Fundamental Freedoms, in so far as they are relevant to the rights and freedoms flowing from the said principles' (Article 19), although the Convention may not be construed as limiting or derogating from any other human right or fundamental freedom which may be ensured under the laws of the State, or under any other agreement to which the State is a Party (Article 22). The rights of members of national minority groups are, therefore, additional to the universal human rights provisions accepted by the State and not an alternative to such provisions. The substantive provisions provided by the framework Convention will now be examined.

Non-Discrimination

Recognising that members of national minority groups are often the subject of discrimination and hostility by the State authorities and the majority population at large, the framework Convention obliges Parties to take appropriate action to protect persons belonging to a national minority group from being subject to acts of hostility or violence on the basis of their ethnic, cultural or religious identity (Article 6(2)) and prohibits discrimination against an individual on the basis of that person 'belonging to a national minority' group (Article 4(1)). Article 4 prohibits all direct discrimination on the basis of a person belonging to a national minority and any indirect discrimination which has no 'objective and reasonable justification', or is not proportionate to the aims sought to be realised (*Belgian Linguistics Case*). The *Explanatory Report on the Framework Convention* (Council of Europe 1994, para 40), notes that it was not felt necessary to provide separate provisions dealing specifically with equal opportunities or other freedoms, including that of movement, as such rights would be implicit within Article 4.

The framework Convention, recognising that the mere imposition of an obligation of non-discrimination will not deal with past and institutionalised discrimination within society, permits Parties to:

> 'adopt, where necessary, adequate measures in order to promote . . . full and effective equality between persons belonging to a national minority and those belonging to the majority.' (Article 4(2))

Whilst such measures of positive discrimination will have most impact in the context of access to employment, particularly in access to public sector employment, the right to positive discrimination in Article 4 is applicable in all areas and may, arguably be mandated where institutionalised discrimination against the national minority group is apparent. Such positive discrimination must be proportionate and limited, as appropriate, in time and scope to avoid violating the rights of the majority but it is the responsibility of the State to determine the necessity and extent of such measures.

The right to develop the culture and maintain and promote the identity of the national minority

The framework Convention provides a general obligation on the parties to 'foster knowledge of the culture, history, language and religion of their national minorities and of the majority' (Article 12(1)) for the promotion of mutual understanding and respect and to promote such conditions as are necessary for the national minority to, 'maintain and develop their culture, and to preserve the essential elements of their identity, namely their religion, language, traditions and cultural heritage' (Article 5(1)). Beyond this general obligation, the right of the national minority group to preserve and promote its identity is guaranteed through the provision of language rights, rights in the context of education and the right to maintain and develop contacts with other members of the national minority group outside of the State. These will be examined in turn.

Language rights

It has been a common practice for States to deny a national minority the right to utilise and express themselves in the minority language as part of a programme of assimilation of the minority group into the majority. The Kurdish minority population in Turkey has been a particular victim of this policy. Recognising the importance of this issue, the framework Convention demands that every person belonging to a national minority be allowed the right to use his or her minority language both in private and in public and the right not to be discriminated against in equal access to the media. The framework Convention requires that each person belonging to the national minority has the right to recognition of their minority name, the right to display signs in the minority language, and in areas inhabited by substantial numbers belonging to the national minority, and subject to limitations, the right to have local names and street signs displayed in the minority language (Article 11).

In criminal matters, members of the national minority have the right to be informed, in a language which they understand, of the reasons for any arrest. Moreover, members of the national minority have the right to defend themselves in the same language – which could include the majority language – but if necessary with the assistance of an interpreter (Article 10(3)).

More generally, in areas inhabited traditionally, or in substantial numbers, by the national minority, if such persons so request and where such a request corresponds to a real need, the State may allow members of the national minority group to use the minority language in their relations with the administrative authorities (Article 10). The framework Convention deliberately provides no definition of 'substantial numbers' or 'real need' granting a large margin of appreciation to the State permitting the authorities to take into account financial and technical problems (involved in interpretation) relating to the provision of language rights, and making any challenge to a State's provision of language rights difficult to sustain in all but the most extreme of circumstances.

The provisions on national minority language rights in the framework Convention appear vaguely defined and limited in contrast with those measures adopted by the Council of Europe's own European Charter for Regional or Minority Languages in 1992. The Charter recognises that the minority language is an integral part of the expression of the cultural wealth of the minority group and calls for resolute action for the promotion of such minority languages. To this end, the use of the minority language in public and in private is to be facilitated and encouraged and appropriate provision made available for the teaching and study of the minority language. No distinction, exclusion or restriction relating to the use of the minority language is permitted where such a restriction is intended to discourage its development (Article 7). It is clearly disappointing that the drafters of the framework Convention felt unable to outline, in greater detail, the specific obligations required of a State in the protection and promotion of the national minority culture through that group's spoken and written language.

Educational rights

The right of the national minority group to preserve its identity requires that characteristics of the group in terms of religion, culture and language be passed on to the children of the members of the group so as to ensure that the majority culture does not supplant, for those children, the minority one. In this context the right of the national minority group to appropriate education for its children is essential. Recognising this fact, to a somewhat limited extent, the framework Convention obliges Parties, where appropriate, to take measures in the field of education to foster knowledge of the culture, history, language and religion of the national minority and the majority (Article 12(1)). Appropriate opportunities for teacher training and access to textbooks are to be provided and contacts between both staff and students of different communities is to be facilitated by the State. The framework Convention does not, however, attempt, to force cross cultural understanding by the establishment of a unitary and homogeneous education system – which has been the primary mechanism by which States have attempted to assimilate national minority groups – recognising the right of the national minority to establish separate private education institutions (Article 13) to enable the preservation and promotion of the national minority culture.

More generally, where there is sufficient demand, the framework Convention requires that Parties endeavour to ensure that members of the national minority have adequate opportunities in the education system (at primary, secondary and University level) to be taught in the minority language and the right to learn the minority language. In areas inhabited traditionally, or in large numbers, by the national minorities, if there is sufficient demand, as far as possible and within the framework of their education system, State parties shall ensure that persons belonging to the national minority have the opportunity to be taught in the minority language without prejudicing the learning of the majority (State) language, which is stated to be a factor of social cohesion within the State (Article 14). Such ambiguities in the posited obligations grant almost absolute discretion to the State concerned in deciding the appropriate level of minority language provision and, again, it would be difficult for any national minority group or other interested party to allege bad faith on the part of the State in its implementation of the framework Convention, reflecting a continuing reluctance on the part of States to surrender exclusive domestic responsibility for dealings with national minority groups to international concern and supervision.

The right to connections with citizens in third States

Recognising that a national minority will often have ethnic connections with a third state, the Framework Convention obliges Parties, 'not to interfere with the right of persons belonging to national minorities to establish and maintain free and peaceful contacts across frontiers with persons lawfully staying in other States, in particular those with whom they share an ethnic, cultural, linguistic or religious identity, or a common cultural heritage' (Article 17(1)). States are encouraged, where necessary, to conclude bilateral and multilateral agreements with other States, in particular neighbouring States, in order to ensure the protection of persons belonging to the national minorities concerned (Article 18).

Section III – The interpretation and application of the framework Convention

The express intention of the framework Convention is the achievement of, preservation and promotion of, the national minority culture within the existing State, that is the granting of the right of self-realisation not self-determination. In particular, in Article 21, the framework Convention rejects any right of the national minority group to external self-determination, that is a right to secession and independence or the (re) joining with what Mullerson describes as the ethnically similar 'Motherland' States (Mullerson 1994, pp 113–4). In return for the granting of such a right to self-realisation by the State (in the context of education, language and cultural rights), persons belonging to the national minority are required, in return, to obey the national legislation of the State and respect the rights of other citizens. In particular, in areas in which the national minority forms the majority, it must respect the rights of individuals belonging to the majority or other national minorities – the oppressed may not become the oppressor (Article 20).

Section IV – Monitoring and Implementation

As a framework Convention, the responsibility for the implementation of the rights and obligations within the instrument lies primarily with the relevant State Party who must implement the rights in good faith. The rights within the framework Convention may not be relied upon by individual members of the national minority group themselves who must rely on the internal provisions adopted by the State to challenge the implementation of the framework Convention's principles.

The Committee of Ministers of the Council of Europe (Article 24) enjoys a limited monitoring role with no potential role of oversight for the European Court on Human Rights. The framework Convention adopts a reporting mechanism by way of implementation and does not allow the possibility of individual petition or petition by a national minority group alleging violation of the provisions. State parties are required to submit a first comprehensive report on legislative and other measures undertaken in the implementation of the framework Convention within one year of becoming a party, thereafter, Parties are obliged to submit reports on a periodical basis and whenever the Committee requests information to enable that information to be kept up to date (Article 25). The Committee of Ministers is assisted by an advisory committee of recognised experts in the field whose composition and procedure is to be determined by the Committee of Ministers one year after the Convention's entry into force (Article 26). The function of the Committee of Ministers is to review the implementation of the rights and obligations created by the framework Convention but the exact nature of its role is unclear and will only become apparent in the operation of the reporting system. The monitoring of the implementation of the framework Convention is intended, as far as possible, to be transparent with consequential publication of reports and other texts resulting from the monitoring expected (Council of Europe 1994, para 97). Such mechanisms for review of implementation, where utilised by other human rights instruments have tended to avoid direct confrontation with the State Parties, with the body charged with reviewing implementation of the rights preferring to make general comments rather than directed individual criticisms. If the experience of the workings of the Committee of Ministers in relation to the European Convention on Human Rights is indicative, the Committee will tend to defer to the expert legal opinion of the body of experts except where the issue is one of emergency or highly political (likely in cases involving national minorities) when the Committee will be paralysed by indecision. The monitoring of the framework Convention is clearly inadequate reflecting the political tensions involved in any re-ordering of the internal political structure of the State between the national minority and the central authorities. This is disappointing, but unsurprising in the context of the Council of Europe, as the European Court of Human Rights has, itself, consistently refused to consider the internal political arrangements of member States (Marquand 1994, p 362).

The Right to Political Participation in the framework Convention

The framework Convention grants rights to individual members of national minority groups and not to the national minority groups themselves, although it is recognised that the individual rights may be enjoyed, 'in community with others' (Article 3(2)). The framework Convention gives each individual the right to associate or not with the national minority, with no disadvantage resulting from the exercise of that choice (Article 3(1)). As well as the right to promote and preserve the identity of the national minority group through education, language and cultural rights the framework Convention requires that:

> 'The Parties shall create the conditions necessary for the effective participation of persons belonging to the national minorities in cultural, social and economic life and in public affairs, in particular those affecting them.' (Article 15)

Article 15 of the Convention builds upon a more general right to popular participation, evidenced in Article 25 of the International Covenant on Civil and Political Rights [1966].[5] However, for a national minority group – numerically disadvantaged in terms of the electorate – it is insufficient to restrict the right to political participation to a periodic right to vote in free and fair elections. An effective right to political participation requires formal inclusion of the national minority within the decision making process of the State to enable it to make direct representation. On this continuing aspect of the right to political participation, the framework Convention recognises the right of members of a national minority group to play an active part in the work of appropriate non-governmental organisations (Article 17(2)) whilst the *Explanatory Report* to the framework Convention issued by the Council of Europe (1994) suggests the measures which

5 Article 25 of the ICCPR reads, 'Every citizen shall have the right and the opportunity . . . (a) to take part in the conduct of public affairs, directly or through freely chosen representatives; (b) to vote and to be elected at genuine periodic elections . . . guaranteeing the free expression of the will of the electors.'

a State may adopt in its implementation of Article 15. These include, *inter alia*, consultation by the State with members of the national minority group through representative institutions when the State is contemplating administrative or legislative measures likely to have a direct effect on the national minority; involving the national minority in the preparation and implementation of regional development activity likely to affect them; allowing effective participation by persons belonging to the national minority into the decision making process at national and regional level; and decentralised or local forms of government (Council of Europe 1994, para 80).

It would be insufficient to simply grant such a right to political participation to individual members of the national minority group (as suggested by Article 15) and the measures suggested by the *Explanatory Report* would inevitably involve the State in the recognition of representatives of the national minority in the granting of the right to political inclusion and dialogue – such a right would, consequently, be collective not individual. Whilst the framework Convention has undertaken only tentative steps in the recognition of a collective human right to political inclusion and dialogue reflecting the political nature of the emerging right, the Organisation for Security and Co-Operation in Europe has gone further, in this context, advocating:

> 'appropriate democratic participation of persons belonging to national minorities or their representatives in decision-making or consultative bodies [as constituting] an important part of effective participation in public affairs.' (OSCE, Geneva Meeting of Experts Report 1991, Section III)

The Organisation for Security and Co-operation in Europe's High Commissioner on National Minorities

Pre-eminent in the New Europe's attempt at preventing and containing ethnic conflicts has been the Organisation for Security and Co-Operation in Europe (OSCE) process begun with the signing of the Helsinki Final Act in 1975. Whilst the OSCE and its subsidiary organs, notably the High Commissioner on National Minorities, is a political organisation, issuing non-binding provisions, its decisions and recommendations have a strong normative value influencing the development of international practice and the developing general international law. Initially the process was not concerned with the protection of national minorities (as it was preoccupied with preventing the Cold War in Europe escalating into conflict and ensuring respect for universal human rights in Eastern Europe) until the second meeting of the Conference of the Human Dimension at Copenhagen in 1990 (29 ILM (1990) 1318) moved the issue to the OSCE agenda. The Copenhagen Meeting was followed by a Meeting of Experts in Geneva and the Moscow meeting of the Human Dimension 1991 which established a system of fact-finding missions of independent experts and rapporteurs, to include consideration of national minority issues (30 ILM (1991)1670). The OSCE process culminated in the Helsinki Follow-Up Meeting in 1992 where a High Commissioner on National Minorities was established to address national minority issues in a constructive manner, by peaceful means and through dialogue among all parties on the basis of OSCE principles and commitments. Formally, the High Commissioner's function is to provide an early warning in situations which exhibit:

'tensions involving national minority issues which have not yet developed beyond an early warning stage, but, in the judgement of the High Commissioner, have the potential to develop into a conflict within the OSCE area, affecting peace stability or relations between participating states.' ([O]SCE Helsinki Document [1992], Para II(2), 31 ILM (1992) 1385).

The High Commissioner may collect and receive information regarding national minority issues from any source (including the parties involved, the media and non-governmental organisations), assess the various roles of the parties involved, the nature of the tensions and any potential consequences of the escalating tensions. If, on the basis of the information received and following meetings with the parties involved, the High Commissioner believes there to be a *prima facie* risk of potential conflict he may issue an early warning which will be communicated to the appropriate OSCE political body. The OSCE may then, at its discretion, undertake further measures.

The formal role of the High Commissioner is complemented by an informal function as an independent outsider with an international mandate able to play a significant role in the early resolution of problems involving national minorities, possibly leading to a resolution of the underlying issues in the conflict. The High Commissioner has published a number of reports on national minority issues in a variety of States, in particular in Central and Eastern Europe. In these reports, the High Commissioner has recommended that States undertake similar measures to those required for compliance with the provisions of the framework Convention but has gone further in the context of the right to political participation calling for the establishment of:

'specialised organ[s] with adequate minority representation and participation. . . . [with] real competencies with regard to legislation touching upon minority issues . . . specifically of the competence to discuss legislative concepts before they are submitted to parliament, to suggest amendments to existing legislation, and also to advise on or even propose themes and concepts for new legislation.' (Letter of [O]SCE High Commissioner on National Minorities to Slovak Republic, CSCE Communication No. 36, Vienna, 14 November 1994).

The purpose of such a body would be to establish a visible policy of dialogue to ensure that rumours and speculation about prospective administrative and legislative decisions can be prevented from causing friction and dispute and to achieve the effective inclusion of the national minority group into the political life of the State. This explicit recommendation by the OSCE's High Commissioner is in direct contradiction to the vague requirements of Article 15 of the framework Convention and reflects to some extent the political, aspirational and programmatic nature of such a right were it to evolve and the fact that such a right is more easily provided within the context of political rather than legal institutions.

Conclusion

The framework Convention and its limited provisions on linguistic, educational and cultural rights has been described as, 'a weak first attempt [for the guarantee of minority rights in Europe]' (Gilbert 1996, p 189) with vaguely defined provisions and inadequate enforcement mechanisms. It is unlikely that such a minimalistic approach to the granting of national minority rights and exhortation of the inclusion of the national minority into the public life of the State will provide the basis for the solution of long standing ethnic disputes, particularly given the refusal of the drafters of the framework Convention to recognise an explicit collective right of national minority groups to political participation and the establishment of procedural mechanisms to inculcate the minority demands and aspirations into the decision making processes of the State. The absence of such a requirement and of an effective system of review and monitoring will ensure that the framework Convention remains largely ineffectual in the resolution of disputes between the State and the national minority. It is to be hoped that such a missed opportunity is not regretted.

Bibliography

Council of Europe (1994), *Explanatory Report on the framework Convention for the Protection of National Minorities*, Council of Europe H(94)10, Strasbourg, November.

Crawford, J (ed.) (1988), *The Rights of Peoples* (Oxford: Clarendon)

Deshenes, J (1985) *United Nations Sub-Commission on Prevention of Discrimination and Protection of Minorities: Proposal concerning a definition of the term 'minority' submitted by Mr. Jules Deshenes*, UN Doc E/CN.4/Sub.2/1985/31 & Corr. 1

Gilbert, G (1996) 'The Council of Europe and Minority Rights' 18 *Human Rights Quarterly* 160.

Marquand, C (1994) 'Human rights protection and minorities' *Public Law* 359.

Mullerson, R (1994) *International law, Rights and Politics* (London; Routledge).

Wright, J (1996) 'The OSCE and the Protection of Minority Rights' 18 *Human Rights Quarterly* 190.

£39.95